1001 4-INGREDIENT RECIPES

1001

4-INGREDIENT

RECIPES

Gregg Gillespie

PHOTOGRAPHS BY PETER BARRY

BLACK DOG
& LEVENTHAL
PUBLISHERS

Author's Acknowledgments

It seems that each time I do a new book, the list of people and companies I have to thank grows and grows. I must again start with my assistant, Gordon Allan. Even when I was down and unwilling to continue with this project, he kept prodding me, kept me going.

Then there is John Darrack and Stacy at Dirgio Corporation, the processors of Cunningham Spice and Herbs. They are so patient with me, and so willing to give me assistance . . . it is unbelievable.

Next comes the kind people at King Arthur Flour company catalog department. They have given me real assistance as to what is openly available in the marketplace.

Next are the unknown, unnamed people who were willing to take home and eat the dishes I prepared while testing these recipes.

Lastly, I would like to give special thanks to all of you who have taken the time to send me your kind words, and sometimes not-so-kind messages, over the Internet. I take it all constructively. As most of you know, I try to answer all of the messages I receive, but there have been a few times this wasn't possible, and for this I apologize. For anyone who would like to contact me by email, my address is gregoree@worldnet.att.net.

Published by
Black Dog & Leventhal Publishers, Inc.
151 West 19th St.
New York, NY 10011

Distributed by
Workman Publishing Company
708 Broadway
New York, NY 10003

Printed in Spain by Artes Gráficas Toledo S.A.U.
D.L. TO: 1001-2001

ISBN 1-57912-207-8

Library of Congress CIP data is on file at the offices of Black Dog & Leventhal.

Additional acknowledgments: Iris Bass, Reeve Chace, Sasha Disko, Judy Hoffman, Gail Kinn, Brad Walrod
Food stylists: Pip Cole, Jacqui Bellefontaine, Mandy Phipps, Vicky Smallwood

Designed by Martin Lubin Graphic Design

j i h g f e d c b a

CONTENTS

INTRODUCTION

I love cooking and eating great food but, like everyone else, I don't have the time to juggle complex, multi-ingredient recipes on a daily basis. However, I don't give up easily on what I love. Instead, I came up with a way to have my cake and eat it too, so to speak: a quick and easy way of cooking, using a minimum amount of ingredients to create maximum flavor. One day, I went into the kitchen and didn't come out until I'd devised the absolutely simplest way to prepare great homemade foods. I stood at the counter, tossing and turning chickens, potatoes, pasta, pork, and any of the basics I could get my hands on, along with wonderfully prepared (store-bought and homemade) sauces and seasonings. Fewer ingredients mean more time at home and less time at the market; more time with family and friends and less time washing, peeling, cutting, chopping, slicing, and dicing. With fewer ingredients, you don't need so much counter space! And you save money.

In the end, I created more than 1,000 dishes, using only four ingredients, without sacrificing any flavor.

I'm sure that you feel the same way I do about eating well without all the fuss. Well, you've come to the right place. Here are more than 1,000 great-tasting dishes from my test-kitchen which you can prepare morning, noon, and night, to serve up delicious homemade cooking every day.

Quick, satisfying, and easy. From appetizers and snacks, soups and salads, fish and seafood . . . to poultry, meat, pasta, side dishes, vegetables, and desserts, there's no reason for anyone to slave over any meal again. And you can see what each dish will look like in the pictures accompanying every recipe. Try a savory, quick Frittata Italiana or Waffle Stacks to start your day. How do Potato Tortillas or an Israeli Eggplant Salad sound for lunch? For dinner, out of only four simple ingredients, create a world of flavor, including Honeyed Lamb, Loin of Pork Smothered in Onions, or Sweet and Savory Salmon Steaks. There are mouthwatering side dishes, such as Lebanese Rice with Cucumbers, Normandy Potatoes, or Polenta-Stuffed Peppers. And then there's dessert, from Quick Chocolate Rice to Apricot Kumquat Balls. Hungry yet?

How can such great food be made with only four ingredients? Easy. Cooking great food is never dependent on the quantity of ingredients you use. In fact, the simpler the cooking, the better the food. The main ingredient in simple and quick cooking is knowing the basics about how to create flavor and texture. Once you realize how well garlic imparts great taste and bacon adds moisture . . . once you understand poultry's versatility and how olive oil yields more taste than vegetable oil . . . and once you know how vinegar and lemon can perk up a sauce, and how flour thickens it, you can cook with less because you know how each ingredient contributes to making a balanced recipe.

Today, it's easier than ever to be a 4-Ingredient cook. Our grocery stores and supermarkets stock an enormous variety of quality dressings, easy-to-use canned beans, zesty salsas and sauces. With a jar of Creamy Ginger Dressing and quick-cooking Shanghai noodles, you can transform shrimp into Chinese Pasta. Canned cooked chickpeas, puréed in a blender with lemon juice and just the right seasonings, makes a tart and creamy Hummus spread, for either a party dip or an afternoon lunch, along with a salad. Sesame oil, soy sauce, flavored vinegars and oils, and all the ingredients listed in our 4-Ingredient Pantry, will kick up the flavor in everything you cook.

It all comes down to one truth: When it comes to cooking, less can definitely be more.

Enjoy all the great food to come—and all of your new spare time. Now you can confidently prepare homemade foods every day of the year.

GLOSSARY

Al dente: An Italian phrase meaning "to the tooth." It is usually used to describe pasta that is cooked until it is just tender, not soft, and certainly not overdone.

Ale: Usually refers to a type of beer.

Anaheim chile: A long and narrow member of the pepper family, usually a medium green color. Chiles can be purchased most everywhere, either canned or fresh.

Angel hair pasta: Also known as capelli d'angelo; it is a very thin and delicate pasta, and should only be served with a delicate sauce.

Anjou pears: A winter fruit that is sweet and adaptable to both cooking and eating.

Basmati rice: A fine-textured, long grain rice with a nut-like flavor and aroma.

Calvados: Apple brandy.

Cannelloni: Tube-shaped pasta.

Chickpeas: Also known as chick peas and garbanzo beans. Irregular-shaped legumes with a nut-like flavor.

Game birds: Usually refers to small or medium-sized fowl, which include pheasants, doves, quails, pigeons, and mud hens.

Garam Masala: A combination of dry roasted spices, usually 10 or more, that may be obtained at specialty stores and shops carrying Indian foods.

Idaho potatoes: Also known as russet and russet Burbank potatoes, they have low moisture and high starch content. Recommended for baking.

Ratatouille: A popular French dish that combines various vegetables mixed together.

Rigatoni: Short, grooved pasta tubes, usually cut diagonally at each end.

Risotto: An Italian rice dish made by stirring hot stock into a mixture of rice and onions that has been sautéed in butter.

Rotelle: Small, round pasta that resembles a wheel.

Rotini: Short spaghetti spiral pasta.

Roux: Usually a mixture of flour and butter or oil that has been heated together, until it becomes pasty; it is used to thicken sauces and soups.

Tamari: A sauce made from soybeans, but thicker than the usual soy sauce. It is used effectively in basting and for dipping sauces.

THE 4-INGREDIENT PANTRIES

The 4-Ingredient Pantry which follows actually consists of two pantries: The Basic Pantry and the Optional Pantry. The Basic Pantry contains products such as sugar, salt, dried herbs, seasonings, soy sauce, and a few other non-perishables; foods you should try to keep in stock at all times. Stocking these products will simplify your cooking life; you won't have to run to the store every time you cook a meal. To make preparation easy, where relevant, you'll find a separate "pantry" list of ingredients in the recipes—in addition to the 4-or-less ingredients list—taken from the Basic Pantry, so you'll know exactly what you'll need to prepare any recipe. These pantry ingredients are not "counted" as any of the four ingredients, as they will be readily available to you once you've set up your kitchen. And, of course, water is not listed as an ingredient; it is indicated in the directions.

The Optional Pantry lists items which would be convenient to keep on hand, but not necessary to have around at all times, such as canned beans, bottled salsas, and seasoning blends. And, in case your local store doesn't carry a Honey Soy Sauce or Ginger Dressing, with this list in mind, you'll be alert to picking up these items whenever you come across them. But you needn't overstock your pantry; therefore, these are simply recommendations.

THE BASIC PANTRY

EVERYDAY ESSENTIALS

butter or margarine
milk
mayonnaise
ketchup
soy sauce
honey
canned or bottled tomato sauce
fresh garlic

VINEGARS

distilled white vinegar
white wine vinegar
red wine vinegar
rice vinegar

DRY INGREDIENTS

salt
pepper
cornstarch
sugar
flour
allspice
cayenne pepper
celery salt
chili powder
cinnamon
cumin
curry powder
crushed red pepper flakes
dried Italian dressing
dried pizza seasoning
garlic powder
garlic salt
onion powder
onion salt
paprika
prepared mustard

DRY HERBS

basil
bay leaves
chives
cloves
dill weed
fennel
fenugreek
garlic
ginger
horseradish
marjoram
mustard
oregano
parsley
rosemary
sage
tarragon
thyme

OILS

canola
vegetable
olive
sesame

THE OPTIONAL PANTRY

CANNED FOODS

A selection of beans, including chickpeas, black beans, and white beans

BOTTLED AND CANNED FLAVORINGS

Caesar salad dressing
creamy ginger dressing
French dressing
chili sauce
Mirin sauce
barbecue sauce
banana ketchup
chili oil
oyster sauce
Southwestern chili mix
tahini
chutney
pepper jelly

SEASONINGS

firmly packed dark-brown sugar
light-brown sugar
fresh herbs
lemon

STAPLES

rice
pasta (all shapes and sizes)
bread crumbs
baking soda
baking powder
Cooking alcohols
red and white wine
dry sherry
bourbon or whiskey
vermouth

HOMEMADE PANTRY: SEASONING BLENDS

Mastering the art of 4-Ingredient cooking is all about knowing where the great flavor can be found—and having it on hand. The following recipes are for terrific mixes, rubs, and butters. If they require more than four ingredients, they are not included in the body of the book. But, because they are so versatile and deliver so much great taste to food, I wanted you to have them. Prepare a few of these recipes and use them when you want to add spice and punch to a particular dish. Where appropriate, make recipes in advance and store them in your pantry. You'll be glad you did.

ALL-PURPOSE SEASONING MIX

makes about 10 tablespoons

½ teaspoon crushed dried coriander

½ teaspoon crushed dried dill weed

½ teaspoon crushed dried rosemary

½ teaspoon crushed dried thyme

½ teaspoon dry mustard powder

1 teaspoon celery seed

1 teaspoon crushed dried basil

1 teaspoon crushed dried bay leaf

1 teaspoon crushed dried marjoram

1 teaspoon crushed dried spearmint

2 tablespoons crushed dried parsley flakes

2 tablespoons sesame seed

2 teaspoons onion powder

2 teaspoons crushed dried oregano

2 teaspoons garlic powder

In the container of a blender or food processor, combine all of the ingredients, and process on high speed until reduced to a fine powder. Transfer to a container with a tight-fitting cover and use as desired.

CAJUN SEASONING MIX

makes about ¼ cup

2 teaspoons white pepper

2 teaspoons garlic powder

2 teaspoons onion powder

2 teaspoons cayenne powder

2 teaspoons paprika

2 teaspoons ground black pepper

In the container of a blender or food processor, combine all of the ingredients, and process on high speed until reduced to a fine powder. Transfer to a container with a tight-fitting cover and use as desired.

CREOLE MEAT SEASONING

makes about 2 cups

½ cup salt

½ cup granulated garlic

½ cup ground black pepper

½ cup cayenne pepper

5 tablespoons cumin powder

In the container of a blender or food processor, combine all of the ingredients, and process on high speed until reduced to a fine powder. Transfer to a container with a tight-fitting cover and use as desired.

Curry Paste

makes about ¼ cup

½ teaspoon cumin powder
½ teaspoon coriander powder
1 large Anaheim chile pepper, stemmed, seeded and chopped
1 garlic clove, chopped
1 tablespoon cardamom seed
2 teaspoons olive oil

In the container of a blender or food processor, combine all of the ingredients, and process on high speed until a smooth paste is formed. Transfer to a container with a tight-fitting cover and refrigerate until needed. Use as desired.

Curry Powder

makes about 1 cup

1 teaspoon cayenne pepper
1 teaspoon ginger powder
1 teaspoon red pepper flakes
2 teaspoons cardamom powder
2 teaspoons coriander seed
2 teaspoons cumin seed
2 teaspoons fenugreek seed
2 teaspoons whole cloves
2 teaspoons black pepper

In the container of a blender or food processor, combine all of the ingredients, and process on high speed until reduced to a fine powder. Transfer to a container with a tight-fitting cover and use as desired.

Curry Powder #2

makes about ½ cup

1 tablespoon coriander seed
1 teaspoon cumin seed
1 teaspoon fenugreek seed
1 teaspoon turmeric powder
1 teaspoon black pepper
1 teaspoon cayenne pepper
1 teaspoon dry mustard powder
2 tablespoons tamarind
2 tablespoons onion powder

In the container of a blender or food processor, combine all of the ingredients, and process on high speed until reduced to a fine powder. Transfer to a container with a tight-fitting cover and use as desired.

Curry Powder #3

makes about ½ cup

1 3-inch piece cinnamon, crushed
1 large dried Anaheim chile, stemmed, seeded and chopped
1 tablespoon cumin seed
1 tablespoon mustard seed
1 teaspoon cardamom seed
1 teaspoon nutmeg seed
⅛ teaspoon cayenne powder
2½ teaspoons fenugreek
2 tablespoons turmeric powder
3 tablespoons coriander seed
6 whole cloves

In the container of a blender or food processor, combine all of the ingredients, and process on high speed until reduced to a fine powder. Transfer to a container with a tight-fitting cover and use as desired.

1 cup crushed dried chervil
½ cup chopped dried chives
1 cup crushed dried flat leaf parsley
½ cup crushed dried tarragon

In the container of a blender or food processor, combine all of the ingredients, and process on high speed until reduced to a fine powder. Transfer to a container with a tight-fitting cover and use as desired.

FINE HERBS

makes about 3 cups

---

5 teaspoons anise seed
5 teaspoons star anise
2 tablespoons whole cloves
1 5-inch piece cinnamon stick, crushed
7 teaspoons fennel seed

In the container of a blender or food processor, combine all of the ingredients, and process on high speed until reduced to a fine powder. Transfer to a container with a tight-fitting cover and use as desired.

FIVE SPICE POWDER

makes about ¼ cup

---

2 teaspoons salt
2 teaspoons crushed dried oregano
1½ teaspoons onion powder
1½ teaspoons garlic powder
1 teaspoon cornstarch or arrowroot
1 teaspoon ground black pepper
1 teaspoon beef bouillon granules
1 teaspoon crushed dried parsley
½ teaspoon ground cinnamon
½ teaspoon ground nutmeg or mace

In the container of a blender or food processor, combine all of the ingredients, and process on high speed until reduced to a fine powder. Transfer to a container with a tight-fitting cover and use as desired.

GREEK BLEND SEASONING MIX

makes about ¼ cup

½ teaspoon cayenne pepper
1 teaspoon crushed dried basil
1 teaspoon crushed dried savory
1 teaspoon crushed dried thyme
1 teaspoon garlic powder
1 teaspoon onion powder

In the container of a blender or food processor, combine all of the ingredients, and process on high speed until reduced to a fine powder. Transfer to a container with a tight-fitting cover and use as desired.

HERB BLEND SEASONING MIX

makes about 2 tablespoons

DISH SIZES

1½-quart casserole measures 8½ x 6½ x 2 inches

1½-quart round casserole measures 6¾ x 1½ inches

1½-quart round casserole measures 7½ x 2½ inches

2-quart casserole measures 8 x 8 x 2 inches

2-quart round casserole measures 8 x 3 inches

2½-quart casserole measures 9 x 9 x 2 inches

3-quart casserole measures 13 x 9 x 2 inches

4-quart round Dutch oven measures 9½ x 4 inches

LEMON-HERB SEASONING MIX

makes about ¾ cup

4½ tablespoons crushed dried basil
3¾ tablespoons crushed dried oregano
1½ tablespoons finely ground black pepper
1½ tablespoons granulated onion
1½ tablespoons celery seed
½ teaspoon granulated garlic
1½ tablespoons dried grated lemon zest

In the container of a blender or a food processor, combine all of the ingredients, and process on high speed until reduced to a fine powder. Transfer to a container with a tight-fitting cover and use as desired.

ORIENTAL SPICE MIX

makes about 3 tablespoons

½ teaspoon crushed dried thyme
½ teaspoon onion powder
½ teaspoon garlic powder
½ teaspoon celery seed
½ teaspoon crushed dried marjoram
¼ teaspoon crushed dried dill weed
½ teaspoon curry powder
1 tablespoon paprika

In the container of a blender or food processor, combine all of the ingredients, and process on high speed until reduced to a fine powder. Transfer to a container with a tight-fitting cover and use as desired.

PORK SEASONING MIX

makes about ¾ cup

⅛ teaspoon crushed dried thyme
¼ teaspoon sage powder
½ teaspoon crushed dried bay leaves
½ teaspoon crushed dried chervil
½ teaspoon ginger powder
½ teaspoon ground celery seed
¾ teaspoon crushed dried cilantro
1 teaspoon dry mustard powder
1 teaspoon paprika
2 tablespoons cayenne pepper
2 tablespoons garlic powder
2 tablespoons onion powder
2 teaspoons ground black pepper

In the container of a blender or food processor, combine all of the ingredients, and process on high speed until reduced to a fine powder. Transfer to a container with a tight-fitting cover and use as desired.

The Use of Salt

The American Heart Association recommends that sodium intake should be limited to 2400 milligrams per day.

¼ teaspoon salt = 500 mg sodium

½ teaspoon salt = 1000 mg sodium

¾ teaspoon salt = 1500 mg sodium

1 teaspoon salt = 2000 mg sodium

1 teaspoon baking soda = 1000 mg sodium

1 tablespoon butter = 140 mg sodium

1 tablespoon margarine = 140 mg sodium

1 tablespoon soy sauce = 1319 mg sodium

1 can (10½ ounces) cream-style chicken soup = 2411 mg sodium

Lemon makes a great salt substitute for many foods. As you can see from the above list, we're eating far too much salt. Stock up on lemons!

---

2 sticks (½ pound) unsalted butter or margarine, at room temperature
2 garlic cloves, mashed
1 teaspoon crushed dried rosemary
1 teaspoon crushed dried oregano
1 teaspoon crushed dried lemon thyme1 teaspoon sage powder
Salt and pepper to taste

In a bowl, blend together all of the ingredients. Transfer to a container with a tight-fitting cover and refrigerate until needed. Use as desired.

Poultry Butter

makes about ½ pound

---

1 tablespoon black pepper
1 tablespoon cayenne pepper
1 tablespoon chili powder
1 tablespoon cornstarch or arrowroot
1 tablespoon crushed dried marjoram
1 tablespoon lemon pepper
1 tablespoon onion salt
1 tablespoon sage powder
2 tablespoons celery salt
3 tablespoons light-brown sugar

In the container of a blender or food processor, combine all of the ingredients, and process on high speed until reduced to a fine powder. Transfer to a container with a tight-fitting cover and use as desired.

Poultry Rub

makes about 1 cup

---

1 tablespoon crushed dried marjoram
1 tablespoon crushed dried savory
1 tablespoon crushed dried thyme
1 tablespoon sage powder
1 teaspoon ground allspice
1 teaspoon ground nutmeg
3 tablespoons salt
1 tablespoon ginger powder

In the container of a blender or a food processor, combine all of the ingredients, and process on high speed until reduced to a fine powder. Transfer to a container with a tight-fitting cover and use as desired.

Poultry Seasoning Mix

makes about ½ cup

SEASONING SALT

makes about ¾ cup

¼ cup paprika
½ teaspoon crushed dried basil
½ teaspoon crushed dried oregano
½ teaspoon crushed dried thyme
1 tablespoon celery salt
1 tablespoon ground white pepper
1 teaspoon ground ginger
2 tablespoons garlic powder
2 tablespoons mustard powder
2 tablespoons salt

In the container of a blender or food processor, combine all of the ingredients, and process on high speed until reduced to a fine powder. Transfer to a container with a tight-fitting cover and use as desired.

SOUTHWESTERN CHILI MIX

makes about ¼ cup

½ teaspoon cumin powder
½ teaspoon granulated garlic
½ teaspoon red pepper flakes
1½ teaspoons chili powder
1 tablespoon all-purpose flour
1 teaspoon dark brown sugar
1 teaspoon onion salt
2 tablespoons granulated onion

In the container of a blender or food processor, combine all of the ingredients, and process on high speed until reduced to a fine powder. Transfer to a container with a tight-fitting cover and use as desired.

Appetizers and Snacks

ROASTED PEPPERS

These tempting and tasty appetizers and snacks demonstrate how well a minimum of ingredients can be transformed into a maximum of flavor.

Whip ham with mayonnaise, mustard, and horseradish, and *voilà*, you have Ham Pâté. Boil kielbasa sausage in red currant jelly for an irresistible hors d'oeuvre. Turn a simple chicken

sandwich into a festive treat by adding cranberry sauce.

Stock your pantry with a variety of breads and crackers of every shape and kind, from refrigerated flaky biscuits and dough to croissants and tortillas. With these "foundations" on hand, you're free to roam through the multitude of fabulous finger foods that follow, from Parmesan-flavored Biscuit Focaccia to Corn

SUPER NACHOS

MANDARIN PANCAKES

Quesadillas, to feed family and guests on the spur of any moment. The gustatory possibilities in using only four ingredients, for a cocktail party or the cocktail hour before the big feast, are almost infinite. And there's a bonus here. Many of these dishes can be made into wonderful main courses, as well!

15-Minute Seafood Salad

makes about 3 to 4 servings

½ cup packaged cheese tortellini, cooked and drained
½ pound deli-style marinated mixed vegetables
1 cup imitation crabmeat, cubed

In a medium bowl, blend together the pasta, the vegetables, and the crabmeat. Cover with plastic wrap, and refrigerate for at least 1 hour before serving.

Akkra (Bean Fritters)

makes about 24 servings

1 cup black-eyed peas
2 pieces hot red pepper, stemmed, seeded and minced
½ cup bread crumbs
1 egg, beaten

PANTRY
2 teaspoons salt
½ cup vegetable oil

1 Place beans in bowl and cover with water. Set aside for 15 minutes. Drain, and rub off the skins. Replace in the bowl, add water, and soak for about 2 hours.

2 Place beans in the container of a blender or food processor and purée until smooth. Blend in the peppers, and process on high speed until blended.

3 In a bowl, blend together the bean mixture, the egg, and the bread crumbs.

4 In a skillet, heat the oil and add the mixture by tablespoons, forming little patties. Cook for about 15 minutes, or until both sides are lightly browned. Transfer to a rack covered with paper towels, drain, and serve.

Antipasto Rolls

makes about 15 rolls

1 can (8 ounces) pitted black olives, drained
1 jar (4 ounces) Italian roasted red peppers, drained and cut into thin strips
15 slices prosciutto, thinly sliced

1 On a flat surface, lay out the prosciutto slices. Place one end of the pepper strips in the holes of the olives. Place chives in the centers of the prosciutto. Roll up jelly-roll fashion, and fasten with a toothpick.

2 Transfer to a dish, cover with plastic wrap, and refrigerate until ready to serve

Asparagus Wraps

makes about 5 to 10 servings

10 asparagus spears, trimmed
10 slices pressed ham

PANTRY

2 tablespoons prepared mustard
1 tablespoon mayonnaise

1 In a saucepan, add the asparagus, and cover with boiling water. Drain immediately.

2 In a small bowl, blend together the mustard and the mayonnaise. Spread the mixture evenly on the pressed ham slices, and top with an asparagus spear. Wrap and place seam side down on a microwave-proof platter.

3 Cover and microwave on medium heat for about 1 to 2 minutes, or until thoroughly heated. Remove from the oven, and serve.

Cooking note: This dish can also be served cold.

Atjar Tumis Djamur (Pickled Mushroom)

makes about 4 servings

8 ounces fresh mushrooms, trimmed and sliced
3 ounces shallots, peeled and slivered

PANTRY

3 cups distilled white vinegar
1 teaspoon cumin powder

1 In a saucepan, add the vinegar and the cumin powder. Bring to a boil and reduce to a simmer. Cover, cook for about 3 to 4 minutes, or until thoroughly heated.

2 In another saucepan, add the mushrooms and the shallots. Blend in the vinegar mixture, bring to a boil, and reduce to a simmer. Cover and cook for about 8 to 9 minutes, or until the mushrooms are tender.

3 Remove from the heat and drain. Pour the mixture into a bowl, cover with plastic wrap, and refrigerate for about 2 hours before serving.

Bacon Roll-Ups

makes about 15 servings

5 tablespoons cream cheese with chives
15 slices mixed grain bread, crust removed
15 bacon slices

PANTRY

1 tablespoon butter or margarine
1 tablespoon milk

1 Position the rack in the center of the oven and preheat to 350 degrees F. Lightly grease a baking or cookie sheet.

2 In a bowl, using a wire whisk or an electric mixer, blend together the milk and the cheese.

3 Spread a thin layer of this mixture evenly on both sides of the bread. Roll up jelly-roll fashion, wrap with the bacon, and fasten with a toothpick. Repeat. Arrange seam side down on the prepared baking sheet. Bake for about 20 minutes, or until the bacon starts to brown. Remove from the oven, and serve.

Bacon Sticks

makes about 4 servings

10 thin bread sticks
5 bacon slices, cut in half lengthwise
½ cup grated Parmesan or Romano cheese

Dredge the bacon in the cheese, and wrap candy-cane fashion around the bread sticks. Arrange on a microwave-proof platter lined with paper towels. Microwave on high heat for about 4 to 6 minutes. Remove from the microwave, roll the breadsticks in the cheese, and serve.

Baked Olive Bundles

makes about 4 to 6 servings

1 cup grated mozzarella
1 small can tomato purée
24 pimiento-stuffed olives, drained and dried

PANTRY

2 tablespoons butter or margarine, at room temperature
½ cup flour

1 Position the rack in the center of the oven and preheat to 400 degrees F. Lightly grease a baking or cookie sheet.

2 In a bowl, blend together the cheese, the purée, and the butter. Blend in the flour, a little at a time, to form a sticky dough.

3 Drop by tablespoons onto the prepared baking sheet, and form into patties. Press the olives into the centers, and pull the dough up to completely cover. Bake for about 15 minutes, or until golden-brown. Remove from the oven, and serve.

Cooking note: Pepper cheese can be substituted for the mozzarella.

1 piece (about 2 pounds) round
   steak, trimmed and cut into
   4 x 2-inch pieces
1 large dill pickle, cut
   lengthwise into 8 pieces
4 bacon slices, cut in half
   lengthwise
2 small white onions, thinly
   sliced

PANTRY
2 tablespoons vegetable oil
2 tablespoons flour

1 Place the pickles in the centers of the meat, and top with
the bacon and the onion. Roll
up jelly-roll fashion and fasten with a toothpick.

2 In a skillet, heat the oil, add
meat rolls, and sauté for
about 10 minutes, or until
lightly browned on all sides.
Add enough water to just
cover. Bring to a boil, and
reduce to a simmer. Cover,
and cook for about 2 hours, or
until tender. Transfer to a
warming plate.

3 In the same skillet, add the
flour, and cook, stirring frequently, for about 3 minutes,
or until thickened. Remove
from the heat, and serve on
the side with the meat.

BEEF AND BACON ROLLS

makes about 4 servings

---

1 package (10 ounces)
   refrigerated flaky biscuits
1 large egg, beaten
1 tablespoon grated fresh
   Parmesan or Romano cheese
2 teaspoons pizza seasoning or
   dried Italian dressing

PANTRY
1 tablespoon butter or margarine

1 Position the rack in the center of the oven and preheat to
375 degrees F. Lightly grease a
baking or cookie sheet.

2 Open the biscuit package
and separate into 10 biscuits.
Split each biscuit in half to
make 20 rounds. Arrange the
rounds on the baking sheet.
Brush with the egg, and top
with cheese and the pizza seasoning. Bake for about 8 to 12
minutes, or until the cheese
has melted. Remove from the
oven, and serve.

Cooking note: Although
dried Parmesan cheese can be
used, it is not recommended
for this recipe.

BISCUIT FOCACCIA

makes about 20 biscuits

BOURBON-FLAVORED COCKTAIL FRANKS

makes about 24 servings

1 package miniature cocktail franks
1 cup bourbon or whiskey
1 cup dark brown sugar

PANTRY
1 bottle (14 ounces) ketchup

In a saucepan, add the ketchup and the bourbon. Cook for 1 minute and blend in the brown sugar. Cover, and simmer, stirring occasionally, for about 20 minutes. Blend in the franks, cover, and continue to cook for about 10 minutes, or until thoroughly heated. Remove from the heat, and serve.

Cooking note: For variation, use banana ketchup when cooking.

BREAD STICKS ITALIANO

makes about 32 servings

1 package (10 ounces) refrigerated pizza dough
⅓ cup grated Romano or Parmesan cheese

PANTRY
2 tablespoons melted butter or margarine
¼ cup flour

1 Position the rack in the center of the oven and preheat to 425 degrees F. Lightly grease a baking or cookie sheet.

2 On a lightly floured surface, roll out the pizza dough to form a 12 x 8-inch rectangle (⅛-inch thick). Brush evenly with the butter, and sprinkle with the cheese. Cut into 32 sticks (6 x ½-inch), and arrange on the prepared sheet. Bake for about 7 minutes or until lightly browned. Remove from the oven, and serve.

1 package (10 ounces)
  refrigerated pizza dough
1 large egg, beaten
1 tablespoon grated Parmesan
  cheese
Calzone Filling (see page 412)

PANTRY
1 tablespoon butter or margarine

1 Position the rack in the center of the oven and preheat to 425 degrees F. Lightly grease a baking or cookie sheet.

2 On a lightly floured surface, roll out the pizza dough to form a 10 x 15-inch rectangle. Cut the dough into six ½-inch squares.

3 Divide the calzone filling among all the squares, and brush the edges with water. Fold the dough over, stretching as necessary, to cover the filling, and press to seal on all sides.

4 Arrange the dough on the prepared baking sheet, prick the tops, brush with the egg, and sprinkle on the cheese. Bake for about 8 to 10 minutes, or until a light golden-brown. Remove from the oven, cool slightly, and serve.

CALZONES

makes about 6 servings

8 slices cinnamon raisin bread
½ pound cheddar cheese, sliced
8 bacon slices, cooked and
  drained

PANTRY
2 tablespoons butter or margarine, at room temperature

1 On a flat surface, lay out the 8 slices of bread and butter. Place 4 slices on a baking sheet, buttered side down. Layer the cheese and the bacon on the bread, and top with the remaining 4 slices, buttered side up.

2 Preheat a nonstick skillet, add the sandwiches, and cook for about 10 minutes, or until both sides are toasted, and the cheese has melted. Remove from the heat, and serve.

CHEDDAR AND BACON SANDWICH

makes about 4 servings

CHEESE-SALAMI CROISSANTS

makes about 4 to 8 servings

4 croissants, partially sliced
2 ounces Italian-style salami, sliced thin
4 ounces Gruyère cheese, sliced

PANTRY

1½ tablespoons butter or margarine, at room temperature

1 Position the rack in the center of the oven and preheat to 350 degrees F. Lightly grease a baking or cookie sheet.

2 Spread the butter on one side of the croissants, arrange the salami on the bottoms of the croissants, top with the cheese, and sandwich them.

3 Arrange on the prepared baking sheet, and bake for about 10 minutes or until the cheese has melted. Remove from the oven, cut in half, and serve.

CHEESY CHICKEN PIZZA

makes about 4 servings

¼ pound ground chicken
½ cup chopped scallions
1 cup shredded Monterey Jack cheese
1 prebaked store-bought pizza crust

PANTRY

1 tablespoon vegetable oil
¾ cup canned spaghetti sauce
Salt and pepper to taste

1 Position the rack in the center of the oven and preheat to 400 degrees F. Lightly grease a round pizza tray.

2 In a skillet, heat the oil, add the chicken, and sauté, stirring occasionally, for about 20 minutes, or until tender. Blend in the spaghetti sauce, and adjust the seasoning to taste.

3 Place the crust on the prepared pizza tray, top with the chicken mixture, and sprinkle with the scallions and the cheese. Bake for about 20 minutes, or until the cheese has melted, and pizza is lightly browned. Remove from the oven, cut into wedges, and serve.

Cooking note: Various types of cheeses can be substituted for the Monterey Jack. Vegetables of choice may also be added to the sauce.

1 piece (about ½ pound) chicken breast, cooked and shredded
¼ cup chopped onion
¼ cup chopped celery
¼ cup shredded cheese of choice

PANTRY
½ cup mayonnaise

1 Position the rack in the center of the oven and preheat to 350 degrees F. Have a baking or cookie sheet available.

2 In a bowl, blend together the chicken, the onion, the celery, and the mayonnaise.

3 Arrange the crackers on the baking sheet, top with the chicken mixture, and sprinkle on the cheese. Bake for about 10 to 15 minutes, or until the cheese has melted. Remove from the oven, and serve.

WARM CHICKEN SALAD HORS D'OEUVRES

makes about 15 servings

---

2 cups shredded cheddar cheese
1 cup cooked diced ham
¼ cup sliced scallions (whites only)
6 small flour (or corn) tortillas

PANTRY
1 tablespoon butter or margarine

1 Position the rack in the center of the oven and preheat to 375 degrees F. Lightly grease a baking or cookie sheet.

2 In a bowl, blend together the cheese, the ham, and the onions.

3 On a flat surface, lay out the 6 tortillas, spread the mixture evenly between them, and fold in half.

4 Arrange on the prepared baking sheet, and bake for about 8 to 10 minutes, or until the edges are lightly browned, and the cheese has melted. Remove from the oven, and serve.

CHEESY HAM TRIANGLES

makes about 2 servings

---

1 piece (about 2 to 3 pounds) boneless chicken breast, trimmed and cut into bite-sized pieces
¾ cup flaked coconut

PANTRY
1 tablespoon butter or margarine
2 tablespoons prepared mustard
2 tablespoons honey

1 Position the rack in the center of the oven and preheat to 400 degrees F. Lightly grease a baking or cookie sheet.

2 In a small bowl, blend together the mustard and the honey. Dip the chicken into the mustard mixture, and roll in the coconut.

3 Arrange on the prepared baking sheet, and bake, turning occasionally, for about 15 to 20 minutes, or until the lightly browned. Remove from the oven, and serve.

CHICKEN COCONUT BITES

makes about 20 servings

CHICKEN CRESCENT ROLLS

makes about 4 serving

2 cups cubed cooked chicken
1 package (4 ounces) cream cheese, room temperature
1 package (8 ounces) crescent rolls, separated

PANTRY
2 tablespoons milk

1 Position the rack in the center of the oven and preheat to 350 degrees F. Have a baking or cookie sheet available.

2 In a bowl, using a wire whisk or an electric mixer, blend together the milk and the cheese. Blend in the chicken.

3 Place the chicken mixture in the centers of the rolls, and pull the corners up to the center and seal. Arrange on the baking sheet, and bake for about 20 to 25 minutes, or until a light golden-brown. Remove from the oven, and serve.

CHICKEN SALAD SANDWICHES

makes about 4 to 8 servings

1 piece (about 1 pound) boneless chicken breast, cooked and shredded
¼ cup chopped celery
8 small dinner rolls

PANTRY
½ cup mayonnaise

1 In a bowl, blend together the chicken, the mayonnaise, and the celery.

2 Cut the tops of the rolls, scoop out the interior, and top with the chicken mixture. Replace the tops, and serve.

Cooking note: For variation, top with sliced onions, tomatoes, or olives.

CHILI CHICKEN WINGS

makes about 6 to 12 servings

12 chicken wings, separated and trimmed

PANTRY
2 tablespoons melted butter or margarine
2 tablespoons distilled white vinegar
2 tablespoons chili powder

1 Position the broiler rack about 4 inches from the heat.

2 In a bowl, blend together the chicken, the butter, the vinegar, and the chili powder.

3 Arrange the chicken on the broiler pan, and broil, turning occasionally, for about 15 to 20 minutes, or until golden-brown. Remove from the oven, and serve.

2 frankfurters
⅓ cup (canned) chili with beans
2 frankfurter buns, split
1 small onion, chopped

1 Wrap the frankfurters in paper towels, and microwave on high heat for about 20 seconds.

2 Put frankfurters in the buns, arrange on a microwave-proof plate, and top with the chili. Cook over high heat for about 40 seconds, or until thoroughly heated. Remove from the oven, sprinkle with the onions, and serve.

CHILI DOGS

makes about 2 servings

---

4 cups pecan halves

PANTRY
1 cup sugar
2 cups vegetable oil

1 In a large bowl, add the pecans, 6 cups of boiling water, and set aside about 5 minutes. Drain the liquid and blend in the sugar.

2 Arrange the pecans on a baking tray, making sure that they don't touch. Set aside for about 24 hours.

3 In a saucepan, heat the oil, add the pecans, and sauté, stirring frequently, for about 10 to 15 minutes, or until lightly browned. Remove from the heat, transfer to a rack covered with paper towels, drain, and serve.

CHINESE FRIED PECANS

makes about 10 servings

---

1 pound cooked roast beef, thinly sliced
½ cup (bottled) barbecue sauce
1 medium green bell pepper, stemmed, seeded and cut into thin strips
4 hard French rolls, split and toasted

In a saucepan, add the meat and the barbecue sauce. Cook for about 2 minutes, blend in the peppers and reduce to a simmer. Cover, and cook for about 15 minutes, or until tender. Remove from the heat, fill the rolls with the mixture, and serve.

CHUCKWAGON SANDWICHES

makes about 4 servings

COCKTAIL WEINERS

makes about 6 servings

1 package (16 ounces) chicken franks, cut into bite-sized pieces
1 jar (10 ounces) currant jelly

PANTRY
Prepared mustard to taste

In a saucepan, add the franks and the jelly. Cook over low heat for about 2 minutes, and blend in the mustard. Cook for about 10 to 15 minutes, or until thoroughly heated. Remove from the heat, and serve.

Cooking note: This recipe can also be prepared with store-bought cocktail sausages.

COLD MARINATED MUSHROOMS

makes about 12 servings

1 pound whole fresh white mushrooms, washed and trimmed
¼ cup (bottled or canned) spaghetti sauce
fresh parsley, chopped

PANTRY
1 tablespoon red wine vinegar

1 In a 3-quart saucepan, fill halfway with water, and bring to a boil. Add the mushrooms, and reduce to a simmer. Cook for about 3-5 minutes, or until tender.

2 In a bowl, blend together the mushrooms, the sauce, and vinegar. Cover with plastic wrap, and refrigerate for at least 2 hours.

3 Blend the mixture, garnish with parsley, and serve.

CORN QUESADILLAS

makes about 4 to 6 servings

½ cup frozen whole kernel corn, cooked and drained
4 flour tortillas, (6 inches each)
½ cup shredded mozzarella or cheddar cheese
1 tablespoon bottled salsa

1 On a flat surface, lay out 2 tortillas. Spread evenly with the corn, sprinkle with the cheese, and top with the salsa. Add the second tortilla to form a quesadilla.

2 Place the quesadillas on a microwave-proof plate, and cook on high heat for about 45 to 60 seconds, or until the cheese has melted. Remove from the microwave, cut into quarters, and serve with the remaining salsa on the side.

Cooking note: For variation, use different types of salsa.

CRABMEAT AND EGGS

makes about 4 servings

1 package (10 ounces) frozen crabmeat, thawed, cleaned and drained
1 tablespoon dry sherry
4 large eggs
1 scallion, trimmed and diced

PANTRY
Salt and pepper to taste

1 In a bowl, blend together the crabmeat and the sherry.

2 In another bowl, using a wire whisk or an electric mixer beat the eggs until thick and light colored. Blend in the scallions, the crabmeat, and the seasoning to taste.

3 Pour the mixture into a cold skillet, and cook over medium heat for about 3 minutes, or until the mixture has set. Turn to other side. Cook over low heat for about 3 minutes, or until set, and thoroughly heated. Remove from the heat, cut into wedges, and serve.

CRANBERRY CHICKEN SANDWICHES

makes about 4 sandwiches

4 frozen breaded chicken patties, cooked
1 cup shredded lettuce
4 tablespoons (canned or bottled) whole cranberry sauce
4 sandwich buns, split and warmed

Spread half of the lettuce on the bottom half of the buns, and top with the patties and the sauce. Sprinkle on the remaining lettuce, sandwich with the tops of the buns, and serve.

Cooking note: For variation, use Indian-style chutney in the sandwiches.

CRESCENT GARLIC TOAST

makes about 8 servings

1 package (8 ounces) refrigerated crescent dinner rolls, separated
½ cup (bottled) Caesar salad dressing
3 tablespoons grated Parmesan cheese

PANTRY
¼ teaspoon crushed dried basil

1 Position the rack in the center of the oven and preheat to 375 degrees F. Have a baking or cookie sheet ready.

2 In a small bowl, blend together the cheese and the basil.

3 Arrange the crescent rolls on the baking sheet. Brush with the salad dressing, and top with the cheese mixture. Bake for about 10 to 12 minutes, or until the cheese has melted, and rolls are light golden-brown. Remove from the oven, and serve.

Cooking note: For variation, try different types of salad dressing.

CROSTINI

makes about 18 to 20 servings

1 loaf (1 pound) fresh Italian bread

PANTRY
½ cup olive oil
2 garlic cloves, halved
¼ cup crushed dried rosemary

1 Position the rack in the center of the oven and preheat to 350 degrees F. Lightly grease a baking or cookie sheet.

2 Slice the bread into twenty ½-inch thick slices. Rub one side of the slices with the garlic, brush with the oil, and sprinkle the top with the rosemary.

3 Arrange the bread on the prepared baking sheet, and bake for about 20 minutes, or until both sides are lightly browned. Remove from the oven, and serve.

CRUSTY BASIL LOAF

makes about 16 servings

¼ cup fresh chopped basil
2 tablespoons fresh chopped oregano
1 loaf French bread, cut in half lengthwise, and cut into 1-inch slices

PANTRY
½ cup butter or margarine, room temperature

1 Position the rack in the center of the oven and preheat to 350 degrees F. Lightly grease a baking or cookie sheet.

2 In a bowl, blend together the butter, the basil, and the oregano. Cover with plastic wrap and refrigerate for about 2 to 3 hours.

3 Spread the butter over one side of the bread slices, and reassemble into original loaf shape. Arrange on the prepared baking sheet, and bake for about 20 minutes, or until the butter has melted, and loaf is lightly browned. Remove from the oven, cool slightly, and serve

6 slices Muenster cheese, cut lengthwise to make 12 strips
12 frankfurters, partially slit lengthwise
12 bacon slices

PANTRY
2 tablespoons vegetable oil
3 tablespoons prepared mustard

DEVILED FRANKFURTERS

makes about 6 servings

1 Spread the inner surfaces of the franks with mustard, and place a piece of the cheese in the slits. Wrap with a slice of bacon, and fasten with a toothpick.

2 In a skillet, heat the oil, add the franks, and sauté, turning frequently for about 10 minutes, or until the bacon is crisp. Remove from the heat, and serve.

Cooking note: For variation, try different types of cheese. You can also substitute honey mustard sauce for the mustard.

1¼ cups tortilla chips, finely crushed
1 package (1¼ ounces) taco spice and seasoning
2 dozen small chicken drumsticks, rinsed in water

PANTRY
1 tablespoon butter or margarine

DRUMSTICK APPETIZERS

makes about 24 servings

1 Position the rack in the center of the oven and preheat to 350 degrees F. Lightly grease a 13 x 9-inch baking pan.

2 In a bowl, blend together the chips and the seasoning. Blend in the chicken.

3 Arrange in the prepared baking pan, and bake for about 40 to 45 minutes, or until crispy. Remove from the oven, and serve.

Cooking note: Drumsticks make a great lunch or served as a side dish.

---

1 can (10¼ ounces) frozen clam chowder, thawed and drained
1 package (8 ounces) cream cheese, at room temperature

EASY CLAM-FLAVORED DIP

makes about 2 cups

In a bowl, using a wire whisk or an electric mixer, blend together the chowder and the cheese. Cover with plastic wrap, and refrigerate until ready to use.

Cooking note: For variation, blend in minced onions and ketchup.

ENDIVE WITH BLUE CHEESE

makes about 24 servings

1 package (3 ounces) cream cheese, at room temperature
1 package (3 ounces) blue cheese, crumbled, at room temperature
½ cup heavy cream
2 large bunches of Belgian endive, separated

PANTRY
¼ cup melted butter

1 In the container of a blender or food processor, combine the two cheeses and the cream. Process on high speed until smooth. Blend in the butter, and process on high speed until thickened.

2 In a flat dish, arrange the endive leaves, and top with the cheese mixture. Cover with plastic wrap, and refrigerate until ready to serve.

ENGLISH-STYLE BACON SANDWICH

makes about 4 servings

16 slices honey-cured bacon, cooked
8 slices bread
1 teaspoon cracked peppercorns

PANTRY
4 tablespoons butter or margarine, at room temperature
2 tablespoons (bottled) ketchup

1 Spread the butter on the bread slices, and top with the peppercorns.

2 In a skillet, add the bacon, and sauté for about 5 minutes, or until crispy. Transfer to a warming plate covered with paper towels.

3 In the same skillet, add the bread slices, and fry, buttered side down, for about 5 minutes, or until lightly browned.

4 In a casserole dish, arrange 4 of the bread slices, toasted side down, and add the bacon and the ketchup. Top with the second slice, cut in half diagonally, and serve.

ENGLISH-STYLE DILLY SQUARES

makes about 1 or 2 servings

2 slices bread, toasted
1 large kosher dill pickle, sliced
½ cup grated cheese of choice

PANTRY
1 tablespoon butter or margarine, at room temperature

1 Position the broiler rack about 4 inches from the heat.

2 Spread butter on the toasted bread. Add the pickles, and top with the cheese.

3 Arrange the bread on the broiler pan, and broil for about 5 minutes, or until the tops of the cheese are bubbly and lightly browned. Remove from the oven, and serve.

2 large eggs, beaten
1 cup bread crumbs
6 equal portions Camembert cheese

PANTRY
1 cup vegetable oil

1 Preheat a deep-fryer to about 350 degrees F.

2 Dip the cheese into the eggs, and roll in the bread crumbs until coated. Repeat the process until double coated.

3 Place the cheese in the hot oil, and cook for about 10 minutes, or until both sides are lightly browned. Transfer to a rack covered with paper towels, drain, and serve.

FRIED CAMEMBERT

makes about 6 servings

½ pound sesame seeds, washed
4 cups glutinous rice flour
4 chicken bouillon cubes

PANTRY
½ pound butter or margarine
½ pound sugar

1 In a dry skillet, add the seeds and cook, stirring frequently, for about 3 to 5 minutes, or until lightly browned.

2 In the container of a blender or food processor, add the seeds. Process on high speed until finely ground.

3 In a bowl, blend together the seeds, the butter, and the sugar. Pinch off small pieces, and shape into balls.

4 In another bowl, add the flour, and enough water to form a smooth dough. On a lightly floured surface, roll out the dough to a thickness of ¼ inch. Cut out circles about 1½-inches in diameter, and place the butter balls in the center. Pull up the edges to seal.

5 In a large saucepan, add 4 cups of water and bring to a boil. Add the bouillon, and the dumplings. Cook for about 10 to 15 minutes, or until the dumplings float to the top. Remove from the heat, and serve in their own liquid.

FULL MOON DUMPLINGS

makes about 4 servings

GARLIC CHEESE BREAD

makes about 4 servings

2 tablespoons grated Parmesan cheese

4 slices French bread, diagonally cut 1-inch thick

PANTRY

2 tablespoons butter or margarine, at room temperature

⅛ teaspoon garlic powder

1 Position the broiler rack about 6 inches from the heat.

2 In a bowl blend together the butter, the cheese, and the garlic powder.

3 Arrange the bread on the broiler pan, and broil for about 4 to 6 minutes per side, or until both sides are lightly toasted.

4 Spread the bread slices with the cheese mixture, and broil for about 1 to 2 minutes, or until lightly browned. Remove from the oven and serve.

GARLIC FINGER SANDWICHES

makes about 4 servings

2 bunches fresh parsley, finely chopped

4 slices white bread

PANTRY

2 garlic cloves, crushed

½ cup mayonnaise

1 In a bowl, blend together the parsley, the garlic and the mayonnaise.

2 Spread the mixture on two slices of bread, and sandwich them with the remaining slices. Cut each sandwich into four pieces and serve.

Cooking note: This spread should be made and used the same day.

GARLIC MUFFINS

makes 8 muffin halves

3 tablespoons prepared garlic spread

4 English muffins, split, and toasted

2 tablespoons grated Parmesan cheese

PANTRY

3 tablespoons butter or margarine

1 Position the broiler rack about 6 inches from the heat.

2 In a bowl, blend together the garlic spread and the butter.

3 Spread the mixture on the muffins, and place on the broiler pan. Broil for about 4 to 6 minutes, or until the cheese starts to bubble. Remove from the oven, and serve.

GLAZED BACON

makes about 6 to 8 appetizer servings

12 ounces sliced bacon, cut in half crosswise

½ cup firmly packed light-brown sugar

2 tablespoons burgundy or dry red wine

PANTRY

1 tablespoon prepared mustard

1 Position the rack in the center of the oven and preheat to 350 degrees F. Have a 15 x 10-inch jelly-roll baking pan available.

2 In a bowl, blend together the sugar, the wine, and the mustard.

3 Arrange the bacon in the baking pan, and bake for about 10 minutes, or until just crispy. Drain the juices, and brush the bacon with the sugar mixture. Bake for about 10 minutes, or until glazed. Remove from the oven, and serve.

GOLDEN CHICKEN TEMPURA BITS

makes about 4 servings

1 piece (about 2 to 3 pounds) boneless chicken breast, cut into bite-sized pieces

3 tablespoons (bottled) Oriental-style marinade of choice

1 large egg, beaten

1½ cups Japanese-style bread crumbs (also known as Panko)

PANTRY

1 cup vegetable oil

1 In a bowl, blend together the chicken and the marinade. Cover with plastic wrap, and refrigerate for about 1 hour. Remove the chicken from the sauce.

2 In a deep fryer, heat the oil to about 350 degrees F.

3 Dip the chicken into the egg, roll in the bread crumbs, and place in the hot oil. Cook, turning occasionally, for about 8 to 10 minutes or until golden-brown. Transfer to a rack covered with paper towels, drain, and serve.

Cooking note: For variation, serve with a dipping sauce on the side.

GRILLED CHEESE AND PEANUT BUTTER SANDWICHES

makes about 6 servings

12 slices bread of choice
¼ cup creamy-style peanut butter
6 slices American cheese

PANTRY
1 tablespoon butter or margarine, room temperature

1 Lightly grease a stove-top grill, and preheat.

2 Spread the peanut butter on 6 slices of bread, top with a slice of cheese, and sandwich with the second slice of bread. Place on the prepared grill and cook for about 8 to 10 minutes, or until both sides are lightly browned. Remove from the grill, and serve.

Cooking note: Cooking time for grilling recipes depends on the heat source.

HAM AND CHUTNEY SPREAD

makes about 1 cup

½ cup minced cooked ham
½ cup (bottled) chutney

In a bowl, blend together the ham and chutney. Cover with plastic wrap, and refrigerate for at least 1 hour before using.

Cooking note: This spread can be used on celery, and a wide variety of baked goods.

HAM PÂTÉ

makes about 4 servings

1 piece baked ham (about 10 ounces), diced
1 teaspoon prepared horseradish

PANTRY
2 tablespoons mayonnaise
2 teaspoons prepared mustard
Salt and pepper to taste

1 In the container of a blender or food processor, add the mayonnaise, the mustard, and the horseradish, and process on high speed until smooth. Add the ham, and the salt and pepper to taste. Continue to blend until incorporated.

2 Transfer to a dish, cover with plastic wrap and refrigerate for at least 1 hour before serving.

Cooking note: To deepen the flavor, add 2 teaspoons of white port wine or dry sherry.

1 honeydew melon
4 slices of cooked ham
4 medium pickles, cut
   lengthwise into four pieces
4 slices buttered pumpernickel
   bread

1 Cut the melon in half,
scoop out the seeds, peel, and
cut each half into 4 wedges.

2 Cut the ham slices in half,
wrap around the melon
wedges, arrange on top of the
pickles, and serve with the
bread on the side.

HAM WRAPPED MELON

makes about 4 servings

---

8 corn tortillas, cut into 6
   wedges

PANTRY
½ cup vegetable oil

1 In a deep fryer, heat the oil
to about 375 degrees F.

2 Place the tortilla wedges in
the hot oil, and cook for about
5 to 7 minutes, or until crispy
and a light golden-brown.
Transfer to a wire rack covered with paper towels, drain,
and serve.

Cooking note: Do not allow
the wedges to become a dark
brown.

HOMEMADE TORTILLA CHIPS

makes 48 chips

2½ pounds chicken wings,
   separated and trimmed
1 bottle (6 ounces) hot sauce

PANTRY
¾ cup vegetable oil for deep
   frying

1 In a deep fryer, heat the oil
to about 350 degrees F.

2 Add the wings to the hot
oil, and stir-fry for about 15 to
20 minutes, or until crispy.
Transfer to a rack covered
with paper towels, drain, and
serve with the hot sauce on
the side.

HOT CHICKEN WINGS

makes about 6 servings

ITALIAN PRESTO STROMBOLI

makes about 4 servings

1 package (10 ounces) refrigerated pizza dough

2 ounces of pepperoni, thinly sliced

1 package (6 ounces) provolone cheese, thinly sliced

1 tablespoon sesame seeds

PANTRY

¼ cup flour

1 Position the rack in the center of the oven and preheat to 350 degrees F. Lightly grease a baking or cookie sheet.

2 On a lightly floured surface, roll out the pizza dough to form a 12 x 10-inch rectangle.

3 Arrange the pepperoni and cheese over the pizza up to 2 inches from the edges. Starting at a long side, roll up jelly-roll fashion, pinching to seal the seam. Place seam-side down on the prepared baking sheet, and cut 3 diagonal slits in the top of the Stromboli for steam to escape. Brush very lightly with water, and sprinkle with the sesame seeds.

4 Bake for about 25 minutes, or until golden-brown. Remove from the oven, cool, cut into 1-inch slices, and serve.

KIELBASA APPETIZER

makes about 10 to 12 appetizers

1¼ pounds kielbasa sausage, thinly sliced

1 jar (10 ounces) red currant jelly

In a saucepan, add the jelly, and cook for about 3 minutes, or until melted. Blend in the sausages, and cook, stirring frequently, for about 5 minutes. Bring to a boil, and reduce to a simmer. Cover, and cook for about 10 minutes, or until thoroughly heated. Remove from the heat, and serve.

1¼ cups flour

PANTRY
¼ cup sesame oil

1 Preheat a stove-top griddle.

2 In a bowl, blend together the flour and ⅔ cup of boiling water. Blend in ⅓ cup of cold water, and knead into a smooth dough. Set aside for about 10 minutes.

3 On a lightly floured surface, work the dough into a baguette, and cut into eight pieces. Flatten the pieces into 4-inch round pancakes and brush them with the oil. Sandwich the oiled side pieces together, until you have four pancakes. Roll out to 6-inch rounds with a rolling pin, and place on the griddle. Cook for about 5 minutes, or until the underside starts to bubble. Turn over, and cook other side.

4 Remove from the heat, separate the pancakes, fold into quarters, and serve.

Cooking note: The pancakes can be reheated and served with fruits and sauces.

MANDARIN PANCAKES

makes about 4 to 6 servings

---

1 piece (about 1½ to 2 pounds) shoulder-cut boneless pork, cut to bite-sized pieces
8 to 10 warm tortillas (on the side)
½ cup (bottled) tomato salsa

PANTRY
1 tablespoon butter or margarine
¼ teaspoon garlic powder
Salt and pepper to taste

1 Position the rack in the center of the oven and preheat to 350 degrees F. Lightly grease a 13 x 9-inch baking dish.

2 Arrange the pork in the prepared baking dish, sprinkle with the garlic powder, and season to taste. Pour in about ½-inch of water, and bake for about 2 hours, or until most of the water has evaporated, and the meat has started to brown.

3 In a bowl, blend together the meat and the salsa, and serve with tortillas on the side.

MEAT TIDBITS

makes about 8 to 10 servings

MEXICAN PIMIENTO DIP

makes about 2½ cups

1 package (8 ounces) cream cheese, room temperature

1 jar (8 ounces) Mexican pasteurized processed cheese spread

1 jar (4 ounces) chopped pimiento, drained

1 scallion, trimmed and sliced

In a bowl, using a wire whisk or an electric mixer, blend together the cream cheese, the cheese spread, and the pimientos. Garnish with scallion and serve.

MINUTE STEAK SANDWICH

makes about 4 servings

4 individual-sized minute steaks

8 slices textured brown bread

PANTRY

2 to 4 tablespoons of butter or margarine

Salt and pepper to taste

1 In a skillet, melt the butter, add the steaks, and sauté for about 5 to 10 minutes, or until both sides are browned. Transfer to a warming plate and adjust the seasoning to taste.

2 In the same skillet, sauté the bread in the drippings, turning frequently, for about 5 minutes or until both sides are crispy. Remove from the heat, sandwich with the meat, and serve.

MOLDED SHRIMP PURÉE

makes about 2 to 4 servings

2 cups cooked shrimp

PANTRY

½ cup butter or margarine

Celery salt to taste

Cayenne pepper to taste

1 Position the rack in the center of the oven and preheat to 350 degrees F. Have a small loaf pan available.

2 In the container of a blender or food processor, purée the shrimp. Add the butter, season to taste and process on high speed until smooth.

3 Pour the mixture into the loaf pan and bake for about 30 minutes or until thoroughly heated. Remove from the oven, invert, slice and serve.

1 package (8 ounces) cream
  cheese, room temperature
1 can (7 ounces) crabmeat,
  drained and flaked
1 tablespoon Worcestershire
  sauce
1 tablespoon lemon juice

1 Position the rack in the center of the oven and preheat to
350 degrees F. Have a baking
dish available.

2 In a bowl, blend together
the cream cheese, the crabmeat, the sauce, and the
lemon juice.

3 Pour the mixture into the
baking dish, and bake for
about 15 to 20 minutes, or
until it releases its own liquid.
Remove from the oven and
serve.

Cooking note: Serve
with crackers or
toast.

NEW ENGLAND CRABMEAT

makes about 6 servings

---

1 package (8 ounces) cheddar
  cheese
36 pimiento-stuffed olives

PANTRY
1 tablespoon butter or margarine
1½ cups flour
½ cup melted butter or margarine

1 In a bowl, using a wire
whisk or an electric mixer,
blend together the cheese and
the flour. Blend in butter until
smooth. Pinch off small pieces
of the dough and roll into
balls. Press an olives into the
center of each ball, and
rework the dough so that it
covers the olive completely.
Arrange the balls about 1½ to
2 inches apart on a lightly
greased baking sheet. Cover,
and refrigerate for at least 2
hours.

2 Position the rack in the center of the oven and preheat to
400 degrees F.

3 Bake for about 15 to 20
minutes or until light golden-
brown. Remove from the
oven and serve.

OLIVE-CHEESE BALLS

makes about 4 servings

PANTRY SANDWICH

makes about 6 servings

12 slices toast, cut in half
  diagonally
1 pound cold cuts
1 can (10¾ ounces) mushroom
  gravy
1 can (8 ounces) pineapple
  tidbits, drained

PANTRY
1 tablespoon butter or margarine

1 Position the rack in the center of the oven and preheat to 350 degrees F. Lightly grease a baking or cookie sheet.

2 In a saucepan, combine the gravy and the pineapple, and cook for about 5 to 10 minutes, or until thoroughly heated.

3 Arrange the cold cuts on the prepared baking sheet and bake for about 5 to 10 minutes, or until thoroughly heated. Remove from the oven, arrange on the toast, top with the pineapple mixture, and serve.

PARTY CHEESE PUFFS

makes about 48 servings

2 cups grated sharp cheddar
  cheese
2 cups whole wheat flour
4 cups Rice Krispies™

PANTRY
1 cup butter or margarine

1 Position the rack in the center of the oven, and preheat to 400 degrees F. Lightly grease a baking or cookie sheet.

2 In a bowl, using a wire whisk or an electric mixer, blend together the flour, the butter, and the cheese. Blend in the Rice Krispies and form into a smooth dough. Pinch off small pieces and roll into balls.

3 Arrange the balls on the prepared baking sheet and bake for about 10 minutes, or until lightly browned. Remove from the oven, cool, and serve.

1 large banana, mashed
¼ cup seedless grapes, mashed
½ cup pecans, finely chopped
Fresh orange juice
4 slices white or dark bread

PANTRY
2 tablespoons butter

1 In a bowl, blend together the banana, the grapes, and the pecans. Add enough orange juice to make a paste.

2 Butter 2 slices of the bread, top with the banana mixture, sandwich with the second slice, and serve.

PECAN AND BANANA SANDWICHES

makes about 2 servings

---

1 loaf focaccia, unsliced
1 cup shredded provolone cheese
¼ teaspoon dried crushed red pepper flakes
½ cup sliced ripe olives

1 Position the rack in the center of the oven and preheat to 375 degrees F. Have a baking or cookie sheet available.

2 Place the focaccia on the baking sheet, sprinkle with the cheese and the pepper flakes, and top with the olives. Bake for about 6 to 8 minutes, or until the cheese has melted, and focaccia is warm. Remove from the oven, cool, cut into 12 wedges, and serve.

RED PEPPER AND PROVOLONE-TOPPED FOCACCIA

makes about one loaf or 12 wedges

---

1 French baguette, cut in half lengthwise

PANTRY
½ cup butter or margarine, room temperature
2 teaspoons garlic powder

1 Position the broiler rack about 6 inches from the heat.

2 In a bowl, blend together the butter and the garlic powder. Cover with plastic wrap and refrigerate for about 1 hour before using.

3 Cut the bread in half crosswise, and score, without cutting through, each section into 5 pieces. Spread the garlic butter on the bread. Broil for about 5 to 10 minutes or until golden-brown. Remove from the oven and serve.

QUICK GARLIC BREAD

makes about 20 servings

Quick Microwave Tortilla

makes about 1 serving

1 flour tortilla, about 6-inch diameter
1 tablespoon processed cheese
1 tablespoon chopped red pepper
1 teaspoon sliced scallion

Spread the cheese in the center of the tortilla, top with the red peppers and scallions, and fold in half. Place on a microwave-proof plate, cover and cook on high heat for about 15 to 20 seconds, or until the cheese has melted. Remove from the oven and serve.

Red Hot Chicken Wings

makes about 4 servings

2½ pounds chicken wings, separated and trimmed
2 tablespoons cider vinegar
5 tablespoons (bottled) hot sauce

PANTRY
3 tablespoons canola oil

1 Position the broiler rack about 6 inches from the heat. Lightly oil the broiler pan.

2 In a bowl, blend together the hot sauce, the oil and the vinegar. Add the wings, toss to coat, cover with plastic wrap and refrigerate for at least 2 hours.

3 Remove wings from sauce and arrange on the broiler pan. Brush with sauce and cook for about 10-15 minutes. Turn wings over, brush with sauce and cook additional 10-15 minutes or until thoroughly cooked and crispy. Remove from the oven and serve.

6 large red, green, or yellow bell peppers
1 cup Italian dressing
½ cup fresh basil, chopped

PANTRY
½ teaspoon black pepper

1 Position the broiler rack about 4 inches from the heat.

2 In the broiler pan, arrange the peppers and broil, turning occasionally, for about 20 minutes, or until the peppers are blackened. Remove from the oven and transfer into a large paper bag. Set aside for about 30 minutes.

3 Under cold running water, peel the skins off the peppers, core and cut into julienne strips.

4 In a bowl, blend together the peppers, the dressing, the basil and the black pepper. Cover with plastic wrap and refrigerate for about 4 hours before serving.

Cooking note: This dish should be served at room temperature.

ROASTED PEPPERS

makes about 3 cups roasted peppers

---

1 package (6 ounces) salami, sliced
1 small honeydew melon, peeled, seeded and cut into 6 wedges
¼ cup black olives, sliced
¼ cup green olives, sliced

On a serving platter, arrange the salami with the melon wedges, sprinkle olives slices on top, and serve.

SALAMI WITH FRUIT ANTIPASTO

makes about 6 servings

---

1 cup (canned) salmon, skinned, boned and flaked
2 tablespoons yellow onion, minced
1 tablespoon lemon juice

PANTRY
½ cup mayonnaise

1 In the container of a blender or food processor, combine the salmon, the mayonnaise, the onion, and the lemon juice. Process on medium speed until smooth.

2 Transfer the mixture to a bowl, cover with plastic wrap and refrigerate for at least 2 hours before using.

SALMON MOUSSE

makes about 1½ cups

SAUERKRAUT CORNED BEEF CRESCENTS

makes about 8 servings

1 can refrigerated quick crescent rolls, separated into 8 triangles
1 cup sauerkraut, drained
1 teaspoon caraway seeds
8 slices cooked corned beef

1 Position the rack in the center of the oven and preheat to 375 degrees F. Have a baking or cookie sheet available.

2 In a bowl, blend together the sauerkraut and the caraway seeds.

3 Arrange the triangles of dough on the baking sheet. Place a slice of meat on each triangle, top with 2 tablespoons of the sauerkraut mixture and roll up to form crescents. Bake for about 10 minutes or until light golden-brown. Remove from the oven and serve.

SAUSAGE APPETIZER IN PASTRY

makes about 20 servings

1 package (8 ounces) cream cheese, room temperature
1 pound sausage, cut into ½-inch pieces

PANTRY
1 cup butter or margarine
2 cups flour

1 Position the rack in the center of the oven and preheat to 400 degrees F. Lightly grease a baking or cookie sheet.

2 In a bowl, using a wire whisk or an electric mixer, blend the cheese and the butter. Blend in the flour and shape the mixture into a ball. Cover with plastic wrap and refrigerate for at least 1 hour.

3 Divide the ball in half and roll out to a rectangle of 12 x 15 inches on a lightly floured surface. Cut into 3-inch squares. Place a piece of sausage in the center of each square, pull up the edges, and press the tops to seal.

4 Arrange on the prepared baking sheet and bake for about 20 minutes, or until the pastry is golden-brown. Remove from the oven and serve.

1 pound sausage
2 cups grated sharp cheddar cheese
3 cups Bisquick™
⅓ cup unsweetened apple juice

PANTRY
1 tablespoon butter or margarine

1 Position the rack in the center of the oven and preheat to 350 degrees F. Lightly grease a baking or cookie sheet.

2 In a bowl, blend together the sausage, the cheese, the Bisquick, and the juice. Pinch off small pieces and roll into balls.

3 Arrange balls on the prepared baking sheet and bake, turning occasionally, for about 20 to 25 minutes or until lightly browned. Remove from the oven and serve.

SAUSAGE BALLS

makes about 5 dozen

1½ cups biscuit mix
1 pound grated cheddar cheese
1 pound sausage

1 Position the rack in the center of the oven and preheat to 350 degrees F. Have a baking or cookie sheet available.

2 In a bowl, blend together the biscuit mix, the cheese, and the sausage. Pinch off small pieces and roll into balls.

3 Arrange the balls on the baking sheet and bake, turning occasionally, for about 25 minutes or until lightly browned. Remove from the oven and serve.

SAUSAGE-CHEESE BALLS

makes about 4 servings

SESAME SHRIMP TOAST

makes about 4 to 6 servings

1 pound medium raw shrimp, cleaned
2 large egg whites, beaten until stiff
½ cup sesame seeds
4 slices day-old bread, cut in half and crusts removed

PANTRY
1 teaspoon cornstarch
Salt to taste
1 cup vegetable oil

1 In the container of a blender or food processor, process shrimp on high speed until finely chopped.

2 In a bowl, blend together the shrimp and the sesame seeds. Blend in the egg whites, the cornstarch, and the salt to taste.

3 Spread the shrimp mixture evenly on the bread and set aside for about 10 minutes.

4 In a skillet, heat the oil, and add the bread, shrimp side down. Cook for about 10 to 20 seconds, and turn to brown other side. Remove from the heat and serve.

Cooking note: Do not leave toast unattended while frying; it burns easily.

SOMERSET RAREBIT

makes about 1 to 2 servings

1½ cups grated cheddar or Monterey Jack cheese
1 tablespoon prepared mustard
2 tablespoons unsweetened apple cider
2 slices bread, toasted

In the top of a double boiler, over boiling water, blend together the cheese, the mustard, and the cider. Cook, stirring frequently, for about 5 minutes, or until the cheese has melted and the mixture is smooth. Spread the mixture on the toasted bread and serve.

SOY BEAN CURD ROLLS

makes about 3 to 4 servings

1 tablespoon sherry
3 dried bean curd rolls, cut into 1-inch lengths

PANTRY
¼ cup soy sauce
2 teaspoons sugar

1 In a saucepan, combine the soy sauce, the sugar, and the sherry. Bring to a boil and blend in ½ cup of water and the bean curd. Bring to a boil and reduce to a simmer. Cover and cook for about 15 minutes or until thoroughly heated. Remove from the heat and drain.

2 Pour the mixture into a bowl, cover with plastic wrap, and refrigerate until ready to use.

1 pound sausage, ground

1 package (8 ounces) cream cheese, room temperature

36 fresh mushroom caps, stemmed

PANTRY
Salt and pepper to taste

1 Position the rack in the center of the oven and preheat to 350 degrees F. Have a baking sheet available.

2 In a skillet, sauté the sausage for about 10 minutes, or until it loses its pinkish color.

3 In a bowl, using a wire whisk or an electric mixture, mix the cheese until smooth. Blend in the sausage and season to taste.

4 Press a small amount of the sausage cheese mixture into the mushroom caps and arrange on the baking sheet. Bake for about 10 minutes.

5 Position the broiler rack about 6 inches from the heat. Broil the mushrooms for about 2 minutes or until light golden-brown. Remove from the oven and serve.

STUFFED MUSHROOMS

makes about 18 to 36 servings

---

1 jar (7 ounces) oil-packed sun-dried tomatoes

1 package (8 ounces) cream cheese, room temperature

6 slices dark rye bread

1 small cucumber, peeled and sliced

PANTRY
2 garlic cloves, minced

1 Drain the tomatoes, reserving 2 teaspoons of the oil.

2 In the container of a blender or food processor combine the tomatoes, the cheese, the garlic, and the reserved oil. Process on high speed until smooth.

3 Spread the mixture on the bread, top with sliced cucumbers and serve.

SUN-DRIED TOMATO OPEN SANDWICH

makes about 4 to 6 servings

Super Nachos

makes about 6 servings

2 dozen corn tortillas, cut into triangles
½ pound sharp cheddar cheese
1 can (4 ounces) sliced jalapeño peppers

PANTRY
¾ cup milk
Chili powder to taste
4 tablespoons vegetable oil

1 In a saucepan, blend the cheese and the milk, and cook for about 2 minutes. Add chili powder to taste, and cook for about 2 minutes or until thickened.

2 In a skillet, heat the oil and fry the tortillas for about 5 minutes or until light golden-brown. Remove from the heat, top with the sauce, garnish with jalapeño peppers, and serve.

Chili Pork Strips

makes about 2 to 4 servings

½ cup bread crumbs
1 boneless pork chop, about ½-inch thick, cut into narrow strips

PANTRY
1 tablespoon chili powder

1 In a bowl, blend together the bread crumbs and the chili powder. Stir in the meat and arrange on a microwave-proof plate.

2 Cover and cook on low heat for about 2 minutes. Turn over and continue to cook for about 3 minutes. Remove from oven and serve.

Texas Grilled Toast

makes about 6 servings

6 slices bread, cut 1-inch thick
2 teaspoons fresh chives, chopped
1 teaspoon barbecue seasoning

PANTRY
⅓ cup melted butter or margarine

1 Position the broiler rack about 4 inches from the heat.

2 In a bowl, blend the butter and the barbecue seasoning. Brush the mixture on both sides of the bread and sprinkle them with the chives. Arrange bread on the broiler pan and broil, turning only once, for about 4 to 6 minutes or until the bread is lightly toasted.

5 slices bread
1 tablespoon prepared mustard
½ pound ground beef
1 tablespoon yellow onion, minced

PANTRY
¾ cup milk
¼ cup melted butter or margarine
Salt and pepper to taste

1 Position the broiler rack about 6 inches from the heat.

2 In a bowl, blend the beef, the milk, and the onion. Season to taste.

3 Arrange the bread on the broiler pan and broil for about 2 minutes or until lightly toasted. Turn over, brush with the butter and mustard, and spread with the meat mixture. Drizzle on a little butter and broil for about 10 to 15 minutes or until lightly browned. Remove from the oven and serve.

THE 5-MINUTE OPEN STEAK SANDWICH

makes about 4 to 5 servings

---

8 slices bread, lightly buttered
4 teaspoons A1™ steak sauce
1 can (16 ounces) baked beans in sauce
½ cup grated Tillamook cheese

PANTRY
1 tablespoon butter or margarine

1 Sprinkle four bread slices with the steak sauce, add the beans, and top with the cheese. Sandwich with the second slice of bread and press gently.

2 Lightly grease a stove-top grill pan and grill the sandwiches for about 8 minutes or until both sides are lightly browned. Remove from the grill and serve.

Cooking note: Cooking time for grilling recipes depends on the heat source.

TOASTED BAKED BEANS AND CHEESE SANDWICH

makes about 4 servings

---

6 slices bread, toasted on one side
¾ pound corned beef, sliced
2 small white onions, sliced

PANTRY
¼ cup butter or margarine
¼ cup vegetable oil

1 Butter the untoasted sides of the bread and top with the corned beef.

2 In a skillet, heat the oil and sauté prepared bread, meat-side down for about 5 minutes or until thoroughly heated. Remove from the heat, garnish with white onion slices, and serve.

TOASTED OPEN CORNED BEEF SANDWICH

makes about 4 to 6 servings

TOMATO AND MOZZARELLA

makes about 4 servings

4 large beefsteak tomatoes, sliced

8 ounces sliced mozzarella cheese

16 fresh basil sprigs

PANTRY

4 tablespoons olive oil

Salt and pepper to taste

On a serving platter, spread out the tomato slices and season to taste. Top with the mozzarella and the basil sprigs. Drizzle on olive oil and serve.

TOMATO CHEESE TIDBITS

makes about 4 to 6 servings

1 can (10 ounces) cream of tomato soup

2 cups shredded Monterey Jack cheese

1 large egg, beaten

1 box (8 ounces) crackers (on the side)

PANTRY

½ teaspoon dry mustard

In a saucepan, blend the soup and the cheese. Cook, stirring frequently, for about 5 minutes or until the cheese has melted. Blend in the mustard and the egg and continue to cook, stirring occasionally, for about 3 minutes or until thoroughly heated. Remove from the heat and serve with the crackers on the side.

TORTILLA ROLL-UPS

makes about 6 servings

2 packages (8 ounces each) cream cheese, at room temperature

1 can (8 ounces) tomatoes, drained

4 scallions with greens, finely chopped

1 package jumbo-sized flour tortillas

PANTRY

1 tablespoon chili powder

1 In the container of a blender or food processor, combine the cheese, the tomatoes, and the scallions. Process on high speed until smooth.

2 Spread the mixture on the tortillas and roll them up in jelly-roll fashion. Place them in a dish, cover with plastic wrap and refrigerate for about 1 hour before serving.

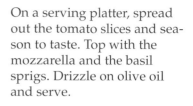

8 large stale corn tortillas,
broken into 1-inch pieces

PANTRY
½ cup vegetable oil
2½ teaspoons chili powder
½ teaspoon salt

In a skillet, heat the oil and
stir-fry the tortillas for about 5
minutes or until they become
crispy and golden-brown.
Drain the oil from the skillet
and sprinkle the tortillas with
the chili powder and salt.
Continue to cook, stirring frequently, for about 2 minutes
or until thoroughly heated.
Transfer to a rack covered
with paper towels, drain,
cool, and serve.

TOSTADITOS
makes about 6 to 8 servings

1 box (8½ ounces) corn muffin
mix, prepared
½ cup frozen mixed vegetables,
thawed and drained
¼ cup grated pepper cheese

PANTRY
1 tablespoon butter or margarine

1 Position the rack in the center of the oven and preheat to
350 degrees F. Lightly grease a
9-inch square baking pan.

2 In a bowl, blend together
the muffin mix and the vegetables. Pour the mixture into
the prepared baking pan and
bake for about 20 minutes.
Sprinkle with cheese and continue to bake for 5 minutes or
until the cheese has melted
and a cake tester inserted in
the center comes out clean.
Remove from the oven and
serve.

VEGETABLE CORNBREAD
makes about 4 servings

6 small white onions, chopped
4 hard-boiled eggs
¼ cup walnuts, finely chopped

PANTRY
2 tablespoons vegetable oil

1 In a skillet, heat the oil,
sauté the onions for about 5
minutes or until lightly
browned.

2 In the container of a
blender or food processor,
process the onions, eggs, and
walnuts on high speed until
smooth.

3 Pour the mixture into a
bowl, cover with plastic
wrap, and refrigerate until
ready to use.

Cooking note: Serve on toast
or crackers.

VEGETARIAN LIVER
makes about 8 servings

VEGETABLE PIZZA

makes about 4 servings

2 English muffins, split
4 tablespoons cream cheese, at room temperature
1 cup broccoli florettes, chopped
1 cup grated pepper cheese

1 Position the broiler rack about 4 inches from the heat.

2 Spread the cream cheese on the muffins and top with the broccoli and the cheese.

3 Place the muffins on the broiler pan and broil for about 3 to 4 minutes or until the cheese has melted. Remove from the oven and serve.

VEGETARIAN TOSTITOS

makes about 2 servings

2 whole wheat tortillas
2 heaping tablespoons refried beans
2 tablespoons grated cheddar cheese
1 tablespoon (bottled) mild tomato salsa

1 Position the rack in the center of the oven and preheat to 350 degrees F. Have a baking or cookie sheet available.

2 Spoon the beans over the tortillas and sprinkle with cheese. Fold the tortillas in half and fasten with a toothpick.

3 Arrange the tortillas on the baking sheet and bake for about 10 minutes or until lightly browned. Remove from the oven, top with the salsa and serve.

Eggs and Dairy

Eggs and dairy offer us some of our most comforting meals, and in 4-Ingredient cooking, they're not just for breakfast. With the addition of a few simple but lively flavors, you can transform an egg into a light meal that will satisfy everyone's appetite morning, noon or night.

If you've never enjoyed the taste of broiled eggs, try Eggs Carmelo, where aromatic rosemary and pungent tomatoes are blended with eggs and then cooked under the broiler to perfection. Eggs, crabmeat, and ginger steamed inside green peppers will make Green Peppers Stuffed with Eggs a quick and easy "standard" on your menu. Here you'll find eggs prepared in just about every way, from a multitude of omelets to a variety of international treats. They all include sauces and chilis and other great flavor enhancers.

In the dairy section you'll find recipes for amazing dishes made with cheese. You won't be able to resist prepar-

EGGS IN BREAD CUPS

ing Greek Fried Cheese, where kasseri cheese is fried until it becomes golden-brown and crusty, and lemon juice sprinkled on top brings out enormous flavor. Mouthwatering dishes, such as Honey-Nut Baked Brie and Mexican Cheese Spread, are all prepared with astonishing ease. They will not only transform the way you cook but the way you eat.

EASY CHEESE SOUFFLÉ

Asparagi à la Fiorentina

makes about 4 to 6 servings

4 eggs
1 package (10 ounces) frozen asparagus tips, cooked and drained
2 tablespoons grated Romano cheese

PANTRY
1½ tablespoons butter or margarine

1 In a saucepan, melt the butter and scramble the eggs.

2 In a skillet, melt the butter and add the asparagus. Stir-fry for about 2 to 3 minutes or until lightly browned. Remove from the heat, garnish with grated Romano cheese, and serve with the scrambled eggs.

Cheesy Eggs

makes about 4 servings

1 can (11 ounces) nacho cheese soup
8 large eggs
Watercress sprigs

In a microwave-proof bowl, blend together the soup and the eggs. Cover and cook on high heat, stirring frequently, for about 6 minutes or until the mixture has nearly set. Remove from the oven, garnish with watercress, and serve.

Cottage Cheese Salad

1½ cups cottage cheese
1 pint fresh blueberries, washed and dried
Watercress
Sliced peaches

1 In a bowl combine the cheese and blueberries.

2 On a flat surface, lay out 6 salad plates and arrange a generous helping of watercress on each plate. Mound the cheese mixture on top of the cress and garnish with sliced peaches.

½ cup grated sharp cheddar
  cheese
2 tablespoons heavy cream
5 large eggs, beaten until thick

PANTRY
2 tablespoons butter or
  margarine
Salt and pepper to taste

In the top of a double boiler over steaming water, blend the butter, the cheese, the cream, and 2 tablespoons water. Cook, stirring occasionally, for about 3 minutes or until the cheese has melted and the mixture is smooth. Blend in the eggs and cook, stirring frequently for about 5 to 7 minutes or until thoroughly heated. Remove from the heat, season to taste and serve.

CREAMY EGGS AND CHEESE

makes about 4 servings

1 cup Brie cheese, at room
  temperature
2 tablespoons heavy cream

PANTRY
Salt and pepper to taste

In a bowl, using a wire whisk or an electric mixer, blend together the cheese and the cream until it becomes the consistency of soft butter. Season to taste, cover with plastic wrap and refrigerate for at least 2 hours before serving.

Cooking note: For variation, substitute the brie cheese with other kinds of soft cheese.

DUTCH-STYLE CHEESE SPREAD

makes about 1¼ cups

3 large eggs
½ cup heavy cream
¾ cup powdered sugar

PANTRY
1 tablespoon butter or margarine
½ teaspoon salt
½ cup flour

1 Position the rack in the center of the oven and preheat to 350 degrees F. Lightly grease an 8-inch square baking pan.

2 In a bowl, using a wire whisk or an electric mixer, beat the eggs until lightly colored. Blend in the salt, the flour and the cream.

3 Pour the mixture into the prepared baking pan and bake for about 20 to 25 minutes or until the top is golden-brown. Remove from the oven and serve with the powdered sugar on the side.

DUTCH-STYLE PANCAKES

makes about 4 servings

Easy Cheese Soufflé

makes about 6 servings

1 can (10½ ounces) cream of asparagus soup
1 cup shredded Monterey Jack cheese
6 large eggs, separated

PANTRY
1 tablespoon butter or margarine

1 Position the rack in the center of the oven and preheat to 300 degrees F. Lightly grease a 3-quart casserole baking dish.

2 In a small bowl, beat the egg yolks.

3 In another bowl, using a wire whisk or an electric mixer, beat the egg whites until stiff but not dry.

4 In a saucepan, pour in the soup and cook for about 8 to 10 minutes or until thoroughly heated. Blend in the cheese and cook for about 8 minutes or until melted. Blend in the egg yolks and remove from the heat. Set aside for about 10 minutes or until cooled and blend in the egg whites.

5 Pour the mixture into the prepared baking dish and bake for about 1 hour or until set. Remove from the oven and serve.

Savory Eggs and Cauliflower

makes about 4 servings

1 medium head cauliflower, cut into the florettes, cooked and drained
2 hard-boiled eggs, shelled and sliced
1 cup Basic White Sauce (see page 398)
1 tablespoon watercress, chopped

PANTRY
1 teaspoon salt

1 Prepare the White Sauce and keep warm.

2 On a serving platter, arrange the florettes, top with sliced eggs, pour on the sauce, garnish with watercress, and serve.

8 large eggs
¼ cup light cream
1 small avocado, peeled, seeded and diced

PANTRY
¼ cup butter or margarine
Salt and pepper to taste

1 In a bowl, using a wire whisk or an electric mixer, blend together the eggs and the cream, and season to taste.

2 In the top of a double boiler, over boiling water, melt the butter and blend in the egg mixture. Cook, stirring occasionally, for about five minutes and blend in the avocado. Cook for another five minutes or until thoroughly heated. Remove from the heat and serve.

EGG AVOCADO SCRAMBLE

makes about 4 servings

---

3 large eggs
1 cup bean sprouts, washed and trimmed
½ cup chopped cooked pork
1 tablespoon white onion, chopped

PANTRY
2 tablespoons vegetable oil
Soy sauce to taste

1 In a bowl, using a wire whisk or an electric mixer, beat the eggs until thickened. Blend in the bean sprouts, the pork, the onions, and the soy sauce to taste.

2 In a wok, heat the oil and spoon in the mixture, forming into small pancakes. Cook for about 5 minutes or until the eggs have set. Fold "pancakes" in half, and cook for about 2 minutes or until lightly browned. Remove from heat and serve.

EGG FOO YONG

makes about 4 servings

---

2 large red bell peppers, stemmed, seeded and cut in half crosswise
8 large eggs

PANTRY
1 tablespoon butter or margarine
1 cup (canned) tomato sauce

1 Position the rack in the center of the oven and preheat to 375 degrees F. Lightly grease a baking pan.

2 In a saucepan, cover the peppers with lightly salted water and bring to a boil.

Cook for about 5 minutes until just tender.

3 Arrange the peppers in the prepared baking pan and break 2 eggs into each pepper half. Top with the butter and fill the pan with ¾ inch of water.

4 Bake for about 4 to 5 minutes or until the eggs have set. Top with the tomato sauce and bake for about 10 minutes or until thoroughly heated. Remove from the oven and serve.

EGGS BAKED IN PEPPERS

makes about 4 servings

Eggs Baked in Sour Cream

makes about 3 to 6 servings

1½ cups sour cream
6 large eggs
½ cup bread crumbs

PANTRY
2 tablespoons melted butter or
   margarine
Salt and pepper to taste

1 Position the rack in the center of the oven and preheat to 350 degrees F. Lightly grease a shallow baking dish.

2 In a bowl, blend together the bread crumbs and 1½ tablespoons butter.

3 In a bowl, using a wire whisk or an electric mixer, blend together the eggs and ½ tablespoon butter. Pour the mixture into the prepared baking dish and top with the bread crumbs. Bake for about 20 minutes or until the top is lightly browned. Remove from the oven. Season to taste and serve.

Eggs Boiled in Soy Sauce

makes about 4 servings

5 hardboiled eggs

PANTRY
¼ cup soy sauce
1 teaspoon sugar
1 teaspoon sesame oil

In a saucepan, blend the soy sauce, the sugar, and the oil. Bring to a boil, add ¼ cup of water and blend in the eggs. Cook over low heat for about 5 minutes or until thoroughly heated. Remove from the heat and set aside for about 30 minutes. Drain and reserve the liquid. Cut the eggs into quarters and serve with the sauce on the side.

Eggs Boiled with Tea Leaves

makes about 4 servings

10 small eggs
4 tea bags
5 aniseed cloves

PANTRY
2 tablespoons soy sauce

In a saucepan, cover the eggs with water and bring to a boil. Cook for about 10 minutes. Drain, crack the eggs all over without removing the shells, and return to the pan. Cover with ice cold water and add the tea bags, the aniseed cloves, and the soy sauce. Bring to a boil and cook for about 20 minutes. Remove from the heat and cool. Remove the shells, slice and serve.

Cooking note: These are also called marbelized tea eggs.

6 ripe plum tomatoes, thinly
sliced
12 large eggs

PANTRY

¼ cup butter or margarine
1 tablespoon crushed dried
rosemary

1 Position the broiler rack
about 6 inches from the heat.
Lightly grease a shallow baking pan.

2 In a saucepan, melt the butter and add the rosemary. Stir-
fry for about 2 minutes or
until well-coated. Blend in the
tomatoes and cook for about 5
to 7 minutes or until thoroughly heated.

3 In a bowl, using a wire
whisk or an electric mixer,
beat the eggs until foamy and
blend in the tomato mixture.

4 Pour the mixture into the
prepared baking pan and
broil for about 3 minutes or
until the eggs have set.
Remove from the oven and
serve.

EGGS CARMELO

makes about 6 to 12 servings

1½ pounds fresh spinach,
washed, dried and trimmed
4 large eggs
4 tablespoons grated Pecorino
cheese

PANTRY

3 tablespoons olive oil
Salt and pepper to taste

1 Position the rack in the center of the oven and preheat to
350 degrees F. Lightly grease 4
individual ramekin dishes.
Have a baking or cookie sheet
available.

2 In a saucepan, heat the oil
and add the spinach. Cover
and simmer for about 10 to 12
minutes or until tender. Season to taste.

3 Arrange the spinach in the
prepared ramekins. Top each
of them with an egg, without
breaking the yolks, and sprinkle with the cheese.

4 Arrange ramekins on the
baking sheet and bake for
about 3 to 5 minutes or until
the egg whites are firm but
the yolks are still soft.
Remove from the oven and
serve.

EGGS FLORENTINE

makes about 4 servings

EGGS IN A NEST

makes about 1 to 2 servings

2 large eggs
2 slices day-old bread

PANTRY
1 tablespoon butter or margarine
Salt and pepper to taste

1 Spread the butter evenly on both sides of the bread and, using a 2¼-inch round cookie cutter, cut out a hole in the center of the bread.

2 In a heated skillet, toast the bread and the cutouts, until both sides are lightly browned. Transfer the cutouts to a warming plate, and break the eggs into the holes in the bread, without breaking the yoke. Cover and cook over low heat for about 2 to 3 minutes, or until the whites are firm but the yokes are still soft. Remove from the heat, season to taste, top with the cutouts and serve.

EGGS IN BREAD CUPS

makes about 4 to 6 servings

6 slices bread, crusts removed
6 large eggs

PANTRY
¼ cup melted butter or margarine
Salt and pepper to taste

1 Position the rack in the center of the oven and preheat to 400 degrees F. Lightly grease a 6-cup muffin pan.

2 Roll out the bread slices until flattened and brush with the butter. Press into the prepared muffin cups and top with the eggs without breaking the yolk. Season to taste and top with a drop of butter.

3 Bake for about 15 or 20 minutes or until the whites of the eggs are set and the edges of the bread are toasted. Remove from the oven and serve.

6 large eggs
1 tablespoon sumac

PANTRY
4 tablespoons olive oil
Salt and pepper to taste

In a skillet, heat the oil and add the eggs without breaking the yolk. Sprinkle the tops with the sumac, cover, and cook over low heat for about 2 to 3 minutes, or until the whites are firm, but the yolks are still soft. Season to taste and serve.

EGGS IN OIL WITH SUMAC

makes about 3 to 6 servings

---

4 large green peppers, stemmed, seeded and cut into julienne strips
5 large eggs, beaten

PANTRY
5 tablespoons olive oil
1 garlic clove, minced

In a skillet, heat the oil and add the garlic and the peppers. Sauté for about 3 minutes and reduce to a simmer. Cover and cook for about 15 minutes, or until tender. Blend in the eggs and cook, stirring frequently, for about 5 minutes or until thoroughly heated. Remove from the heat and serve.

EGGS WITH GREEN PEPPERS

makes about 4 servings

---

4 large eggs, beaten
12 large ripe Italian olives, pitted
2 ounces provolone cheese, diced into ½-inch pieces

PANTRY
3 tablespoons olive oil
Salt and pepper to taste

In a skillet, heat the oil, add the olives and sauté for about 2 minutes. Blend in the cheese and cook, stirring frequently, for about 1 minute. Blend in the eggs and season to taste. Cook, stirring frequently, for about 5 minutes or until thoroughly heated. Remove from the heat and serve.

EGGS WITH OLIVES AND PROVOLONE

makes about 2 servings

Eggs with Sweet and Sour Sauce

makes about 4 servings

6 large eggs

PANTRY
2 tablespoons vegetable oil
1 tablespoon soy sauce
1 tablespoon vinegar
1 tablespoon sugar

In a skillet, heat the oil and add the eggs without breaking the yolk. Cook for about 5 minutes or until the eggs are set. Fold in half and blend in the soy sauce, the vinegar, and the sugar. Bring to a boil and reduce to a simmer. Cook for about 1 minute or until thoroughly heated. Remove from the heat and serve.

Frittata Italiana

makes about 4 servings

2 large sweet onions, thinly sliced
6 eggs

PANTRY
¼ cup olive oil
Salt and pepper to taste

1 In a skillet, heat the oil, add the onions and sauté for about 5 minutes or until translucent.

2 In a bowl, blend together the eggs, the onions, and season to taste.

3 In the same skillet, heat the oil, and add the egg mixture. Cover and cook over low heat for about 4 minutes or until the eggs are just set. Turn over and cook for about 2 minutes or until lightly browned. Remove from the heat and serve.

Ginger-Peach Yogurt

makes about 1 cup

1 carton (8 ounces) peach yogurt
1½ tablespoons orange marmalade
2 tablespoons (bottled) ginger preserves

In a bowl, blend together the yogurt, the marmalade, and the preserves. Cover with plastic wrap and refrigerate for at least 2 hours before using.

GREEK FRIED CHEESE

makes about 4 servings

⅓ pound kasseri cheese, cut into bite-sized pieces
1 tablespoon lemon juice

PANTRY
2 tablespoons butter or margarine

In a skillet, melt the butter and add the cheese. Stir-fry for about 8 to 10 minutes or until crusty and lightly browned. Top with the lemon juice and cook for about 1 minute or until thoroughly heated. Remove from the heat and serve.

GREEN PEPPERS STUFFED WITH EGGS

makes about 4 servings

1 can (4 ounces) water-packed crab meat, drained and flaked
4 medium green bell peppers, stemmed, seeded and cut in half sideways
8 hardboiled eggs, shelled and chopped
1 teaspoon ginger juice

PANTRY
Salt and pepper to taste
1 tablespoon sesame oil

1 In a bowl, blend together the eggs, the crab meat, the ginger juice, and season to taste. Press the mixture evenly into the pepper halves.

2 In a bamboo steamer, steam the peppers over a pot of boiling water for about 10 minutes and sprinkle with the oil. Continue to steam for about 5 minutes or until tender. Remove from the heat and serve.

HOMEMADE MUESLI

makes about 12 ounces

4 ounces rolled oats
4 ounces seedless raisins
4 ounces pecans or walnuts, chopped
2 ounces light-brown sugar

In a bowl, blend together the oats, the raisins, the nuts, and the sugar. Place in an airtight container and use as desired.

Cooking note: For a thick cereal soak the Muesli in milk and refrigerate until morning.

Honey-Nut Baked Brie

makes about 16 to 20 servings

¼ cup coarsely chopped pecans
1 wheel (14-ounces, about 5-inches in diameter) Brie cheese
1 tablespoon brandy

PANTRY
1 tablespoon butter or margarine
¼ cup honey

1 Position the rack in the center of the oven and preheat to 500 degrees F. Lightly grease a 9-inch round baking dish.

2 In a bowl, blend together the honey, the pecans and the brandy.

3 Place the cheese in the prepared baking pan and bake for about 4 minutes or until the cheese starts to soften. Drizzle the top with the honey mixture and continue to bake for about 3 minutes or until thoroughly heated but not melted. Remove from the oven and serve.

Huevos Rancheros

makes about 4 servings

1 cup (bottled) thick salsa, heated
8 large eggs, beaten
4 corn tortillas, heated

PANTRY
1 tablespoon butter or margarine

1 In a skillet, sauté the eggs in melted butter for about 3 to 5 minutes or until firm.

2 Top the tortillas with the eggs and the salsa, fold over to hold the mixture and serve.

Jellied Eggs and Bacon

makes about 4 servings

1 can (10½ ounces) condensed beef consommé, chilled
4 hardboiled eggs
4 slices Canadian bacon, fried and chopped
1 tablespoon parsley, chopped

Place the eggs in 4 ramekin dishes, sprinkle on the bacon, and top with the consommé. Garnish with parsley and refrigerate for about 30 minutes before serving.

1 can (4 ounces) chopped green chiles, drained

1 package (8 ounces) Neufchatel cheese, room temperature

PANTRY

1 tablespoon milk

In a bowl, using a wire whisk, or an electric mixer, blend together the cheese, the chiles, and the milk until the consistency resembles soft butter. Cover with plastic wrap and refrigerate for at least 1 hour before using.

Mexican Cheese Spread

makes about 2 cups

---

6 large eggs, separated

1 teaspoon fresh parsley, snipped

1 teaspoon anchovy paste

PANTRY

1 tablespoon butter or margarine

Salt and pepper to taste

1 Position the rack in the center of the oven and preheat to 350 degrees F.

2 In a bowl, using a wire whisk or an electric mixer, beat the egg yolks until thick and lightly colored. Blend in the parsley, the anchovy paste and season to taste.

3 In another bowl, using a wire whisk or an electric mixer, beat the egg whites until stiff but not dry. Blend in the egg yolk mixture.

4 In a skillet, cook the egg mixture in melted butter for about 3 minutes or until the bottom is lightly browned.

5 Bake for about 3 minutes or until the top is lightly browned. Remove from the oven and serve.

New England Sailor's Omelet

makes about 6 servings

One Egg Hamlet

makes 1 serving

1 large egg
1 slice American cheese
1 hamburger roll, split
1 slice cooked ham

PANTRY
Salt and pepper to taste

1 In a microwave-proof bowl, beat egg until smooth. Cover and cook on high heat, stirring once, for about 1½ minutes or until firm.

2 Place the roll on a microwave-proof dish and top with the cheese, the ham, and the egg. Season to taste and sandwich with the top of the roll. Cover and cook on high heat for about 15 to 20 seconds or until thoroughly heated. Remove from the oven and serve.

Onion Omelet

makes about 4 servings

4 large eggs, beaten
1 large yellow onion, thinly
   sliced

PANTRY
3 tablespoons olive oil

1 In a skillet, sauté the onions in olive oil for about 5 minutes or until lightly browned. Transfer to a warming plate.

2 In the same skillet, cook the eggs in oil for about 5 minutes or until firm. Top with the onions, fold in half and continue to cook for about 2 minutes or until thoroughly heated. Remove from the heat and serve.

Poached Eggs and Spinach

makes about 2 to 4 servings

1 package (10 ounces) frozen
   chopped spinach, cooked and
   drained
4 eggs
¾ cup (bottled) hollandaise
   sauce

PANTRY
1 tablespoon butter or margarine
Salt and pepper to taste

1 Position the rack in the center of the oven and preheat to 350 degrees F. Lightly grease a baking dish.

2 Arrange the spinach in the prepared baking dish, season to taste and top with the eggs without breaking the yolks. Cover and bake for about 3 to 5 minutes, or until the whites are firm but the yolks are still soft. Remove from the oven and serve with the hollandaise sauce on the side.

1 can (4¾ ounces) chicken
  spread
3 English muffins, split and
  toasted
6 poached eggs
Chopped chives

PANTRY
½ teaspoon ground thyme

In a bowl, blend together the chicken and the thyme. Spread the mixture on each muffin half, top with an egg, garnish with chives, and serve.

POACHED EGGS ON CHICKEN MUFFINS

makes about 3 to 4 servings

1 cup (bottled) salsa
6 eggs, partially beaten
½ cup sour cream

PANTRY
1 tablespoon butter or margarine

In a skillet, heat the salsa and blend in the eggs. Cook, stirring frequently, for about 5 minutes or until the eggs have set. Remove from the heat and serve with the sour cream on the side.

SALSA SCRAMBLED EGGS

makes about 3 to 4 servings

¼ pound bacon, diced
2 cups whole kernel corn
3 large eggs, beaten

PANTRY
Salt and pepper to taste

In a skillet, sauté the bacon for about 5 minutes or until browned. Blend in the corn, cook for about 2 minutes and blend in the eggs. Cook for about 5 minutes or until the eggs have set. Remove from the heat, season to taste, and serve.

SCRAMBLED EGGS AND CORN

makes about 2 to 3 servings

SCRAMBLED EGGS AND FRANKFURTERS

makes about 4 servings

4 frankfurters, cut into small pieces
8 eggs, beaten
2 tablespoons vegetable juice

PANTRY
1 tablespoon vegetable oil

1 In a bowl, blend together the eggs and the juice.

2 In a skillet, sauté the franks in oil for about 2 minutes or until lightly browned. Blend in the egg mixture and cook for about 5 minutes or until the eggs have set. Remove from the heat, cut into wedges, and serve.

Cooking note: For variation, add chopped ripe olives to the mixture.

SCRAMBLED EGGS WITH SPINACH

makes about 3 to 4 servings

5 large eggs, beaten
1 package (10 ounces) chopped frozen spinach thawed and drained

PANTRY
¼ cup vegetable oil
Salt and pepper to taste

1 In a wok, stir-fry the eggs in oil for about 2 minutes or until the eggs are firm. Transfer to a warming plate.

2 In the same wok, sauté the spinach in oil for about 5 minutes. Blend in the eggs and cook for about 1 minute or until thoroughly heated. Remove from the heat, season to taste, and serve.

6 large eggs, separated
⅓ cup pancake mix
⅓ cup unflavored yogurt or
** sour cream**

PANTRY
1 tablespoon vegetable oil

SOUFFLÉ PANCAKES

makes about 4 to 6 servings

1 Lightly oil and preheat a griddle.

2 In a bowl, using a wire whisk or an electric mixer, beat the egg yolks until thick and lightly colored. Blend in the pancake mix and the yogurt.

3 In another bowl, using a wire whisk or an electric mixer, beat the egg whites until stiff but not dry. Blend in the egg yolk mixture.

4 Drop the mixture, by tablespoons onto the prepared griddle, and cook for about 5 to 8 minutes or until both sides are light golden-brown. Remove from the heat and serve.

---

1 eggplant (about 8 inches long),
** washed and stemmed**
2 large eggs, beaten
3 tablespoons leeks, minced

PANTRY
¼ cup vegetable oil
3 tablespoons soy sauce

STEAMED EGGPLANT WITH EGGS

makes about 2 to 3 servings

1 In a bamboo steamer or a pot of boiling water, steam the eggplant for about 15 minutes or until tender. Cut the eggplant into 8 to 10 slices.

2 In a bowl, blend together the eggs, the leeks, and the soy sauce.

3 In a skillet, sauté the egg mixture in oil, stirring frequently, for about 5 minutes or until the eggs have set.

4 Remove from the heat and serve with the eggplant slices.

STEAMED QUAIL EGGS

makes about 6 servings

¼ **pound lean ground pork**
1 **teaspoon rice wine**
14 **quail eggs**
Chopped parsley (for garnish)

PANTRY
1 teaspoon butter or margarine
¼ teaspoon cornstarch or
   arrowroot
Salt and pepper to taste

1 In a bowl, blend together the pork, the wine and the cornstarch. Lightly grease 14 Chinese-style porcelain cups and spoon the pork mixture into the prepared cups.

2 Crack an egg over each cup of pork mixture. Place the cups in a bamboo steamer over a pot of boiling water for about 10 minutes.

3 Transfer to a serving platter, garnish and serve.

Cooking note: This dish can be served cold. For variation, garnish with chopped mushrooms.

SUPPER EGG BOWL

makes about 3 to 4 servings

6 **hot hard-boiled eggs, shelled
   and sliced**
4 **scallions with greens, trimmed
   and chopped**
4 **slices of cooked ham, cut into
   strips**

PANTRY
2 tablespoons melted butter or
   margarine
Salt and pepper

Slice the hot eggs into heated serving dishes. Drizzle on the butter and add the scallions and ham. Season to taste, toss gently, and serve immediately.

TEXAS-STYLE CHILI AND EGGS

makes about 4 servings

4 **thick slices bread, crusts
   removed**
3 **cups (canned) chili and beans**
8 **poached eggs**

PANTRY
1 tablespoon melted butter or
   margarine

1 Spread the butter on both sides of the bread.

2 In a skillet, sauté the bread for about 5 minutes or until both sides are lightly browned. Transfer to a warming plate.

3 In a saucepan, cook the chili for about 5 minutes until thoroughly heated.

4 Spread the chili over the bread, top with the eggs, and serve.

3 large eggs
1 cup grated American cheese

PANTRY
1 tablespoon butter or margarine
¼ teaspoon dry mustard
½ cup milk
Salt and pepper to taste

1 Position the rack in the center of the oven and pre-heat to 375 degrees F. Lightly grease a small casserole dish, and sprinkle the mustard, salt, and pepper to taste on the bottom of the dish.

2 In a bowl, using a wire whisk or an electric mixer, blend together the eggs, the cheese and the milk.

3 Pour the mixture into the prepared baking dish, set the dish in a pan of hot water and bake for about 35 minutes or until firmly set. Remove from the oven and serve.

TOASTED CHEESE CASEROLE

makes about 3 servings

---

1 medium cucumber, pared, diced, and patted dry
1 tablespoon fresh mint leaves, snipped
1 cup unflavored yogurt
6 pita breads

PANTRY
1 medium garlic clove, crushed
Salt and pepper to taste

In a bowl, combine the cucumber, the garlic, the mint leaves, and the yogurt. Season to taste and serve with the pita bread on the side.

Cooking note: For variation, garnish with mint sprigs.

TZATZIKI

makes about 6 servings

WAFFLE STACKS

makes about 2 servings

1 package of 4 frozen waffles, toasted

2 large eggs, cooked as desired

2 slices cooked ham

½ cup lettuce, shredded

Top 2 waffles with the ham and the eggs and sprinkle on the lettuce. Sandwich with the second slice and serve.

Salads

Move over lettuce and tomatoes! Here comes an array of fast and fantastic salads, guaranteed to change your definition of salad. In this collection, you'll find everything from side salads to main courses. Included

JICAMA-SPINACH SALAD

in this terrific assortment are: Apple and Fennel Salad, which blends the sweetness of apples with aromatic fennel, each with a satisfying crunch. There's an exotic and

richly-flavored Szechwan Cucumber Salad, and a fresh and sweet Chicken Salad with Grapes. There are also a slew of palate-pleasing cole slaws, among them Cilantro Slaw with Dressing, German Cabbage Salad and Hawaiian Country Slaw. What a great way to get healthful greens into your diet.

ORIENTAL PASTA SALAD

GRAPE AND GRAPEFRUIT SALAD

APPLE AND FENNEL SALAD

makes about 6 servings

5 ounces fresh spinach, washed
   trimmed and torn into
   bite-sized pieces
1 small head of fennel, sliced
2 medium Granny Smith apples,
   peeled, cored and diced
1 small red onion, sliced
½ cup dressing of choice

In a bowl, combine the spinach, the fennel, the apples and the onion. Drizzle on the dressing and serve.

BEETS AND POTATO SALAD

makes about 4 to 6 servings

3 medium-sized red-skinned
   potatoes, cooked and sliced
3 beets, cooked and sliced
¼ cup oil and vinegar dressing

PANTRY
4 teaspoons ground coriander
Salt and pepper to taste

1 In a small bowl, blend together the dressing and the coriander.

2 In another bowl, blend together the potatoes and the beets. Blend in the dressing, season to taste and serve.

CARROT SALAD

makes about 4 to 6 servings

1 pound carrots, trimmed, pared, and grated
1 bunch fresh chives, minced
2 teaspoons tarragon vinegar

PANTRY
1 cup mayonnaise

In a bowl, combine together the carrots, the chives, the mayonnaise, and the vinegar. Cover with plastic wrap and refrigerate for at least 15 minutes before serving.

CAULIFLOWER SALAD

makes about 6 to 8 servings

1 medium head of cauliflower, trimmed and cored
2 cups (prepared) guacamole
½ cup shredded cheddar cheese
radish roses

1 In a saucepan, cover the cauliflower with 1 cup of lightly salted water. Bring to a boil and cook for about 15 to 20 minutes or until tender.

2 Place the cauliflower in a bowl, cover with plastic wrap and refrigerate for about 1 hour. Top with the guacamole, sprinkle on the cheese, garnish with radish roses, and serve.

CHICKEN AND APPLE SALAD

makes about 4 to 6 servings

4 cups cooked chicken, diced
2 cups Macintosh apples, diced
1 cup celery, diced

PANTRY
½ cup mayonnaise

In a bowl, combine the chicken, the apples, the celery, and the mayonnaise. Cover with plastic wrap and refrigerate for at least 2 hours before serving.

CHICKEN AND PINEAPPLE SALAD

makes about 1 serving

½ cup (canned) crushed pineapple, drained
10 ounces cooked chicken, flaked

PANTRY
4 tablespoons mayonnaise

In a bowl, combine the pineapple, the chicken, and the mayonnaise. Cover with plastic wrap and refrigerate for at least 2 hours before serving.

CHICKEN SALAD WITH GRAPES

makes about 4 servings

4 cups salad greens, torn into bite-sized pieces and chilled
10 ounces cooked chicken, flaked
1 cup seedless grapes, halved
½ cup (bottled) Italian dressing

In a bowl, toss the salad greens, the chicken, the grapes, and the dressing. Cover with plastic wrap and refrigerate for about 1 hour before serving.

Cooking note: For variation, garnish with thinly sliced lemons.

CILANTRO SLAW WITH DRESSING

makes about 6 servings

1 small head of cabbage, finely shredded
2 tablespoons fresh cilantro, minced
1 medium cucumber, peeled, seeded and cut into 3-inch pieces
1 small yellow onion, minced
½ cup (bottled) garlic salad dressing

In a bowl, toss the cabbage, the onion, the cilantro, the cucumbers, and the salad dressing. Cover with plastic wrap and refrigerate for about 1 hour before serving.

½ pound bacon

1 medium head of cabbage, cored and shredded

2 cups white onions, chopped

½ cup sour cream or unflavored yogurt

1 In a skillet, sauté the bacon for about 10 minutes or until crispy. Transfer to a rack covered with paper towels and drain.

2 In the same skillet, sauté the onions for about 5 minutes and blend in the sour cream. Cook, stirring occasionally, for about 5 minutes and blend in the cabbage. Cook for about 10 minutes or until just tender. Blend in the bacon and cook for 3 to 5 minutes or until thoroughly heated. Remove from the heat and serve.

Cooking note: For variation, add some minced garlic while cooking.

DANISH-STYLE CABBAGE SALAD

makes about 6 to 8 servings

---

3 medium celery roots, trimmed, pared, and cut into paper-thin slivers

½ cup heavy cream, whipped

1 teaspoon prepared mustard

PANTRY

½ cup mayonnaise

1 Cut the celery root slivers crosswise into very thin strips.

2 In a bowl, using a wire whisk or an electric mixer, blend together the celery roots, the cream, the mayonnaise and the mustard. Cover with plastic wrap and refrigerate for about 2 hours before serving.

Cooking note: The celery roots should be about the size of toothpicks.

DANISH-STYLE CELERY ROOT SALAD

makes about 4 servings

FRENCH-STYLE CABBAGE SALAD

makes about 6 to 8 servings

½ pound bacon, chopped
2 cups yellow onions, chopped
1 medium head of cabbage, cored and shredded

PANTRY
1 tablespoon vinegar
Salt and pepper to taste

In a skillet, sauté the bacon until crispy. Transfer to a rack covered with paper towels to drain. Place the onion in the same skillet and cook until tender and golden. Add the vinegar. Cook over low heat and blend in the cabbage and the bacon. Remove from the heat, adjust the seasoning and serve.

FRESH VEGETABLE SALAD

makes about 6 to 8 servings

1 tablespoon tarragon leaves, snipped
2 cups broccoli florettes
2 cups cauliflower florettes
½ cup Italian-style dressing

PANTRY
Salt and pepper to taste

In a bowl, blend together the tarragon, the broccoli, and the cauliflower. Drizzle on the dressing and cover with plastic wrap. Refrigerate for at least 1 hour. Adjust the seasoning to taste and serve.

4 large red onions
1 tablespoon cider vinegar

PANTRY
2 tablespoons canola oil
Salt to taste

1 Position the rack in the center of the oven and preheat to 350 degrees F. Lightly grease a baking pan.

2 Arrange the onions in the prepared baking pan, and add 1 cup water or stock.

3 Bake for about 20 to 30 minutes or until the onions are fork tender. Remove from the oven and cool slightly.

4 Remove the outer skins and carefully slice the onions. Return to the pan, sprinkle with salt, and set aside undisturbed for at least 1 hour.

5 Drain and discard any liquid. In a cup combine the oil and the vinegar, season to taste, and pour over the onions.

Cooking note: A strong meat stock will give more flavor to this dish.

GEBACKENER ZWIEBEL SALAT

makes about 6 to 8 servings

½ pound bacon
2 cups red onions, chopped
½ cup cider vinegar
1 medium head of cabbage, cored and shredded

In a skillet, sauté the bacon until crisp. Transfer to a rack covered with paper towels and crumble. In the same skillet, sauté the onions until tender and lightly colored. Add the vinegar, turn heat to low, and add the cabbage and bacon, tossing lightly to incorporate. Remove from the heat and serve.

GERMAN-STYLE CABBAGE SALAD

makes about 6 to 8 servings

German Chicken Salad

makes about 6 to 8 servings

1½ cups cooked chicken, shredded
1 can (8 ounces) crushed pineapple, drained
1 can (13 ounces) green peas, drained

PANTRY
1 cup mayonnaise
Salt and pepper to taste

In a bowl, combine the chicken, the pineapple, the peas, and the mayonnaise. Season to taste and serve.

Grape and Grapefruit Salad

makes about 4 servings

2 cups black grapes
2 large ripe grapefruits
¼ cup (bottled) French dressing
1 tablespoon fresh parsley, snipped

1 Cut the grapefruit in half and remove the segments. Reserve the rind.

2 In a bowl, combine the grapes and the grapefruit. Drizzle on the dressing, cover with plastic wrap and refrigerate for at least 2 hours. Place the fruit mixture in the reserved grapefruit rinds, garnish with parsley, and serve.

Hawaiian Country Slaw

makes about 4 to 6 servings

1 can (20 ounces) pineapple chunks, drained
1 package (16 ounces) cole slaw salad mix
½ cup sunflower seeds
½ cup dressing of choice

In a bowl, combine the pineapple, the salad mix, and the seeds. Drizzle on the dressing, cover with plastic wrap and refrigerate for at least 2 hours before serving.

½ cup yellow onion, minced
1 medium head of cabbage, shredded
½ cup dressing of choice

PANTRY
3 tablespoons butter or margarine

In a saucepan, sauté the onion in butter for about 5 minutes until tender. Add the cabbage and 1 tablespoon of water. Cover and steam for about 3 to 5 minutes or until tender. Remove from the heat, blend in the dressing, and serve.

HOT CABBAGE SLAW

makes about 4 servings

---

8 cups (loosely packed) spinach leaves, torn into bite-sized pieces
1 cup fresh strawberries, sliced
1 medium jicama, peeled, cut into julienne strips
½ cup dressing of choice

In a bowl, combine the spinach, the strawberries and the jicama. Cover with plastic wrap and refrigerate for at least 1 hour. Drizzle on the dressing before serving.

JICAMA-SPINACH SALAD

makes about 6 servings

---

3 cups (canned) sauerkraut, drained and chopped
1 cup (bottled) French dressing
1 tablespoon white onions, minced
Fresh parsley

PANTRY
½ clove garlic, minced

In a bowl, combine the sauerkraut, the dressing, the onions, and the garlic. Cover with plastic wrap, and refrigerate for about 30 minutes. Garnish with parsley and serve.

KALTER KRAUT SALAT

makes about 8 to 10 servings

ORANGE AND CHICORY SALAD

makes about 4 servings

1 bunch chicory, about 8 ounces, trimmed and thinly sliced

1 large Valencia orange, peeled and separated into segments

½ cup seedless grapes, halved

¼ cup (bottled) French dressing

PANTRY
Salt and pepper to taste

In a bowl, toss the chicory and the orange segments with the dressing, and season to taste. Cover with plastic wrap and refrigerate for about 1 hour before serving.

Cooking note: For variation, add dark bread croutons.

ORIENTAL PASTA SALAD

makes about 4 servings

2 cups broccoli florettes

1½ cups cooked spaghetti

¾ cup red bell pepper, thinly sliced

PANTRY
2 tablespoons soy sauce
1 tablespoon sesame oil

1 In a bamboo steamer over a pot of boiling water, steam the broccoli for about 5 minutes or until just tender.

2 In a bowl, combine the broccoli, the spaghetti, the peppers, the soy sauce, and the oil. Cover with plastic wrap and refrigerate for at least 2 hours before serving.

PEA SALAD FRANÇAISE

makes about 4 servings

2 packages (10 ounces each) frozen green peas, thawed and drained

4 scallions, trimmed, (white part only)

1 small head of lettuce, sliced

1 mint leaf

PANTRY
1 medium garlic clove, minced
¼ cup olive oil
2 tablespoons red wine vinegar

1 In a saucepan, cover the peas with water and bring them to a boil. Add the mint leaf and cook for 15 to 20 minutes or until tender. Drain and rinse under cold water.

2 In a small bowl, blend together the oil and vinegar.

3 In another bowl, combine the garlic, the lettuce, and the peas. Drizzle on oil mixture, cover with plastic wrap and refrigerate for about 1 hour before serving.

1 large red bell pepper,
  stemmed, halved and seeded
1 large green bell pepper,
  stemmed, halved and seeded
18 pimiento-stuffed green
  olives, sliced
Parsley, chopped

PANTRY
3 garlic cloves, chopped
¼ vegetable oil

1 Position the broiler rack
about 6 inches from the heat.

2 Place the peppers on the
broiler tray and broil for
about 8 to 10 minutes or until
the skin starts to sear. Place
the peppers under running
water, pull off the skins, and
dice.

3 In a skillet, sauté the peppers and the garlic in oil for
about 2 minutes. Reduce to a
very low simmer and cover.
Cook, stirring occasionally,
for about 15 minutes or until
tender and thoroughly heated.

4 Pour the entire mixture,
including the oil, into a bowl.
Cool to room temperature
and add the olives. Cover
with plastic wrap and refrigerate for at least 1 hour. Garnish with parsley, and serve.

Pepper and Olive Salad

makes about 4 servings

1 cup pickled beets
¼ cup red onion, thinly sliced
¾ cup seedless cucumber, diced
2 teaspoons fresh dill weed,
  chopped

In a bowl, combine the beets,
the onion, the cucumber, and
the dill weed. Cover with
plastic wrap and refrigerate
until ready to serve.

Pickled Beets with Cucumbers

makes about 2 servings

PICKLED CUCUMBER SALAD

makes about 4 to 6 servings

1 large cucumber
3 tablespoons vinegar
Dill weed, snipped

PANTRY
2 tablespoons sugar
Salt and pepper to taste

1 Trim the ends from the cucumber and score down the sides with a fork. Using a sharp knife cut into thin diagonal slices, sprinkle with salt,

place in a plastic bag, seal, and refrigerate for about 2 hours.

2 Place the slices on a flat surface covered with paper towels and press all of the moisture from them. Transfer to a bowl.

3 Combine the vinegar and the sugar, and salt and pepper to taste. Drizzle over the cucumber slices, toss to coat, and garnish with dill. Serve immediately.

POTATO AND BRUSSELS SPROUT SALAD

makes about 4 to 6 servings

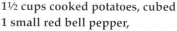

1½ cups cooked potatoes, cubed
1 small red bell pepper, stemmed, seeded and cut into bite-sized pieces
1 package (9 ounces) frozen Brussels sprouts, thawed
1 jar (6 ounces) marinated artichokes hearts, drained

PANTRY
Salt and pepper to taste

In a bamboo steamer over a pot of boiling water, steam the potatoes, the peppers, the Brussels sprouts, and the artichokes for about 10 minutes or until thoroughly heated. Remove from the heat, season to taste and serve.

RADISH AND CELERY SALAD

makes about 4 servings

1 cup radishes
1 cup celery, thinly sliced
1 cup lettuce leaves, torn into bite-sized
¼ cup (bottled) French dressing

In a bowl, combine the radishes, the celery, and the dressing. Cover with plastic wrap, and refrigerate for at least 1 hour. Top with the lettuce leaves and serve.

1 cup seedless raisins
1½ cup carrots, shredded
½ cup celery, minced
½ cup pecans or hazelnuts, chopped

PANTRY
¼ cup mayonnaise
Salt and pepper to taste

In a bowl, combine the raisins, the carrots, the celery, the pecans, and the mayonnaise and season to taste. Cover with plastic wrap and refrigerate for about 1 hour before serving.

RAISIN CARROT SALAD

makes about 4 to 6 servings

---

2 heads of romaine lettuce, stemmed and separated

PANTRY
½ cup warm honey
1¼ cups white wine vinegar

1 In a saucepan, bring the honey and the vinegar to a boil and cook for about 10 minutes or until thickened to a syrup. Remove from the heat, cool slightly and add ½ cup of warm water.

2 Tear the lettuce into bite-sized pieces and serve with the dressing on the side.

ROMAINE LETTUCE WITH SWEET SYRUP DRESSING

makes about 6 to 8 servings

---

1 small head of cabbage, cut into bite-sized pieces
4 dried red peppers

PANTRY
¼ teaspoon soy sauce
¼ teaspoon rice wine vinegar
1 teaspoon sesame oil

1 In the container of a blender or food processor, combine the peppers, the soy sauce, and the vinegar. Add the sesame oil and process on high speed until smooth.

2 In a saucepan, cook the mixture for about 2 minutes. Blend in the cabbage and cook for about 10 minutes or until just tender.

3 Pour the mixture into a bowl, cover with plastic wrap and refrigerate for about 1 day before serving.

SPICY CABBAGE SALAD

makes about 4 servings

SPINACH AND BACON SALAD

makes about 6 servings

8 bacon slices, fried and crumbled

2 bunches of spinach, torn into bite-sized pieces

¾ cup (bottled) French dressing

PANTRY
2 garlic cloves, quartered

1 In a small bowl, blend together the garlic and the dressing. Cover with plastic wrap and refrigerate for about 2 hours.

2 In a bowl, toss the spinach and the bacon with the dressing and serve.

Cooking note: For variation, garnish with sliced hard-boiled eggs.

SPRING SALAD

makes about 4 servings

1 can (16 ounces) grapefruit sections, drained

4 scallions, trimmed and thinly sliced

½ cup radishes, sliced

½ cup cucumbers, sliced

½ cup (bottled) Roquefort or other creamy-style dressing

In a bowl, combine the grapefruit, the scallions, the radishes, the cucumbers, and the dressing. Cover with plastic wrap and refrigerate for at least 2 hours before serving.

STEIRISCHER KRAUT SALAT

makes about 6 to 8 servings

1 medium head of cabbage, cored and finely sliced

3 teaspoons caraway seeds

1 cup (bottled) Roquefort or other creamy-style dressing

PANTRY
Salt and pepper to taste

In a bowl, combine the cabbage, the caraway seeds, salt and pepper to taste, and the dressing. Cover with plastic wrap and refrigerate for at least 1 hour before serving.

Cooking note: For variation, add diced cranberries.

1 tablespoon fresh savory, snipped

1 wheel (4½ ounces—about 3 inches in diameter) Brie cheese

1 can (7 ounces) baby pear tomatoes

PANTRY

1 tablespoon vegetable oil

1 teaspoon pepper

1 Lightly grease a 9-inch microwave-proof pie dish.

2 Place the cheese in the prepared dish, score the top in a diamond pattern, and sprinkle with pepper. Microwave on high heat for about 2 minutes or until the cheese starts to melt.

3 Arrange the tomatoes around the cheese and cook on high heat for about 1 minute or until the tomatoes are thoroughly heated. Remove from the microwave, cut into wedges and serve.

SWISS-STYLE TOMATOES AND BRIE

makes about 4 servings

---

2 tablespoons dried woodear mushrooms

2 small cucumbers, trimmed, seeded and thinly sliced lengthwise

4 red, hot peppers, stemmed, seeded and finely sliced

1 teaspoon Chinese white vinegar

PANTRY

2 tablespoons sesame oil

1 tablespoon soy sauce

¼ teaspoon sugar

Salt and pepper to taste

1 Place the mushrooms in a bowl, cover with boiling water and set aside for about 15 minutes. Drain and cut into thin slices.

2 In a bowl, combine the mushrooms, the cucumbers, the peppers, and the oil. Blend in the soy sauce, the vinegar, and the sugar, and season to taste. Cover with plastic wrap and refrigerate for at least 1 hour before serving.

SZECHWAN CUCUMBER SALAD

makes about 2 to 3 servings

---

2 large beefsteak tomatoes, thinly sliced

2 scallions, trimmed and chopped

½ cup (bottled) French dressing

Cilantro, chopped

PANTRY

¼ teaspoon sugar

In a dish, arrange the tomato slices in overlapping layers. Sprinkle with the sugar and top with the scallions. Cover with plastic wrap and refrigerate for at least 1 hour. Drizzle on the dressing, garnish with cilantro, and serve.

Cooking note: For variation, garnish with chopped parsley.

TOMATO SALAD

makes about 4 servings

TROPICAL SALAD

makes about 4 to 6 servings

3 pink grapefruit, peeled and separated into sections

1 large papaya, peeled, seeded and thinly sliced

3 avocados, peeled, seeded and thinly sliced

Citrus zest

PANTRY

3 tablespoons olive oil

Salt and pepper to taste

In a bowl, combine the grapefruit, the papaya, and the avocado. Cover with plastic wrap and refrigerate for at least one hour. Drizzle on the oil, season to taste, garnish with citrus zest, and serve.

WARMER ERDAPFEL SALAT (HOT POTATO SALAD)

makes about 4 to 6 servings

3 pounds Idaho potatoes, boiled in skins

1 cup chicken stock

2 tablespoons white onions, minced

PANTRY

1 teaspoon wine vinegar

¼ cup oil to taste

Salt and pepper to taste

1 In a saucepan, bring stock to a boil.

2 Pare and slice the potatoes while still warm. Place in a bowl and pour the stock over them. Set aside for 30 minutes. Add the onions. Drizzle with the oil and vinegar, season to taste, and serve.

Cooking note: This dish can be served cold.

WILTED ROMAINE SALAD WITH OYSTER SAUCE

makes about 4 servings

2 tablespoons peanut oil

1 tablespoon premium oyster sauce

1 head of romaine lettuce, separated

PANTRY

1 tablespoon salt

1 In a small bowl, blend together the oil and the oyster sauce.

2 In a two gallon-sized pot, bring lightly salted water to a boil. Dip the lettuce leaves in the boiling water for about 20 seconds and immediately dip them into a bath of cold water. Drain, and tear into bite-sized pieces.

3 In a bowl, toss the lettuce with the oyster sauce and serve.

Cooking note: For variation, add seedless raisins.

Soups

You'll never approach soup the same way again after you've prepared it the 4-Ingredient way. Here are rich, flavorful and satisfying soups that can be made without the time and effort of preparing homemade stocks. Canned broth makes a great substitute for homemade stocks,

BEEF SOUP WITH QUAIL EGGS

and allows you the great freedom of putting together a pot of warm soup for your family at a moment's notice. Our Chicken Soup with Lima Beans uses crumbled bacon for extra special flavor; hearty Finnish Pork Goulash can be prepared in minutes; and a light Italian Consommé makes an excellent first course. On the cooler

EASY CHICKEN TOMATO SOUP

side, refresh yourself with our Soft Fruit Soup, which can be whipped up in a blender.

Serve these soups and you'll receive ovations for your dedication to great cooking—there's no need to tell anyone they were made with only four ingredients!

ITALIAN CONSOMMÉ

BEEF SOUP WITH QUAIL EGGS

makes about 4 to 6 servings

1 piece (about ½ to 1 pound) beef, thinly sliced
6 hardboiled quail eggs
10 snow peas

PANTRY
Salt and pepper to taste

In a saucepan, bring 6 cups of water to a boil. Add the beef and cook, skimming off the top, for about 20 minutes or until tender. Blend in the eggs and the peas, and season to taste. Cook for about 5 minutes or until thoroughly heated. Remove from the heat and serve.

CHAYOTE SOUP

makes about 6 serving

1 medium chayote, peeled and diced
1 cup soy milk
2 cans (14½ ounces each) diced tomatoes
1 tablespoon fresh ginger

PANTRY
Salt and pepper to taste

1 In a saucepan, blend together the chayotes and the soy milk. Bring to a boil and reduce to a simmer. Cover and cook for about 10 to 15 minutes or until tender.

2 In the container of a blender or food processor, purée the chayotes a little at a time. Blend in the tomatoes and process on high speed until smooth.

3 Pour the mixture back into the saucepan. Blend in the ginger and season to taste. Cook for about 5 minutes or until thoroughly heated and serve.

Cooking note: For variation, garnish with toasted whole wheat croutons.

1 can (10¾ ounces) condensed
  chicken vegetable soup
1 cup cooked lima beans
3 tablespoons bacon, crumbled
  or bacon bits

PANTRY
1 cup milk

In a saucepan, combine the
soup and the milk. Bring to a
boil and stir in the beans.
Cook for almost 5 minutes or
until thoroughly heated.
Remove from the heat, garnish with crumbled bacon,
and serve.

CHICKEN SOUP WITH LIMA BEANS
makes about 4 servings

1 can (10¾ ounces) condensed
  tomato soup
1 cup creamy peanut butter

PANTRY
1¼ cups milk

In a saucepan, using a wire
whisk or an electric mixer,
blend together the soup and
the peanut butter. Blend in
the milk and cook on a low
simmer, stirring occasionally,
for about 10 minutes, or until
heated without coming to a
boil. Remove from the heat
and serve.

CREAMY PEANUT BUTTER SOUP
makes about 3 to 4 servings

1 can (10¾ ounces) condensed
  cream of chicken soup
1 can (10½ ounces) condensed
  tomato soup

PANTRY
1 cup milk

1 In a saucepan, blend the
chicken and the tomato soup
and cook for about three minutes. Blend in 1 cup of water
and the milk. Cook for about
7 minutes or until thoroughly
heated. Remove from the heat
and serve.

EASY CHICKEN TOMATO SOUP
makes about 4 to 6 servings

EGG DROP SOUP

makes about 4 to 5 servings

1 large egg
2 cans (10½ ounces each) condensed beef broth
1 medium bay leaf
6 slices of bread, toasted (on the side)

1 In a bowl, beat the egg until the yolk is just blended.

2 In a saucepan, blend together the soup and 1¾ cups of water. Add the bay leaf. Bring to a boil and swirl in the egg, pouring in a narrow stream. Remove from the heat, discard the bay leaf, and serve with the toast on the side.

Cooking note: The egg in the soup should form thin threads.

FINNISH-STYLE PORK GOULASH

makes about 4 servings

1 piece (about ½ pound) pork, thinly sliced
1 white onion, chopped

PANTRY
2 tablespoons vegetable oil
2 tablespoons flour
Salt and pepper to taste

1 In a skillet, sauté the meat in the oil, turning frequently, for about 5 minutes or until browned. Transfer to a warming plate.

2 In the same skillet, blend the flour with the meat juices to make a roux. Blend in the onion, and cook, stirring frequently, for about 5 minutes or until tender. Add 3 cups of boiling water, stirring after each cup. Cook for about 5 minutes or until thickened. Stir in the meat and simmer, stirring occasionally, for about 30 minutes or until tender. Remove from the heat and serve.

Cooking note: For variation, try with the traditional tomato purée stirred in.

2 cups frozen green peas,
  cooked and drained
5 cups ham or pork stock
½ cup chopped cooked ham

PANTRY
¾ cup milk
Salt and pepper to taste

1 In the container of a blender or food processor, process the peas on high speed until smooth.

2 In a saucepan, bring the stock to a boil. Blend in the peas, the ham and the milk. Cook for about 5 minutes or until thoroughly heated. Remove from the heat, season to taste and serve.

GREEN PEA AND HAM SOUP

makes about 4 servings

1 can (10½ ounces) beef
  consommé
2 tablespoons dry red wine
⅓ cup shell pasta, cooked
  al dente and drained
2 tablespoons Parmesan cheese,
  grated

In a saucepan, combine the consommé and the wine and cook for about 2 minutes. Stir in the pasta. Cook for about 8 minutes or until thoroughly heated. Remove from the heat, sprinkle with the cheese, and serve.

ITALIAN CONSOMMÉ

makes about 4 servings

LOTUS ROOT AND PORK SOUP

makes about 4 servings

1 pound lotus root, trimmed, pared, halved, and thinly sliced
1½ pounds pork spareribs, separated
6 cups of broth (base from spareribs)
1 leek stalk, diced

PANTRY
¼ cup rice vinegar
Salt and pepper to taste

1 In a bowl, sprinkle the roots with the vinegar and add enough water to just cover.

2 In a large saucepan, cover the ribs with water and bring to a boil. Reduce to a simmer, skimming off the top for about 30 minutes. Add the lotus root, the leek, and season to taste. Continue to simmer for about 20 to 30 minutes or until the meat is tender. Remove from the heat and serve.

PASSOVER MATZO BALL SOUP

makes about 3 to 4 servings

MATZO BALLS
¼ cup matzo meal
1 tablespoon potato starch

SOUP
6 chicken bouillon cubes

PANTRY
1 tablespoon butter or margarine
¼ teaspoon salt

1 Position the rack in the center of the oven and preheat to 350 degrees F. Lightly grease a baking or cookie sheet.

2 In a bowl, blend together the matzo meal, the potato starch, ⅓ cup of water, and the salt. Cover with plastic wrap and refrigerate for about 30 minutes. Remove from the refrigerator, and when it has become room temperature, pinch off pieces of the dough and roll into balls.

3 In a saucepan bring 6 cups of water to a boil and add the bouillon cubes. Cook for about 3 minutes or until dissolved.

4 Add the matzo balls to the boiling broth and boil for about 10 minutes.

5 Place the matzo balls on the prepared baking sheet and bake for about 10 minutes or until firm. Remove from the oven, stir into the soup and serve.

Cooking note: For variation, serve with vegetable soup.

1 can (10¾ ounces) beef noodle
soup
½ cup cooked whole kernel corn
1 tablespoon fresh oregano,
snipped

PANTRY
⅛ teaspoon chili powder

In a saucepan, blend the soup
and 1 cup of water and cook
for about 2 minutes. Stir in
the corn, the oregano, and the
chili powder, and cook for
about 5 minutes or until the
corn is just tender. Bring to a
slow boil, remove from the
heat and serve.

PHOENIX-STYLE
CHILI SOUP

makes about 2 to 3 servings

---

4 cups fresh fruit

PANTRY
½ cup sugar
3¾ cups milk or half and half,
scalded and cooled

1 In the top of a double boiler
over boiling water, cook the
fruit for about 5 minutes or
until softened.

2 In the container of a
blender or food processor,
process the fruit and the
sugar on high speed until
smooth.

3 Pour the mixture into a
bowl and blend in the milk.
Cover with plastic wrap and
refrigerate for about 1 hour
before serving.

SOFT FRUIT SOUP

makes about 4 servings

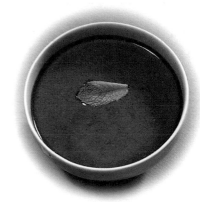

---

1 medium butternut squash,
peeled and diced
1 cup soy milk
2 cans (14½ ounces each) diced
tomatoes
1 tablespoon fresh ginger

PANTRY
Salt and pepper to taste

1 In a saucepan, combine the
squash and the soy milk.
Bring to a boil and reduce to a
simmer, cover, and cook for
about 10 to 15 minutes, or
until tender.

2 In the container of a
blender or food processor,
process the squash and the
tomatoes on high speed until
smooth.

3 Pour the mixture back into
the saucepan. Cook for about
10 minutes, or until thoroughly heated. Blend in the ginger,
season to taste and serve.

Cooking note: For variation,
garnish with toasted whole
wheat croutons.

TOMATO
BUTTERNUT SOUP

makes about 6 servings

TOMATO RICE SOUP WITH FRANKFURTERS

makes about 2 to 3 servings

2 chicken frankfurters, thinly sliced
2 tablespoons minced onion
1 can (10¾ ounces) condensed tomato rice soup

PANTRY
1 tablespoon butter or margarine

In a saucepan, combine the franks and the onions and sauté, stirring occasionally for about 5 minutes or until the onion is tender. Blend in the soup and 1 cup of water and bring to a slow boil. Remove from the heat and serve.

VEGETABLE CHICKEN SOUP WITH GINGER

makes about 2 servings

1 can (16 ounces) chicken broth
1 cup frozen mixed vegetables, thawed
1 cup diced cooked chicken
1 teaspoon dry sherry

PANTRY
1 teaspoon ginger powder

In a 1½ quart microwave-proof dish, combine the broth and ginger. Microwave on high heat for about 2 minutes. Add the vegetables and the chicken. Cover and microwave on high heat for about 3 minutes or until the vegetables are just tender. Remove from the microwave, blend in the sherry, and serve.

1 large yellow onion, minced

1 large green bell pepper, stemmed, seeded and chopped

1 medium head of red cabbage, cored and chopped

PANTRY

Salt and pepper to taste

1 Position the rack in the center of the oven and preheat to 350 degrees F.

2 In a Dutch oven, combine the onion, the pepper, the cabbage, and 1 cup of water. Cover and bake for about 30 minutes or until the cabbage has wilted. Remove from the oven, season to taste and serve.

VEGETABLE GOULASH

makes about 2 to 4 servings

Fish and Seafood

Fish and seafood are the quick cook's best friend. Not only are they versatile, tasty, and nutritious, but they cook in only minutes. Since fish does take so little time, be sure not to overcook. Fish cooked just right is at its peak: moist and flavorful. Another

BROILED SHRIMP SCAMPI

4-Ingredient staple, fish can be made simply and with a variety of sauces and seasonings. Included here are garnishes and sauces, such as cilantro pesto, sour cream stuffing, Cajun spice mix, chili sauce and, of course, that great all-around flavor enhancer, lemon.

Whether it's Chili Shrimp or Corn-Crab-meat Scramble, Creamed Herring or Crispy Fish, you'll find every conceivable preparation to satisfy every taste, and all requiring only four ingredients or less. In many cases there's a great deal of flexibility, in that one fish can be substituted for another, similar variety.

SWEET AND SAVORY
SALMON STEAKS

BLACKENED CHAR

Baked Halibut with Cilantro Pesto

makes about 6 servings

1 tablespoon Cilantro Pesto (see page 401)
6 halibut steaks, 1-inch thick
2 tablespoons fresh lemon juice

PANTRY
2 tablespoons melted butter or margarine

1 Position the rack in the center of the oven and preheat to 400 degrees F. Have a 13 x 9-inch baking pan available.

2 In a bowl, blend together the butter and the lemon juice.

3 Arrange the fish in the baking pan and pour the butter-lemon mixture over the top. Bake for about 20 minutes or until the fish flakes easily. Remove from the oven and serve with the pesto on the side.

Cooking note: For variation, try different pesto flavorings.

Baked Red Snapper with Stuffing

makes about 4 servings

1 piece (about 4 pounds) red snapper, dressed and lightly salted
Sour Cream Stuffing (see page 410)

PANTRY
1½ teaspoons salt
2 tablespoons melted butter or margarine

1 Position the rack in the center of the oven and preheat to 350 degrees F. Lightly grease a 13 x 9-inch baking pan.

2 Fill the fish loosely with the stuffing and close the opening with toothpicks.

3 Arrange the fish on the prepared baking pan. Brush with the butter and bake, basting occasionally, for about 40 to 50 minutes or until the fish becomes flakey. Remove from the oven and serve.

1 piece (about 3½ pounds)
  salmon
2 lemons, thinly sliced

PANTRY

2 tablespoons vegetable oil
1 tablespoon melted butter or
  margarine
Salt and pepper to taste

1 Position the rack in the center of the oven and preheat to 350 degrees F. Line a baking pan with aluminum foil and brush the foil with the oil.

2 Arrange some of the sliced lemons in the prepared baking pan. Add the salmon, top with lemon, and drizzle with the butter. Pull up the edges of the foil and fold over fish.

3 Bake for about 30 minutes, or until the salmon is flakey. Remove from the oven, season to taste and serve.

BAKED SALMON IN FOIL

makes about 4 to 6 servings

---

1 pound fresh jumbo shrimp,
  cleaned, shelled and deveined
1 cup flat beer or ale
¼ cup fresh lemon juice

PANTRY

½ cup vegetable oil for frying
1 cup flour
1½ teaspoons paprika

1 In a deep-fryer, preheat the oil to 350 degrees F.

2 In bowl, blend together the flour and the paprika. Using a wire whisk or an electric mixer, blend in the beer until smooth. Cover with plastic wrap and refrigerate for about 30 minutes.

3 Cut the shrimp lengthwise, but do not cut all the way through. Form into a butterfly shape and sprinkle with the lemon juice. Roll in the batter and place in the hot oil. Fry, stirring frequently, for about 5 minutes or until shrimp becomes golden brown. Transfer to a rack covered with paper towels, drain and serve.

BEER-BATTERED SHRIMP

makes about 4 to 6 servings

Blackened Char

makes about 3 to 4 servings

1 Arctic char (about 4½ pounds)

2 medium lemons, cut into wedges

1 tablespoon Cajun Seasoning (see page 399)

ons butter or
ne

In a skillet, melt the butter and sprinkle with the spice. Add the fish and squeeze lemon juice on top. Cook for about 5 minutes, or until both sides are blackened. Remove from the heat, squeeze lemon juice over the fish and serve with the remaining lemon wedges on the side.

Cooking note: Almost any type of fish can be used with this recipe.

Broccoli Stems with Shrimp

makes about 4 servings

2 pounds broccoli stems, pared and cut diagonally into ¼-inch slices

¼ tablespoon fermented soy beans, rinsed

¼ cup (canned) tiny deveined shrimp, drained, washed, and chopped

½ cup chicken stock

2 tablespoons peanut oil

PANTRY

4 garlic cloves, minced

1 tablespoon cornstarch

Salt and pepper to taste

1 In a bowl, mash the soy beans and the garlic until smooth.

2 In another bowl, combine the shrimp and the stock.

3 In a wok, stir-fry the broccoli in the oil for about 1 minute. Add the garlic mixture, the shrimp, and the stock. Cook, stirring frequently, for about 20 minutes or until the broccoli is tender.

4 Remove the shrimp and the broccoli and transfer to a warming plate.

5 Blend the cornstarch with the juices in the wok and cook for about 5 minutes or until thickened. Add the shrimp and the broccoli. Cook for about 5 minutes or until thoroughly heated. Remove from the heat, season to taste, and serve.

4 catfish fillets (4 to 6 ounces each)
2 tablespoons freshly grated Parmesan or Romano cheese
4 tablespoons (bottled) ranch-style dressing

PANTRY

Salt and pepper to taste
2 tablespoons butter or margarine

BROILED CATFISH

makes about 4 servings

1 Position the broiler rack about 4 inches from the heat. Lightly grease the broiler pan.

2 Arrange the fillets on the prepared broiler pan, drizzle some of the dressing over the fillets, and season to taste.

3 Broil for about 1 minute, sprinkle with the cheese and broil 1 more minute. Turn over, sprinkle with cheese, and broil for 3 to 5 minutes, or until the cheese starts to bubble. Add the remaining dressing and cheese, season to taste, and broil for about 6 to 8 minutes or until the fish is completely opaque. Remove from the broiler and serve.

½ cup creamy garlic dressing
1 tablespoon lemon juice
1 pound fresh shrimp, cleaned, shelled, and deveined

BROILED SHRIMP SCAMPI

makes about 3 servings

1 Position the broiler rack about 4 inches from the heat.

2 In a bowl, blend together the dressing and the lemon juice.

3 Arrange the shrimp on the broiler pan and drizzle the dressing over the top. Broil, turning only once and basting, for about 7 to 10 minutes or until lightly browned.

BUTTERFLY SHRIMP

makes about 4 servings

1 pound fresh shrimp, cleaned, shelled, and deveined
1 large egg

PANTRY
½ cup cornstarch
⅔ cup flour
½ cup vegetable oil

1 In a deep fryer, heat the oil to about 350 degrees F.

2 Cut shrimp lengthwise, but do not cut all the way through, and form into a butterfly shape.

3 In a small bowl, coat shrimp with the cornstarch.

4 In a bowl, using a wire whisk or an electric mixer, blend together the flour, the egg, and ⅔ cup water.

5 Dip the shrimp, into the batter, and place in the hot oil. When the shrimp rise to the top, turn and continue to cook for about 1 to 2 minutes or until golden-brown. Transfer to a wire rack covered with paper towels, drain and serve.

CHILI SHRIMP

makes about 2 servings

½ pound fresh shrimp, cleaned, shelled, and deveined
1 large onion, sliced
3 tablespoons (bottled) chili sauce

PANTRY
3 tablespoons vegetable oil

In a wok, heat the oil and add the shrimp and the onions. Stir-fry for about 3 minutes, and blend in the chili sauce. Continue to stir-fry for about 4 minutes or until the onions are lightly browned. Remove from the heat and serve.

1 pound fresh shrimp, cleaned, shelled, and deveined
2 egg whites beaten until foamy
¼ cup (bottled) sweet and sour sauce

PANTRY

½ teaspoon salt
1 cup cornstarch
4 cups vegetable oil

CHINESE-STYLE POPCORN SHRIMP

makes about 4 servings

1 In a small bowl, combine the cornstarch and the salt.

2 Cut the shrimp in half lengthwise, coat with the egg whites and dredge in the cornstarch. Transfer to a dish and refrigerate for at least 2 hours.

3 In a deep fryer, heat the oil to about 350 degrees F. Add the shrimp and fry. When the shrimp rise to the top, turn and continue to cook for about 1 to 2 minutes or until golden-brown. Remove from the oil and drain. Toss the shrimp in the sweet and sour sauce and serve.

---

3 large eggs, slightly beaten
1 can (4 ounces) chopped tiny deveined shrimp, drained
3 tablespoons rice wine
1 cup cooked rice, cold
⅓ cup barbecued pork, cooked and chopped

PANTRY

1 to 2 tablespoons vegetable oil
Salt and pepper to taste
½ cup soy sauce

1 In a skillet, fry the eggs in the oil, tilting the pan to spread the eggs as thin as possible. Remove from the heat and cut into narrow strips.

CHINESE-STYLE SHRIMP FRIED RICE

makes about 4 servings

2 In the same skillet, sauté the shrimp for about 3 to 4 minutes or until thoroughly heated. Add the wine and the rice, and season to taste. Cook, stirring frequently, for about 2 to 3 minutes or until the rice is completely coated. Add the pork and continue to cook, stirring frequently, for about 2 to 3 minutes or until thoroughly heated. Remove from the heat and serve with the soy sauce on the side.

CORN CRABMEAT SCRAMBLE

makes about 4 servings

1½ cups whole kernel corn
1 can (6½ ounces) crabmeat, flaked
6 large eggs

PANTRY
2 tablespoons butter or margarine
¼ cup milk
Salt and pepper to taste

1 In a skillet, sauté the corn and the crabmeat in the butter for about 3 to 4 minutes or until thoroughly heated.

2 In a bowl, using a wire whisk or an electric mixer, beat the eggs until thick and foamy. Blend in the milk and the corn mixture.

3 In the same skillet, cook corn-crabmeat-egg mixture for about 5 minutes or until the eggs are set.

Cooking note: For variation, add a pinch of curry powder and turmeric to the eggs.

CREAMED HERRING

makes about 4 servings

4 ounces pickled herring
1 cup sour cream or unflavored yogurt
½ cup winesap apples, diced
1 tablespoon white onion, minced

In the container of a blender or food processor, purée the herring until smooth. Add the sour cream, the apples, and the onion, and process on high speed until smooth. Pour the mixture into a bowl, cover with plastic wrap and refrigerate for at least 1 hour before serving.

CRISPY FISH

makes about 2 servings

2 flounder fillets (about 3 ounces each)
⅓ cup milk
⅓ cup crushed corn flakes
½ teaspoon safflower oil

1 Position the rack in the center of the oven and preheat to 400 degrees F. Lightly grease a 9-inch square baking pan.

2 Dip the fillets in the milk and dredge in the corn flakes. Set aside for about 10 minutes. Arrange the fillets in the prepared baking pan and bake for about 10 minutes, or until both sides are light golden-brown. Remove from the oven and serve.

4 to 5 crabs (about 2 pounds), cooked, cleaned and cracked

½ cup sliced pickled ginger

3 to 4 teaspoons prepared wasabi

PANTRY

¾ cup soy sauce

1 In a bowl, blend together the soy sauce and the wasabi.

2 Serve the crab meat with the sauce and the ginger on the side.

Cooking note: The wasabi and pickled ginger can usually be found in well-stocked supermarkets or Asian food markets.

Dungeness Crab with Wasabi Soy and Pickled Ginger

makes about 4 to 6 servings

---

2 cups potatoes, cooked and diced

2 cups cooked fish, flaked

¼ teaspoon onion, minced

PANTRY

1 tablespoon vegetable oil

Salt and pepper to taste

1 In a bowl, combine the potatoes, the fish, and the onion, and season to taste.

2 In a skillet, heat the oil and add the fish and potato mixture. Cook over low heat until the bottom is browned. Remove from the heat and serve.

Fish Potato Hash

makes about 2 to 4 servings

---

2 cups lobster meat, cooked and cubed

PANTRY

¼ cup butter or margarine

2 tablespoons vinegar or lemon juice

In a saucepan, cook the lobster in butter, stirring occasionally, for about 5 minutes or until thoroughly heated. Stir in the vinegar, remove from the heat and serve.

Fried Lobster

makes about 2 to 3 servings

GEBRADEN SCHELVISCH (DUTCH-STYLE BAKED HADDOCK)

makes about 6 servings

6 slices haddock, 2 inches thick
6 slices lemon
1½ cups dry bread crumbs

PANTRY
1 tablespoon butter or margarine
Salt and pepper to taste

1 Position the rack in the center of the oven and preheat to 350 degrees F. Lightly grease a 13 x 9-inch baking pan.

2 Arrange the fish in the prepared baking pan. Place a slice of lemon on each portion, sprinkle with the bread crumbs, and season to taste.

3 Cover and bake for about 45 minutes or until the fish becomes flakey. Remove from the oven and serve.

GRILLED SHRIMP

makes about 2 servings

2 tablespoons chili sauce
2 teaspoons fresh parsley, chopped
2 teaspoons lemon juice
½ pound medium size fresh shrimp, cleaned, shelled, and deveined

1 Position the grill about 6 inches from the heat.

2 In a bowl, blend together the chili sauce, the parsley, and the lemon juice. Stir in the shrimp, cover with plastic wrap, and refrigerate for about 30 minutes.

3 Arrange the shrimp on the grill and cook, turning occasionally, for about 3 to 4 minutes or until the shrimp turns pink. Remove from the grill and serve.

Cooking note: Cooking time for grilling recipes depends on the heat source.

GRILLED SWORDFISH

makes about 4 servings

4 swordfish steaks, (1 inch thick)
½ cup teriyaki sauce

PANTRY
2 tablespoons sesame oil
2 tablespoons honey

1 Position the grill about 6 inches from the heat.

2 In a bowl, blend the teriyaki sauce, the oil and the honey.

3 Arrange the steaks in a dish and pour the sauce over the top. Cover with plastic wrap and refrigerate, turning occasionally, for about 8 hours or overnight.

4 Arrange the fish on the grill and cook for about 5 minutes on both sides, or until the fish is flakey. Remove from the grill and serve.

Cooking note: Cooking time for grilling recipes depends on the heat source.

½ cup (bottled) clam juice

3 tablespoons fresh lemon juice

3 tablespoons fresh tarragon, snipped

6 whitefish fillets with skin (about 8 ounces)

PANTRY

¾ cup olive oil

Salt and pepper to taste

1 Position the grill about 6 inches from the heat.

2 In a saucepan, bring the clam juice to a boil for about 5 minutes, or until reduced to about 2 tablespoons.

3 In the container of a blender or food processor, combine the clam juice, the lemon juice, the tarragon, and the oil. Process on high speed until smooth.

4 Place the fish on the grill, brush with a little oil, and season to taste. Grill without turning, for about 5 minutes, or until the fish becomes flakey. Remove fillets from the grill, drizzle with the sauce, and serve.

Cooking note: Cooking time for grilling recipes depends on the heat source.

GRILLED WHITEFISH WITH TARRAGON SAUCE

makes about 6 servings

1 can (14¾ ounces) salmon, drained, skinned, boned and flaked

2 cans (16 ounces each) crushed tomatoes

1 bunch scallions, trimmed and minced

1 cup crushed ice

In a bowl, combine the salmon, the tomatoes and the scallions. Cover with plastic wrap, and refrigerate for at least 2 hours before serving.

HAWAIIAN ICED SALMON

makes about 3 servings

KOREAN TUNA STEAKS

makes about 4 servings

1 tuna steak (about 1 pound)
2 teaspoons peanut oil

PANTRY
2 teaspoons melted butter or
  margarine
2 teaspoons soy sauce

1 Position the broiler rack about 4 inches from the heat.

2 In a small bowl, blend together the oil, the butter and the soy sauce.

3 Arrange the fish on the broiler pan and brush with the oil mixture. Broil for about 4 minutes and turn over. Brush with the oil mixture and broil for additional 3 to 5 minutes or until the fish becomes flakey. Remove from the oven and serve.

MUSTARD GLAZED SALMON

makes about 2 servings

¾ pound fresh salmon fillets
¼ cup balsamic vinegar
1 tablespoon Dijon mustard

PANTRY
1 tablespoon vegetable oil
Salt and pepper to taste

1 In a skillet, sauté the salmon in oil on high heat for about 6 minutes or until both sides are lightly browned. Transfer to a warming plate.

2 In the same skillet, boil the vinegar on high heat for about 5 minutes or until most of the liquid has evaporated. Add the mustard and the salmon, and season to taste. Cook for about 2 minutes or until thoroughly heated. Remove from the heat and serve.

PRINSEFISK

makes about 4 servings

1½ pounds fresh cod fillets
1 package (10 ounces) frozen asparagus spears, thawed and drained
3 large egg yolks, beaten until thick
2 cups Basic White Sauce (see page 398)

PANTRY
1 tablespoon butter or margarine
¼ cup milk

1 Position the broiler rack about 4 inches from the heat. Lightly grease a baking dish.

2 In a bowl, using a wire whisk or an electric mixer, beat the egg yolks into the white sauce.

3 Arrange the fish in the prepared baking dish, and cover with the milk. Set dish on the stovetop, bring to a boil, and reduce to a simmer. Cook for about 5 to 7 minutes or until the fish becomes flakey. Drain, arrange the asparagus over the fish, and top with the sauce. Broil for about 2 minutes or until the top is lightly browned. Remove from the oven and serve.

2 cups potatoes, cooked and
  mashed
2 cups (canned) salmon,
  skinned, boned and flaked
¼ cup grated American cheese

PANTRY
1 tablespoon butter or margarine
Salt and pepper to taste

1 Position the rack in the center of the oven and preheat to
350 degrees F. Lightly grease a
baking dish.

2 In a bowl, combine the
potatoes and the salmon, and
season to taste.

3 Pour the fish and potato
mixture into the prepared
baking dish and sprinkle
the cheese. Bake for about
30 minutes or until the top is
lightly browned. Remove
from the oven and serve.

Salmon and Potato Bake

makes about 6 servings

---

2 cups Basic White Sauce (see
  page 398)
1 can (6 ounces) salmon,
  drained, skinned, boned and
  flaked
1 cup green peas, cooked
2 cups potatoes, cooked and
  mashed

PANTRY
1 tablespoon butter or margarine

1 Position the rack in the center of the oven and preheat to
450 degrees F. Lightly grease a
baking dish.

2 In a bowl, combine the
white sauce, the salmon, and
the peas.

3 Pour the salmon mixture
into the prepared baking dish
and top with the potatoes.
Dot with butter. Bake for
about 15 minutes or until
lightly browned. Remove
from the oven and serve.

Cooking note: Add 1 tablespoon of chopped chives to
the potatoes.

Salmon and Potato Pie

makes about 4 to 6 servings

---

6 potatoes, cooked and chopped
2 cups (canned) salmon,
  skinned, boned and flaked
1 large egg
Tartar Sauce (see page 411)

PANTRY
¼ cup vegetable oil
Pepper to taste
Celery salt to taste

1 In a bowl, combine the
potatoes, the salmon, and the
eggs, and season to taste.
Shape into 6 patties.

2 In a skillet, sauté the patties
for about 10 minutes or until
both sides are light golden-
brown. Remove from the
heat and serve with the
Tartar Sauce on the side.

Salmon Cakes

makes about 6 servings

SALMON CROQUETTES

makes about 4 servings

1 can (14¾ ounces) salmon, skinned, boned and flaked
1 cup bread crumbs
1 large egg, beaten

PANTRY
1 tablespoon canola oil
Salt and pepper to taste

1 In a bowl, combine the salmon and the bread crumbs and season to taste. Form into 4 patties.

2 In a skillet, sauté the patties for about 10 minutes or until both sides are light golden-brown. Remove from the heat and serve.

SALMON LOAF

makes about 4 serving

2 cups cooked salmon, flaked
2 large eggs, beaten
⅓ cup bread crumbs

PANTRY
¼ cup butter or margarine, room temperature

1 Position the rack in the center of the oven and preheat to 350 degrees F. Lightly grease a 6 x 5-inch loaf pan.

2 In a bowl, combine the salmon, the eggs, the bread crumbs and the butter.

3 Press the mixture into the prepared loaf pan and bake for about 40 minutes or until lightly browned. Remove from the oven, invert, slice and serve.

SAUTÉED TUNA

makes about 4 servings

4 tuna steaks, skinned
1 tablespoon fresh parsley, snipped
1 lemon, cut into wedges (on the side)

PANTRY
1 tablespoon vegetable oil
1 tablespoon butter or margarine
1 garlic clove, chopped
Salt and pepper to taste

In a skillet, sauté the steaks in the oil and butter for about 5 minutes. Turn over and sprinkle with the garlic and the parsley, and season to taste. Cover and cook for about 8 to 10 minutes or until the fish becomes flakey. Remove from the heat and serve with the lemon wedges on the side.

SAUTÉED SCALLOPS ON A BED OF GREENS

makes about 4 servings

2 tablespoons peanut oil
2 pounds fresh scallops
¼ cup creamy ginger dressing
1 medium head of lettuce, separated

PANTRY
1 garlic clove, mashed

In a skillet, heat the oil and add the scallops and garlic. Cook, stirring frequently, for about 3 minutes or until lightly browned. Remove from the heat, arrange on a bed of lettuce, and serve with the dressing on the side.

SEAFOOD AU GRATIN

makes about 3 to 4 servings

1 can (10¾ ounces) cheddar cheese soup
2 cups white fish, cooked and flaked
1 tablespoon fresh parsley or cilantro, snipped
¼ cup dry bread crumbs

PANTRY
¼ cup milk

1 Position the rack in the center of the oven and preheat to 400 degrees F.

2 In a casserole dish, blend together the soup and the milk. Add in the fish and the parsley, and top with the bread crumbs. Bake for about 30 minutes, or until lightly browned. Remove from the oven and serve.

SEARED SALMON

makes about 4 servings

4 salmon fillets (about 8 ounces each)
2 tablespoons vegetable relish of choice

PANTRY
3 tablespoons vegetable oil
Salt and pepper to taste

In a skillet, sauté the salmon in the oil for about 5 minutes or until sides are browned. Remove from the heat, top with relish, season to taste and serve.

SHRIMP SAUTÉED WITH SPINACH

makes about 3 servings

2 tablespoons canned shrimp, minced

1 package (10 ounce) frozen spinach, thawed

PANTRY

1 small garlic clove, crushed

2 tablespoons vegetable oil

In a saucepan, combine the shrimp, the oil, and the garlic, and cook over medium heat for about 2 to 3 minutes. Add the spinach. Cover and cook for about 3 to 4 minutes or until the spinach wilts. Remove from the heat and serve.

SIMPLE SWEET AND SOUR SHRIMP

makes about 4 servings

3 cups rotelli pasta

1 package (10 ounces) frozen cooked shrimp

1 package (10 ounces) frozen Japanese-style vegetables

1 jar (9 ounces) sweet and sour sauce

In a 3-quart microwave-proof casserole, blend together 1 cup of water and the pasta. Cover and microwave on medium, stirring occasionally, for about 10 minutes. Add the shrimp and the vegetables, cover, and continue to cook,

stirring occasionally, for about 5 to 8 minutes or until the pasta is al dente. Stir in the sweet and sour sauce, and cook for about 2 minutes or until thoroughly heated. Remove from the oven and serve.

Cooking note: For variation, garnish with chopped peanuts.

STEAMED PRAWNS

makes about 2 servings

4 fresh prawns, washed and deveined

1 tablespoon white rice wine

PANTRY

Salt to taste

In a bamboo steamer, over a pot of boiling water, place the prawns and sprinkle with the wine. Steam for about 20 minutes or until tender. Remove from the heat, slice in half lengthwise, salt to taste, and serve.

3 cups unsweetened pineapple
  juice
6 salmon steaks (about 6½
  ounces each)

PANTRY
2 tablespoons soy sauce

Sweet and Savory Salmon Steaks

makes about 6 servings

1 In a saucepan, bring the juice to a boil and reduce to a simmer. Cook for about 10 minutes or until reduced by half. Cool to room temperature.

2 Pour the juice into a bowl and add the steaks. Cover with plastic wrap and refrigerate for about 2 hours. Drain, reserving marinade.

3 Heat a nonstick skillet, and sear the fish steaks for about 6 minutes or until both sides are browned. Transfer to a warming platter.

4 In a saucepan, bring marinade to a boil, reduce to a simmer, and cook for about 5 minutes or until reduced by half. Remove from the heat, brush the steaks with the sauce, and serve with the remaining sauce on the side.

---

1 can (7 ounces) tuna, drained
  and flaked
1½ cups Basic White Sauce (see
  page 398)
1 package (10 ounces) frozen
  mixed vegetables
½ cup bread crumbs

PANTRY
2 tablespoons butter or
  margarine
Salt and pepper to taste

Tuna Casserole

makes about 4 servings

1 Position the broiler rack about 6 inches from the heat. Lightly grease a shallow baking dish

2 In a bowl, combine the fish, the white sauce, and the vegetables, and season to taste.

3 Pour the mixture into the prepared baking dish and sprinkle with bread crumbs. Broil for about 10 minutes, or until thoroughly heated, and the bread crumbs are toasted. Remove from the oven and serve.

Cooking note: For a variation, add grated cheese to the bread crumbs.

TUNA GRILL

makes about 4 servings

1 tuna steak (about ½-inch thick)

PANTRY
2 teaspoons olive oil
2 teaspoons melted butter or margarine
2 teaspoons soy sauce

1 Position the grill rack about 4 inches from the heat.

2 In a bowl, blend together the oil, the butter, and the soy sauce until smooth.

3 Arrange the fish on the grill, brush with soy mixture, and cook for about 4 minutes. Turn over, brush with the mixture, and cook for about 3 to 5 minutes or until the fish is flakey. Remove from the grill and serve.

Cooking note: Cooking time for grilling recipes depends on the heat source.

WHITEFISH TEMPURA

makes about 4 to 6 servings

1½ pounds white fish fillets, cut into bite-sized pieces
1 box (8 ounces) tempura batter mix, prepared

PANTRY
½ cup vegetable oil
¼ cup soy sauce

1 In a deep fryer, heat the oil to about 375 degrees F.

2 Roll the fish in the batter until well-coated. Place in the hot oil and cook, turning occasionally, for about 5 to 7 minutes or until both sides are golden-brown. Transfer to a rack covered with paper towels, drain, and serve with soy sauce on the side.

WRAPPED FISH STICKS

makes about 6 to 8 servings

1 can (8 ounces) refrigerated crescent dinner rolls
8 frozen fish sticks, slightly thawed
½ cup sliced ripe olives
Tartar Sauce (see page 411)

1 Position the rack in the center of the oven and preheat to 375 degrees F. Have a baking or cookie sheet available.

2 Separate the dough into 4 rectangles, firmly pressing the perforations to seal. Cut each rectangle lengthwise into 2-inch strips, forming a total of eight 6 x 2-inch rectangles. Place a fish stick on each rectangle. Fold the dough over the fish and press to seal the edge.

3 Arrange on the baking sheet and bake for about 15 to 17 minutes or until deep golden-brown. Remove from the oven, garnish and serve with the sauce on the side.

Poultry

It was difficult to get out of the kitchen once we began devising 4-Ingredient recipes for poultry. Chicken is so versatile there's hardly an ingredient it doesn't like. We marinated it in everything from sherry, wine and vermouth to Caesar, French, and Russian dressings. We topped it with chili sauce, peanut butter, and a variety of fruits. We shook it and baked it in tortilla chips, corn flakes, and good old-fashioned bread crumbs. From

CHICKEN ASPARAGUS MARINARA

basic recipes, such as Easy Chicken Casserole, where comforting cream of mushroom soup and a perky dash of Worcestershire sauce bring soulful satisfaction, to an exotic Chicken à la Moambe, where tomato sauce and peanut butter give new meaning to flavor, every dish in this abundant chapter delivers on the

promise of great taste using a minimum of ingredients. Whether baked, broiled, sautéed, fried, tempura'd, or grilled, with sauces from curries to teriyakis, the 4-Ingredient chicken is always a "special" on the menu. Remember: always wash chicken thoroughly and pat it dry before preparing.

CHICKEN À LA MOAMBE

SMOKED CHICKEN

APRICOT GLAZED CHICKEN

makes about 6 to 8 servings

1 medium (about 3 to 3½ pounds) chickens washed and quartered
1 small jar apricot marmalade
1 package (1¼ ounce) onion soup mix
8 ounces (bottled) Russian dressing

1 Position the rack in the center of the oven and preheat to 350 degrees F. Have a shallow baking dish available.

2 In a bowl, blend together the marmalade, the onion soup mix, and the dressing. Place the chicken in the baking dish and top with the marmalade sauce. Cover with plastic wrap and refrigerate for at least 8 hours.

3 Bake the chicken, basting occasionally, for about 40 to 50 minutes or until tender. Remove from the oven and serve.

ASPARAGUS CHICKEN

makes about 2 servings

1 whole boneless, skinless, chicken breast, cut into bite-sized pieces
1 large egg white
1½ pounds fresh asparagus, trimmed and cut into bite-sized pieces
1 tablespoon dry sherry

PANTRY
2 garlic cloves, minced
Salt and pepper to taste
4 tablespoons vegetable oil
1 teaspoon sugar

1 In a bowl, combine the sherry, the egg, the chicken and season to taste.

2 In a skillet, sauté the garlic in the oil for about 1 minute and blend in the sugar. Transfer to a warming plate.

3 In the same skillet, sauté the chicken in the oil for about 3 minutes. Add the asparagus and the sherry mixture. Cook, stirring frequently, for about 15 minutes or until the chicken is tender. Remove from the heat and serve.

BACON FRIED CHICKEN

makes about 4 servings

1 small (about 2 to 2½ pounds) chicken, cut into serving-sized pieces
¼ pound bacon, minced

PANTRY
Salt and pepper to taste

Place the bacon in a skillet, lay the chicken pieces on top, and sauté over low heat, turning occasionally, for about 50 minutes, or until the chicken is tender and light golden-brown. Remove from the heat, season to taste and serve.

Cooking note: The bacon bits can be used as a garnish over an accompanying dish or salad.

1 package (7 ounces) seasoned
   stuffing mix, prepared
1 medium (about 3 pounds)
   frying chicken, skinned and
   quartered
1 teaspoon lemon pepper

PANTRY
1 tablespoon butter or margarine

1 Position the rack in the center of the oven and preheat to
350 degrees F. Lightly grease a
large baking dish.

2 Place the stuffing mix in the
prepared baking dish, top
with the chicken pieces, and
sprinkle with the lemon pepper. Cover and bake for about
30 minutes. Remove the cover
and continue to bake for
about 30 minutes or until the
chicken is tender. Remove
from the oven and serve.

BAKED CHICKEN AND STUFFING

makes about 4 to 5 servings

---

8 chicken thighs, skinned
3 cups crushed corn flakes
3 tablespoons sesame seeds

PANTRY
3 tablespoons vegetable oil
Sa and peppeto taste

1 Position the rack in the center of the oven and preheat to
350 degrees F. Lightly grease a
baking or cookie sheet.

2 In a bowl, combine the corn
flakes and the sesame seeds.
Brush the chicken with the oil
and dredge in the corn flakes
mixture until thoroughly
coated.

3 Arrange the chicken on the
prepared baking sheet and
bake for about 25 minutes or
until tender and crispy.
Remove from the oven and
serve.

BAKED CHICKEN IN CORNFLAKES

makes about 4 to 6 servings

---

1 pound chicken livers, cleaned
   and pierced

PANTRY
½ teaspoon dried thyme, crushed
½ teaspoon dried sage, crushed
½ teaspoon dry mustard

1 In a small bowl, combine
the thyme, the sage and the
mustard.

2 Arrange the livers in a 1-
quart microwave-proof dish,
and sprinkle the herb mixture
on top. Cover and microwave
on high heat for about 2 minutes. Lower to medium heat
and continue to cook, turning
occasionally, for about 5 to 7
minutes or until thoroughly
heated. Remove from the
oven, cool and serve.

BAKED CHICKEN LIVERS

makes about 4 to 5 servings

BAKED CHICKEN REUBEN

makes about 6 to 8 servings

4 whole chicken breasts, split, skinned and boned

1 can (16 ounces) sauerkraut, drained

4 slices (6 x 4-inches) Swiss cheese

1¼ cups (bottled) Thousand Island dressing

PANTRY

Salt and pepper to taste

1 Position the rack in the center of the oven and preheat to 325 degrees F. Lightly grease a baking dish.

2 Arrange the chicken in the prepared baking dish and season to taste. Top with the sauerkraut, the cheese, and the dressing. Cover and bake for about 65 to 70 minutes or until the chicken is tender. Remove from the oven and serve.

BAKED CHICKEN WITH MUSHROOMS

makes about 4 servings

1 medium (about 3 to 3½ pounds) chicken, quartered

4 strips bacon, chopped

¼ cup fresh mushrooms, chopped

1 large white onion, chopped

1 Position the rack in the center of the oven and preheat to 375 degrees F. Have a baking or cookie sheet available.

2 In a bowl, combine the bacon, the mushrooms and the onions.

3 Lay the pieces of chicken out on individual foil sheets. Spread the bacon mixture evenly over the chicken pieces. Pull up the sides of the foil, sealing it on top to create an envelope. Place on a baking sheet and bake for about 40 to 50 minutes. Open the top of the foil and continue to bake for about 10 minutes or until the chicken is tender and lightly browned. Remove from the oven and serve.

2 to 3 pounds chicken, cut into bite-sized pieces

1 can (10¾ ounces) cream of celery soup

PANTRY

1 tablespoon dried parsley, crushed

2 tablespoons melted butter or margarine

1 Postion the rack in the center of the oven and preheat to 400 degrees F. Lightly grease a 13 x 9-inch baking pan.

2 Arrange the chicken in the prepared baking pan. Top with the butter and bake for about 20 minutes. Turn over and bake for an additional 20 minutes. Pour on the soup, sprinkle with parsley, and bake, turning and basting, for about 10 minutes or until tender and lightly browned. Remove from the oven and serve.

BAKED GOLDEN CHICKEN

makes about 4 to 6 servings

---

6 boneless squab breasts

6 bacon slices

PANTRY

Salt and pepper to taste

1 Position the rack in the center of the oven, and preheat to 350 degrees F. Lightly grease a 13 x 9-inch baking pan.

2 Wrap each breast with a bacon slice and arrange in the prepared baking pan. Season to taste, add 1 cup of water, and cover. Bake for about 65 to 70 minutes or until tender. Remove from the oven, adjust the seasoning, and serve.

Cooking note: This recipe can be used to bake game hens.

BAKED SQUAB WITH BACON

makes about 6 servings

---

1 medium (about 4 to 5 pounds) duck

¼ cup white port wine

3 oranges, peeled and sliced

PANTRY

2 tablespoons melted butter or margarine

Salt and pepper to taste

1 In a baking dish, place the duck, season to taste, and drizzle on the wine. Cover with plastic wrap and refrigerate for at least 8 hours.

Remove from refrigerator, unwrap, and spread the duck with the butter.

2 Position the rack in the center of the oven and preheat to 375 degrees F.

3 Bake, basting frequently, for about 2½ to 3 hours or until tender and lightly browned. Remove from the oven, garnish with orange slices, and serve.

BRAZILIAN DUCK WITH ORANGE

makes about 4 servings

BROILED CHICKEN SMOTHERED IN FRENCH DRESSING

makes about 4 servings

1 medium (about 3 to 3½ pounds) chicken, cut into serving-sized pieces
½ cup (bottled) creamy French dressing
¼ cup dry white wine

1 In a 2-quart microwave-proof baking dish, combine the dressing, the wine, and the chicken. Cover with plastic wrap, and refrigerate for at least 2 hours. Drain the liquid and reserve.

2 Cover the baking dish with plastic wrap and microwave on high heat for about 10 minutes.

3 Position the broiler rack about 6 inches from the heat.

4 Arrange the chicken on the broiler pan, brush with the marinade sauce, and broil, turning only once, for about 15 to 20 minutes or until tender and lightly browned. Remove from the oven and serve.

CHICKEN AND GRAVY DINNER

makes about 4 servings

1 medium (about 3 pounds) chicken, cut into serving-sized pieces
1 can (10½ ounce) cream of mushroom soup
¼ cup white port wine
4 ounces fresh mushrooms

1 Thoroughly wash the chicken, season to taste and place in a crockpot.

2 In a bowl, blend together the soup and wine, and pour over the chicken. Arrange the mushrooms on top and cook on low for about 4 to 6 hours, or until the chicken is cooked through. Remove the chicken from the crockpot and serve, with the liquids from the pot in a bowl on the side.

Cooking note: Add more vegetables to the crockpot if desired.

1 cup turkey, cooked and diced
1 cup chicken, cooked and diced
1 package (10 ounces) frozen broccoli, thawed
2½ cups cooked pasta

PANTRY
2 tablespoons sesame oil
Salt and pepper to taste

In a wok, heat the oil and add the turkey and chicken. Stir-fry for about 3 minutes, or until well-coated. Add the broccoli and stir-fry for about 4 minutes or until just tender. Add the pasta, season to taste, and stir-fry for about 3 minutes or until thoroughly heated. Remove from the heat and serve.

Cooking note: For variation, sprinkle the dish with an Oriental-style sweet and sour sauce.

CHICKEN AND TURKEY STIR-FRY

makes about 4 to 6 servings

1 medium (about 3 to 3½ pounds) chicken, cut into serving-sized pieces
1 can (6 ounces) tomato purée
½ cup creamy-style peanut butter

PANTRY
3 tablespoons sesame oil
Salt and pepper to taste

1 In a bowl, combine the tomato puree and ¼ cup of water.

2 In a skillet, heat the oil and add the chicken. Sauté, turning occasionally, for about 15 minutes or until lightly browned. Stir in the tomato mixture, bring to a boil, and reduce to a simmer. Cook, turning occasionally, for about 10 minutes. Blend in the peanut butter, season to taste, and cover. Simmer for about 20 minutes or until tender. Remove from the heat and serve.

CHICKEN À LA MOAMBE

makes about 4 to 6 servings

1 jar (30 ounces) spaghetti sauce
1 cup chicken, cooked and diced
1 package (10 ounces) frozen asparagus, thawed
½ pound pasta, cooked

In a saucepan, combine the sauce, the chicken, and the asparagus. Bring to a boil and reduce to a simmer. Cook for about 5 to 7 minutes or until thoroughly heated. Remove from the heat, pour over the pasta, and serve.

CHICKEN ASPARAGUS MARINARA

makes about 4 servings

CHICKEN BREASTS WRAPPED IN BACON

makes about 4 to 6 servings

¼ **pound dried beef**
4 boneless chicken breasts
4 thick bacon slices
1 pint sour cream

PANTRY
1 tablespoon butter or margarine

1 Position the rack in the center of the oven and preheat to 300 degrees F. Lightly grease a 13 x 9-inch baking pan.

2 Line the prepared baking pan with the dried beef. Wrap each breast with a bacon slice and arrange on top of the beef. Spread the sour cream over the chicken and cover. Bake for about 2½ hours. Remove the cover and bake for about 30 minutes or until tender and lightly browned. Remove from the oven and serve.

CHICKEN CASSEROLE WITH MUSHROOM STUFFING

makes about 2 servings

2 cups cooked chicken, cut into bite-sized pieces
1 cup mushrooms, sliced
1 can (10½ ounces) cream of mushroom soup
1 package stuffing mix

PANTRY
1 tablespoon butter or margarine

1 Position the rack in the center of the oven and preheat to 350 degrees F. Lightly grease a baking dish.

2 In a bowl, combine the chicken, the mushrooms, and half of the soup.

3 Pour the chicken mixture into the prepared baking dish, top with the stuffing mix, and bake for about 20 minutes. Add the remaining soup and bake for about 5 minutes or until thoroughly heated. Remove from the oven and serve.

CHICKEN DIVAN

makes about 4 servings

2 large boneless chicken breasts
¾ cup sherry or white port
¾ cup (bottled) Caesar dressing

PANTRY
1 tablespoon butter or margarine
1 tablespoons dried parsley, crushed

1 Position the rack in the center of the oven and preheat to 350 degrees F. Lightly grease a 13 x 9-inch baking pan.

2 In a bowl, blend together the wine, the dressing, and the parsley.

3 Arrange the chicken in the prepared baking dish and top with the wine mixture. Bake, basting occasionally, for about 45 to 50 minutes or until tender. Remove from the oven and serve.

⅔ cup dressing of choice

2 small (about 2 to 2½ pounds each) chickens, cut into serving-sized pieces

1¾ cups crushed cereal

PANTRY

1 tablespoon butter or margarine

3 tablespoons honey

1 Position the rack in the center of the oven and preheat to 375 degrees F. Lightly grease a 13 x 9-inch baking pan.

2 In a bowl, blend together the dressing and the honey. Dip the chicken into the dressing mixture and roll in the crushed cereal until well-coated.

3 Arrange the chicken in the prepared baking pan and bake for about 35 to 40 minutes or until tender and lightly browned. Remove from the oven, arrange in a paper-lined basket, and serve.

CHICKEN IN A BASKET

makes about 4 to 6 servings

1 medium (about 3 pounds) chicken, cut into serving-sized pieces

1 can (14½ ounces) whole peeled tomatoes, drained; reserve liquid

1 envelope onion soup mix

⅓ cup white port

PANTRY

1 tablespoon butter or margarine

1 In a bowl, blend together the tomatoes, the soup mix, the wine, and the reserved tomato juice.

2 Arrange the chicken in a lightly greased microwave-proof baking dish. Microwave on high heat, turning occasionally, for about 12 minutes. Drain the juices. Pour the tomato mixture over the chicken, cover, and microwave on high heat for about 15 minutes or until tender. Remove from the microwave and serve.

CHICKEN IN A SKILLET

makes about 4 servings

CHICKEN IN CREAM SAUCE

makes about 4 servings

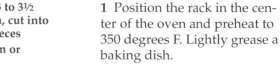

1 medium (about 3 to 3½ pounds) chicken, cut into serving-sized pieces
1½ cups sour cream or buttermilk

PANTRY
½ cup flour
3 tablespoons butter or margarine
Salt and pepper to taste

1 Position the rack in the center of the oven and preheat to 350 degrees F. Lightly grease a baking dish.

2 Sprinkle the chicken with the seasoning to taste and dredge in the flour.

3 In a skillet, sauté the chicken in butter for about 10 minutes or until lightly browned.

4 Place the chicken in the prepared dish, top with the cream and cover. Bake for about 20 minutes, remove the cover and continue to bake for about 15 minutes or until tender. Remove from the oven and serve.

CHICKEN KIEV

makes about 6 servings

6 boneless chicken breasts
2 cups bread crumbs
3 large eggs, beaten until yellow

PANTRY
¼ cup vegetable oil
1½ sticks chilled butter or margarine, halved lengthwise, and cut into 2-inch pieces

1 Position the rack in the center of the oven and preheat to 400 degrees F. Lightly grease a baking or cookie sheet.

2 Place a piece of butter in the center of the breast, roll up, folding in the sides and secure the flap with a toothpick. Roll in the bread crumbs, dip into the eggs, and roll again in the bread crumbs.

3 In a deep fryer, heat the oil to about 350 degrees F. Add the chicken and fry for about 10 to 15 minutes or until golden-brown.

4 Arrange the chicken on the prepared baking sheet and bake for about 5 to 7 minutes or until tender. Remove from the oven and serve.

1 bag (16 ounces) frozen chicken nuggets
4 to 8 strips lean bacon, fried crisp and drained
2 large bananas, peeled, halved lengthwise and quartered

PANTRY
2 tablespoons vegetable oil

1 Prepare the chicken nuggets according to the package directions.

2 Heat the oil in a skillet and sauté the bananas, stirring and turning until just softened. Transfer to a wire rack covered with paper towels to drain.

3 Arrange the chicken, bacon, and bananas on a serving plate.

CHICKEN MARYLAND

makes about 4 servings

2 boneless chicken breasts, cut into bite-sized pieces
1½ cups (bottled) honey mustard sauce
½ cup crushed pretzels

1 Position the rack in the center of the oven and preheat to 375 degrees F. Lightly grease a baking or cookie sheet.

2 Dip the chicken in the sauce, roll in the crushed pretzels, and arrange on the prepared baking sheet. Bake for about 15 to 20 minutes or until tender. Remove from the oven and serve with the remaining sauce on the side.

CHICKEN NUGGETS WITH HONEY AND MUSTARD SAUCE

makes about 4 servings

3 chicken quarters
1 medium yellow onion, sliced
3 large tomatoes, sliced
2 tablespoons grated cheese

PANTRY
1 tablespoon vegetable oil
Salt and pepper to taste

1 Position the rack in the center of the oven and preheat to 375 degrees F. Lightly grease a baking dish.

2 Brush the chicken with the oil and season to taste.

3 Arrange the chicken in the prepared baking dish, and top with a layer of the onions and the tomatoes. Sprinkle with the cheese and cover. Bake for about 50 to 60 minutes, or until the chicken is tender. Remove the cover and bake for an additional 5 minutes or until the cheese begins to bubble. Remove from the oven and serve.

CHICKEN PORTUGUESE

makes about 3 servings

CHICKEN RAGOUT

makes about 4 servings

2 cups leftover chicken gravy
1 tablespoon currant jelly
2 cups cooked chicken, cut into strips

PANTRY
Salt and pepper to taste

In a saucepan, combine the gravy, the jelly, and chicken. Heat through, season to taste and serve.

CHICKEN STEAMED WITH LEEKS AND GINGER

makes about 8 to 10 servings

1 whole chicken (about 2 pounds)
1 leek, trimmed and chopped
5 thin slices ginger root
5 tablespoons rice wine

PANTRY
soy sauce for dipping

1 Thoroughly wash the chicken and rub inside and out with salt. Place the leek and ginger inside the chicken.

2 Place the chicken in a bamboo steamer over a pot of boiling water and steam for at least 30 minutes or until fork tender.

3 Remove the chicken from the steamer, let cool, remove the skin and slice the meat very thin. Serve at once with soy sauce on the side.

CHICKEN STUFFED POTATO

makes about 4 servings

1 large russet potato
1 package (4 ounces) frozen chicken à la king
Chives, chopped

PANTRY
Salt to taste

1 Scrub the potato and stab several times with a fork. Microwave on high for about 3 minutes.

2 Open the cooking pouch of the chicken, snip off a small corner of the package, and place in the microwave next to the potato. Microwave on high for about 3 to 4 minutes.

3 Cut the potato almost in half lengthwise, pressing to open the potato. Sprinkle with salt and spoon the chicken into the potato. Sprinkle with chopped chives and serve immediately.

½ cup tempura batter mix, prepared

10 chicken wings, separated and tips removed

½ cup (bottled) sweet and sour sauce

PANTRY

¾ cup vegetable oil

CHICKEN TEMPURA

makes about 4 servings

1 In a deep fryer, heat the oil to about 375 degrees F.

2 Dip the chicken into the batter, and place into the hot oil. Cook, turning occasionally, for about 10 to 12 minutes or until tender and golden-brown. Transfer to a rack covered with paper towels, drain, and serve with the sauce on the side.

6 boneless, skinless chicken breast halves

1 jar (12 ounces) teriyaki sauce

2 medium green bell peppers, stemmed, seeded and halved

6 slices canned pineapple, drained

CHICKEN TERIYAKI

makes about 6 servings

1 In a shallow baking dish, combine the chicken and teriyaki sauce, tossing lightly to coat. Cover with plastic wrap and refrigerate for about 2 hours.

2 Position the grill rack 6 inches from the heat source and preheat.

3 Remove the chicken from the sauce, reserving the sauce.

4 On the prepared grill, lay out the chicken, peppers, and pineapples and cook, turning and basting, for about 15 minutes, until the chicken is cooked through and the juices run clear.

5 Remove the chicken, peppers, and pineapples from the grill. Arrange on serving plates and serve with the sauce on the side.

Cooking note: The sauce may be served hot or cold.

CHICKEN WITH BUTTER AND VERMOUTH

makes about 4 servings

2 boneless chicken breasts
¼ cup dry vermouth

PANTRY
¼ cup butter or margarine
1 teaspoon onion powder
1 teaspoon garlic powder

1 Position the rack in the center of the oven and preheat to 350 degrees F. Lightly grease a baking dish.

2 Arrange the chicken on the prepared dish, sprinkle with the onion and garlic powder, and dot with the butter. Cover and bake for about 30 minutes. Remove the cover, add the vermouth, and continue to bake for about 15 minutes or until tender. Remove from the oven and serve.

CHICKEN WITH CHEESE TORTILLAS

makes about 4 servings

1 envelope nacho cheese soup mix
2 cups cooked chicken, cut into bite-sized pieces
4 corn tortillas
Sliced olives

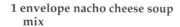

PANTRY
1¼ cups milk

1 In a saucepan, blend together the soup mix and the milk. Bring to a boil and reduce to a simmer. Cover and cook for about 5 minutes. Stir in the chicken and cook for about 5 minutes or until thoroughly heated.

2 Arrange the tortillas in a dish, add about one half of the chicken mixture, garnish with olives, top with the remaining chicken, and serve.

Cooking note: For variation, top with chopped onions.

CHICKEN WITH CUCUMBERS IN OYSTER SAUCE

makes about 2 servings

2 boneless chicken thighs
1 large cucumber, peeled and cut into thin strips
¼ cup (bottled) oyster-flavored sauce

1 In a saucepan, cover the chicken with water and bring to a boil. Reduce to a simmer, cover, and cook for about 30 minutes or until tender. Drain the liquid and cover with ice water. Set aside to cool for about 1 hour. Drain and shred the chicken.

2 In a bowl, combine the chicken, the cucumbers, and the sauce, and serve.

4 boneless chicken breasts,
  thinly sliced
4 slices cooked ham
4 ounces grated Gruyère cheese
1 tomato, thinly sliced

PANTRY

1 tablespoon melted butter or
  margarine

1 Position the boiler rack about 6 inches from the heat.

2 Brush the chicken with the butter and arrange on the boiler pan. Broil for about 5 minutes on each side and top with the ham and cheese. Continue to cook for about 3 minutes or until the cheese has melted. Remove from the oven, garnish with tomato, and serve.

CHICKEN WITH HAM AND GRUYÈRE

makes about 4 servings

2 boneless chicken breasts
1 large onion, quartered
1½ cups heavy cream
⅓ cup grated fresh Parmesan
  cheese

PANTRY

Salt and pepper to taste

1 Position the rack in the center of the oven and preheat to 350 degrees F. Have a baking dish available.

2 Arrange the chicken in the baking dish, add the onions and season to taste. Pour the cream over the top and sprinkle with the cheese. Bake for about 45 to 50 minutes or until tender. Remove from the oven and serve.

CHICKEN WITH PARMESAN CREAM

makes about 4 servings

8 boneless chicken breasts,
  halved
½ cup dry white wine
¾ cup ripe mango, chopped

PANTRY

4 tablespoons butter or
  margarine

1 Position the rack in the center of the oven and preheat to 350 degrees F. Lightly grease a shallow baking dish.

2 Arrange the chicken in the prepared baking dish and dot with the butter. Cover and bake, basting occasionally, for about 30 minutes. Remove the cover, add the wine, and continue to bake for about 15 to 20 minutes, or until tender. Sprinkle with the mango and cook for about 3 minutes or until thoroughly heated. Remove from the oven and serve.

CHICKEN WITH WINE AND MANGO

makes about 8 servings

CHICKEN WORCESTERSHIRE

makes about 4 to 6 servings

2 tablespoons Worcestershire sauce
1 small (about 2½ pounds) chicken, cut into 8 pieces
¼ cup bread crumbs

PANTRY
½ cup flour
½ cup vegetable oil
Salt and pepper to taste

1 Arrange the chicken in a dish and brush with the sauce. Cover with plastic wrap and refrigerate for about 1 hour.

2 In a bowl, combine the flour, the bread crumbs, and the chicken, and season to taste.

3 In a skillet, heat the oil and add the chicken. Fry, turning occasionally, for about 20 to 25 minutes or until tender and lightly browned. Transfer to a rack covered with paper towels, drain and serve.

CHILI CHICKEN

makes about 6 servings

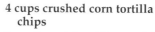

4 cups crushed corn tortilla chips
1 medium (about 3 pounds) chicken, cut into serving-sized pieces

PANTRY
2 teaspoons chili powder
⅓ cup mayonnaise

1 In a bowl, combine the chips and the chili powder.

2 Coat the chicken with the mayonnaise and roll in the chip mixture.

3 Arrange the chicken in a 13 x 9-inch microwave-proof dish so that the pieces do not touch. Cover and microwave on high heat for about 10 minutes. Remove the cover and continue to microwave for about 10 minutes or until tender. Remove from the microwave and serve.

CHILI LIVERS

makes about 4 servings

4 bacon slices
1 pound chicken livers, chopped
1 can (10½ ounces) cream of onion soup
¾ cup (bottled) chili sauce

PANTRY
1 tablespoon flour

1 In a skillet, sauté the bacon for about 8 to 10 minutes or until crisp. Remove and crumble.

2 Lightly dust the livers with the flour.

3 In the same skillet, sauté the liver for about 5 minutes or until browned. Add the bacon, the soup, and the chili sauce. Cover and simmer for about 20 minutes or until the livers are tender. Remove the cover and continue to cook for about 5 minutes or until thickened. Remove from the heat and serve.

1½ cups chicken breasts, cooked and diced
1 cup White Wine Sauce (see page 411)
1 tablespoon fruit chutney or fruit preserves
1 cup bread crumbs

PANTRY
1 tablespoon butter or margarine

CHUTNEY BAKED CHICKEN

makes about 4 servings

1 Position the broiler rack about 6 inches from the heat. Lightly grease four individual ramekin cups. Have a baking or cookie sheet available.

2 In a small bowl, blend together the sauce and chutney.

3 Divide the chicken among the prepared cups, spoon on the sauce, and sprinkle the tops with the bread crumbs. Arrange on a baking sheet and broil for about 5 minutes or until the tops are toasted. Remove from the oven and serve.

Cooking note: If the chutney comes in large chunks, it should be finely chopped before using.

1 medium (about 3 pounds) chicken, cut into serving-sized pieces
1 can (10¾ ounces) cream of chicken soup

PANTRY
2 tablespoons vegetable oil
⅛ teaspoon dried thyme, crushed

CREAMY HERBED CHICKEN

makes about 4 servings

In a skillet, sauté the chicken in the oil, turning occasionally, for about 10 minutes or until browned. Add the soup and the thyme. Bring to a boil and reduce to a simmer. Cover and continue to cook for about 30 minutes or until tender. Remove from the heat and serve.

CRISPY CHICKEN

makes about 6 servings

3 whole boneless, skinless, chicken breasts, halved
¾ cup Miracle Whip™ salad dressing
1 cup crushed corn flakes
½ cup grated Parmesan cheese

PANTRY

1 tablespoon butter or margarine
Salt and pepper to taste

1 Position the rack in the center of the oven and preheat to 350 degrees F. Lightly grease a 13 x 9-inch baking pan.

2 Brush the chicken with salad dressing, dredge in the corn flakes, and roll in the cheese. Season to taste.

3 Arrange the chicken in the prepared baking pan and bake for about 60 minutes or until tender and lightly browned. Remove from the oven and serve.

CRISPY SQUAB

makes about 4 servings

2 squabs (about 1 pound each)

PANTRY

2 tablespoon vegetable oil
Salt and pepper to taste
2 tablespoons soy sauce
2 tablespoons honey

1 In a deep fryer, heat the oil to about 375 degrees F.

2 Rub the inside and the outside of the squab with soy sauce and season to taste. Brush the outside with honey.

3 Place the squabs in the hot oil and fry for about 25 minutes or until tender and golden-brown. Remove from the heat, cut into serving-sized pieces and serve.

CROCKPOT CHICKEN AND GRAVY

makes about 4 servings

1 medium (about 3 pounds) chicken
1 can (10½ ounces) cream of mushroom soup
⅓ cup dry white wine
1 can (4 ounces) tiny button mushrooms, undrained

PANTRY

Salt and pepper to taste

1 Rub the inside and outside of the chicken with seasoning to taste.

2 In a bowl, blend together the soup and wine, and pour over the chicken.

3 Place in a crockpot and cook on high heat for 2 hours. Blend in the mushrooms and mushroom juice. Cook for 1 hour or until tender. Remove from the heat and serve.

Cooking note: For variation, add different kinds of vegetables during cooking.

4 boneless chicken breasts, flattened

½ cup Curry Paste, at room temperature (see page 10)

PANTRY

Salt and pepper to taste

1 Position the broiler rack about 6 inches from the heat.

2 Brush both sides of the chicken with the Curry Butter and place in the broiler pan. Broil, turning once, for about 20 minutes or until tender. Remove from the oven, season to taste and serve.

CURRIED CHICKEN

makes about 4 servings

---

4 boneless chicken breasts

1 cup white rice, washed and drained

PANTRY

2 tablespoons curry powder

¼ cup butter or margarine

Salt and pepper

1 In a skillet, cover the chicken with about 2 to 2½ cups of water and blend in the curry. Bring to a boil and reduce to a simmer. Cover and cook for about 20 minutes or until tender. Reserve 2 cups of the liquid.

2 In a saucepan, combine the rice and the butter. Cook, stirring frequently, for about 5 minutes or until well-coated.

3 Position the rack in the center of the oven and preheat to 350 degrees F. Lightly grease a baking dish.

4 Arrange the chicken in the prepared baking dish, pour the reserved liquid over the top, add the rice, and season to taste. Bake for about 15 to 20 minutes, or until most of the liquid has evaporated and the rice is tender. Remove from the oven and serve.

CURRIED CHICKEN PILAF

makes about 4 servings

Drunken Sweet Turkey

makes about 4 servings

1 half fresh turkey
½ cup Kahlua
½ cup apricot preserves

PANTRY
1 tablespoon melted butter or margarine

1 Position the rack in the center of the oven and preheat to 450 degrees F. Lightly grease a roasting pan.

2 In a bowl, blend together the Kahlua and the apricot preserves.

3 Place the turkey in the prepared roasting pan. Brush with the butter and cover with a piece of butter-soaked cheesecloth. Reduce the heat to 350 degrees F. Cook, brushing with the glaze frequently, for about 3½ hours or until tender. Remove from the oven, peel off the cheesecloth, cool and serve with the pan juices on the side.

Easy Chicken Casserole

makes about 4 servings

1 large (about 4 to 5 pounds) chicken, cut into serving-sized pieces
1 cup yellow onions, chopped
1 tablespoon Worcestershire sauce
1 can (10¾ ounces) cream of mushroom soup

PANTRY
1 tablespoon butter or margarine

1 Position the rack in the center of the oven and preheat to 350 degrees F. Lightly grease a baking dish.

2 In a bowl, blend together the sauce and the soup.

3 Arrange the onion in the prepared baking dish and place the chicken on top. Pour the soup mixture over the chicken and cover. Bake, turning occasionally, for about 1½ to 2 hours or until tender. Remove from the oven and serve.

1 can (10½ ounces) chicken à la king
2 hardboiled eggs, sliced
½ cup cooked green beans
4 slices buttered toast

In a saucepan, cook the chicken, the eggs, and the beans for about 10 minutes or until thoroughly heated. Remove from the heat and serve over toast.

FAST, EASY CHICKEN À LA KING

makes about 2 to 4 servings

---

1 small (about 4 to 5 pounds) turkey, cut into serving-sized pieces
¼ teaspoon Poultry Seasoning (see page 13)

PANTRY
¼ cup vegetable oil
½ cup flour
Salt and pepper to taste

1 In a Dutch oven, preheat the oil to about 350 degrees F.

2 In a bowl, combine the flour, the poultry seasoning, and the turkey, and salt and pepper to taste. Stir until the turkey is well-coated.

3 Place the turkey in the hot oil and fry, turning occasionally, for about 15 to 20 minutes or until browned. Pour the juice off, add ¼ cup of water, and cover. Cook over low heat for about 1 hour or until tender. Remove from the heat and serve.

FRIED TURKEY

makes about 4 to 6 servings

---

8 small squabs (about 1 pound each), halved
4 medium pears, stemmed, pared, cored and halved

PANTRY
½ cup olive oil

1 Position the grill about 6 inches from the heat.

2 Brush the squab with the oil and place on the grill skin-side down. Grill for about 10 minutes or until the skin is crispy. Turn over and grill for about 4 minutes. Place the pears on the grill. Grill for about 1 minute or until the squab is tender and the pears are heated. Remove from the grill and serve.

GRILLED SQUAB AND PEARS

makes about 8 servings

HERBED ROAST CHICKEN

makes about 4 servings

1 medium (2½ to 3 pounds) chicken, cut into serving-sized pieces

1 envelope Lipton's™ savory herbs with garlic

PANTRY

1 tablespoon vegetable oil

1 Position the rack in the center of the oven and preheat to 375 degrees F. Lightly grease a 13 x 9-inch baking pan.

2 In a small bowl, blend together the herb mix, 2 tablespoons water and the oil.

3 Arrange the chicken in the prepared baking pan and pour the herb mixture over the top. Bake, basting occasionally, for about 50 to 60 minutes or until tender. Remove from the oven and serve.

HONEY'S CHICKEN

makes about 4 servings

4 boneless chicken breasts, halved

PANTRY

2 tablespoons warm honey

½ teaspoon dried rosemary, crushed

Salt and pepper to taste

1 Position the broiler rack about 6 inches from the heat. Lightly grease the broiler pan.

2 In a small bowl, blend together the honey and the rosemary. Season to taste.

3 Brush both sides of the chicken with the honey-herb mixture and arrange on the prepared broiler pan. Broil for about 15 minutes. Turn over and broil for about 10 minutes or until tender. Remove from the oven and serve.

1 small head of green cabbage, cored and sliced ½ inch thick
3 boneless chicken breasts

PANTRY
Paprika to taste
¼ cup butter or margarine
Salt and pepper to taste

1 Position the rack in the center of the oven and preheat to 375 degrees F. Lightly grease a 13 x 9-inch baking pan.

2 Place the cabbage in a bowl, salt to taste, and set aside for about 2 minutes. Sprinkle with the paprika to taste.

3 In a skillet, sauté the chicken in butter for about 5 minutes. Cover and reduce to a simmer. Cook, turning occasionally, for about 20 minutes or until tender.

4 Arrange the cabbage in the prepared baking pan, pepper to taste, and cover. Bake for about 15 minutes and top with the chicken. Cover and bake for about 20 minutes or until thoroughly heated. Remove from the oven and serve.

HUNGARIAN-STYLE BAKED CHICKEN

makes about 6 servings

---

1 (about 3½ pounds) fryer chicken, cut into serving-sized pieces
1 envelope onion soup mix
¾ cup bread crumbs

PANTRY
½ cup mayonnaise

1 Position the broiler rack about 6 inches from the heat.

2 In a bowl, combine the soup mix, and the bread crumbs.

3 Brush the chicken with the mayonnaise, roll in the bread crumb mixture, and arrange on the broiler pan. Bake for about 40 to 50 minutes or until tender and golden-brown. Remove from the oven and serve.

MOIST AND CRISPY ONION CHICKEN

makes about 4 servings

MOIST CHICKEN IN CREAM SAUCE

makes about 4 servings

1 piece (about 2½ to 3 pounds) chicken, cut into serving-sized pieces

1 can (10¾ ounces) condensed cream of chicken soup

1 tablespoon celery, minced

1 tablespoon fresh parsley, snipped

1 In a bowl, combine the soup, the celery, and the parsley.

2 Arrange the chicken in a microwave-proof baking dish and pour the soup mixture over the top. Cover and cook on high heat, basting occasionally, for about 20 to 25 minutes or until tender. Remove from the oven and serve.

MUSTARD ALMOND CHICKEN

makes about 4 servings

2 tablespoons prepared mustard

2 boneless chicken breasts, halved

½ cup chopped almonds

PANTRY
2 tablespoons melted butter or margarine

1 Position the rack in the center of the oven and preheat to 375 degrees F. Lightly grease a 10 x 6-inch baking dish.

2 In a bowl, blend together the butter and the mustard.

3 Dip the chicken in the mustard mixture and coat with the almonds. Place in the prepared baking dish and bake for about 30 to 40 minutes or until tender. Remove from the oven and serve.

ORANGE GLAZED CHICKEN

makes about 4 servings

¾ cup Italian dressing

½ cup orange marmalade

1 medium chicken (about 3 to 3½ pounds) cut into serving-sized pieces

PANTRY
2 teaspoons ground ginger
1 tablespoon butter or margarine

1 Position the rack in the center of the oven and preheat to 375 degrees F. Lightly grease a 13 x 9-inch baking dish.

2 In a bowl, blend together the dressing, the marmalade, and the ginger.

3 Arrange the chicken, skin side up, in the prepared baking dish. Brush with the glaze. Bake, brushing occasionally, for about 1 hour or until tender. Remove from the oven and serve.

¼ teaspoon garlic salt

1 medium chicken (about 3 to 3½ pounds), cut into serving-sized pieces

2 cups crushed potato chips

PANTRY

½ cup melted butter

Salt and pepper to taste

1 Position the rack in the center of the oven and preheat to 375 degrees F. Lightly grease a 13 x 9-inch baking dish.

2 In a bowl, combine the garlic salt and the potato chips and pepper to taste.

3 Brush the chicken with the butter and roll it around in the potato chip mixture.

4 Arrange the chicken in the prepared baking dish and bake for about 1 hour or until tender and lightly browned. Remove from the oven and serve.

OVEN-FRIED CHICKEN

makes about 4 servings

---

4 boneless chicken breasts, halved

1 bottle (6 ounces) Chinese plum sauce

PANTRY

1 tablespoon butter or margarine

1 Position the rack in the center of the oven and preheat to 400 degrees F. Lightly grease a 13 x 9-inch baking pan.

2 Arrange the chicken in the prepared baking pan and top with the sauce. Bake, basting occasionally, for about 40 minutes or until tender. Remove from the oven and serve with the pan juices on the side.

PLUM CHICKEN

makes about 4 servings

½ cup apple juice

Nutmeg to taste

4 boneless chicken breasts, halved

PANTRY

¼ teaspoon cinnamon

In a large skillet, blend and bring to a boil together the apple juice, the cinnamon, and the nutmeg. Add the chicken, bring to a boil, and reduce to a simmer. Cover and continue to cook for about 25 to 30 minutes or until tender. Remove from the heat and serve.

POACHED CHICKEN BREASTS

makes about 4 servings

Pot au Feu

makes about 4 to 6 servings

1 large (about 4 to 5 pounds) roasting chicken
2 large carrots, trimmed, pared and sliced
1 large yellow onion, sliced
2 stalks celery, sliced
1 cup (canned) onion gravy

PANTRY
1 teaspoon salt

In a Dutch oven, place the chicken and cover with lightly salted water. Put lid on and simmer for about 20 minutes. Add the carrots, the onions, and the celery. Cover and continue to cook for about 30 to 40 minutes or until tender. Remove from the heat and cool. Remove the bones and skin. Shred the chicken and serve with gravy on the side.

Potted Turkey

makes about 4 to 6 servings

1½ cups cooked turkey, finely ground
⅓ cup cooked ham, finely chopped
1 small white onion, minced

PANTRY
1 tablespoon vegetable oil
2 tablespoons melted butter or margarine
Salt and pepper to taste

1 In a skillet, sauté the onion in oil until tender but not browned.

2 In the container of a blender or food processor, combine the turkey, the ham, the onion, and the butter, and season to taste. Process on high speed until smooth.

3 Pour the mixture into a bowl, cover with plastic wrap, and refrigerate for about 2 hours before serving.

Roast Goose

makes about 6 to 8 servings

1 medium (about 8 to 9 pounds) goose

PANTRY
Salt and pepper to taste

1 Position the rack in the center of the oven and preheat to 375 degrees F. Lightly grease a shallow baking pan.

2 Place the goose in the prepared baking pan and season to taste. Bake for about 2½ to 3 hours or until tender. Remove from the oven, slice and serve.

Cooking note: This goes very well with fruit-based dishes.

4 boneless chicken breasts, halved
2 large lemons, thinly sliced

PANTRY
¼ cup butter or margarine
Salt and pepper to taste

1 Position the rack in the center of the oven and preheat to 350 degrees F. Lightly grease a shallow baking pan.

2 Arrange the chicken in the prepared baking pan, dot with the butter, and cover with the lemon slices. Bake, basting occasionally, for about 50 minutes or until tender. Remove from the oven and serve.

ROASTED CHICKEN BREASTS WITH LEMON SLICES

makes about 4 servings

---

6 anchovies, mashed
3½ to 4 pound roasting chicken

PANTRY
¼ cup butter or margarine

1 Position the rack in the center of the oven and preheat to 350 degrees F. Lightly grease a Dutch oven.

2 In a bowl, blend together the anchovies and the butter until smooth.

3 Thoroughly wash the chicken under running water and pat dry using paper towels. Spread evenly with the anchovy butter and arrange in the prepared roasting pan. Cover and bake for about 1½ hours, basting, or until fork tender and the juices run clear. Remove from the oven, cut into serving size pieces, and serve immediately.

ROASTED CHICKEN WITH ANCHOVY BUTTER

makes about 4 to 6 servings

ROASTED PHEASANT

makes about 4 to 6 servings

2 large (2 to 2½ pounds each) pheasants
1 tablespoon onion, minced

PANTRY

4 garlic cloves, minced
1 tablespoon butter or margarine
Salt and pepper to taste

1 Position the rack in the center of the oven and preheat to about 350 degrees F. Have a baking sheet available.

2 In a bowl, blend together the butter, the garlic and the onion.

3 Rub the pheasant inside and outside with the seasoning. Brush the outside with butter and stuff with the prepared mixture.

4 Place in a brown paper bag, secure the end, and place on the baking sheet. Bake for about 1½ to 2 hours or until tender. Remove from the oven and serve.

Cooking note: This recipe can also be used for chicken.

SAUTÉED DUCK WITH PORT

makes about 4 servings

1 whole duck breast
1 tablespoon white port wine
1 tablespoon red currant jelly

PANTRY
Salt and pepper to taste

1 Sprinkle a large skillet with salt. Add the duck, skin-side down, and simmer for about 5 minutes or until the fat starts to trickle from the skin. Turn over and continue to cook for about 5 minutes. Remove from the skillet, cut into serving-sized pieces, and transfer to a warming plate.

2 Add the wine to the skillet, bring to a boil and cook for about 1 minute or until reduced by half. Reduce to a simmer, add the jelly and the duck, and season to taste. Cook, basting occasionally, for about 30 minutes or until tender. Remove from the heat and serve with the pan juices on the side.

Cooking note: Add water to the sauce if it becomes too thick.

1 medium (about 2½ to 3 pounds) chicken
1½ tablespoons light-brown sugar

PANTRY
Salt and pepper to taste
2 teaspoons sesame oil

1 In a large skillet, sprinkle 1 tablespoon of the brown sugar. Place a wire meat rack in the skillet. Arrange the chicken on the rack, cover and over low heat smoke the chicken in the fumes of the burning sugar for about 15 minutes. Transfer to a warming plate.

2 Remove the burned sugar and replace with the remaining sugar. Return the chicken to the rack, cover and continue to smoke for about 10 minutes or until tender. Remove the chicken from the pan, brush with the sesame oil, and cut into serving-sized pieces.

Cooking note: If you place aluminum foil in the bottom of the pan, it will make it easier to remove the burned sugar.

SMOKED CHICKEN

makes about 4 to 6 servings

---

1 medium tomato, peeled, cored, and chopped
1 cup chicken, cooked and chopped
1 can (4 ounces) green chile peppers, drained, rinsed, and minced
1 teaspoon cider vinegar

PANTRY
Salt and pepper to taste

1 In a bowl, blend together the tomatoes, the chicken, the peppers, and the vinegar, and season to taste. Cover with plastic wrap and refrigerate for at least 2 hours before using.

Cooking note: The chicken can be served in pita bread with lettuce and cheese.

SPICED CHICKEN FOR SANDWICHES

makes about 2 servings

---

1 piece (about 4 to 5 pounds) turkey breast, boned
1 package dried fruit
½ cup unsweetened apple juice
½ teaspoon dried mint leaves, crushed

PANTRY
1 tablespoon butter or margarine

1 Position the rack in the center of the oven and preheat to 375 degrees F. Lightly grease a shallow baking pan.

2 In a saucepan, combine the fruit, the apple juice, and the mint. Bring to a boil and reduce to a simmer. Cook for about 5 minutes or until the liquid has evaporated.

3 Stuff the fruit mixture under the skin of the turkey. Place in the prepared baking pan and bake for about 2 hours or until tender. Remove from the oven and cool. Remove the skin, cut into thin slices, and serve.

STUFFED TURKEY BREAST

makes about 10 to 12 servings

SOUTHWESTERN CHICKEN SANTA FE

makes about 4 servings

2 whole boneless, skinless chicken breasts

2 sweet red bell peppers, stemmed, roasted, skinned, seeded, and cut into strips

Marinade of choice

4 tablespoons melted jalapeño pepper jelly

1 Place chicken between two pieces of parchment or wax paper and, using a meat tenderizer, flatten to ¼-inch thickness. Place the chicken in a plastic bag, add the marinade, and refrigerate for about 1 hours. Remove the chicken from the bag and let it come to room temperature.

2 Position the broiler rack 6 inches from the heat source and preheat.

3 Arrange the chicken on a broiler pan, brush liberally with the remaining marinade and broil, turning and brushing with marinade, for about 8 minutes per side or until tender and the juices run clear.

4 Remove from the broiler and brush with the melted jelly. Cover chicken with pepper strips and spoon any remaining jelly over the top. Return to the broiler until the chicken is glazed. Remove form the broiler and serve immediately.

SWEET AND SOUR CHICKEN

makes about 4 servings

1 medium (about 3 to 3½ pounds) chicken, cut into serving-sized pieces

1 can (8½ ounces) crushed pineapple in syrup

¼ cup prepared mustard

½ cup chopped chutney

PANTRY

1 tablespoon butter or margarine

Salt and pepper to taste

1 Position the rack in the center of the oven and preheat to 350 degrees F. Lightly grease a 13 x 9-inch baking pan.

2 In a bowl, blend together the pineapple (with syrup), the mustard, and the chutney.

3 Place the chicken in the prepared baking pan, season to taste, and pour the pineapple mixture over the top. Bake, basting occasionally, for about 1 hour or until tender. Remove from the oven and serve.

1 medium (about 3 to 3½ pounds) chicken
3 tablespoons fresh lemon juice
1 tablespoon tandoori spice mix

PANTRY
1 tablespoon melted butter or margarine

1 In a bowl, blend together the lemon juice, the spice mix, and the butter.

2 Slice about ¼-inch deep cuts in the chicken and rub in the paste. Place the chicken in a lightly greased baking dish, cover with plastic wrap and refrigerate for at least 24 hours.

3 Position the rack in the center of the oven and preheat to 400 degrees F.

4 Remove the plastic wrap, and bake, basting occasionally, for about 45 to 55 minutes or until tender. Remove from the oven and serve.

TANDOORI CHICKEN

makes about 4 servings

1 medium (3 to 3½ pounds) chicken, cut into serving-sized pieces
1 small onion, thinly sliced
1 jar (12 ounces) chunky salsa

PANTRY
1 tablespoon butter or margarine

1 Position the rack in the center of the oven and preheat to 350 degrees F. Lightly grease a 13 x 9-inch baking dish.

2 Arrange the chicken in the prepared baking dish, cover with the onion slices and top with the salsa. Bake, basting occasionally, for about 1 hour or until tender. Remove from the oven and serve.

TEX-MEX CHICKEN

makes about 4 to 5 servings

1 piece (about 6 pounds) turkey breast
⅓ cup beer

PANTRY
1 tablespoon melted butter or margarine
½ teaspoon chili powder

1 Position the rack in the center of the oven and preheat to 325 degrees F. Lightly grease a roasting pan.

2 In a bowl, blend together the butter and the chili powder.

3 Place the turkey in the prepared pan, brush with the chili mixture and pour the beer over the top. Bake for 2 to 2½ hours or until tender. Remove from the oven and set aside for at least 20 to 30 minutes. Slice and serve.

TURKEY BORRACHOS

makes about 4 to 6 servings

TURKEY FLORENTINE

makes about 6 to 8 servings

1 Butterball™ turkey breast (about 5 to 6-pounds)

1 package (6 ounces) wild rice mix, cooked

1 package (10 ounces) frozen chopped spinach, thawed and cooked

¾ cup diced cooked ham

1 Position the rack in the center of the oven and preheat to 325 degrees F. Lightly grease a roasting pan.

2 In a bowl, combine the rice, the spinach, and the ham. Transfer to a baking dish and cover. Bake for about 15 to 20 minutes or until thoroughly heated.

3 Place the turkey in the prepared roasting pan and cover. Bake for about 2½ to 3 hours or until tender. Remove from the oven, set aside for about 20 to 30 minutes, slice, and serve with the rice.

Cooking note: Rice mixture can be placed in the oven for about 20 minutes until the turkey is ready.

TURKEY WINGS FRICASSEE

makes about 2 to 4 servings

4 turkey wings

½ cup dry sherry

PANTRY

¾ cup vegetable oil

⅓ cup flour

Salt and pepper to taste

1 Preheat the oil in a skillet to 350 degrees F.

2 In a bowl, combine the flour, the seasoning to taste, and the wings. Stir until the wings are well-coated.

3 Place the wings in the hot oil and cook, turning occasionally, for about 10 minutes or until golden-brown. Drain the liquid and pour in the sherry. Cover and simmer for about 40 minutes or until tender. Remove from the heat and serve.

Meat

No single food is more adaptable to the recipes in this book than meat. There are so many cuts available, each of them delivering different flavor and different texture. Still, we had a great time inventing easy new ways of preparing the foods we love, and, once again you'll find an abundance of interesting recipes, all requiring a minimum

GRILLED PORK SPARERIBS

of fuss. Here's a little sampling of what's to come: Braised Brisket in Beer, Orange Glazed Corned Beef, Pork Barbecue, Potato Coated Pork Fillets, Quick Lamb Fricassee, Sausage and Spaghetti, and the list goes on.

The most important thing to know about preparing great dishes with meat is to choose quality. If you buy the very best cuts of meat you can afford, you don't have to do much more than cook them well. And the recipes in this book will help you do just that.

CURRIED MUTTON

BRAISED BRISKET IN BEER

ACORN SQUASH WITH SAUSAGE

makes about 4 servings

2 medium acorn squash, halved, seeded and pith removed

1 cup packed brown sugar

1 pound bulk sausage

1 Position the rack in the center of the oven and preheat to 350 degrees F. Lightly grease a baking or cookie sheet.

2 Arrange the squash on the prepared baking sheet and spoon the sugar into each half.

3 Form sausage into 4 patties. Place the patties on the squash.

4 Bake for about 30 to 45 minutes or until tender. Remove from the oven and serve.

AFELIA

makes about 4 servings

1 piece (about 1¼ to 2 pounds) pork tenderloin, thinly sliced

1 teaspoon coriander seeds, finely crushed

1 teaspoon light-brown sugar

1 cup dry red wine

PANTRY

2 tablespoons vegetable oil

1 In a small bowl, combine the coriander and the sugar. Rub the meat slices with the sugar mixture and set aside for about 15 minutes.

2 In a skillet, sauté the pork slices in the oil for about 15 minutes or until both sides are lightly browned. Blend in the wine, bring to a boil, and cook for about 2 minutes. Reduce to a simmer and continue to cook for about 15 minutes, or until tender and most of the liquid has evaporated. Remove from the heat and serve.

4 center cut or rib pork chops, trimmed, reserving the fat

2½ pounds fresh spinach, stemmed

4 medium sweet potatoes, pared and sliced

¼ cup butter or margarine

Salt and pepper to taste

1 teaspoon ground nutmeg

ALOHA PORK CHOPS WITH SPINACH

makes about 4 servings

1 Position the rack in the center of the oven and preheat to 350 degrees F. Lightly grease a 13 x 9-inch baking dish.

2 In a skillet, place reserved fat and sauté, stirring frequently, for about 3 to 4 minutes. Add the chops and sauté for about 15 minutes or until both sides are lightly browned.

3 Arrange half of the spinach in the prepared baking dish, sprinkle with the nutmeg, add the pork chops, and top with the remaining spinach and the yams. Season to taste and dot with the butter. Bake for about 40 minutes or until tender. Remove from the oven and serve.

---

1 corned beef (about 4 to 5 pounds)

1 cup packed brown sugar

5 whole cloves

BAKED CORNED BEEF

makes about 6 to 8 servings

1 In a saucepan, cover the beef with water and bring to a boil. Reduce to a simmer and cook, skimming off the fat, for about 3 to 4 hours or until tender.

2 Position the rack in the center of the oven and preheat to 325 degrees F. Lightly grease a baking pan and place a meat rack in the pan.

3 Place the corned beef on the rack. Rub with the sugar and press the cloves into the meat. Bake for about 40 to 50 minutes or until tender and golden-brown. Remove from the oven and serve.

BAKED HAM AND RICE

makes about 2 to 4 servings

1 cup uncooked rice, washed and drained
2 slices of ham, diced

PANTRY

1 tablespoon butter or margarine
3 cups milk

1 Position the rack in the center of the oven and preheat to 350 degrees F. Lightly grease a baking dish.

2 Arrange half of the rice in the prepared baking dish, top with the ham and top with the remaining rice. Pour the milk over the ham, cover and bake for about 20 minutes. Remove the cover, and continue to bake for about 20 minutes, or until all the liquid has evaporated and the rice is tender. Remove from the heat, fluff and serve.

BAKED LAMB CHOPS IN CHEESE SAUCE

makes about 4 servings

4 thick loin lamb chops
6 scallions, trimmed and thinly sliced
¼ cup light cream
2 tablespoons grated Swiss cheese

PANTRY

1 tablespoon butter or margarine
Salt and pepper to taste

1 Position the rack in the center of the oven and preheat to 350 degrees F. Lightly grease a baking dish.

2 Arrange the chops in the prepared baking dish, top with the onions, and pour on the cream. Season to taste and bake for about 40 minutes. Sprinkle on the cheese and continue to bake for about 10 to 15 minutes or until the cheese has melted. Remove from the oven and serve.

BAKED LAMB CHOPS WITH VEGETABLES

makes about 4 servings

4 thick boneless loin lamb chops
1 large green peppers, stemmed, seeded and sliced
1 small white onion, sliced
2 large tomatoes, sliced

PANTRY

2 tablespoons vegetable oil
Salt and pepper to taste

1 Position the rack in the center of the oven and preheat to 375 degrees F. Lightly grease a baking dish.

2 In a skillet, heat the oil and add the lamb chops. Sear over high heat sear on both sides.

3 Arrange the chops in the prepared baking dish and top with the peppers, the onions, and the tomatoes. Cover and bake for about 30 minutes. Remove the cover, season to taste, and continue to bake for about 10 to 20 minutes or until tender. Remove from the oven and serve.

1 pork roast (about 2 to 2½ pounds)
27 ounces fresh sauerkraut

PANTRY
1 tablespoon butter or margarine

1 Position the rack in the center of the oven and preheat to 325 degrees F. Lightly grease a roasting pan.

2 Place the pork in the center of the prepared roasting pan and arrange the sauerkraut around the meat. Add 3 cups of water and cover.

3 Bake for about 2½ hours or until tender. Remove from the oven and serve.

BAKED PORK AND SAUERKRAUT

makes about 4 to 6 servings

---

1 to 2 pounds pork tenderloin, cut into bite-sized strips
1 cup oriental-style marinade

PANTRY
1 tablespoon honey

1 In a cup, blend together the honey and 2 tablespoons of boiling water. Set aside.

2 In a bowl, combine the pork and the marinade. Cover with plastic wrap and refrigerate for about 3 to 4 hours. Remove the pork and reserve the sauce.

3 Position the rack in the center of the oven and preheat to 425 degree F. Lightly grease a 13 x 9-inch baking pan and place a wire rack in the pan.

4 Arrange the pork on the wire rack. Pour ⅔ cup of boiling water into the pan and bake for about 15 minutes. Lower the temperature to 350 degrees F and cook, basting with the reserved marinade, for an additional 10 minutes or until tender. Remove from the oven and brush with the honey.

5 Position the broiler rack about 4 to 5 inches from the heat. Broil the pork for about 4 minutes or until glazed. Remove from the oven and serve on a bed of lettuce with the pan juices on the side.

BARBECUED PORK TENDERLOIN

makes about 2 to 4 servings

BEEF AND POTATO CAKES

makes about 4 servings

2½ cups leftover cooked ground beef

1½ cups leftover seasoned mashed potatoes

1 teaspoon prepared thick meat sauce

2 teaspoons white onion, minced

PANTRY

¼ cup flour

2 tablespoons vegetable oil

Salt and pepper to taste

1 In a bowl, combine the beef, the potatoes, the meat sauce, and the onion. Shape into 6 patties. Dredge the patties in the flour.

2 In a skillet, sauté the patties in the oil for about 25 minutes or until both sides are browned. Remove from the heat, season to taste, and serve.

BEEF AU JUS SPECIAL

makes about 12 to 15 sandwiches

1 boneless chuck roast (about 5 to 6 pounds), trimmed

2 envelopes (¼ ounce each) dry onion soup mix

2 jars (about 4 ounces each) sliced mushrooms, undrained

PANTRY

1 tablespoon butter or margarine

Salt and pepper to taste

1 Position the rack in the center of the oven and preheat to 300 degrees F. Lightly grease a roasting pan.

2 Place the meat in the prepared baking pan, sprinkle with the soup mix, and cover. Bake for about 3½ hours, top with the mushrooms and season to taste. Cook for an additional 30 minutes, or until tender. Remove from the oven, slice, and serve with the pan juices on the side.

BEEF CHUCK WITH WINE SAUCE

makes about 10 servings

1 piece (about 3½ to 4 pounds) beef chuck, trimmed and cut into bite-sized pieces

1 cup dry red wine

1 can (10½ ounces) mushroom soup

PANTRY

Salt and pepper to taste

1 Position the rack in the center of the oven and preheat to 350 degrees F. Lightly grease a shallow baking pan.

2 Arrange the beef in the prepared baking pan, season to taste, and pour the wine and the soup over the top. Cover and bake for about 2 hours or until tender. Remove from the oven and serve.

1½ pounds beef heart, trimmed and cut into cubes

1 small yellow onion, peeled and quartered

1 egg

Salt and pepper to taste

2 tablespoons vegetable oil

1 In the container of a blender or a food processor, combine the meat, the onions and the egg. Process on high speed until finely ground. Transfer to a bowl, season to taste and form into patties.

2 In a skillet, sauté the patties in the oil for about 25 minutes or until both sides are browned.

Cooking note: Beef heart tends to be dry; additional oil may be needed while sautéing.

BEEF HEART PATTIES

makes about 4 to 8 servings

1 roast beef (about 3 to 4 pounds)

1 tablespoon vegetable oil

2 tablespoons flour

¼ cup milk

Salt and pepper to taste

1 Position the rack in the center of the oven and preheat to 325 degrees F. Lightly grease a roasting pan and place a meat rack in the pan.

2 Arrange the meat on the rack. Drizzle the oil over the roast and season to taste. Add about 1 cup of water, cover, and bake for about 1½ hours. Remove the cover and continue to bake for about 30 minutes or until tender. Transfer to a warming plate.

3 In a small bowl, blend together the milk and the flour.

4 Place the roasting pan on the stove top and heat. Blend in the mixture, season to taste and bring to a boil. Cook, stirring frequently, until the sauce is thickened. Add the meat, coat with the sauce, and cook for about 5 minutes or until thoroughly heated. Remove from the heat and serve.

ROAST BEEF WITH GRAVY

makes about 6 servings

BEEF ROASTED IN DRIED FRUIT

makes about 4 to 6 servings

1 rump roast (about 5 pounds)
2 tablespoons mixed pickling spice
1 container (16 ounces) mixed dried fruit

PANTRY
2 tablespoons vegetable oil
Salt and pepper to taste

1 In a skillet, sauté the meat in the oil for about 15 minutes or until both sides are lightly browned. Transfer to a warming plate.

2 Place a meat rack in a large roasting pan. Place the meat on the rack and add 2 cups water. Bring to a boil, blend in the pickling spice, and reduce to a simmer. Cover and cook for about 2 to 2½ hours. Add the fruit and season to taste. Simmer over low heat for an additional 1 hour or until tender. Remove from the heat, slice, garnish with the fruit, and serve.

BEEF STROGANOFF

makes about 4 servings

1 piece (about 2 pounds) boneless beef steak, cut into narrow strips
½ cup yellow onion, chopped
1 can (10¾ ounces) cream of mushroom soup
½ cup sour cream

PANTRY
Salt and pepper to taste

1 In a 2-quart microwave-proof dish, combine the meat and the onions. Cover and microwave on high heat, stirring occasionally, for about 5 minutes, or until the beef loses its pinkish color.

2 In a bowl, blend together the soup and the sour cream. Pour over the beef, cover, and microwave on medium heat for about 5 to 7 minutes, or until tender and thoroughly heated. Remove from the oven, season to taste, and serve.

BEEF WITH WINE

makes about 8 to 10 servings

1 piece (about 3½ to 4 pounds) beef chuck, trimmed and cut into bite-sized pieces
1 can (10¾ ounces) mushroom soup
1 cup dry red wine

PANTRY
Salt and pepper to taste

1 Position the rack in the center of the oven and preheat to 325 degrees F. Have a baking dish available.

2 Season the meat to taste and place in the baking dish. Pour the soup and wine over the meat, cover, and bake for about 3 hours or until tender. Remove from the oven and serve.

1 pound fresh bratwurst
1 can (12 ounces) beer
1 medium yellow onion, peeled
   and sliced
10 whole black peppercorns

1 In a saucepan, combine the bratwurst, the beer, the onion, and the peppercorns. Cook, stirring occasionally, for about 5 minutes or until bubbles start to form around the edge of the pan. Reduce to a simmer, cover, and cook for about 10 minutes or until the onions are tender.

2 Position the rack of a grill about 6 inches from the heat.

3 Arrange the bratwurst on the rack and grill, turning for about 6 to 10 minutes or until browned on all sides. Remove from the rack and serve with sliced onions on the side.

Cooking note: Cooking time in grilling recipes depends on the heat source.

BEER AND BRATWURST

makes about 4 servings

1 shoulder of mutton (about 3
   pounds), boned and rolled
2 large white onions
2 large carrots, trimmed and
   pared
2 turnips, trimmed and pared

1 In a soup kettle or Dutch oven, cover the mutton with lightly salted water. Bring to a boil, skimming the fat from the top of the water. Add the onions, the carrots, and the turnips, and return to the boil. Reduce to a simmer, cover and cook for about 2 to 2½ hours or until tender.

2 Remove from the heat, slice and serve.

BOILED MUTTON

makes about 4 to 6 servings

BRAISED BRISKET IN BEER

makes about 8 to 10 servings

1 medium (about 5 to 6 pounds) beef brisket
1 can (12 ounces) beer or ale
½ cup homemade or prepared marinade of choice

PANTRY
1 tablespoon flour
Salt and pepper to taste

1 Position the rack in the center of the oven, and preheat to 350 degrees F.

2 In a Dutch oven, blend together the beer and the marinade.

3 Rub the beef with the flour and season to taste. Place in the Dutch oven, cover, and bake for about 3 to 4 hours or until tender. Remove from the oven, season to taste, slice, and serve with the pan juices on the side.

Cooking note: Use a non-tomato based marinade for this dish.

BRAISED HAM HOCKS (PIG'S KNUCKLES)

makes about 4 to 6 servings

2½ to 3 pounds fresh ham hocks
3 cups sauerkraut, fresh or canned
2 large potatoes, pared and quartered
1 teaspoon caraway seeds

PANTRY
Salt and pepper to taste

In a Dutch oven, just cover the ham hocks with lightly salted water. Bring to a boil, and reduce to a simmer. Cook for about 2 to 2½ hours. Add the sauerkraut, the potatoes, and the caraway seeds. Continue to cook for about 30 minutes or until tender. Remove from the heat, season to taste and serve.

Cooking note: When using cured ham hocks, cut back on the salt.

BRAISED LAMB AND GREEN PEAS

makes about 4 servings

1 medium yellow onion, thinly sliced
4 lean lamb cutlets
2 small turnips, pared and diced
1 package (10 ounces) frozen green peas, drained

PANTRY
1 teaspoon sugar
Salt and pepper to taste

1 Position the rack in the center of the oven and preheat to 375 degrees F. Lightly grease a shallow baking dish.

2 Arrange the onions in the bottom of the prepared baking dish and lay the cutlets on top. Add the turnips, sprinkle lightly with the sugar, and season to taste. Fill the baking dish halfway with water, and cover. Bake for about 30 minutes or until tender. Remove from the oven and serve.

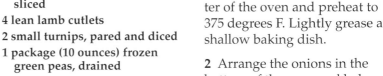

4 loin lamb chops (¾-inch thick)
¼ cup (bottled) stir-fry sauce
1½ teaspoons five spice powder

PANTRY
1 tablespoon butter or margarine

BRAISED LAMB CHOPS

makes about 4 servings

1 In a bowl, blend together the sauce, the spice powder, and ⅔ cup water.

2 In a skillet, fry the chops in the butter for about 5 minutes or until the lamb loses its pinkish color and both sides are lightly browned. Add the sauce, bring to a boil and reduce to a simmer. Cover and continue to cook for about 20 to 30 minutes or until tender. Remove from the heat and serve with the pan juices on the side.

---

1 pound liverwurst, casing removed and cut into ½-inch slices
2 tablespoons bacon drippings
8 slices pre-fried tomatoes
8 slices pre-fried onions

BRAISED LIVER SAUSAGE

makes about 4 servings

In a skillet, sauté the liverwurst in the bacon drippings for about 10 to 15 minutes or until both sides are lightly browned. Remove from the heat, and serve with the tomatoes and the onions on the side.

---

4 pork loin chops (½-inch thick)
3 tablespoons (bottled) black bean sauce
¾ cup chicken broth
2 scallions, trimmed and chopped

PANTRY
2 tablespoons vegetable oil
2 teaspoons cornstarch or arrowroot

BRAISED PORK CHOPS

makes about 4 servings

1 In a skillet, fry the chops in the oil for about 5 minutes, or until the pork loses its pinkish color and both sides are lightly browned. Add in the broth, the sauce, and the scallions. Bring to a boil and reduce to a simmer. Cover and cook for about 30 minutes or until tender.

2 In a small bowl, blend together the cornstarch and 2 tablespoons of water. Stir into the juices in the pan. Cook, stirring frequently, for about 5 minutes or until thickened. Remove from the heat, pour over the meat, and serve.

Braised Short Ribs

makes about 6 to 8 servings

Beef short ribs (about 3 to 4 pounds), cut into serving-sized pieces

PANTRY
2 tablespoons canola oil
¼ cup flour
Salt and pepper to taste

1 Position the rack in the center of the oven and preheat to 300 degrees F. On the stove top, preheat the oil in a roasting pan with a cover.

2 Roll the ribs in the flour and season to taste.

3 Arrange the ribs in the prepared roasting pan, add 1 cup of water and cover. Bake, turning and basting, for about 1½ to 2 hours or until tender. Remove from the oven and serve.

Cooking note: Make sure there's enough water in the pan while cooking.

Braised Veal Goulash

makes about 2 to 4 servings

1 piece veal (about 1½ to 2 pounds), trimmed and cut into bite-sized pieces
1 medium yellow onion, chopped

PANTRY
1 tablespoon paprika
2 tablespoons canola oil
Salt and pepper to taste

In a Dutch oven, sauté the onions in the oil for about 5 minutes or until translucent. Add the paprika and the meat. Reduce the heat to a slow simmer and cover. Continue to cook for about 45 minutes or until tender. Remove from the heat, season to taste, and serve.

Bratwurst with Apples

makes about 6 servings

4 medium Cortland apples, peeled, cored and sliced
1 pound bratwurst links, halved crosswise
⅓ cup packed brown sugar
1 teaspoon caraway seeds

In a crockpot, place the apples and the bratwurst. Add the sugar, the caraway seeds, and ¼ cup of water. Cover and cook on low heat for about 3 to 4 hours or until tender. Remove from the heat and serve.

¼ **pound braunschweiger sausage, casing removed and broken into bite-sized pieces**

1 pound ground beef

¼ **cup sour cream or unflavored yogurt**

2 tablespoons white onion, minced

1 Position the broiler rack about 5 inches from the heat.

2 In a bowl, combine the sausage, the beef, the sour cream, and the onion. Stir until smooth. Form into ¾-inch thick patties.

3 Place the meat in the broiler pan. Cook, turning once, for about 15 to 20 minutes or until tender. Remove from the oven and serve.

Cooking note: Braunschweiger is also known as liver sausage.

BRAUNBURGERS

makes about 3 to 4 servings

¾ **cup bread crumbs**

1 large egg, beaten

2 tablespoons sherry or white port

Pork tenderloins (about 3 pounds), cut into serving-sized pieces

PANTRY

1 tablespoon flour

Salt and pepper to taste

1 tablespoon garlic powder

1 tablespoon vegetable oil

1 In a bowl, blend together the flour and the salt and pepper to taste. In another bowl, place the bread crumbs. In a third bowl, blend together the egg and the wine.

2 Sprinkle the meat with the garlic. Roll meat in the flour, dip into the egg mixture, and coat with the bread crumbs.

3 In a skillet, sauté the meat in the oil for about 15 minutes or until both sides are golden-brown. Reduce to a low simmer and cover. Continue to cook for about 20 minutes or until tender. Remove from the heat and serve.

BREADED PORK TENDERLOIN

makes about 4 to 6 servings

BREADED VEAL CUTLETS

makes about 6 servings

6 veal cutlets, (about ½-inch thick)
1 cup bread crumbs
2 eggs, lightly beaten

PANTRY
2 tablespoons butter or margarine
Salt and pepper to taste

1 Season the cutlets to taste, and coat with the bread crumbs, dip into the eggs and roll in the crumbs.

2 In a skillet, sauté the cutlets in butter over low heat for about 15 to 20 minutes, or until tender and both sides are lightly browned. Remove from the heat and serve.

BROILED CALF'S LIVER

makes about 4 to 6 servings

6 slices (about 1½ to 2 pounds) calf's liver
1 can (8 ounces) sliced mushrooms
¼ cup (bottled) French dressing

1 Position the broiler rack about 4 inches from the heat. Lightly grease a broiler pan.

2 Brush both sides of the liver with the French dressing and place on the prepared broiler pan. Broil for about 4 minutes on each side. Top with the mushrooms and broil for about 2 to 3 minutes or until thoroughly heated. Remove from the broiler and serve.

BURGUNDY NUT BURGERS

makes about 4 servings

1 pound ground beef
½ cup pecans, coarsely chopped
⅓ cup red Burgundy wine

PANTRY
1 tablespoon butter or margarine
Salt and pepper

1 In a bowl, combine the meat and the nuts. Shape into eight patties.

2 In a skillet, sauté the patties in the butter for about 10 minutes or until both sides are browned. Add the wine and season to taste. Cover and continue to cook for about 15 minutes or until tender. Remove from the heat and serve.

CALF'S LIVER IN TOMATO SAUCE

makes about 4 servings

1 pound calf's liver
1 teaspoon Worcestershire sauce

PANTRY
¾ cup tomato sauce
Salt and pepper to taste

1 Position the rack in the center of the oven and preheat to 350 degrees F. Lightly grease a baking dish.

2 Arrange the liver in the prepared baking dish. Top with the tomato sauce, season to taste, and cover. Bake for about 20 minutes or until tender. Remove from the oven, sprinkle with the Worcestershire sauce, slice and serve.

CHERRY GLAZED HAM

makes about 8 servings

1 cured ham (about 3 to 4 pounds)
1 can (21 ounces) cherry pie filling
2 tablespoons brandy or rum

PANTRY
1 tablespoon butter or margarine

1 Position the rack in the center of the oven and preheat to 325 degrees F. Lightly grease a shallow baking pan.

2 Arrange the ham in the prepared baking pan, and bake, turning once, for about 30 minutes or until it loses its pinkish color. Top with the pie filling and continue to bake for about 30 to 40 minutes or until tender. Remove from the oven, cut into serving-sized pieces, drizzle on the brandy, and serve.

Cooking note: If you choose to flambé, use caution with the open flame.

CHERRY PORK CHOPS

makes about 6 servings

6 boneless pork chops (about ½-inch thick), trimmed
1 cup (canned) cherry pie filling
2 teaspoons fresh lemon juice
1 tablespoon instant chicken bouillon granules

PANTRY
1 tablespoon vegetable oil

1 Preheat a slow cooker on high.

2 In a skillet, heat the oil and sauté the chops for about 10 minutes or until the pork loses its pinkish color.

3 In a bowl, blend together the pie filling, the lemon juice and the bouillon granules.

4 Arrange the pork chops in the prepared slow cooker and top with the fruit mixture. Cover and cook over low heat for about 4 hours or until tender. Remove from the heat and serve with the gravy on the side.

Chinese Beef Kebabs

makes about 4 servings

1 piece (about 2 to 3 pounds) beef, trimmed and cut into bite-sized pieces

2 large green, red or yellow peppers, cut into squares

6 cherry tomatoes

6 pineapple wedges

1 cup (bottled) marinade of choice

1 In a bowl, combine the meat, the peppers, the tomatoes, and the pineapple wedges. Pour the marinade over the meat, vegetable, and fruit mixture, cover with plastic wrap, and refrigerate for at least 8 hours.

2 Position the rack of a grill about 4 to 5 inches from the heat.

3 Remove the meat, vegetables and fruit from the marinade and reserve the liquid.

4 Arrange the meat, the pepper, the tomato, and the pineapple on the skewer. Repeat.

5 Place the skewers on the grill and cook for about 10 to 15 minutes, or until the meat is tender and the peppers are crispy. Remove from the heat and serve with the marinade on the side.

Cooking note: Cooking time for grilling recipes depends on the heat source.

Chinese Mapo Tofu

makes about 2 servings

¼ pound ground pork

1 tablespoon (bottled) black bean garlic sauce

1 teaspoon red chili paste

1 package (8 ounces) fresh tofu, diced

PANTRY

2 tablespoons vegetable oil

Salt and pepper to taste

In a wok, blend the oil, the garlic sauce, and the chili paste. Add the pork and stir-fry for about 5 minutes or until it loses its pinkish color. Add the tofu and stir-fry for about 5 to 8 minutes or until the meat is tender. Remove from the heat, season to taste, and serve.

Cooking note: For variation, add chopped onions while cooking.

1 chuck roast (about 3 pounds), trimmed
½ cup (bottled) stir-fry sauce
½ cup burgundy wine
½ pound fresh white mushrooms, trimmed

PANTRY
1 tablespoon vegetable oil
1 tablespoon cornstarch

CHINESE POT ROAST

makes about 6 to 8 servings

1 In a Dutch oven, sauté the meat in the oil for about 15 minutes or until both sides are lightly browned. Blend in the sauce and the wine, and cover. Cook for about 1¾ to 2 hours or until tender. Add the mushrooms, cover, and cook for about 10 minutes or until thoroughly heated. Transfer the roast to a warming plate.

2 In a small bowl, blend together the cornstarch and ¼ cup of water; blend with pan juices. Cook for about 3 minutes or until thickened.

3 Cut the meat into thin slices and serve with the mushrooms and gravy on the side.

---

1 cup fresh beef stock
1 cup beef, diced
¼ cup (bottled) red curry sauce
1 cup broccoli, chopped

PANTRY
1 tablespoon sesame oil

CHINESE-STYLE STEW

makes about 2 to 4 servings

In a wok, stir-fry the beef in the oil for about 5 minutes or until it loses its pinkish color. Add the sauce and simmer for about 30 minutes or until tender. Add the broccoli, increase the heat, and stir-fry for about 5 minutes, or until the broccoli is just tender. Remove from the heat and serve.

---

1 pound chorizo or Italian sausage, casing removed and broken into bite-sized pieces
1 medium tomato, peeled, seeded and chopped
¼ cup grated Parmesan cheese

PANTRY
1 tablespoon olive oil

CHORIZO FILLING

makes 2 to 3 servings

In a skillet, sauté the sausage in the oil for about 5 to 10 minutes or until it loses its pinkish color. Drain the liquid and add the tomatoes and the cheese. Cook for about 10 minutes or until thoroughly heated. Remove from the heat and serve.

Cooking note: This is traditionally used as a filling for sandwiches.

CIDER GLAZED PORK

makes about 4 servings

1 boneless tri-tip pork roast (about 3 pounds)
½ cup apple cider

PANTRY
¼ cup olive oil
¼ cup prepared mustard
¼ cup soy sauce

1 Position the rack in the center of the oven and preheat to 350 degrees F. Lightly grease a roasting pan.

2 In a bowl or cup, blend together the cider, the mustard and the soy sauce.

3 Brush the pork with the oil and arrange in the prepared roasting pan. Top with the mustard mixture and bake, basting frequently, for about 60 to 70 minutes or until tender. Remove from the oven and serve.

CORNBREAD FRANKFURTERS

makes about 4 servings

1 box (8½ ounces) corn muffin mix, prepared
4 jumbo franks, cooked
1 tablespoon (bottled) mild salsa

PANTRY
1 tablespoon butter or margarine

1 Position the rack in the center of the oven and preheat to 350 degrees F. Lightly grease an 8-inch square baking pan.

2 In a bowl, combine the muffin mix and the salsa. Pour into the prepared baking pan and top with the franks.

3 Bake for about 20 to 25 minutes or until a cake tester inserted into the center comes out clean. Remove from the oven and serve.

CORNED BEEF HASH

makes about 4 servings

2 cups ground corned beef
3 cups potatoes, boiled and minced
1 large yellow onion, minced
4 tablespoons vegetable shortening

1 In a bowl, combine the beef, the potatoes and the onions.

2 In a skillet, sauté the beef mixture in the shortening, stirring frequently, for about 10 minutes or until slightly browned. Remove from the heat and serve.

Cooking note: For variation, top with poached eggs and serve with toast.

1 round steak (about 2 pounds), thinly sliced and cut into bite-sized squares
⅔ cup apple cider

PANTRY
⅓ cup flour
3 tablespoons butter or margarine
Salt and pepper to taste

1 Sprinkle the steak with seasoning to taste, and rub with the flour.

2 In a skillet, sauté the steak in the butter for about 10 to 15 minutes or until both sides are browned. Reduce to a simmer and stir in the cider. Cover and cook for about 30 minutes or until tender. Transfer the steak to a warming plate. Blend in the flour with the gravy in the pan and stir until thickened. Serve with gravy on the side.

COUNTRY FRIED STEAK

makes about 4 servings

---

1 piece (about 2 pounds) center cut ham, trimmed
4 whole cloves
1½ cups fresh cranberries

PANTRY
1 tablespoon butter or margarine
¾ cup warm honey

1 Position the rack in the center of the oven and preheat to 350 degrees F. Lightly grease a shallow baking dish.

2 In a bowl, combine the cranberries and the honey.

3 Arrange the ham in the prepared baking dish and insert the cloves in the top of the ham. Pour the cranberry mixture over the top.

4 Bake, basting frequently, for about 40 minutes or until tender. Remove from the oven and serve.

CRANBERRY HAM

makes about 4 to 6 servings

¼ pound dried beef, torn into bite-sized shreds
1 tablespoon chives or watercress, chopped
6 slices bread, toasted

PANTRY
¼ cup butter or margarine
3 tablespoons flour
2 cups milk

1 In the top of a double boiler over boiling water, cook the meat in the butter for about 10 to 15 minutes, until the edges start to curl. Blend in the flour, increase the heat and pour in the milk, stirring frequently, until blended. Continue to cook, stirring occasionally, for about 10 minutes or until thickened.

2 Remove from the heat, garnish with watercress, and serve with the bread on the side.

Cooking note: For variation, add different types of vegetables to the sauce.

CREAMED CHIPPED BEEF

makes about 2 to 4 servings

CREAMED CHIPPED BEEF WITH MUSHROOOMS

1 jar (4 ounces) chipped beef
2 cans (10½ ounces each) cream of mushroom soup
½ cup cream

PANTRY
2 tablespoons butter or margarine

1 In a bowl, cover the beef with boiling water. Set aside for about 5 minutes, drain and tear into bite-sized pieces.

2 In the top of a double boiler over boiling water, cook the meat in the butter for about 10 to 15 minutes or until the meat starts to sizzle. Blend in the soup and the cream. Cook, stirring frequently, for about 10 minutes or until thoroughly heated. Remove from the heat and serve.

CREAMY FRANKS AND CORN

makes about 4 servings

1 pound frankfurters, sliced
1 can (16 ounces) whole kernel corn, drained
1 can (10½ ounces) cream of mushroom soup

PANTRY
3 tablespoons butter or margarine
Salt and pepper to taste

In a saucepan, sauté the franks and corn in the butter for about 2 minutes. Reduce to a simmer and cover. Cook, stirring frequently, for about 10 minutes or until tender. Blend in the soup and cook for about 10 minutes or until thoroughly heated. Remove from the heat, season to taste and serve.

Cooking note: For variation, try different kinds of sausages.

CRISPY FRANKFURTERS

makes about 4 to 5 servings

6 to 8 frankfurters, cut lengthwise
1 package (5 ounces) potato chips, crushed

PANTRY
½ cup mayonnaise

1 Position the broiler rack about 4 inches from the heat.

2 Brush the franks with the mayonnaise, roll in the potato chips, and arrange on the broiler pan.

3 Broil, turning occasionally, for about 5 to 10 minutes until light golden-brown. Remove from the oven and serve.

1 beef chuck roast (about 4 to 5 pounds)
2 Roma tomatoes, chopped
1½ envelopes dry spaghetti sauce mix

PANTRY
Salt and pepper to taste

1 Sprinkle the meat with the salt and pepper to taste and the sauce mix and rub gently into the meat.

2 In a crockpot, place the meat, top with tomatoes, and cover. Cook on low heat for about 7 to 9 hours or until tender. Remove from the heat, slice, top with the pan juices, and serve.

CROCKPOT ROAST
makes about 4 to 6 servings

1 package (10 ounces) green peas with cream sauce
1½ cups ham, cooked and cut into thin strips

PANTRY
¾ cup milk
½ teaspoon curry powder

In a saucepan, combine the peas and the milk. Bring to a boil and reduce to a simmer. Cover and cook for about 10 minutes. Remove from the heat and cool slightly. Stir in the curry powder and the ham. Cover and cook for an additional 10 minutes or until thoroughly heated. Remove from the heat and serve.

Cooking note: More curry can be added for a spicier flavor.

CURRIED HAM AND PEAS
makes about 4 servings

4 to 8 lamb chops
½ cup Curry Paste, at room temperature (see page 10)

PANTRY
Salt and pepper to taste

1 Position the broiler rack about 4 to 6 inches from the heat source and preheat.

2 Arrange the chops on the broiler pan and brush with the butter. Broil, basting frequently, for about 20 minutes or until tender and both sides lightly browned. Remove from the oven, season to taste and serve.

CURRIED LAMB
makes about 4 servings

CURRIED MUTTON

makes about 2 to 4 servings

1 piece (about 1½ pounds) breast of mutton, cut into bite-sized pieces
4 small red onions, sliced
4 small tomatoes, sliced

PANTRY
2 tablespoons butter or margarine
½ teaspoon curry powder
Salt and pepper to taste

In a saucepan, sauté the onions in the butter for about 5 minutes or until tender. Stir in the curry powder and meat and cook, stirring frequently, for about 5 minutes or until lightly browned. Blend in ¼ cup of water and season to taste. Cover and cook for about 1 to 1½ hours or until tender. Remove from the heat and serve with the tomatoes.

Cooking note: More curry can be added for a spicier flavor.

CURRIED PORK AND BEANS

makes about 2 to 3 servings

1 small white onion, sliced
1 can (16 ounces) pork and beans in tomato sauce
½ cup (canned) pineapple chunks, drained

PANTRY
1 tablespoon butter or margarine
½ teaspoon curry powder

In a skillet, sauté the onion in the butter for about 5 minutes or until tender. Add the curry powder and the beans. Cook, stirring frequently, for about 10 minutes or until thoroughly heated. Remove from the heat, garnish with pineapple chunks, and serve.

Cooking note: More curry can be added for a spicier flavor.

DANISH-STYLE HAM IN MADEIRA SAUCE

makes about 4 servings

1 can (about 2 pounds) Danish ham, gelatin removed
2 tablespoons Madeira wine
½ cup dark-brown sugar

PANTRY
1 tablespoon butter or margarine

1 Position the rack in the center of the oven and preheat to 350 degrees F. Lightly grease a baking pan and place a meat rack in the pan.

2 In a bowl, blend together the sugar and the wine.

3 Place the ham on the meat rack and top with the sugar mixture.

4 Bake for about 30 minutes or until thoroughly heated. Remove from the oven, slice, and serve with pan drippings on the side.

¼ cup celery, sliced
1 can (10 ounces) beef stew
½ cup cooking apples, diced

PANTRY
1 tablespoon butter or margarine

EASY BEEF STEW

makes about 2 to 3 servings

In a skillet, sauté the celery in the butter for about 10 minutes or until tender. Blend in the stew and the apples. Cook, stirring occasionally, for about 10 minutes or until the apples are just tender. Remove from the heat and serve.

1½ cups leftover cooked beef
1 tablespoon white onions, minced
1 cup Basic White Sauce (see page 398)
¼ cup bread crumbs

PANTRY
1 tablespoon butter or margarine

ENGLISH-STYLE DAY AFTER CUPS

makes about 4 servings

1 Position the broiler rack about 6 inches from the heat. Lightly grease four individual ramekin cups.

2 In a small bowl combine the sauce and onions.

3 Spoon the beef evenly among the ramekin cups, top with the sauce and sprinkle with the bread crumbs.

4 Broil for about 5 to 10 minutes or until toasted on top. Remove from the broiler and serve.

---

1 medium bunch of kale, cooked and chopped
6 medium Idaho potatoes, peeled, cooked and mashed
1 pound smoked sausages, cooked and diced

PANTRY
3 tablespoons melted butter or margarine
Salt and pepper to taste

FARMER'S CABBAGE WITH SMOKED SAUSAGES

makes about 6 servings

In the container of a blender or food processor, combine the kale and ¼ cup of water. Process on high speed until thickened. Add the potatoes, the sausages, and the butter, and process on high speed until smooth. Pour the mixture into a bowl, season to taste, and serve.

FLORENTINE PORK ROAST

makes about 6 servings

1 boneless pork loin (about 2 pounds), rolled and tied
2 tablespoons fresh rosemary leaves, snipped
⅔ cup white wine of choice

PANTRY
1 tablespoon vegetable oil
2 garlic cloves, minced

1 Position the rack in the center of the oven and preheat to 375 degrees F. Lightly grease a shallow baking pan, and place a meat rack in the pan.

2 In a bowl, blend together the rosemary and the garlic, and rub into the roast.

3 Place the roast on the rack in the prepared baking pan and drizzle with the oil. Bake in the oven for about 5 minutes. Pour the wine over the top and continue to cook, basting and turning frequently, for about 1 hour or until tender. Remove from the oven, slice and serve.

FRANKFURTER RAMEKINS

makes about 4 servings

4 chicken or beef frankfurters, sliced
1 cup Basic Parmesan Cheese Sauce (see page 398)
1 tablespoon pickle or pepper relish
1 cup bread crumbs

PANTRY
1 tablespoon butter or margarine

1 Position the broiler rack about 6 inches from the heat source. Lightly grease four individual ramekin cups.

2 In a small bowl, blend the sauce and the relish.

3 Divide the franks evenly among the cups, top with the sauce, and sprinkle with the bread crumbs.

4 Broil for about 5 to 10 minutes or until the tops are toasted on top. Remove from the oven and serve.

1 package (12 ounces) jumbo
  chicken frankfurters
½ cup (bottled) French dressing
  (1 tablespoon reserved)

PANTRY

2 tablespoons butter or
  margarine

1 In a bowl, combine the franks and the dressing. Cover with plastic wrap and refrigerate for about 1 hour. Remove the franks from the sauce.

2 In a skillet, sauté the franks in the butter and the reserved dressing, turning frequently, for about 10 minutes or lightly browned. Remove from the heat and serve.

FRANKFURTERS FRANÇAISE

makes about 4 servings

6 frankfurters, cooked and
  partially cut lengthwise
4 cups (canned) pork and beans
2 tablespoons yellow onions,
  minced
¼ cup (bottled) pickle relish

1 Position the rack in the center of the oven and preheat to 400 degrees F. Lightly grease a 1½-quart baking dish.

2 Fill the franks with the relish, cut in half crosswise, and arrange in the prepared baking dish. Top with the beans and the onions. Repeat layering, ending with the franks on top.

3 Bake for about 40 minutes or until thoroughly heated. Remove from the oven and serve.

Cooking note: For an alternative, sprinkle the top with grated cheese of choice.

FRANK AND BEAN CASSEROLE

makes about 6 servings

FRENCH FRIED HOT DOGS

makes about 4 servings

1 cup packaged pancake mix
2 tablespoons corn meal
10 to 12 frankfurters, cooked

PANTRY
1½ cups vegetable oil for deep frying
1 tablespoon sugar

1 Place the oil in a deep fryer and preheat to 350 degrees F.

2 In a bowl, combine the pancake mix, the corn meal and the sugar. Blend in enough water to make a thick batter.

3 Dip the franks in the batter and place in the hot oil. Fry for about 5 minutes or until golden-brown. Transfer to a rack covered with paper towels, drain, and serve.

GARLIC-BUTTERED FRANKFURTERS

makes about 4 servings

1 pound frankfurters, sliced

PANTRY
¼ cup butter or margarine
2 garlic cloves, minced

In a skillet, sauté the garlic in the butter for about 5 minutes or until lightly browned. Add the franks and sauté, turning frequently, for about 5 to 7 minutes or until thoroughly heated. Remove from the heat and serve.

GEDUNSTETES LAMMFLEISCH

makes about 8 servings

1 lamb shoulder (about 4 pounds), trimmed

PANTRY
1 cup melted butter or margarine
1 garlic clove, halved

1 Position the rack in the center of the oven and preheat to 300 degrees F. Have a roasting pan with a cover available.

2 Rub the meat with the garlic and place in the roasting pan. Drizzle the butter over the top, add 1 cup of water, and cover.

3 Bake for about 2 to 2½ hours or until tender. Remove from the oven, slice, and serve.

Cooking note: Make sure there's enough water in the pan while cooking.

4 (about 4 ounces each) boneless beef strip steaks
½ teaspoon lemon pepper

PANTRY
½ teaspoon onion powder
¼ teaspoon garlic salt

1 Position the grill about 6 inches from the heat.

2 In a bowl, blend the onion powder, the lemon pepper, and the garlic salt. Rub this mixture on the steaks and set aside for about 15 minutes.

3 Arrange the steaks on the grill and cook for about 15 to 20 minutes or until both sides are browned. Remove from the grill and serve.

Cooking note: Cooking time for grilling recipes depends on the heat source.

GRILLED LEMON PEPPER STEAK

makes about 4 servings

---

1 piece (about 1 pound) center cut ham, cooked
½ cup orange marmalade
1 teaspoon prepared mustard

1 Position the grill about 6 inches from the heat.

2 In a small bowl, blend the marmalade and the mustard.

3 Arrange the ham on the grill and brush with the glaze. Cook, brushing and turning, for about 10 minutes or until thoroughly heated. Remove from the grill and serve.

Cooking note: Cooking time for grilling recipes depends on the heat source.

GRILLED ORANGE-GLAZED HAM STEAK

makes about 4 servings

---

4 pounds pork spareribs or back ribs, cooked and cut into serving-sized pieces
1¼ cups (bottled) barbecue sauce

1 Position the grill about 6 inches from the heat.

2 Arrange the ribs on the grill and brush with the sauce. Cook, brushing and turning, for about 10 minutes or until thoroughly heated. Remove from the grill and serve.

Cooking note: Cooking time for grilling recipes depends on the heat source.

GRILLED PORK SPARERIBS

makes about 4 servings

GRILLED SIRLOIN STEAK AND POTATOES

makes about 4 servings

1 boneless beef top sirloin steak (about 1 pound)

2 large baking potatoes, cut lengthwise into wedges

4 thick slices of red onion

PANTRY
2 tablespoons canola oil

1 Position the grill about 4 to 6 inches from the heat.

2 Brush the meat and the cut side of the potatoes with oil and arrange on the grill. Cook, brushing and turning, for about 25 to 30 minutes or until tender. Remove the meat from the grill, trim, slice, and serve with the potatoes.

Cooking note: Cooking time for grilling recipes depends on the heat source.

GRILLED SMOKED SAUSAGES

makes about 4 servings

1½ pounds pork or beef sausages

1 cup apricot or pineapple preserves

1 tablespoon lemon juice

1 cup apricot or pineapple, sliced

1 Position the grill about 6 inches from the heat.

2 In a saucepan, cook the preserves for about 5 minutes or until bubbles start to form around the edge of the pan. Strain through a fine sieve into a small bowl, pressing with a spoon to extract the juices. Blend in the lemon juice.

3 Arrange the sausages on the grill. Cook, brushing and turning, for about 15 minutes or until lightly browned. Remove from the grill and serve with the fruit slices on the side.

Cooking note: Cooking time for grilling recipes depends on the heat source.

6 veal chops
1 tablespoon safflower oil
1 cup Mushroom Sauce (see
   page 406)

PANTRY
Salt and pepper to taste

1 Position the grill about 6 inches from the heat.

2 Rub the veal with the oil, salt and pepper to taste, and arrange on the grill. Cook for about 15 minutes or until both sides are browned.

3 Position the rack in the center of the oven and preheat to 400 degrees F.

4 Arrange the veal in a shallow baking pan, and bake for about 20 minutes or until tender. Remove from the oven and serve with the sauce on the side.

Cooking note: Cooking time for grilling recipes depends on the heat source.

GRILLED VEAL WITH MUSHROOM SAUCE

makes about 6 servings

177

Meat

---

1 small head of green or red
   cabbage, cored and shredded
1 pound ground beef
3 cups potatoes, sliced

PANTRY
1 tablespoon butter or margarine
1 cup milk
Salt and pepper to taste

1 Position the rack in the center of the oven and preheat to 350 degrees F. Lightly grease a baking dish.

2 Arrange the cabbage in the prepared baking dish. Top with the potatoes and the beef, and season to taste. Pour the milk over the top and bake for about 60 minutes or until the potatoes are tender and the meat is thoroughly cooked. Remove from the oven and serve.

Cooking note: If you make a larger portion, continue to add the ingredients in layers.

GROUND BEEF WITH CABBAGE AND POTATOES

makes about 2 to 4 servings

Ham Baked in Claret

makes about 4 servings

1 slice (about 1-inch thick) center cut ham
2 cups cooking apples, chopped
½ cup packed dark-brown sugar
1 cup claret

PANTRY
1 tablespoon butter or margarine

1 Position the rack in the center of the oven and preheat to 350 degrees F. Lightly grease a shallow baking pan.

2 Arrange the ham in the prepared baking pan. Top with the apples, sprinkle with the sugar, and pour on the claret. Cover and bake for about 40 minutes. Remove the cover and continue to bake for about 30 minutes or until tender and slightly browned. Remove from the oven and serve.

Cooking note: For a tart taste, blend in a teaspoon of mustard with the sugar.

Ham Baked in Milk

makes about 4 to 6 servings

1 slice (about 2-inch-thick) center cut ham
4 tablespoons packed brown sugar

PANTRY
1 tablespoon butter or margarine
1 teaspoon dry mustard
½ cup milk
Salt and pepper to taste

1 Position the rack in the center of the oven and preheat to 300 degrees F. Lightly grease a baking dish.

2 In a small bowl, blend the mustard and the sugar.

3 Arrange the ham in the prepared baking dish and spread with the mustard mixture. Add the milk and bake for about 1 hour or until tender. Remove from the oven, season to taste and serve.

Ham Macedoine

makes about 4 servings

2 cups cooked mixed vegetables
1 can (10½ ounces) cream of chicken soup, undiluted
1½ cups ham, diced
2 tablespoons bread crumbs

PANTRY
1 tablespoon butter or margarine

1 Position the rack in the center of the oven and preheat to 350 degrees F. Lightly grease a 2-quart baking dish.

2 In the prepared baking dish, combine the vegetables, the soup, and the ham. Sprinkle the top with the bread crumbs and bake for about 30 minutes or until toasted on top. Remove from the oven and serve.

1 can (15 ounces) pitted purple
   plums, drained, reserving ⅓
   cup of liquid
4 slices (about 1-inch think)
   cooked ham
½ cup packed light-brown sugar
4 to 8 whole cloves

1 Position the rack in the center of the oven and preheat to
300 degrees F. Lightly grease a
13 x 9-inch baking pan.

2 Insert the cloves in the ham
and arrange in the prepared
baking pan. Sprinkle with the
sugar and pour the reserved
juice on top.

3 Bake for about 50 minutes
and top with the plums. Continue to bake for about 10
minutes or until tender.
Remove from the oven and
serve.

Ham Topped with Plums and Cloves

makes about 4 servings

1 cooked meaty ham bone
4 pounds curly kale, torn into
   bite-sized pieces
½ cup pearl barley

PANTRY
Pepper to taste

1 In a saucepan, just cover
the ham with water and bring
to a boil. Drain. Cover with
water, bring to a boil and
drain again, reserving the liquid.

2 In a soup kettle, combine
the kale and the reserved liquid. Cook over low heat for
about 5 minutes. Add the barley and pepper to taste. Cover
and simmer, stirring occasionally, for about 1½ hours, or
until tender and most of the
liquid has evaporated.

3 Remove the bone and cut
off the meat. Return the meat
to the pot and cook for about
3 minutes or until thoroughly
heated. Remove from the heat
and serve.

Cooking note: The ham bone
can be left over from a previ-
ous meal.

Ham with Kale and Barley

makes about 4 to 6 servings

HAWAIIAN PORK COOKED IN WINE

makes about 3 servings

1½ cups ham or pork, cooked and diced

2 tablespoons white wine or water

1 package (10 ounces) Hawaiian-style frozen vegetables, thawed and drained

PANTRY

2 tablespoons butter or margarine

In a skillet, combine the butter, the meat, the wine and the vegetables. Simmer, stirring occasionally, for about 7 to 10 minutes or until the vegetables are tender. Remove from the heat and serve.

HAWAIIAN ROAST PORK

makes about 6 servings

1 boneless pork shoulder roast (about 3 pounds), cut lengthwise in half

1 teaspoon (bottled) Hoisin sauce

PANTRY

½ cup soy sauce

1 In a bowl, combine the meat, the soy sauce and the Hoisin sauce. Cover with plastic wrap and refrigerate for about 8 hours or overnight. Remove the meat from the sauce.

2 Position the rack in the center of the oven and preheat to 350 degrees F. Have a shallow baking pan available.

3 Arrange the meat in the baking pan and cover. Bake for about 20 minutes, remove the cover and continue to bake for about 40 minutes or until tender. Remove from the oven, slice and serve.

HOISIN STEAK

makes about 4 to 6 servings

1 beef chuck steak (about 1½ to 2 pounds)

¼ cup (bottled) Hoisin sauce

PANTRY

2 tablespoons vegetable oil

1 garlic clove, minced

1 tablespoon soy sauce

1 In a bowl, combine the meat, the soy sauce, and the Hoisin sauce. Cover with plastic wrap and refrigerate for about 8 hours or overnight.

2 In a skillet, heat the oil and add the steak, the marinade, and 1 tablespoon of water. Cook for about 20 to 25 minutes or until tender and both sides are lightly browned. Remove from the heat, slice, and serve with the pan juices on the side.

1 boneless lamb shoulder (about 2 pounds), trimmed and cut into bite-sized pieces
2 cans (16 ounces each) hominy, drained
3 cups chicken broth
1 can (7 ounces) whole chiles, torn into wide strips

PANTRY
Salt and pepper to taste

In a Dutch oven, combine the lamb, the hominy, the broth, and the chiles. Bring to a boil and reduce to a simmer. Cover and cook, skimming off the fat, for about 2 hours or until tender. Remove from the heat, season to taste, and serve.

HOMINY AND LAMB STEW

makes about 4 servings

1 leg of lamb (about 4 pounds)
1 cup unsweetened apple cider
1 sprig of fresh rosemary

PANTRY
1 tablespoon butter or margarine
4 tablespoons honey
Salt and pepper to taste

1 Position the rack in the center of the oven and preheat to 400 degrees F. Lightly grease a baking dish.

2 Place the leg of lamb in the prepared baking dish and brush with the honey. Season with salt and pepper to taste, place the sprig of rosemary on top, cover, and bake for 15 minutes.

3 Lower the heat to 350 degrees F and continue to cook for about 1½ hours or until tender. Remove the cover and cook 20 minutes or until lightly browned. Transfer lamb to a warming plate.

4 Pour the juices from the baking dish into a saucepan, and blend in the cider and the remaining honey. Bring to a boil and cook for about 5 minutes or until reduced by half. Slice the meat and serve with the sauce on the side.

HONEYED LAMB

makes about 6 to 8 servings

Hot and Sweet Andouille Sausage Sauté

makes about 4 to 6 servings

2 pounds Andouille sausages, sliced ¼-inch thick
1 cup dry white wine
1 tablespoon hot mustard

PANTRY
2 tablespoons honey

1 In a small bowl, blend the wine, the honey, and the mustard.

2 In a skillet, combine the sausages and the wine mixture. Cover and cook for about 10 minutes or until tender. Remove from the heat and serve.

Irish Lamb Stew

makes about 4 to 5 servings

5 medium russet potatoes, pared and halved lengthwise
2 to 2½ pounds lean neck of lamb with bones, trimmed
3 large yellow onions, sliced

PANTRY
Salt and pepper to taste

1 In a soup kettle, layer the potatoes, the lamb, and the onions. Cover with 1 quart of water, season to taste and cover. Simmer for about 2 hours or until tender.

2 Remove from the heat, cool to room temperature and refrigerate for about 3 hours. Skim off the fat and cook for about 20 minutes or until thoroughly heated. Remove from the heat and serve.

Island Roast Pork

makes about 6 servings

1 boneless loin of pork (about 2 pounds)
½ teaspoon nutmeg

PANTRY
½ teaspoon olive oil
½ teaspoon cinnamon

1 Position the rack in the center of the oven and preheat to 350 degrees F. Lightly grease a shallow baking pan.

2 In a bowl, blend the oil, the nutmeg, and the cinnamon until smooth.

3 Place the roast in the prepared baking pan, pour the spice mixture on top, and rub in. Bake for about 50 to 60 minutes or until tender. Remove from the oven, slice, and serve.

8 sweet Italian sausages, cut into thirds
1 package (10 ounces) Italian-style vegetables, thawed and drained

PANTRY
1 tablespoon vegetable oil

In a skillet, sauté the sausages in the oil for about 10 minutes or until lightly browned. Add ⅓ cup of water and simmer for about 5 minutes. Add the vegetables, bring to a boil, and reduce to a simmer. Cook, stirring occasionally, for about 5 minutes or until thoroughly heated. Remove from the heat and serve.

ITALIAN SAUSAGE SAUTÉ

makes about 4 to 6 servings

1 boneless roast loin of pork (about 4 pounds), rolled and tied
3 cups (bottled) pepper jelly marinade
¾ cup (bottled) pepper jelly
¼ cup cider vinegar

PANTRY
1 tablespoon butter or margarine

1 In a bowl, combine the pork and the marinade. Cover with plastic wrap and refrigerate for at least 24 hours.

2 Position the rack in the center of the oven and preheat to 350 degrees F. Lightly grease a roasting pan and place a meat rack in the pan.

3 In a small bowl, blend together the jelly and the vinegar.

4 Place the meat in the prepared roasting pan. Bake, basting occasionally with the marinade, for about 2 to 2½ hours or until tender. Brush with the jelly mixture and bake for about 20 minutes or until glazed. Remove from the oven and serve.

JELLY GLAZED PORK

makes about 10 to 12 servings

KOREAN-STYLE PORK MEATBALLS

makes about 24 to 30 balls

3 pounds lean ground pork
1½ cups Basmati rice
1 large yellow onion, chopped

PANTRY

1 tablespoon butter or margarine
2 cans (8 ounces each) tomato
    sauce

1 Position the rack in the center of the oven and preheat to 350 degrees F. Lightly grease a shallow baking dish.

2 In a bowl, combine the beef, the onions, and the rice. Shape into balls about the size of walnuts.

3 Arrange the meatballs in the prepared baking dish, pour the tomato sauce over the top, and cover. Bake for about 40 minutes. Remove the cover and continue to bake for about 20 minutes or until thoroughly heated. Remove from the oven and serve.

LAMB CHOPS WITH WINE AND TOMATOES

makes about 4 servings

4 lamb chops (½-inch thick)
4 whole tomatoes
1 cup dry red wine

PANTRY

2 tablespoons vegetable oil
Salt and pepper to taste

In a skillet, sauté the chops in the oil for about 15 minutes or until both sides are lightly browned. Blend in the tomatoes, cover, and simmer for about 10 to 12 minutes. Remove the cover, add the wine, and season to taste. Continue to simmer for about 10 minutes or until thoroughly heated. Remove from the heat and serve.

LAMB CHOPS WRAPPED IN BACON

makes about 4 servings

4 boneless loin lamb chops
    (½-inch thick)
4 bacon strips

PANTRY

¼ cup melted butter or
    margarine
Salt and pepper to taste

1 Position the broiler rack about 4 inches from the heat.

2 Wrap the bacon around the lamb chops and secure with a toothpick.

3 Arrange the meat on the broiler pan, drizzle on the butter, and season to taste.

4 Broil for about 20 minutes or until tender and both sides are lightly browned. Remove from the oven and serve.

2 lamb neck fillets, trimmed
1 tablespoon lime juice

2 tablespoons soy sauce
1 garlic clove, minced
1 tablespoon olive oil

1 In a bowl, combine the lamb, the lime juice, the soy sauce, and the garlic. Add the oil, cover with plastic wrap and refrigerate for about 12 hours. Remove the lamb from the marinade.

2 Position the rack in the center of the oven and preheat to 450 degrees F. Lightly grease a shallow baking dish and place a meat rack in the pan.

3 Place the lamb on the rack in the prepared baking dish. Bake for about 20 to 25 minutes or until tender. Remove from the oven, slice, and serve.

LAMB FILLETS WITH GARLIC AND SOY SAUCE

makes about 4 servings

1½ pounds ground lamb
10 to 12 bacon slices
10 to 12 onion slices
10 to 12 tomato slices

1 tablespoon butter or margarine

1 Shape the ground lamb into about 10 to 12 small patties. Wrap the bacon around the patties and secure with a toothpick.

2 Arrange the meat on the prepared baking pan and broil for about 25 to 30 minutes or until both sides are browned. Remove from the oven, top with the onion and the tomato slices, and serve.

LAMB PATTIES WITH BACON

makes about 6 servings

LIVER, POTATO, AND BACON PIE

makes about 4 servings

1 pound sheep liver, cut in ¼-inch slices

2 pounds russet potatoes, pared and sliced

2 large yellow onions, chopped

6 bacon slices

PANTRY

1 tablespoon butter or margarine

¼ cup flour

1 Position the rack in the center of the oven and preheat to 350 degrees F. Lightly grease a shallow baking dish.

2 Rub the liver slices with the flour.

3 In the prepared baking dish, layer the liver, potatoes, and onion, finishing with a layer of the potatoes. Add enough water to just cover the mixture. Cover and bake for about 50 minutes or until tender. Remove the cover and top with the bacon. Continue to bake for about 10 minutes or until the bacon is crispy. Remove from the oven and serve.

Cooking note: Calf or pork liver can be substituted for sheep liver.

LIVERBURGERS

makes about 4 servings

1 cup ground leftover fried liver

1 cup leftover mashed potatoes

1 large egg, beaten

¼ cup bread crumbs

PANTRY

2 tablespoons vegetable oil

1 In a bowl, combine the liver, the potatoes, and the egg. Shape into 4 patties and dredge in the bread crumbs.

2 In a skillet, sauté the patties in the oil for about 20 minutes or until both sides are lightly browned. Remove from the heat and serve.

LONDON BROIL

makes about 4 to 6 servings

1 flank steak (about 2½ to 3 pounds), trimmed and scored

PANTRY
1 tablespoon butter or margarine
Salt and pepper to taste

1 Position the broiler rack about 3 to 4 inches from the heat. Lightly grease the broiler pan.

2 Place the meat on the prepared broiler pan. Broil for about 10 minutes or until tender and both sides are browned. Remove from the oven, season to taste, slice and serve.

Cooking note: Flank steak is a tough cut of meat and should be served rare and thinly sliced.

MARINATED PORK

makes about 4 to 6 servings

6 pork chops
3 cups (bottled) red chili sauce

PANTRY
3 garlic cloves, minced
2 teaspoons crushed dried oregano

1 Arrange the pork in a 13 x 9-inch baking dish and top with the garlic, the oregano, and the chili sauce. Cover with plastic wrap and refrigerate for about 8 hours.

2 Position the rack in the middle of the oven and preheat to 350 degrees F.

3 Bake for about 60 to 70 minutes or until tender. Remove from the oven and serve.

MOMMA'S LATE NIGHT CASSEROLE

makes about 4 servings

6 medium russet potatoes, pared, cooked and mashed
1 pound ground beef
½ cup white onion, chopped
1 cup grated sharp cheddar cheese

PANTRY
2 tablespoons vegetable oil

1 Position the rack in the center of the oven and preheat to 450 degrees F. Lightly grease a baking dish.

2 In a skillet, sauté the beef and the onions in the oil for about 20 minutes or until thoroughly cooked.

3 Spread the mashed potatoes evenly in the bottom of the prepared baking dish. Make shallow holes in the potatoes and fill with the beef mixture. Sprinkle the cheese over the top and bake for about 10 minutes or until the cheese has melted. Remove from the oven and serve.

MOLDED GROUND PORK AND HAM

makes about 6 servings

½ pound ground cooked ham
1 pound ground pork
¼ cup bread crumbs
1 large egg

PANTRY
1 tablespoon butter or margarine
Salt and pepper to taste

1 Position the rack in the center of the oven and preheat to 350 degrees F. Lightly grease a baking for cookie sheet and 6 individual ring molds.

2 In a bowl, combine the ham, the pork, the bread crumbs, and the egg, and season to taste.

3 Arrange the ring molds on the baking sheet and press the meat mixture into the rings. Bake for about 20 minutes or until both sides are lightly browned. Remove from the oven, cool, remove the rings and serve.

NEW YORK STRIP STEAK

makes about 3 servings

3 strip steaks, trimmed
¼ cup prepared teriyaki marinade sauce

PANTRY
1 garlic clove, minced
⅛ teaspoon black pepper

1 In a bowl, combine the meat, the sauce, the garlic, and the black pepper. Cover with plastic wrap and refrigerate for at least 2 hours.

2 Position the broiler rack about 6 inches from the heat.

3 Place the steaks on the broiler pan. Broil, basting with the marinade sauce and turning, for about 10 minutes or until both sides are lightly browned. Remove from the oven and serve.

ONION BURGERS

makes about 4 servings

3¼ pounds ground beef
2 medium onions, sliced

PANTRY
3 teaspoons butter or margarine
Salt and pepper to taste

1 Shape the ground beef into 4 patties.

2 In a skillet, sauté the onions in the butter for about 5 minutes until translucent. Transfer to a warming plate.

3 In the same skillet, sauté the meat for about 30 minutes or until both sides are lightly browned. Remove from the heat, spread the onion on the patties, season to taste, and serve.

3 pounds corned beef
1 cup orange marmalade
4 tablespoons prepared mustard
¼ cup packed brown sugar

PANTRY
1 tablespoon butter or margarine

1 In a soup kettle, cover the beef with water. Bring to a boil and reduce to a simmer. Cover and cook for about 2 to 2½ hours or until tender.

2 Position the rack in the center of the oven and preheat to 350 degrees F. Lightly grease a shallow baking dish.

3 In a bowl, blend the marmalade, the mustard, and the sugar.

4 Arrange the meat in the prepared baking dish and top with the marmalade mixture. Bake, basting occasionally, for about 30 minutes or until the glaze is a deep golden-brown. Remove from the oven, slice, and serve.

ORANGE-GLAZED CORNED BEEF

makes about 6 to 8 servings

1 boneless ham (about 4 to 5 pounds), cooked and scored
½ cup orange marmalade

1 Position the rack in the center of the oven and preheat to 325 degrees F. Lightly grease a 13 x 9-inch baking pan.

2 Arrange the ham in the prepared baking pan. Bake, brushing frequently with the marmalade, for about 20 minutes or until glazed. Remove from the oven, slice, and serve.

ORANGE-GLAZED HAM

makes about 12 servings

ORANGE-GLAZED STEAK

makes about 4 servings

4 pork steaks
1 tablespoon orange marmalade
1 teaspoon orange juice
1 orange, thinly sliced

PANTRY
½ teaspoon ground ginger
1 tablespoon butter or margarine

1 Position the broiler rack about 4 inches from the heat.

2 In a bowl, blend the marmalade, the ground ginger and the juice.

3 In a skillet, sauté the steaks in the butter for about 3 minutes. Turn and brush with the marmalade mixture. Cook, basting and turning, for about 5 minutes or until both sides are lightly browned. Transfer to the broiler pan.

4 Broil for about 5 to 10 minutes or until tender and glazed. Remove from the oven, garnish with orange slices, and serve.

OVEN-BAKED FRANKFURTERS WITH STEWED TOMATOES

makes about 4 servings

4 frankfurters, diced
1 can (16 ounces) stewed tomatoes
1 cup bread crumbs

PANTRY
Salt and pepper to taste

1 Position the rack in the center of the oven and preheat to 400 degrees F. Lightly grease a baking dish.

2 Arrange the franks in the prepared baking dish and top with the tomatoes and the bread crumbs. Season to taste.

3 Bake for about 20 minutes or until thoroughly heated and toasted on top. Remove from the oven and serve.

Cooking note: For variation, add Romano or Parmesan cheese to the bread crumbs.

1½ pounds ground beef or pork
¼ cup white onions, minced
½ cup bread crumbs

PANTRY
1 tablespoon butter or margarine
¾ cup milk
Salt and pepper to taste

Penny Steak

makes about 4 servings

1 Position the broiler rack about 4 inches from the heat. Lightly grease the broiler pan.

2 In a bowl, combine the meat, the onion, the milk, and the bread crumbs, and season to taste.

3 Arrange the meat on the prepared broiler pan and cook for about 25 to 30 minutes or until both sides are lightly browned. Remove from the broiler and serve.

---

4 medium green bell peppers, tops and seeds removed
5 large frankfurters, diced
½ cup celery, chopped

PANTRY
½ cup mayonnaise
Salt and pepper to taste

Peppers Stuffed with Frankfurters

makes about 4 servings

1 Position the broiler rack about 4 inches from the heat.

2 In a bowl, combine the franks, the celery, and the mayonnaise, and season to taste. Stuff the peppers with this mixture.

3 Arrange the peppers on the broiler pan. Broil for about 10 minutes or until the peppers are lightly toasted. Remove from the broiler and serve.

Cooking note: For variation, sprinkle the tops of the peppers with grated cheese before broiling.

---

1 can (8 ounces) crushed pineapple, drained, syrup reserved
1 slice (about 1½ to 2 pounds) ham
⅔ cup orange marmalade

PANTRY
1 tablespoon butter or margarine

Pineapple and Orange-Glazed Ham

makes about 4 servings

1 Position the rack in the center of the oven and preheat to 350 degrees F. Lightly grease a baking pan.

2 In a bowl, blend the reserved pineapple syrup and the marmalade until smooth.

3 Arrange the ham in the prepared baking pan and brush with the marmalade mixture. Bake, basting occasionally, for about 1 hour or until tender and glazed. Remove from the oven, slice, and serve with the crushed pineapple on the side.

PORK BARBECUE

makes about 4 to 6 servings

1 smoked boneless pork shoulder (about 2 to 3 pounds), scored
3 medium Idaho potatoes, pared and cut into bite-sized cubes
1 cup carrots, sliced
1 cup barbecue sauce

PANTRY
1 tablespoon butter or margarine

1 Position the rack in the center of the oven and preheat to 350 degrees F. Lightly grease a 13 x 9-inch baking pan and place a meat rack inside.

2 Place the meat on the rack in the prepared baking pan. Arrange the potatoes and carrots around the meat, and add about ¼ cup of water. Pour the barbecue sauce over the meat and cover. Bake for about 1 hour, remove the cover and continue to bake for about 20 minutes or until tender. Remove from the oven and serve.

PORK TERIYAKI

makes about 4 servings

2 pounds tri-tip pork roast, trimmed and cut into bite-sized cubes
1 to 1½ cups (bottled) teriyaki marinade

1 In a bowl, combine the marinade and the pork. Cover with plastic wrap and refrigerate for about 6 hours or overnight.

2 Position the rack in the center of the oven and preheat to 400 degrees F. Lightly grease a baking pan and place a meat rack inside.

3 Arrange the meat on the rack in the prepared baking pan. Pour the marinade over the meat. Bake, basting and turning, for about 40 minutes or until tender. Remove from the oven and serve.

PORTERHOUSE AND POTATOES

makes about 2 servings

1 beef porterhouse steak (about 1-inch thick)
1 package (10 ounces) frozen potatoes, any variety
½ teaspoon garlic salt
¼ teaspoon white pepper

1 Cook the potatoes according to the package instructions and keep warm.

2 In a bowl, combine the garlic salt and the white pepper, and rub into both sides of the steak.

3 In a nonstick skillet, sauté the steak for about 20 minutes or until both sides are browned. Remove from the heat, trim, remove the bone, slice, and serve with the potatoes on the side.

1 pot roast (about 3 to 5 pounds)
1 package (1½ ounces) dry
  onion soup
1 can (10½ ounces) cream of
  mushroom soup

POT ROAST DINNER

makes about 4 to 6 servings

1 Position the rack in the center of the oven and preheat to 350 degrees F. Have a baking pan available.

2 In a bowl, blend the onion and the mushroom soups.

3 Place the roast in a baking pan and pour the soup mixture over the top. Cover and bake for about 2½ to 3 hours or until tender. Remove from the oven, slice, and serve.

1 large egg, beaten
4 pork fillets
½ cup crushed potato chips

PANTRY
¼ cup flour
4 tablespoons vegetable oil
Salt and pepper to taste

1 Place the egg in one bowl, the flour in the second bowl, and the potato chips in the third bowl.

2 Dredge the fillets in the flour, dip in the egg, and coat with the potato chips.

3 In a skillet, sauté the meat in the oil for about 15 to 20 minutes or until both sides are lightly browned. Remove from the heat, season to taste, and serve.

Cooking note: For variation, add garlic powder or other herbs to the potato chips.

POTATO-COATED PORK FILLETS

makes about 4 servings

8 jumbo frankfurters, partially
  cut lengthwise and cooked
½ cup grated cheddar cheese
2 cup potatoes, cooked and
  mashed
2 tablespoons prepared mustard

PANTRY
1 tablespoon butter or margarine

1 Position the broiler rack about 4 inches from the heat. Lightly grease the broiler pan.

2 In a bowl, using a wire whisk or an electric mixer, combine the cheese and the potatoes.

3 Arrange the franks in the prepared broiler pan. Brush cut sides of the franks with the mustard and stuff with the potato mixture. Broil for about 7 to 10 minutes or until the potatoes are lightly browned. Remove from the broiler and serve.

POTATO-STUFFED FRANKFURTERS

makes about 4 servings

Pressed Lamb Loaf with Herbs

makes about 6 to 8 servings

1 lamb shoulder (about 4 pounds)
1 teaspoon caraway seeds, crushed

PANTRY
½ teaspoon dried marjoram
½ teaspoon dried thyme

1 In a Dutch oven, cover the meat with lightly salted water. Add the marjoram, the thyme, and the caraway seeds. Bring to a boil and reduce to a simmer. Cover and cook for about 3 hours or until tender.

2 Remove the meat from the Dutch oven and chop finely. Add a little of the broth to moisten and press into a 9 x 5 x 4-inch loaf baking pan. Cover with plastic wrap and refrigerate for at least 12 hours or overnight.

3 Invert the pan onto a serving platter, slice, and serve.

Prosciutto with Pasta Sauce

makes about 2 servings

¼ pound prosciutto, diced
1 cup chopped Italian plum tomatoes
1 cup cooked pasta of choice

PANTRY
1 jar or can (30 ounces) tomato sauce

In a saucepan, combine the tomato sauce, the prosciutto, and the tomatoes. Bring to a boil and reduce to a simmer. Cook for about 10 minutes or until thoroughly heated. Remove from the heat, pour over the pasta, and serve.

Quick Lamb Fricassee

makes about 2 servings

1 envelope onion soup mix
1 cup heavy cream
1½ cup lamb, cooked and diced
1 can (4 ounces) tiny button mushrooms, drained

PANTRY
Salt and pepper to taste

In a saucepan, blend the soup mix and the cream. Add the lamb and the mushrooms, and cook for about 10 minutes or until thoroughly heated. Remove from the heat, season to taste, and serve.

1 can (16 ounces) cooked ham, sliced

1 can (16 ounces) diced tomatoes

1 can (8 ounces) sliced pineapple, drained

¾ cup grated Monterey Jack cheese

1 Position the broiler pan about 4 inches from the heat.

2 Slice the canned ham into 4 steaks. Arrange the ham on a broiler pan and broil for about 5 minutes or until both sides are lightly browned. Top with the tomatoes and pineapple, and sprinkle with the cheese. Continue to cook for about 5 minutes or until the cheese has melted. Remove from the broiler and serve.

QUICK HAM AND PINEAPPLE

makes about 4 servings

---

9 small beets, trimmed, pared, cooked and diced

6 cups potatoes, diced

1½ cups corned beef, chopped

PANTRY

½ cup melted butter or margarine

Salt and pepper to taste

1 Position the rack in the center of the oven and preheat to 350 degrees F.

2 In a Dutch oven, combine the beets, the potatoes, and the beef, and drizzle the butter on top. Bake for about 45 minutes or until tender. Remove from the oven, season to taste, and serve.

RED FLANNEL HASH

makes about 4 to 6 servings

---

1 pound frankfurters, sliced

8 ounces cheddar or Monterey Jack cheese, grated

1½ cups cooked rice

PANTRY

½ cup milk

In the top of a double boiler over boiling water, combine the franks and the cheese, and stir until the cheese has melted. Add the rice and the milk and cook, stirring frequently, for about 10 minutes or until thoroughly heated. Remove from the heat and serve.

Cooking note: For variation, add chopped olives or tomatoes, while cooking.

RICE AND CHEESE WITH FRANKFURTERS

makes about 4 servings

Roast Leg of Lamb

makes about 6 to 8 servings

1 leg of lamb (about 5 pounds)
¼ cup prepared mustard
½ cup seasoned bread crumbs

PANTRY
1 medium garlic clove, minced
1 tablespoon butter or margarine

1 Position the rack in the center of the oven and preheat to 325 degrees F. Lightly grease a roasting pan and place a meat rack in the pan.

2 In a small bowl, blend the mustard and the garlic.

3 Place the lamb on the rack in the prepared roasting pan. Brush the mustard mixture on the lamb and sprinkle the top with the bread crumbs. Bake for about 2½ to 3 hours or until tender. Remove from the oven and serve.

Saucy Frankfurters

makes about 4 to 5 servings

6 frankfurters, sliced
2 cups thick Basic White Sauce (see page 398)
½ cup Burgundy

In the top of a double boiler over boiling water, heat the sauce. Add the wine and the franks. Continue to cook for about 10 minutes or until thoroughly heated. Remove from the heat and serve.

Sausage and Fruit Kebobs

makes about 4 servings

1 pound sausages of choice, sliced 1-inch thick
2 small Macintosh apples, cored and quartered
2 small yellow onions, quartered
2 tablespoons apple jelly

PANTRY
1 tablespoon melted butter or margarine

1 Position the broiler rack about 4 inches from the heat.

2 Lightly grease four metal skewers. In a small bowl, blend the jelly and the butter.

3 Arrange the sausages, the apples, and the onions on the prepared skewers. Brush the jelly mixture over the kebobs.

4 Place the skewers on the broiler pan at an angle to avoid touching the bottom of the pan. Broil, turning occasionally, for about 10 to 15 minutes or until tender. Remove from the broiler and serve.

1 pound sweet Italian sausages,
  sliced into 1-inch pieces
1½ cups cooked rice
1 cup grated fresh Parmesan
  cheese

PANTRY
1 tablespoon butter or margarine
Salt and pepper to taste

In a skillet, sauté the sausages
in the butter for about 10 minutes or lightly browned. Add
the rice and the cheese. Cook
for about 5 minutes or until
the cheese has melted.
Remove from the heat, season
to taste and serve.

SAUSAGE AND RICE ITALIANO

makes about 4 servings

---

1 package (4 ounces) spaghetti,
  cooked al dente and drained
1 pound link pork sausages
1½ cups (canned) crushed
  tomatoes, drained
½ cup grated fresh cheese of
  choice

PANTRY
1 tablespoon butter or margarine

1 Position the rack in the center of the oven and preheat to
400 degrees F. Lightly grease a
baking dish.

2 In a saucepan, cover the
sausages with water. Bring to
a boil and cook for about 5
minutes. Drain the liquid and
continue to cook, turning
occasionally, for about 10
minutes or until lightly
browned. Add the tomatoes
and cook for about 5 minutes
or until thoroughly heated.

3 Arrange the spaghetti in
the prepared casserole, top
with the tomatoes and
sausage, sprinkle with cheese,
and bake for about 20 to 30
minutes or until thoroughly
heated. Remove from the
oven and serve.

SAUSAGE AND SPAGHETTI

makes about 4 to 6 servings

Sausage Chili

makes about 2 to 4 servings

1 pound linguica sausages, casings removed and broken into small pieces
1 can (16 ounces) chili with beans

In a skillet, sauté the sausages for about 5 minutes. Add the chili and cook for about 10 minutes or until thoroughly heated. Remove from the heat and serve.

Sausages Cooked in Milk and Mustard

makes about 4 servings

1 pound pork link sausages, pierced
1 small white onion, minced

PANTRY
1 tablespoon cornstarch
1 teaspoon dry mustard
1 cup plus 5 tablespoons milk
Salt and pepper to taste

1 Using a fork, prick the sausage links all over.

2 In a saucepan, combine 1 cup plus 3 tablespoons milk, the onions, and the sausages and cook, over a low simmer for about 15 minutes. Transfer the sausages to a warming plate.

3 In a small bowl, blend together the cornstarch, the dry mustard, and 2 table-spoons of milk. Add 2 table-spoons of liquid from the saucepan and stir the mixture back into the saucepan. Bring to a boil and cook, stirring fre-quently, for about 5 minutes, or until thickened.

4 Season to taste, add the sausages, and cook for about 5 minutes or until thoroughly heated. Remove from the heat and serve.

1 pound bulk pork sausage
2 cups unsweetened applesauce
2 drops red food coloring

PANTRY
1 tablespoon vegetable oil
½ teaspoon ground cinnamon

SAUSAGE BALLS IN APPLESAUCE

makes about 4 servings

1 Form the sausage meat into balls about the size of walnuts.

2 In a skillet, sauté the sausage balls for about 15 minutes or until evenly browned. Transfer to a wire rack covered with paper towels to drain.

3 In a saucepan, blend the applesauce, the cinnamon, and the food coloring. Cook for about 5 minutes or until thoroughly heated. Remove from the heat and serve with the sausage balls.

1 to 1½ pounds large pork sausages, cooked
1 can (8 ounces) beer

PANTRY
2 tablespoons vegetable oil
1 tablespoon flour

SAUSAGES IN BEER

makes about 4 servings

1 Rub the sausages with flour.

2 In a skillet, heat the oil, sauté the sausages, turning frequently, for about 1 minute or until evenly browned. Transfer to a warming plate.

3 Stir the flour into the juices in the skillet to make a roux. Add the beer, bring to a boil, and reduce to a simmer. Cook for about 2 minutes or until thickened. Remove from the heat, pour the beer sauce over the sausages, and serve.

1 pound Italian sausage, cut into ½-inch slices
1½ cups frozen mixed vegetables, thawed and drained
4 cups cooked pasta of choice

PANTRY
3 cups (bottled) tomato sauce

SAUSAGE WITH PASTA ITALIANO

makes about 4 servings

In a saucepan, sauté the sausage for about 10 to 15 minutes or until it loses its pinkish color. Drain the liquid, and add the tomato sauce and the vegetables. Bring to a boil and reduce to a simmer. Cover and cook for about 10 minutes or until the vegetables are tender. Remove from the heat and serve with the pasta.

SAUTÉED FLANK STEAK

makes about 4 servings

1 flank steak (about 2 to 3 pounds)

PANTRY
1 tablespoon butter or margarine
Salt and pepper to taste

1 Sprinkle the steak with salt and pepper to taste and rub in.

2 In a skillet, sauté the meat in the butter, turning occasionally, for about 25 to 30 minutes or until tender. Remove from the heat, slice, and serve.

SAUTÉED LIVER

makes about 4 to 5 servings

1 pound liver of choice, cut into pieces
1 medium yellow onion, quartered
1 egg, beaten
1 teaspoon onion salt

PANTRY
2 tablespoons canola oil

1 In the container of a blender or food processor, combine the liver and the onion, and process on low speed until ground.

2 Transfer to a bowl and blend in the egg and the onion salt. Form into 4 or 5 patties.

3 In a skillet, sauté the patties in the oil for about 20 minutes or until both sides are lightly browned. Remove from heat and serve.

1 large white onion, chopped
1 can (16 ounces) baked pork and beans
½ cup bread crumbs

PANTRY

1 tablespoon butter or margarine
2 teaspoons sage
Salt and pepper to taste

1 Position the rack in the center of the oven and preheat to 400 degrees F. Lightly grease a small shallow baking dish.

2 In a skillet, sauté the onions in the butter for about 5 minutes or until translucent.

3 In a bowl, combine the onions, the bread crumbs, and the sage, and season to taste. Add just enough water to hold the mixture together.

4 Arrange half of the pork and beans in the prepared baking dish. Top with half of the bread crumb mixture and repeat. Bake for about 20 minutes or until thoroughly heated. Remove from the oven and serve.

SAVORY PORK AND BEAN BAKE

makes about 3 to 4 servings

---

2 sliced red onions, minced
2 cups chopped cooked beef
1 cup Basic White Sauce (see page 398)
¼ cup soft bread crumbs

PANTRY

1 tablespoon butter or margarine
Salt and pepper to taste

1 Position the rack in the center of the oven and preheat to 350 degrees F. Lightly grease a shallow baking dish.

2 In a saucepan, sauté the onion in the butter for about 5 minutes or until lightly browned. Blend in the sauce and cook, stirring frequently, for about 5 minutes or until thickened.

3 Arrange the beef in the prepared baking dish, top with the sauce, season to taste, and sprinkle with the bread crumbs. Bake for about 20 to 25 minutes or until thoroughly heated. Remove from the oven and serve.

SCALLOPED CORNED BEEF

makes about 4 to 5 servings

SCHWEINSBRATEN (ROAST PORK)

makes about 6 servings

1 loin of pork (about 14 ribs)

2 teaspoons caraway seeds, crushed

½ teaspoon white pepper

PANTRY

1 medium garlic clove, mashed

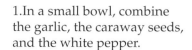

1. In a small bowl, combine the garlic, the caraway seeds, and the white pepper.

2 Arrange the pork in a roasting pan, sprinkle with garlic mixture, and rub in. Cover and refrigerate for at least 1 hour. Add 2 cups of water and cover.

3 Position the rack in the center of the oven and preheat to 350 degrees F.

4 Bake the pork for about 1 hour, turn and continue to bake for about 1 hour or until tender. Remove the cover and bake for about 30 to 40 minutes or until golden-brown. Remove from the oven, cut into serving-sized pieces, and serve.

SHEPHERD'S PIE

makes about 4 servings

2 cups mashed potatoes

2 cups cooked lamb, cut into bite-sized pieces

1½ cups leftover lamb gravy

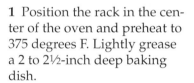

1 Position the rack in the center of the oven and preheat to 375 degrees F. Lightly grease a 2 to 2½-inch deep baking dish.

2 Spread the potatoes in the bottom of the prepared baking dish. Hollow out the center and reserve. Fill the center with the meat, pour on the gravy, and top with the reserved potatoes. Bake for about 20 minutes or until thoroughly heated. Remove from the oven and serve.

1½ pounds frozen meatballs, thawed

1 cup dry or sweet sherry

PANTRY

1 tablespoon butter or margarine

1 cup (bottled) ketchup

1 Position the rack in the center of the oven and preheat to 350 degrees F. Lightly grease a 13 x 9-inch baking dish.

2 In a bowl, blend the ketchup and the sherry.

3 Arrange the meatballs in the prepared baking dish and top with the ketchup mixture.

4 Bake for about 35 to 40 minutes or until thoroughly heated. Remove from the oven and serve.

SHERRY-GLAZED MEATBALLS

makes about 4 servings

6 boneless loin of pork chops, about ½-inch thick

1 medium onion, sliced

1 can (10½ ounces) beef broth

PANTRY

2 tablespoons vegetable oil

2 tablespoons cornstarch or arrowroot

1 In a skillet, sauté the chops in the oil for about 20 to 25 minutes or until tender and both sides are lightly browned. Transfer to a warming plate.

2 In a bowl, using a wire whisk or an electric mixer, blend the cornstarch and the broth.

3 In the same skillet, sauté the onions for about 5 minutes or until tender. Blend in the cornstarch mixture and bring to a boil. Cook, stirring frequently, until thickened. Return the chops to the skillet and cover. Continue to cook for about 5 minutes or until thoroughly heated. Remove from the heat and serve.

SMOTHERED PORK CHOPS

makes about 6 servings

SOUPER BURGER

makes about 8 servings

2 pounds ground beef
**1 envelope (1¼ ounces) dry
    soup mix of choice**
8 toasted hamburger buns

PANTRY
2 tablespoons vegetable oil

1 In a bowl, combine the soup mix, the beef, and ½ cup of water. Form into 8 patties.

2 In a skillet, sauté the patties in the oil for about 25 to 30 minutes or until both sides are lightly browned. Remove from the heat and serve on buns.

Cooking note: For variation, add potatoes and vegetables to this dish and prepare in a casserole.

SOUPY PORK CHOPS

makes about 4 servings

4 loin of pork chops
**1 can (10½ ounces) cream of
    celery soup**

In a skillet, sauté the chops for about 10 minutes or until both sides are browned. Blend in the soup and ⅓ cup of water. Cover and continue to cook, stirring and basting, over a low heat for about 40 minutes or until tender. Remove from the heat and serve with the pan juices on the side.

SPARERIBS AND SAUERKRAUT

makes about 4 servings

**2 pounds pork spareribs, cut
    into serving-sized pieces**
4 cups sauerkraut

PANTRY
1 teaspoon salt

1 Sprinkle the spareribs with the salt.

2 In a large pot, cover the ribs with water. Bring to a boil and cook, skimming the fat from the top, for about 30 minutes. Add the sauerkraut, bring to a boil, and reduce to a simmer. Cover and cook for about 20 minutes or until tender. Remove from the heat and serve.

1 slice ham with bone (about 2 to 3 pounds)

4 whole cloves

2 tablespoons packed brown sugar

2 bananas, peeled and sliced in half lengthwise

2 teaspoons fresh unsweetened lemon juice

1 tablespoon prepared mustard

PANTRY

1 tablespoon butter or margarine

SPICED HAM WITH BANANAS

makes about 4 servings

1 Position the rack in the center of the oven and preheat to 300 degrees F. Lightly grease a shallow baking dish.

2 Arrange the ham in the prepared baking dish and insert cloves in and around the ham. Top with the mustard and 1 teaspoon of the sugar. Add ½ cup of water. Bake for about 40 to 50 minutes or until tender.

3 Arrange the bananas on top of the ham, sprinkle with the remaining sugar, and drizzle on the lemon juice. Continue to cook, basting occasionally, for about 10 minutes or until thoroughly heated. Remove from the oven, slice, and serve.

6 slices loin of pork chops

1 can (6 ounces) condensed frozen orange juice

6 whole cloves

1 tablespoon brown sugar

¼ teaspoon cinnamon

PANTRY

1 tablespoon butter or margarine

SPICY PORK

makes about 4 to 6 servings

1 Press a whole clove in the center of each chop.

2 In a small bowl, blend the orange juice, the sugar, and the cinnamon.

3 In a skillet, sauté the chops in the butter for about 10 minutes or until both sides are browned. Remove the cloves and blend in the orange mixture. Cover and cook, basting occasionally, for about 20 to 25 minutes or until tender. Remove from the heat and serve.

STEAK FONDUE

makes about 4 servings

1½ pounds beef steak
½ cup mild cheddar cheese
¼ cup sherry

PANTRY
1 tablespoon vegetable oil
Salt and pepper to taste

1 Brush both sides of the steak with the oil.

2 In the top of a double boiler over boiling water, cook the cheese until it has melted. Blend in the sherry and season to taste.

3 In a skillet, sauté the steak for about 25 to 30 minutes or until both sides are lightly browned. Remove from the heat, top with the cheese sauce, slice, and serve.

STEAK MILANO

makes about 4 servings

2 garlic cloves, chopped
1 teaspoon fresh unsweetened
    lemon juice
1½ pounds beef steak, trimmed
    and cut into 4 pieces

PANTRY
½ cup olive oil
Salt and pepper to taste

1 In a bowl, blend the garlic, the oil, the lemon juice, and season to taste. Add the meat, cover with plastic wrap, and refrigerate for about 12 hours or overnight.

2 Position the broiler rack about 4 inches from the heat.

3 Arrange the steak on the broiler pan. Broil, basting with the marinade and turning, for about 15 minutes or until both sides are browned. Remove from the broiler and serve.

STEAK TARTAR

makes about 4 servings

1½ pounds lean ground beef
4 egg yolks
1 teaspoon chervil, minced
1 medium yellow onion, minced
Tartar Sauce (see page 411)

Form the meat into 4 patties and make an indentation in the center of each pattie. Place one yolk in each indentation, sprinkle on the chervil and the onions, and serve with the Tartar Sauce on the side.

2 pounds top round steak
¼ cup Burgundy
½ cup V8™ vegetable juice

PANTRY
2 garlic cloves, minced
Salt and pepper to taste

STEAK WITH GARLIC AND WINE

makes about 4 to 6 servings

1 In a bowl, blend the vegetable juice, the wine, the garlic, and salt and pepper to taste. Add the meat, cover with plastic wrap, and refrigerate for at least 4 hours.

2 Preheat a counter-top grill.

3 Remove the steak from the marinade and place on the grill. Cook, basting with the marinade, for about 30 minutes or until both sides are browned. Remove from the grill, slice and serve.

Cooking note: Cooking time for grilling recipes depends on the heat source.

---

1 beef heart (about 1 pound), trimmed
½ cup Basic White Sauce (see page 398)
1 cup roasted chestnuts, skinned and chopped
½ cup cracker crumbs, sifted

PANTRY
1 tablespoon butter or margarine
Salt and pepper to taste

STUFFED BEEF HEART

makes about 2 to 4 servings

1 Position the rack in the center of the oven and preheat to 350 degrees F. Lightly grease a baking or cookie sheet.

2 In a bowl, combine the sauce, the chestnuts, and ¼ cup of the crumbs. Slice the meat along the side without cutting through. Stuff with the chestnut mixture and secure with a toothpick.

3 In a pot of boiling water, boil the meat for about 10 minutes. Reduce to a simmer and cook for about 20 minutes or until tender. Remove from the heat, sprinkle with the remaining crumbs, season to taste and serve.

STUFFED LIVER

makes about 2 servings

1 calf's liver, (about 1 pound)
1 cup (packaged) bread stuffing, prepared
3 strips salt pork

PANTRY
1 tablespoon butter or margarine
¼ cup flour

1 Position the rack in the center of the oven and preheat to 450 degrees F. Lightly grease a baking pan.

2 Slice the liver along the side without cutting through. Stuff with the bread mixture, secure with toothpicks, and rub with the flour.

3 Arrange the liver in the prepared baking pan, place the strips of pork on top, and bake for about 15 minutes. Reduce the heat to 350 degrees F and continue to bake for about 20 minutes or until tender. Remove from the oven and serve.

STUFFED PORK CHOPS

makes about 4 servings

4 boneless pork chops (about 1½-inches thick), trimmed
1½ cups packaged bread stuffing, prepared
1 bottle (12 ounces) chili sauce

PANTRY
1 tablespoon vegetable oil

1 Position the rack in the center of the oven and preheat to 350 degrees F. Lightly grease a 13 x 9-inch baking pan.

2 Cut slits in one side of the chops to create pockets. Fill the pockets with bread stuffing and secure with toothpicks.

3 In a skillet, sauté the chops in the oil for about 15 minutes or until both sides are browned.

4 Arrange the chops in the prepared baking pan, top with the chili sauce, and cover. Bake for about 40 to 50 minutes or until tender. Remove from the oven and serve with the pan juices on the side.

4 pork tenderloins (about
¾-inch thick), trimmed

2 cups (packaged) bread
stuffing, prepared

PANTRY

1 tablespoon butter or margarine

1 garlic clove

1 Position the rack in the center of the oven and preheat to 350 degrees F. Lightly grease a 13 x 9-inch baking dish.

2 Rub chops with garlic. Cut slits in one side of the chops to create pockets. Fill with bread stuffing and secure with toothpicks.

3 Arrange the meat in the prepared baking dish and bake for about 50 minutes to 1 hour or until tender. Remove from the oven and serve.

STUFFED PORK TENDERLOIN

makes about 4 to 6 servings

---

8 slices leftover roasted lamb

¼ cup (bottled) chunky chutney,
finely chopped

1½ cups leftover lamb gravy

In the top of a double boiler, over boiling water, blend together the chutney and the gravy. Add the meat and cook for about 15 to 20 minutes or until thoroughly heated. Remove from the heat and serve.

SUCCULENT LAMB WITH CHUTNEY

makes about 4 servings

---

1 ham with bone (about 2
pounds), trimmed

½ cup packed light-brown sugar

PANTRY

1 teaspoon dry mustard

2 tablespoons white wine vinegar

1 Position the broiler rack about 4 inches from the heat. Have a shallow baking pan available.

2 In a small bowl, blend the mustard, the sugar, and the vinegar.

3 Place the ham in the baking pan and brush with the mustard mixture. Broil for about 7 to 10 minutes or until browned. Turn over and repeat. Remove from the oven, slice and serve.

SWEET AND SAVORY BROILED HAM

makes about 4 servings

SWEET AND SPICY CORNED BEEF

makes about 8 servings

3 pounds corned beef
1 cup orange marmalade
¼ cup packed dark-brown sugar

PANTRY
1 tablespoon butter or margarine
¼ cup prepared mustard

1 In a large saucepan, cover the meat with water, bring to a boil, and reduce to a simmer. Cover and simmer over low heat for about 3 hours or until tender.

2 Position the rack in the center of the oven and preheat to 350 degrees F. Lightly grease a baking pan.

3 In a bowl, blend the marmalade, the mustard, and the sugar.

4 Arrange the beef in the prepared baking pan and coat the entire roast with the marmalade mixture. Bake for about 30 minutes or until the glaze is crispy and light golden-brown. Remove from the oven, slice, and serve.

SWEET AND SOUR MEATBALLS

makes about 4 servings

1 pound ground beef
1 egg, lightly beaten
1 bottle (12 ounces) prepared chili sauce
1 jar (8 ounces) currant jelly

1 In a bowl, combine the beef and the egg. Form into balls about the size of walnuts.

2 In a saucepan, blend the chili sauce, the jelly, and ¼ cup of water. Cook over low heat for about 5 minutes and add the meatballs. Continue to cook for about 30 minutes or until thoroughly cooked. Remove from the heat and serve.

1 pound ground pork sausages, formed into 4 patties

4 large sweet potatoes, pared, cooked and thinly sliced

4 large apples, cored and cut into ½-inch slices

1 tablespoon brown sugar

PANTRY

1 tablespoon butter or margarine

Sweet Potato, Sausage, and Apple Bake

makes about 4 servings

1 Position the rack in the center of the oven and preheat to 350 degrees F. Lightly grease a casserole.

2 Arrange half of the potatoes in the bottom of the prepared casserole. Place the sausage patties on top, add the apples, and cover with the remaining potatoes. Brush the top with water and sprinkle with the sugar. Bake for about 40 minutes or until the potatoes are tender. Remove from the oven and serve.

Cooking note: Use only sweet potatoes, not yams (see glossary).

---

5 pounds pork spareribs, cut into serving-sized pieces

¼ cup yellow onion, finely chopped

PANTRY

¾ cup warm honey

1 cup soy sauce

Salt and pepper to taste

Sweet Spareribs

makes about 6 servings

1 In the container of a blender or food processor, combine the honey, the soy sauce, the onion, and salt and pepper to taste. Process on high speed until smooth.

2 Pour the sweet sauce mixture into a bowl, stir in the meat, cover with plastic wrap, and refrigerate for at least 24 hours.

3 Position the rack in the center of the oven and preheat to 300 degrees F. Lightly grease a shallow baking pan and place a meat rack inside.

4 Arrange the ribs on the meat rack in the prepared baking pan. Bake, basting with the sweet sauce, for about 1½ to 2 hours or until tender. Remove from the oven and serve.

SWISS-STYLE LIVER

makes about 4 servings

2 pounds calf's liver, cut into
   ½-inch strips
3 tablespoons onions, minced
3 tablespoons cilantro, minced
1 cup sour cream or unflavored
   yogurt

PANTRY

3 tablespoons butter
Salt and pepper to taste

In a skillet, sauté the onions and the cilantro in the butter for about 1 minute. Add the liver and cook, stirring frequently, for about 10 minutes or until browned on all sides. Season to taste and blend in the sour cream. Cook for about 10 minutes or until heated but not boiling. Remove from the heat and serve.

Cooking note: The liver should not be overcooked.

TERESA'S LAMB CUTLETS

makes about 4 servings

8 lamb cutlets, thinly sliced
1 tablespoon fresh watercress

PANTRY

2 tablespoons butter or
   margarine
1 garlic clove, chopped
Salt and pepper to taste

In a skillet, sauté the cutlets for about 20 minutes or until both sides are browned. Add the garlic, ¼ cup of water, and salt and pepper to taste. Cover and simmer for about 10 minutes or until tender. Remove from the heat, garnish with watercress, and serve.

1 ham (about 5 pounds), scored
1 bottle (16 ounces) apple cider
½ cup packed light-brown sugar
1 teaspoon prepared mustard
5 whole cloves

PANTRY
2 tablespoons butter or
  margarine

1 Position the rack in the center of the oven and preheat to 350 degrees F. Lightly grease a roasting pan.

2 In a Dutch oven, cover the ham with water and bring to a boil. Drain and cover the meat with the apple cider. Bring to a boil and reduce to a simmer. Cook for about 1½ hours or until tender.

3 In a small bowl, combine the sugar and the mustard.

4 Arrange the ham in the prepared roasting pan, press the cloves into the meat, and top with the sugar mixture. Bake for about 20 minutes or until the glaze is light golden-brown. Remove from the oven, slice, and serve.

TRADITIONAL BAKED HAM

makes about 4 servings

4 pork chops, thinly cut and
  trimmed
1 small can (6 ounces) crushed
  pineapple
1 cup fresh orange juice

PANTRY
1 tablespoon butter or margarine

1 Position the rack in the center of the oven and preheat to 325 degrees F. Lightly grease a 13 x 9-inch baking dish.

2 In a bowl, combine the pineapple and the orange juice.

3 Arrange the chops in the prepared baking pan and top with the fruit mixture. Bake for about 40 minutes or until tender. Remove from the oven and serve.

TROPICAL PORK CHOPS

makes about 4 servings

Two Meat Stir-Fry

makes about 2 to 4 servings

1 cup smoked sausage, sliced
1 cup chicken, cooked and diced
1 package (10 ounces) frozen broccoli florettes, thawed and drained
2½ cups cooked shell pasta

PANTRY

2 tablespoons sesame oil
Salt and pepper to taste

In a wok, stir-fry the sausages in the oil for about 2 minutes or until well-coated. Add the chicken and stir-fry for about 1 minute. Add the broccoli and cook, stirring occasionally, for about 2 to 5 minutes or until the broccoli is just tender. Add the pasta and season to taste. Cook for about 5 minutes or until thoroughly heated. Remove from the heat and serve.

Cooking note: For variation, garnish with diced almonds and serve with an Oriental-style sauce on the side.

Veal à la Roma

makes about 4 servings

1 pound veal cutlets, thinly cut and divided into squares
1 can (10 ounces) spaghetti sauce with mushrooms
½ medium green bell pepper, trimmed, seeded and cut into thin strips

PANTRY

2 tablespoons butter or margarine

In a skillet, sauté the cutlets in the butter for about 5 minutes or until it loses its pinkish color. Add the spaghetti sauce and the pepper, and cover. Simmer over low heat for about 30 minutes or until tender. Remove from the heat and serve.

Veal and Onion Fricassee

makes about 4 servings

1 pound round steak, thinly cut and divided into squares
2 large red onions, chopped
⅔ cup apple cider

PANTRY

2 tablespoons butter or margarine
Salt and pepper to taste
½ cup flour

1 Sprinkle the meat with seasoning to taste and rub with the flour.

2 In a skillet, sauté the onions and the steak in the butter for about 10 minutes or until both sides are lightly browned. Pour in the cider and reduce to a simmer. Cover and cook for about 30 minutes or until tender. Transfer to a warming plate.

3 Heat the juices in the skillet and blend in the flour. Cook for about 5 minutes or until thickened. Remove from the heat and serve the steak with the gravy on the side.

3 pounds veal rump roast, trimmed and cut into cubes

8 bacon slices, cut into 1½ inch strips

PANTRY

1 tablespoon butter or margarine

1 tablespoon dried rosemary

1 Position the broiler rack about 6 inches from the heat. Lightly grease 4 metal skewers.

2 Alternate the veal and the bacon on the skewers and sprinkle with rosemary.

3 Arrange the skewers on the broiler pan. Broil, turning frequently, for about 20 minutes or until tender and lightly browned. Remove from the oven and serve.

VEAL SKEWERS

makes about 4 to 6 servings

---

1 pound ground fresh venison

3 ounces ground pork

PANTRY

1 tablespoon vegetable oil

Salt and pepper to taste

1 Position the grill about 6 inches from the heat.

2 In a bowl, combine the venison, the pork, and season to taste. Shape into 4 patties.

3 Place the meat on the grill and brush with the oil. Grill for about 30 to 40 minutes or until both sides are lightly browned. Remove from the grill and serve.

Cooking note: Cooking time for grilling recipes depends on the heat source.

VENISON AND PORK BURGERS

makes about 4 servings

1½ pounds ground beef

½ cup zucchini, thinly sliced

½ cup Swiss cheese, shredded

2 tablespoons pimento, chopped

PANTRY

Pepper to taste

1 Position the rack in the center of the oven and preheat to 350 degrees F. Have a small loaf pan available.

2 In a bowl, combine the meat and the pepper to taste.

3 Layer the meat, the zucchini, the cheese, and the pimento in the loaf pan. Repeat layers, ending with the meat. Bake for about 1 to 1½ hours or until thoroughly cooked. Remove from the oven, invert the pan, slice, and serve.

ZUCCHINI MEAT LOAF

makes about 4 to 6 servings

Beans, Grains, and Other Side Dishes

BAKED HOMINY

SAVORY BLACK-EYED PEAS

Sometimes I wonder why the protein portion of dinner is called the main course. To me, the big thrill is the side dish. You can do so much with beans, rice, and other grains, and they're so satisfying to eat. Whether you're a vegetarian, or just a side dish afficionado like me, the 4-Ingredient side dish chapter provides simply delicious recipes. Now you can easily prepare such exotic dishes as Lebanese Rice with Cucumbers, in which rice is blended with yogurt, cucumber, and mint leaves, or Korean Rice and Dates, where sweet and savory are combined. You'll also find recipes for other healthful grains here, including Garlic Quinoa, which is high in protein content. Black Beans and Corn is prepared with

VEGETARIAN STUFFED PEPPERS

brown rice and a mild salsa for a picante plate of beans, and Baked Creamed Beans, made with bread crumbs and our Basic White Sauce, is soul-satisfyingly good. No matter what dish you prepare, your family and guests are sure to step up for seconds. I usually take thirds.

ALMOND RICE PILAF

makes about 4 servings

4 cups cooked rice
¼ cup scallions, sliced
2 tablespoons sliced almonds, toasted

PANTRY
¼ cup soy sauce

In a bowl, combine the rice, the scallions, the almonds, and the soy sauce, and serve.

BACON BUBBLE AND SQUEAK

makes about 4 servings

½ small savory cabbage, shredded
8 bacon slices, cooked and crumbled
2 cups mashed potato

PANTRY
1 tablespoon butter or margarine

1 Position the rack in the center of the oven and preheat to 375 degrees F. Lightly grease a shallow baking pan.

2 In a bamboo steamer over boiling water, steam the cabbage for about 10 minutes or until tender.

3 In a bowl, combine the cabbage, the bacon, and the mashed potatoes.

4 Arrange in the prepared baking pan and bake for about 15 minutes or until the top is crispy. Remove from the oven and serve.

BAKED ACORN SQUASH

makes about 4 servings

2 medium acorn squash, cut in half, seeds and pith removed
1 pound sausage, cooked
¼ cup light-brown sugar

PANTRY
1 tablespoon butter or margarine

1 Position the rack in the center of the oven and preheat to 350 degrees F. Lightly grease a baking or cookie sheet.

2 Form the sausage into 4 patties.

3 Arrange the squash, cut side up, on the prepared baking sheet.

4 Sprinkle the sugar on the squash pieces and top with the meat patties.

5 Bake for about 30 minutes or until the squash is tender. Remove from the oven, scoop out the squash, and serve on top of the patties.

1 medium carrot, trimmed, pared and sliced
1 tablespoon brown sugar
½ cup brown rice, washed and drained

Baked Carrots and Rice

makes about 2 servings

1 Position the rack in the center of the oven and preheat to 350 degrees F. Have a baking dish with a cover available.

2 In the container of a blender or food processor, combine the carrot, 1 cup of water, and the sugar. Process on high speed until the carrot is reduced to fine pieces.

3 Pour into the baking dish and stir in the rice. Cover and bake, stirring once, for about 20 to 30 minutes or until the liquid has been absorbed and the rice is tender. Remove from the oven and serve.

---

2 cups navy beans, cleaned, soaked and drained
1¼ cups Basic White Sauce (see page 398)
1 large egg, beaten until foamy
½ cup bread crumbs

PANTRY
1 tablespoon butter or margarine
salt and pepper to taste

Baked Creamed Beans

makes about 6 to 8 servings

1 Position the rack in the center of the oven and preheat to 350 degrees F. Lightly grease a baking pan.

2 In a pot, cover the beans and bring to a boil. Reduce to a simmer, cover and cook for about 2 hours or until tender. Drain and cool.

3 In the container of a blender or food processor, process the beans on high speed until smooth. Blend in the sauce and the egg, and season with salt and pepper to taste.

4 Pour into the prepared baking pan and top with the bread crumbs. Bake for about 30 minutes or until the bread crumbs are toasted. Remove from the oven and serve.

BAKED FRENCH FRIES

makes about 4 to 5 servings

2 large russet potatoes, pared and cut into French fries
Paprika to taste

PANTRY
1 tablespoon vegetable oil
Salt to taste

1 Place the potatoes in a bowl of ice water for about 2 hours before baking. Drain and pat dry.

2 Position the rack in the center of the oven and preheat to 450 degrees F. Lightly grease a 13 x 9-inch baking pan.

3 Arrange the potatoes in the prepared baking pan and sprinkle with the oil. Bake, turning frequently, for about 30 minutes or until light golden-brown. Remove from the oven, sprinkle with the salt and the paprika to taste, and serve.

BAKED HOMINY

makes about 4 servings

1 cup boiled hominy
1 egg, beaten

PANTRY
½ cup milk
1 tablespoon butter or margarine
Salt and pepper to taste

1 Position the rack in the center of the oven and preheat to 350 degrees F. Lightly grease a baking dish.

2 In a saucepan, combine the milk and the butter. Cook for about 5 minutes, add the hominy and the egg, and season to taste.

3 Pour into the prepared baking dish. Bake for about 30 minutes, or until a cake tester inserted into the center comes out clean and the top is light golden-brown. Remove from the oven and serve.

BAKED LIMA BEANS AND CHEESE

makes about 4 to 6 servings

1 package (10 ounces) frozen lima beans, cooked and drained
4 hard-boiled eggs, sliced
1 package (6 ounces) American cheese slices

PANTRY
1 tablespoon butter or margarine
1 cup (bottled) tomato sauce

1 Position the rack in the center of the oven and preheat to 350 degrees F. Lightly grease an 8-inch square baking pan.

2 Arrange the ingredients by layers in the prepared baking pan, using half of the beans, half of the eggs, half of the tomato sauce, and half of the cheese. Repeat.

3 Bake for about 20 to 25 minutes or until the cheese has melted. Remove from the oven and serve.

2 small Idaho potatoes, boiled, peeled and sliced

2 small pears, peeled, cored and cut into ½-inch slices

¼ cup maple-flavored syrup

PANTRY

1½ tablespoons melted butter or margarine

1 Position the rack in the center of the oven and preheat to 350 degrees F. Lightly grease a 12 x 8-inch baking dish.

2 In a skillet, sauté the pears in the butter, turning frequently, for about 15 minutes or until lightly browned.

3 In a bowl, blend the butter and the syrup.

4 Arrange the potatoes and the pears in the prepared baking dish in alternating rows. Top with half of the syrup. Bake for about 30 minutes and pour the remaining syrup over the top. Bake for an additional 20 minutes or until lightly browned. Remove from the oven and serve.

Baked Potatoes and Pears

makes about 2 to 4 servings

¾ cup white rice, washed and drained

2 tablespoons onions, minced

PANTRY

2 tablespoons butter or margarine

1 Position the rack in the center of the oven and preheat to 350 degrees F. Lightly grease a 1½-quart baking dish.

2 Place the rice in the prepared baking dish. Add the butter, the onion, 2 cups of boiling water, and stir. Cover and bake for about 30 minutes or until the liquid has evaporated. Remove from the oven, fluff, and serve.

Baked Savory Rice

makes about 4 servings

BAKED WILD RICE IN CONSOMMÉ

makes about 4 servings

1 cup wild rice, washed and drained

1 can (10¾ ounces) condensed consommé

1 can (8 ounces) sliced mushrooms, drained

PANTRY

1 tablespoons butter or margarine

1 Place the rice in a lightly greased 1½-quart baking dish, add the consommé, cover and set aside for about 3 hours.

2 Position the rack in the center of the oven and preheat to 350 degrees F.

3 Bake the rice for about 40 minutes, reduce the heat to 300 degrees F, and remove the cover. Add the mushrooms and the butter and continue to bake for about 10 minutes or until the liquid has evaporated. Remove from the oven, fluff, and serve.

BASMATI CHAAVAL

makes about 4 servings

2 cups basmati rice, washed and drained

PANTRY

¾ teaspoon salt

1 tablespoon butter or margarine

1 Place the rice in a dish, cover with 4 cups of water and set aside for about 3 hours.

2 In a saucepan, combine the rice, the water, the salt, and the butter. Bring to a boil and reduce to a simmer. Cover and cook for about 20 minutes or until tender. Remove from the heat, fluff, and serve.

1 package (16 ounces) dried red kidney beans, cleaned
1 cup white onions, chopped
1 pound ground beef
1 can (16 ounces) chopped tomatoes

PANTRY
1 tablespoon vegetable oil
Salt and pepper to taste

1 In a soup kettle, cover the beans halfway with lightly salted water. Bring to a boil and cook for about 2 to 3 minutes. Remove from the heat and set aside for about 1 hour.

2 Add the onions, bring to a boil, and reduce to a simmer. Cover and cook for about 1 hour or until tender. Drain and reserve ½ cup of liquid.

3 In a skillet, sauté the beef in the oil, stirring frequently, for about 15 to 20 minutes or until it loses its pinkish color.

Add the tomatoes and season to taste.

4 Position the rack in the center of the oven and preheat to 325 degrees F. Lightly grease a 1½-quart baking dish.

5 In a bowl, combine the beans and the beef mixture. Blend in the reserved liquid.

6 Pour into the prepared baking dish and cover. Bake for about 2 hours, remove the cover and continue to bake for about 30 minutes or until thoroughly heated and the liquid has evaporated. Remove from the oven and serve.

BEAN BAKE ITALIANO

makes about 4 servings

---

1 can (16 ounces) baked beans in tomato sauce
½ cup grated sharp cheddar cheese
¼ cup kosher pickles, chopped

PANTRY
1 tablespoon butter or margarine

1 Position the rack in the center of the oven and preheat to 350 degrees F. Lightly grease a baking dish.

2 Arrange the beans in the prepared baking dish and top with the cheese and the pickles. Bake for about 20 minutes or until thoroughly heated and bubbling. Remove from oven and serve.

BEANS WITH CHEESE

makes about 4 cups

BLACK BEANS AND CORN

makes about 2 servings

1 cup (canned) black beans
1 cup (canned) corn
1 cup brown rice, cooked
2 tablespoons mild salsa

In a microwave-proof dish, combine the beans, the corn, the rice, and the salsa. Cover and microwave on high heat for about 1 to 2 minutes or until thoroughly heated. Remove from the microwave and serve.

BROWNED HOMINY

makes about 4 to 6 servings

1 can (16 ounces) hominy, drained
3 tablespoons leftover bacon drippings

PANTRY
Salt and pepper to taste

In a skillet, sauté the hominy in the drippings for about 5 minutes. Reduce to a simmer, season to taste and cover. Cook for about 20 minutes or until tender. Remove from the heat and serve.

CURRIED RICE WITH PEANUTS

makes about 4 to 5 servings

2 packages (10 ounces each) frozen rice pilaf, thawed
¼ cup raisins
¼ cup chopped peanuts

PANTRY
½ teaspoon curry powder

1 Position the grill about 4 inches from the heat.

2 Arrange the rice on a sheet of aluminum foil, sprinkle with the curry powder, and top with the raisins. Pull the foil up to seal.

3 Place the foil on the grill. Cook, turning once, for about 25 minutes. Open the foil, sprinkle the rice with the nuts, and continue to grill for about 5 minutes or until the rice is tender. Remove from the grill, fluff, and serve.

Cooking note: Cooking time for grilling recipes depends on the heat source. More curry can be added for a spicier flavor.

1 can (15 ounces) cannellini
  beans, drained
1 medium zucchini, trimmed,
  cut in half lengthwise and
  sliced
Cayenne pepper to taste
1 package (8 ounces) pasta of
  choice, cooked and drained

PANTRY
1 bottle (30 ounces) tomato sauce
Salt and pepper to taste

In a large saucepan, combine
the tomato sauce, the beans,
the zucchini, and the cayenne
pepper. Bring to a boil and
reduce to a simmer. Cover
and cook, stirring occasionally, for about 20 minutes or
until the zucchini is tender.
Remove from the heat,
season to taste, pour over
the pasta, and serve.

CANNELLINI BEANS MARINARA

makes about 4 servings

---

1 package (14 ounces) frozen
  French fried potatoes,
  prepared
¼ cup Velveeta™ cheese spread

PANTRY
2 tablespoons milk
¼ teaspoon dry mustard

In the top of a double boiler
over boiling water, blend the
cheese, the milk, and the mustard. Cook for about 5 minutes or until the cheese has
melted. Remove from the
heat, pour over the fries, and
serve.

Cooking note: For variation,
use different types of cheeses.

CHEESY FRIES

makes about 4 to 6 servings

1½ cups minute rice, cooked
1 large egg, beaten
⅓ cup white onion, chopped

PANTRY
3 tablespoons butter or
  margarine
½ cup soy sauce

In a skillet, cook the egg and
the onion in the butter, stirring frequently, for about 5
minutes or until thoroughly
heated. Remove from the
heat, fluff, and serve with the
soy sauce on the side.

CHINESE FRIED RICE

makes about 4 servings

COUNTRY-STYLE POTATO DUMPLINGS

makes about 4 to 6 servings

8 medium russet potatoes, pierced
2 large eggs, beaten

PANTRY
½ cup flour
½ teaspoon salt

1 In a saucepan, cover the potatoes with lightly salted water and bring to a boil. Cook for about 15 to 20 minutes or until tender. Drain, pare, and slice.

2 In the container of a blender or food processor, process the potatoes on high speed until smooth. Pour into a bowl, cover, and let it stand for at least 24 hours.

3 In a bowl, combine the flour, the eggs, and the salt. Stir in the potatoes to form a smooth but lumpy dough. Form into 8 balls.

4 Fill a saucepan halfway with lightly salted water. Bring to a boil and add the potato balls. Cook for about 20 minutes or until thoroughly cooked. Remove from the heat, drain, and serve.

CREOLE RICE

makes about 4 servings

¼ cup (bottled) chili sauce
1 package (12 ounces) frozen Spanish rice, thawed
6 green bell peppers, stemmed, seeded and cut into strips
1 can (2½ ounces) tiny shrimp, drained

1 Position the grill about 4 inches from the heat.

2 Arrange the rice on a sheet of aluminum foil and top with the chili sauce, the peppers, and the shrimp. Pull the foil up to seal.

3 Place the foil on the grill. Cook, turning occasionally, for 30 minutes or until the rice is tender. Remove from the grill, fluff, and serve.

Cooking note: Cooking time for grilling recipes depends on the heat source.

CURRIED RICE

makes about 4 servings

2 cups cooked rice
¼ cup golden raisins

PANTRY
2 tablespoons butter or
  margarine
½ tablespoon curry powder

In the top of a double boiler over boiling water, blend the butter and the curry powder. Heat for about 2 minutes and blend in the rice and the raisins. Cook for about 5 minutes or until thoroughly heated. Remove from the heat and serve.

Cooking note: More curry can be added for spicier flavor.

EASY BROWN RICE

makes about 4 servings

1 cup brown rice, washed and
  drained
2½ cups chicken stock (see note)

PANTRY
1 tablespoon butter or margarine

In a saucepan, sauté the rice in the butter for about 2 to 3 minutes. Pour in the stock, bring to a boil and cover. Cook, stirring occasionally, for about 30 to 40 minutes or until tender and the liquid has been absorbed. Remove from the heat, fluff, and serve.

Cooking note: It is best to use a rendered chicken stock which gels when chilled.

EGGPLANT AND RICE CASSEROLE

makes about 4 servings

1 large white onion, peeled and
  minced
2 cups brown rice, cooked
2 cups eggplant, diced, cooked
  and drained
¾ grated cheese of choice

PANTRY
2 tablespoons melted butter or
  margarine

1 Position the rack in the center of the oven and preheat to about 350 degrees F. Lightly grease a baking dish.

2 In a skillet, sauté the onions in the oil for about 5 minutes or until lightly browned.

3 In a bowl, combine the onions, the rice, and the eggplant.

4 Pour into the prepared baking dish, drizzle on the butter, and sprinkle with the cheese. Bake for about 10 minutes or until the cheese has melted. Remove from the oven and serve.

GARLIC QUINOA

makes about 4 servings

1 cup quinoa, washed and drained
2 cups chicken broth

PANTRY
2 teaspoons olive oil
2 garlic cloves, crushed

In a skillet, sauté the garlic in the oil for about 5 minutes or until lightly browned. Add the quinoa and cook, stirring frequently, for about 2 to 3 minutes. Add the broth and reduce to a simmer. Cover and cook over low heat for about 20 minutes or until tender. Remove from the heat, fluff, and serve.

GINGERED RICE

makes about 4 servings

1 cup short-grain rice
½ teaspoon minced fresh ginger
2 teaspoons peanut oil

In a saucepan, stir-fry the ginger in the oil for about 2 minutes or until fragrant. Add the rice and stir-fry about 1 minute or until coated. Add 2 cups of water, bring to a boil, and reduce to a simmer. Cover and cook, stirring occasionally, for about 15 to 20 minutes or until tender and the liquid has been absorbed. Remove from the heat, fluff, and serve.

GRECIAN RICE

makes about 4 servings

1 cup rice, uncooked
2½ cups chicken stock

PANTRY
¼ cup butter or margarine
Salt and pepper to taste

In a skillet, stir-fry the rice in the butter for about 3 minutes or until lightly browned. Add the stock, season to taste, and reduce to a simmer. Cover and cook, stirring occasionally, for about 20 minutes or until tender and the liquid has been absorbed. Remove from the heat, fluff, and serve.

1½ cups long-grain rice, washed and drained

2 envelopes (3 ounces each) Italian salad dressing mix

PANTRY
1 tablespoon butter or margarine

In a saucepan, stir-fry the rice in the butter for about 3 minutes or until lightly browned. Add 3¼ cups of water, blend in the dressing mix, bring to a boil, and reduce to a simmer. Cover and cook, stirring occasionally, for about 20 minutes or until tender and the liquid has been absorbed. Remove from the heat, fluff, and serve.

ITALIAN RICE

makes about 4 to 6 servings

½ cup pearl barley
1½ cups rice

1 In a saucepan, combine 2 cups of boiling water and the barley. Cover and set aside for about 12 hours.

2 Place the saucepan over medium heat, bring to a boil, and reduce to a simmer. Cook for about 30 minutes and blend in the rice and 2 cups cold water. Return to a boil and cover. Cook for 30 minutes or until tender and the liquid has been absorbed. Remove from the heat, fluff, and serve.

KOREAN RICE AND BARLEY

makes about 6 servings

2 cups white rice, washed and drained
½ cup pitted, chopped dates

In a saucepan, combine the rice, the dates and 4 cups of water. Bring to a boil and reduce to a simmer. Cover and cook for about 30 minutes or until tender and the liquid has been absorbed. Remove from the heat, fluff, and serve.

KOREAN RICE AND DATES

makes about 4 to 6 servings

LEBANESE RICE WITH CUCUMBERS

makes about 2 to 4 servings

1 large cucumber, pared, patted dry and grated
1½ cups rice, cooked
⅔ cup unflavored yogurt or sour cream
2 teaspoons dried mint leaves, crushed

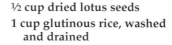

PANTRY
Salt and pepper to taste

1 In a small bowl, combine the yogurt and the mint and season to taste.

2 In another bowl, combine the cucumber and the rice. Top with the yogurt mixture, cover with plastic wrap, and refrigerate for about 1 hour before serving.

LOTUS SEEDS AND GLUTINOUS RICE GONGEE

makes about 4 servings

½ cup dried lotus seeds
1 cup glutinous rice, washed and drained

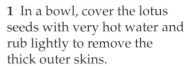

PANTRY
3 tablespoons sugar

1 In a bowl, cover the lotus seeds with very hot water and rub lightly to remove the thick outer skins.

2 In a large saucepan, cover the seeds with 9 cups of water, bring to a boil, and reduce to a simmer. Cover and cook for about 30 minutes. Add the rice and bring to a boil. Cook for about 20 to 30 minutes or until tender and the liquid has been absorbed. Stir in the sugar and cook for about 1 minute or until thoroughly heated. Remove from the heat, fluff, and serve.

1 cup brown rice, washed and
   drained
1 package (4 ounces) Spanish
   rice seasoning mix

PANTRY
2 tablespoons vegetable oil

In a saucepan, sauté the rice
in the oil for about 2 to 3 minutes or until lightly browned.
Add 1¾ cups water and
blend in the seasoning mix.
Bring to a boil and reduce to a
simmer. Cover and cook for
about 25 minutes or until tender and the liquid has been
absorbed. Remove from the
heat, fluff and serve.

MEXICAN
FRIED RICE

makes about 4 to 6 servings

---

1 can (15½ ounces) pinto beans,
   drained and liquid reserved

PANTRY
1 tablespoon olive oil
2 garlic cloves, minced
⅛ teaspoon black pepper

In a microwave-proof dish,
combine the oil and the garlic
and microwave on high heat
for about 45 seconds. Add the
beans, the pepper, and the
reserved liquid, and mash
beans with a potato masher.
Cover and cook on high heat
for about 3 minutes or until
thoroughly heated. Remove
from the oven and serve.

MEXICAN-STYLE
REFRIED BEANS

makes about 4 servings

¼ cup corn oil
2 cups long-grain rice, washed
   and drained
4 cups chicken broth

PANTRY
2 garlic cloves, minced

In a skillet, sauté the garlic
in the oil for about 5 minutes
or until tender. Add the rice
and stir-fry for about 2 to
3 minutes or until lightly
browned. Add the broth,
bring to a boil, and reduce
to a simmer. Cover and cook
for about 20 minutes or until
tender and the liquid has
been absorbed. Remove from
the heat, fluff, and serve.

MEXICAN-
STYLE RICE

makes about 6 servings

MICROWAVE RICE AND VEGGIES

makes about 4 servings

1 cup instant rice

1 package (10 ounces) frozen mixed vegetables

3 tablespoons Tamari soy sauce

In a microwave-proof dish, combine the rice, 2 cups of water, and the vegetables. Cover and microwave on high heat for about 3 to 5 minutes or until tender and the liquid has been absorbed. Remove from the microwave, sprinkle with the soy sauce, fluff, and serve.

PEPPERY RICE BAKE

makes about 4 servings

2 ounces cheddar cheese, cubed

¼ cup light cream

½ cup red bell peppers, diced

1½ cups brown rice, cooked

1 Position the rack in the center of the oven and preheat to 350 degrees F. Have a baking or cookie sheet and 4 individual ramekins available.

2 In a saucepan, blend the cheese and the cream and cook, stirring frequently, for about 3 minutes or until the cheese has melted.

3 In a bowl, combine the peppers, the rice, and the cheese mixture.

4 Divide the mixture evenly among the ramekins and arrange on the baking sheet. Bake for about 25 minutes or until the tops are lightly browned. Remove from the oven and serve.

4 large red or green bell peppers, tops cut off and seeds and pith removed
2 cups polenta, cooked
1½ cups whole kernel corn
6 ounces grated Monterey Jack cheese

PANTRY

1 tablespoon butter or margarine
Salt and pepper to taste

1 Position the rack in the center of the oven and preheat to 350 degrees F. Lightly grease an 8-inch square baking dish.

2 In a bowl, combine the polenta, the corn, and half of the cheese, and season to taste.

3 Spoon into the peppers, sprinkle with the remaining cheese, and arrange in the prepared baking dish. Fill the dish halfway with water.

4 Cover and bake for about 10 minutes. Remove the cover and continue to bake for about 15 minutes or until tender and the cheese has melted. Remove from the oven and serve.

POLENTA STUFFED PEPPERS

makes about 4 servings

---

1 pound fresh green beans, trimmed
1½ cups (canned) plum tomatoes
½ cup (canned) beef bouillon
2 tablespoons grated Parmesan cheese

In a skillet, combine the beans, the tomatoes, and the bouillon. Cover and simmer for about 30 minutes or until the beans are just tender. Remove from the heat, top with the cheese, and serve.

POMPEY'S BEANS

makes about 3 to 4 servings

---

1 package (12 ounces) precooked rice mix
1 can (10½ ounces) onion soup
⅓ cup white port
1 tablespoon grated Romano cheese

PANTRY

Salt and pepper to taste

In a saucepan, blend the soup and the wine. Add the rice mix and bring to a boil. Cover, remove from the heat, and set aside for about 5 minutes. Remove the cover, season to taste, top with the cheese, fluff, and serve.

RICE COOKED IN ONION AND WINE

makes about 4 servings

Rice with Coconut Milk

makes about 4 to 6 servings

2 cups jasmine rice, washed and drained

⅓ cup coconut cream

2⅓ cups coconut milk

PANTRY

2 tablespoons sugar

1 In a small bowl, blend the coconut cream and the coconut milk.

2 In a saucepan, bring the milk mixture to a boil. Add the rice and the sugar and cook, stirring occasionally, for about 5 minutes. Cover, reduce to a simmer and cook for about 20 minutes or until tender and the liquid has been absorbed. Remove from the heat, fluff, and serve.

Rosemary Potatoes

makes about 2 servings

2 large Idaho potatoes, scrubbed and thinly sliced

PANTRY

1 tablespoon melted butter or margarine

½ teaspoon dried rosemary, crushed

Salt and pepper to taste

1 Position the rack in the center of the oven and preheat to 425 degrees F. Lightly grease a baking or cookie sheet.

2 In a bowl, combine the potatoes and the butter.

3 Arrange the potatoes, overlapping, on the prepared baking sheet, sprinkle with the rosemary, and drizzle on the butter. Bake for about 20 to 25 minutes or until tender and lightly browned. Remove from the oven, season to taste, and serve.

Royal Rice

makes about 4 servings

½ cup scallions with tops, finely chopped

3 cups rice, cooked

1 can (4 ounces) sliced mushrooms, drained

PANTRY

2 tablespoons butter or margarine

Salt and pepper to taste

In a skillet, sauté the onion in the butter for about 5 minutes or until tender. Add the rice and the mushrooms, season to taste, and cook for about 10 minutes or until thoroughly heated. Remove from the heat, fluff, and serve.

1 package (10 ounces) frozen mixed vegetables, cooked and drained
2 cups long grain rice, cooked
4 lettuce leaves

PANTRY
2 tablespoons mayonnaise
Salt and pepper to taste

In a bowl, combine the rice, the vegetables, and the mayonnaise and season to taste. Spoon the mixture over the lettuce leaves and serve.

Cooking note: For variation, top with cooked, chopped meat.

RUSSIAN RICE

makes about 4 servings

---

2 cups dried black-eyed peas, soaked overnight, drained and 4 cups of liquid reserved
4 pieces salt pork
4 small white onions, sliced

In a saucepan, combine the peas, the reserved liquid, the pork, and the onions. Bring to a boil and reduce to a simmer. Cover and cook, stirring occasionally, for about 1 hour or until tender. Remove from the heat and serve.

Cooking note: Add boiling water if the peas become dry while cooking.

SAVORY BLACK-EYED PEAS

makes about 4 servings

---

1 cup quick-cooking hominy, uncooked
½ cup green onions, minced

In a saucepan, bring 4 cups of water to a boil. Add the hominy and the onions, bring to a boil, and reduce to a simmer. Cook, stirring occasionally, for about 7 to 10 minutes or until thickened. Remove from the heat and serve.

SAVORY GRITS

makes about 4 servings

Savory Rice with Spaghetti Sauce

makes about 4 servings

1 package (12 ounces) precooked rice mix, prepared

1 can (8 ounces) spaghetti sauce

3 tablespoons grated Parmesan cheese

In a saucepan, combine the rice and the spaghetti sauce, and heat thoroughly. Transfer to a serving platter, top with cheese, and serve.

South American-Style Wild Rice with Quinoa

makes about 3 to 4 servings

½ cup wild rice, washed and drained

½ cup quinoa

PANTRY

4 teaspoons soy sauce

In a saucepan, combine 2½ cups water and the soy sauce. Bring to a boil, add in the rice, reduce to a simmer, and cover. Cook for about 15 minutes and add the quinoa. Cover and continue to cook for about 20 minutes or until tender and the liquid has been absorbed. Remove from the heat, fluff, and serve.

Spanish-Style Rice with Squash and Tomatoes

makes about 4 to 6 servings

1 package (4 ounces) Spanish quick brown rice, prepared

2 cups summer squash, cubed

1 medium bell pepper, stemmed, seeded and chopped

1 can (16 ounces) stewed tomatoes

PANTRY

1 tablespoon butter or margarine

1 Position the rack in the center of the oven and preheat to 350 degrees F. Lightly grease a 13 x 9-inch baking dish.

2 Arrange the rice in the prepared baking dish and top with the squash, the peppers, and the tomatoes. Cover and bake for about 30 minutes or until the squash is tender. Remove from the oven and serve.

Cooking note: Any type of squash can be used.

2 cups (canned) chickpeas, drained, skinned and chopped

2 cups buckwheat groats, cooked

½ cup (canned) beef broth

1 cup unflavored yogurt

PANTRY

1 tablespoon butter or margarine

1 Position the rack in the center of the oven and preheat to 350 degrees F. Lightly grease a 1½-quart baking dish.

2 In a bowl, combine the peas and the buckwheat groats.

3 Arrange the mixture in the prepared baking dish, add the broth and the butter and cover. Bake for about 20 minutes or until the liquid has been absorbed. Remove from the oven, garnish with yogurt, and serve.

Syrian Kasha with Chickpeas

makes about 3 to 6 servings

---

2 cans (16 ounces each) garbanzo beans, drained and ¼ cup liquid reserved

5 tablespoons tahini

¼ cup fresh lemon juice

3 tablespoons apple juice

PANTRY

3 garlic cloves, sliced

In the container of a blender or food processor, combine the garlic, the tahini, the beans, the reserved liquid, the lemon juice, and the apple juice. Process on high speed until smooth and serve.

Tahini Beans

makes about 4 to 6 servings

---

1 cup dry black soybeans, soaked overnight

1 strip kombu, about 2 inches

1 tablespoon peanut oil

2 teaspoons Tamari soy sauce

PANTRY

1 garlic clove, thinly sliced

Salt and pepper to taste

1 Drain the beans, rinse under running water and discard the loose skins.

2 In a saucepan, cover the beans with lightly salted water. Bring to a boil and reduce to a simmer. Cook, skimming the film from the top of the water, for about 5 minutes. Repeat the process two more times. Add the garlic, the kombu, and the oil. Cover and cook for about 1½ hours or until tender. Remove from the heat, add the sauce, season to taste, and serve.

Tamari Black Soybeans

makes about 3 to 4 servings

Thanksgiving Mincemeat Mold

makes about 4 to 6 servings

2 large packages (8 ounces each) cherry-flavored gelatin
½ cup pecans, finely chopped
2 cups moist mincemeat
1 cup sweetened whipped cream

1 In a bowl, combine the gelatin and 3½ cups of boiling water. Stir until dissolved. Pour ¾ cup of the gelatin into a ½-quart mold and refrigerate for about 1 hour or until firm.

2 In another bowl, refrigerate the remaining gelatin until it has started to thicken. Blend in the mincemeat and the nuts. Spread evenly over the top of the firm gelatin. Refrigerate again until firm. Invert the mold, garnish with whipped cream, and serve.

Tomato Rice Bake

makes about 4 to 6 servings

2 cups brown rice, cooked
1 can (13 ounces) crushed tomatoes, drained and liquid reserved
2 large tomatoes, thinly sliced
1 cup bread crumbs

PANTRY
1 tablespoon butter or margarine

1 Position the rack in the center of the oven and preheat to 350 degrees F. Lightly grease a baking dish.

2 In a bowl, combine the rice and the crushed tomatoes.

3 Arrange half of the rice in the prepared baking dish and top with half of the tomato slices. Repeat, add the reserved liquid, and top with the bread crumbs. Bake for about 20 minutes or until the liquid has been absorbed and the top is lightly browned. Remove from the oven and serve.

Vegetable Rice

makes about 4 servings

2½ cups vegetable stock
¾ cup long-grain brown rice, uncooked
¾ cup frozen mixed vegetables, thawed

In a saucepan, bring the stock to a boil. Add the rice and cook for about 15 minutes. Add the vegetables and continue to cook for about 5 minutes or until tender and the liquid has been absorbed. Remove from the heat and serve.

4 red or green bell peppers, stemmed, seeded, tops cut off and reserved
2 cups jasmine rice, cooked
2 tablespoons nuts of choice, chopped

PANTRY
1 tablespoon vegetable oil

VEGETARIAN STUFFED PEPPERS

makes about 4 servings

1 Position the rack in the center of the oven and preheat to 400 degrees F. Lightly grease an 8-inch square baking dish.

2 In a bowl, combine the rice and the nuts. Spoon into the peppers and replace the reserved tops.

3 Arrange in the prepared baking pan and drizzle on the oil. Bake for about 20 minutes or until tender. Remove from the oven and serve.

---

5 medium red onions, chopped
1 cup wild rice, washed and drained

PANTRY
½ tablespoon red wine vinegar
2 tablespoons olive oil

WILD RICE WITH RED ONIONS

makes about 6 servings

1 In a skillet, sauté the onion in the oil for about 1 minute. Add 1 cup of water and the vinegar and bring to a boil. Reduce to a simmer and cook, stirring occasionally, for about 5 minutes or until the onions are a light pink. Drain and reserve the liquid.

2 Combine the reserved liquid and water to measure 2¼ cups.

3 In a saucepan, bring the liquid to a boil. Add the rice, reduce to a simmer and cover. Cook for about 25 to 30 minutes or until the rice is tender and the liquid has been absorbed. Add the onion mixture and cook for about 5 minutes or until thoroughly heated. Remove from the heat, fluff, and serve.

YORKSHIRE PUDDING

makes about 6 servings

3 eggs, well-beaten
1 tablespoon meat drippings

PANTRY
1 cup milk
1 cup sifted flour

1 In a bowl, using a wire whisk or an electric mixer, blend the milk and the eggs until smooth. Add the flour and the meat drippings and let sit for 40 minutes.

2 Position the rack in the center of the oven and preheat to 400 degrees F. Lightly grease and preheat a 9-inch square baking pan.

3 Using a wire whisk or an electric mixer, blend the batter until smooth and pour into the prepared baking pan. Bake for about 20 minutes or until light golden-brown. Remove from the oven, slice, and serve.

BAKED SWEET POTATOES AND APPLES

makes about 4 to 6 servings

2 large sweet potatoes or yams, boiled, pared and sliced
2 large Macintosh apples, peeled, cored and cut into ½-inch slices
½ cup maple-flavored pancake syrup

PANTRY
¼ cup plus 2 tablespoons melted butter or margarine

1 Position the rack in the center of the oven and preheat to 350 degrees F. Lightly grease a 12 x 8-inch baking dish.

2 In a skillet, sauté the apples in ¼ cup butter, turning frequently, for about 10 to 15 minutes or until light golden-brown.

3 In a bowl, blend 2 tablespoons of butter and the syrup.

4 Arrange the potatoes and the apples in the prepared baking dish in alternating rows. Top with half of the syrup, bake for about 30 minutes, and pour the remaining syrup over the top. Bake for an additional 20 minutes or until lightly browned. Remove from the oven and serve.

2 medium large acorn squash, stemmed, seeded and halved

1 package (about 9 ounces) sliced green beans in butter sauce, prepared

¼ cup walnuts or pine nuts, chopped

PANTRY

1 tablespoon butter or margarine

3 tablespoons honey

1 Position the rack in the center of the oven and preheat to 350 degrees F. Lightly grease a shallow baking dish.

2 Arrange the squash in the prepared baking dish cut side down. Bake for 30 to 40 minutes or until tender.

3 In a bowl, combine the beans, the honey, and the walnuts.

4 Turn the squash cut side up and stuff with the bean mixture. Bake for about 5 minutes or until thoroughly heated. Remove from the oven and serve.

BEAN-STUFFED SQUASH

makes about 4 servings

2 cups green peas, cooked and drained

4 medium potatoes, pared, cooked and sliced

¼ cup red bell peppers, chopped

PANTRY

2 tablespoons butter or margarine

Salt and pepper to taste

In a skillet, sauté the peas and the sliced potatoes in the butter, stirring frequently, for about 15 minutes or until the potatoes are light golden-brown. Remove from the heat, season to taste, top with the chopped peppers, and serve.

BHUGIA

makes about 4 to 6 servings

Pasta

SPAGHETTI PIE

There are probably as many different pasta sizes and shapes as there are ways to prepare them. Make sure to check the cooking times for the pasta you are preparing as they vary. Never overcook your pasta or it will turn into mush. Prepare it al dente (from "to the teeth").

Pasta is an enormously satisfying food that has gained tremendous popularity in the last decade. Italian restaurants have sprung up everywhere to serve the appetites of Americans for this Italian staple. You can prepare it at home quite simply. Here you'll find Pasta with Sweet Potatoes, a prized Italian combination; Soba Noodles with Garlic, a Japanese-style pasta; and

SOBA NOODLES WITH GARLIC

MACARONI SAUTÉ

Savory Noodles, where onions sautéed in butter do the trick. Each savory dish delivers its own satisfaction.

Special note: Always be sure you have lots of fresh Parmesan cheese on hand. It is delicious on a variety of pasta dishes.

ASPARAGUS NOODLE BAKE

akes about 2 servings

2 ounces cheddar cheese, cubed

¼ cup heavy cream

½ cup canned asparagus tips, drained

½ cup wide egg noodles, cooked and drained

¼ teaspoon nutmeg

1 Position the rack in the center of the oven and preheat to 350 degrees F. Have a baking or cookie sheet and two individual ramekins ready.

2 In a saucepan, combine the cheese and the cream. Cook, stirring frequently, for about 3 minutes or until the cheese has melted.

3 In a bowl, combine the asparagus, the noodles, and the cheese mixture. Spoon into the ramekins. Arrange on the baking sheet and bake for about 25 minutes or until the tops are a light golden-brown. Remove from the oven, sprinkle with the nutmeg, and serve.

BEEF AND MACARONI

makes about 4 to 6 servings

1 pound ground beef

1 package (7 ounces) macaroni, cooked and drained

½ cup Miracle Whip™

PANTRY

1 can (30 ounces) tomato sauce

In a skillet, sauté the beef for about 15 minutes or until lightly browned. Blend in the mayonnaise and the tomato sauce and cover. Simmer for about 10 minutes and add the macaroni. Cook for about 10 minutes or until thoroughly heated. Remove from the heat and serve.

Cooking note: For variation, use ground pork and beef mixed together and garnish with chopped mushrooms or olives.

1 package (8 ounces) spaghetti, cooked and drained
1 cup grated fresh Parmesan cheese
2 tablespoons fresh chives, snipped
1 loaf of Italian bread, sliced into serving-size pieces

PANTRY
¼ cup butter or margarine

In a saucepan, cook the spaghetti in the butter for about 3 minutes or until thoroughly heated. Add the cheese and the chives, and cook for about 3 to 4 minutes or until cheese has melted. Remove from the heat and serve with the bread on the side.

CHEESE AND CHIVE SPAGHETTI

makes about 4 servings

½ pound fresh shrimp, shelled and deveined
¼ cup ginger dressing
½ pound snow peas, cooked
2 tablespoons wine marinade
1 pound Shanghai noodles, cooked and drained, cut into 4-inch strands

PANTRY
1 tablespoon vegetable oil

1 In a bowl, combine the shrimp and the dressing. Cover with plastic wrap and refrigerate for about 1 hour.

2 In a wok, stir-fry the shrimp in the oil for about 7 minutes. Add the marinade, the noodles, and the peas. Stir-fry for about 5 minutes or until thoroughly heated. Remove from the heat and serve.

Cooking note: For variation, garnish with chopped scallions and cilantro.

CHINESE-STYLE PASTA SALAD WITH GINGER DRESSING

makes about 4 to 6 servings

1¼ cups light cream
½ cup cream cheese, at room temperature
2 cups small shell pasta, cooked and drained

PANTRY
1 tablespoon dried tarragon

In the top of a double boiler over boiling water, combine the cream, the cream cheese, and the tarragon. Add the pasta and cook for about 5 minutes or until thoroughly melted. Remove from the heat and serve.

CREAMY TARRAGON PASTA

makes about 4 servings

DESPERATE DAISY'S DINNER

makes about 4 servings

1 cup cooked broccoli florettes
2 cups wide egg noodles, cooked and drained

PANTRY

2 cups (bottled) tomato sauce
1 garlic clove, minced

In a saucepan, cook the tomato sauce and the garlic for about 5 minutes. Add the broccoli and the noodles, and cook for about 5 to 10 minutes or until thoroughly heated. Remove from the heat and serve.

EGGS AND MACARONI FLORENTINE

makes about 4 to 6 servings

10 ounces macaroni, cooked and drained
2 packages (10 ounces each) frozen chopped spinach, thawed and drained
4 hard-boiled eggs, quartered
½ cup grated cheddar cheese

PANTRY

1 tablespoon butter or margarine
Salt and pepper to taste

1 Position the rack in the center of the oven and preheat to 350 degrees F. Lightly grease a baking dish.

2 Layer the spinach, the macaroni, the hard-boiled eggs, and the cheese in the prepared baking dish.

3 Bake for about 25 minutes or until the cheese has melted. Remove from the oven and serve.

FETTUCCINE ALFREDO

makes about 4 servings

¾ cup grated Parmesan cheese
1 pound fettucini, cooked and drained
1 cup heavy cream

PANTRY

½ cup butter or margarine
Salt and pepper to taste

In a saucepan, combine the butter, the cream, and the cheese. Cook, on low heat, stirring frequently, for about 5 minutes or until the cheese has melted. Remove from the heat, season to taste, pour over the pasta, and serve.

2 cups pasta of choice, cooked and drained

1½ cups diced frozen fruit, thawed

1 cup Basic White Sauce (see page 398)

½ cup cherry tomatoes, quartered

In a bowl, combine the pasta, the fruit, the sauce, and the tomatoes. Cover with plastic wrap and refrigerate for at least 1 hour before serving.

Cooking note: This dish can also be served hot.

Fruit Filled Pasta

makes about 4 servings

---

4 cups broccoli florettes

1 pound fusilli, cooked and drained

PANTRY

⅓ cup olive oil

½ cup sliced garlic

Salt and pepper to taste

1 In a skillet, sauté the garlic in the oil for about 5 minutes or until tender. Add the broccoli and cook, stirring frequently, for about 7 minutes or until just tender.

2 In a bowl, combine the pasta and the broccoli. Season to taste and serve.

Cooking note: This dish can also be served hot.

Fusilli with Broccoli and Garlic

makes about 4 servings

¼ pound feta cheese, grated

1½ pounds spaghetti, cooked and drained

16 Greek Kalamata olives, pitted and chopped

PANTRY

1 stick (¼ pound) butter or margarine

1 In a saucepan, melt the butter and blend in the cheese. Cook for about 5 minutes or until thoroughly heated.

2 In a bowl, combine the pasta, the cheese sauce, the olives, and serve.

Cooking note: This dish can also be served hot.

Greek Makaronia

makes about 4 servings

Ham and Noodle Casserole

makes about 4 servings

1 package (8 ounces) noodles of choice, cooked and drained
1½ cups ham, cooked and diced
2 eggs, beaten

PANTRY
1 tablespoon butter or margarine
1½ cups milk
Salt and pepper to taste

1 Position the rack in the center of the oven and preheat to 350 degrees F. Lightly grease a baking dish.

2 In a bowl, using a wire whisk or an electric mixer, beat together the eggs and the milk.

3 Arrange alternating layers of noodles and ham in the prepared baking dish. Pour the milk and egg mixture over the top, and bake for about 20 minutes or until thoroughly heated. Remove from the oven, season to taste, and serve.

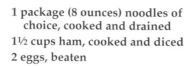

Lazy Lasagna Toss

makes about 4 servings

1 pound hot Italian sausages, casing removed and cut into bite-sized pieces
3 cups (canned) chunky style spaghetti sauce
Basic Parmesan Cheese Sauce (see page 398)
2½ cups cooked pasta shells or fusilli

PANTRY
1 teaspoon olive oil

1 In a skillet, sauté the sausage in the oil for about 5 minutes or until it loses its pinkish color. Drain and add the cheese sauce. Cook for about 3 minutes or until the sauce starts to bubble.

2 In a bowl, combine the shells and the sausage mixture. Top with the cheese sauce and serve.

Cooking note: For variation, garnish with snipped oregano leaves.

Macaroni and Broccoli au Gratin

makes about 4 to 6 servings

1 package (10 ounces) macaroni, cooked and drained
1½ cups blanched broccoli florettes, chopped
1 tablespoon pecans, chopped
½ cup grated cheddar cheese

PANTRY
1 tablespoon butter or margarine

1 Position the rack in the center of the oven and preheat to 350 degrees F. Lightly grease a baking dish.

2 In a bowl, combine the macaroni and broccoli.

3 Arrange the mixture in the prepared baking dish and top with the cheese. Bake for about 20 minutes or until thoroughly heated and the cheese has melted. Remove from the oven, garnish with chopped pecans, and serve.

2 cups elbow macaroni, cooked and drained

1 cup chicken, cooked and diced

1 can (10½ ounces) condensed cream of chicken soup

2 tablespoons white onions, diced

In a saucepan, combine the macaroni, the chicken, the soup, and the onions. Cook for about 10 minutes or until thoroughly heated. Remove from the heat and serve.

MACARONI CHICKEN DINNER

makes about 4 servings

---

1 package (7½ ounces) macaroni and cheese

1 can (16 ounces) chili beans, drained

1 can (10¾ ounces)cream of mushroom soup, prepared

1 can (3½ ounces) French's™ fried onions

PANTRY

1 tablespoon butter or margarine

½ cup milk

1 Position the rack in the center of the oven and preheat to 350 degrees F. Lightly grease a 10 x 6-inch baking pan.

2 Arrange the pasta in the prepared baking pan. Pour in the soup, add the beans, and top with the onions. Bake for about 30 minutes or until thoroughly heated. Remove from the oven and serve.

MACARONI CHILI CASSEROLE

makes about 4 to 6 servings

---

2 cups elbow macaroni, cooked and drained

1 can (15 ounces) chili with beans

1 can (10½ ounce) condensed tomato soup

In a saucepan, combine the macaroni, the beans, and the soup. Cook for about 10 minutes or until thoroughly heated. Remove from the heat and serve.

MACARONI CHILI DINNER

makes about 6 servings

Macaroni Sauté

makes about 4 to 6 servings

1 package (8 ounces) macaroni, cooked and drained

¼ cup leftover bacon or meat drippings

¼ cup broccoli florettes, blanched

PANTRY

1 tablespoon dried marjoram, crushed

Salt and pepper to taste

In a skillet, sauté the florettes in the oil for about 3 minutes or until tender. Add the macaroni and sprinkle on the marjoram. Cook for about 5 minutes or until thoroughly heated. Remove from the heat, season to taste, and serve.

Cooking note: For variation, use other vegetables instead of broccoli.

Maccheroni al Pomodoro

makes about 4 servings

½ pound macaroni, cooked and drained

1 pound tomatoes, quartered

1 small yellow onion, diced

1 sprig of sweet basil

PANTRY

1 tablespoon butter or margarine

1 In a saucepan, sauté the onion in the butter for about 5 minutes or until tender. Transfer to a warming plate.

2 In the same saucepan, combine the tomatoes and the basil, and simmer for about 1 hour or until the tomatoes are reduced to a soft pulp. Drain and work the pulp through a sieve.

3 Pour the tomato pulp back into the saucepan, blend in the onions, and cook for 5 minutes or until thoroughly heated. Remove from the heat, pour over the pasta, and serve.

4 cups wide egg noodles, cooked and drained

2 cups fresh asparagus, cut into 1-inch pieces, cooked and drained

PANTRY

⅓ cup butter or margarine

In a saucepan, combine the butter, the noodles, and the asparagus. Cook for about 10 minutes or until thoroughly heated. Remove from the heat and serve.

Noodles and Asparagus

makes about 4 servings

---

1 package (8 ounces) tagliatelle, cooked and drained

1 teaspoon fresh ground white pepper

⅓ cup grated fresh Parmesan cheese

PANTRY

¼ cup butter or margarine

In a saucepan, combine the butter, the noodles, and the white pepper. Cook for about 10 minutes or until thoroughly heated. Remove from the heat, top with the cheese, and serve.

Nouille Fraiches au Beurre

makes about 4 servings

---

6 thick bacon slices, chopped

1 package (10 ounces) spaghetti, cooked and drained

3 large eggs, beaten

PANTRY

1 garlic clove, minced

Salt and pepper to taste

1 In a large skillet, sauté the bacon and the garlic for about 15 minutes or until browned.

2 In a bowl, combine the bacon mixture, the pasta, and the eggs. Season to taste and serve.

Cooking note: Make sure the spaghetti is hot when the eggs are added.

Pasta Carbonara

makes about 4 servings

Pasta with Shrimp and Tomato

makes about 4 servings

1¼ pounds plum tomatoes, diced

16 large shrimp, cleaned and cooked

¼ cup fresh basil, snipped

1 package (10 ounces) spaghetti, cooked and drained

PANTRY

2 garlic cloves, minced

In a bowl, combine the tomatoes, the shrimp, the basil, and the garlic. Pour over the pasta and serve.

Pasta

Pasta with Vegetable Ribbons

makes about 4 servings

1 large carrot, trimmed, pared and cut into thin ribbons

1 medium zucchini, trimmed and cut into thin ribbons

1 package (8 ounces) tagliatelle

PANTRY

1 tablespoon butter or margarine, room temperature

Salt and pepper to taste

1 In a saucepan, bring 1 quart of lightly salted water to a boil. Add the pasta and cook, stirring occasionally, for about 10 minutes or until the pasta is al dente. Add the carrots and the zucchini, and cook for 1 minute. Drain.

2 In a bowl, combine the pasta, the vegetables, the butter. Season to taste and serve.

Pasta Smothered with Onions and Ham

makes about 4 to 6 servings

2 large onions, cut into thin rings

1 ham steak (about 1 to 1½ pounds), cut into bite-sized pieces

2 cups pasta of choice, cooked

¼ cup freshly grated Parmesan cheese

PANTRY

1 tablespoon butter or margarine

Oregano to taste

1 In a skillet, sauté the onions in the butter for about 5 minutes or until tender. Transfer to a warming plate.

2 In the same skillet, sauté the ham for about 15 minutes or until it loses its pinkish color. Stir in the onion and the oregano to taste.

3 Cook for about 10 minutes or until thoroughly heated. Remove from the heat, pour over the pasta, top with cheese, and serve.

Cooking note: For variation, garnish with chopped parsley, cilantro, or chives

⅓ cup dry sherry
1 package (10 ounces) spaghetti, cooked and drained
¼ cup grated cheese of choice

PANTRY
⅓ cup olive oil
1 garlic clove, minced
Salt and pepper to taste

In a saucepan, sauté the garlic in the oil for about 5 minutes or until tender. Stir in the pasta and the sherry, and season to taste. Cook for about 10 minutes or until thoroughly heated. Remove from the heat, top with cheese and serve.

PASTA WITH GARLIC AND SHERRY

makes about 4 servings

---

1 package (12 ounces) jumbo franks, cut into bite-sized pieces
½ cup (bottled) chili sauce
1 tablespoon prepared mustard
½ cup grape jelly
1 package (10 ounces) pasta of choice, cooked and drained

In a saucepan, combine the chili sauce, the mustard, and the jelly, and cook for about 5 minutes. Add the franks and the pasta. Cook for about 10 minutes or until thoroughly heated. Remove from the heat and serve.

PASTA WITH SPICY FRANKS

makes about 4 to 6 servings

---

1 package (10 ounces) frozen mixed vegetables, cooked and drained
½ cup cooked sweet potato, diced
¼ cup (bottled) fat-free dressing of choice
2 cups cooked shell pasta

PANTRY
Salt and pepper to taste

In a saucepan, combine the vegetables, the potatoes, the dressing, and the pasta. Cook over low heat for about 10 to 15 minutes or until thoroughly heated. Remove from the heat, season to taste, and serve.

Cooking note: For variation, top with grated Parmesan or Romano cheese.

PASTA WITH SWEET POTATOES

makes about 2 servings

Pasta with Tahini Sauce

makes about 4 servings

1 package (8 to 10 ounces) pasta of choice, cooked and drained

1 cup green peas, cooked and drained

6 tablespoons (bottled) tahini

1 tablespoon peanuts or toasted sesame seeds

In a bowl, combine the pasta, the peas, and the tahini. Garnish with peanuts or sesame seeds and serve.

Cooking note: For variation, add cooked shrimp.

Ramen Noodles with Chinese Cabbage

makes about 4 servings

½ cup sliced almonds, toasted

½ head of cabbage, thinly sliced

1 bunch scallions, trimmed and chopped

2 packages (2½ ounces each) chicken ramen noodles

PANTRY

½ cup rice vinegar

1 Cook the noodles according to the package directions (but do not use the seasoning package) and drain.

2 In a small bowl, blend the contents of the seasoning package and the vinegar.

3 In another bowl, combine the almonds, the cabbage, the scallions, and the noodles. Pour the vinegar mixture over the top and serve.

Savory Noodles

makes about 4 servings

½ cup white onion, minced

½ cup green bell pepper, minced

5 cups narrow noodles, cooked and drained

PANTRY

2 tablespoons butter or margarine

1 In a saucepan, sauté the onions in the butter for about 5 minutes or until translucent. Add the peppers and continue to cook, stirring frequently, for about 5 minutes, or until tender.

2 In a bowl, combine the noodles and the vegetables and serve.

1 package (10 ounces) frozen chopped spinach, thawed, cooked and drained

1 can (16 ounces) cannellini beans, rinsed and drained

1¼ cups pasta shells, cooked and drained

PANTRY

1 jar (16 ounces) tomato sauce

In a saucepan, combine the spinach, the beans, and the tomato sauce. Cook for about 5 minutes or until thoroughly heated. Remove from the heat, pour over the pasta, and serve.

Shells with Spinach and Beans

makes about 4 servings

½ package soba noodles, cooked and drained

1 package (1½ ounces) soup mix

2 tablespoons scallions, minced

1 tablespoon sesame seeds

PANTRY

1 large clove garlic, peeled and minced

In a small bowl, combine the pasta, the soup mix, the scallions and the garlic. Garnish with sesame seeds and serve.

Soba Noodles with Garlic

makes about 2 servings

---

1 package refrigerated pizza crust, uncooked

2 to 2½ cups leftover spaghetti with sauce

2 tablespoons sliced ripe olives

3 tablespoons grated cheese of choice

PANTRY

1 tablespoon butter or margarine

1 Position the rack in the center of the oven and preheat to 400 degrees F. Lightly grease a 9 x 5-inch loaf pan.

2 Shape the crust to fit the prepared loaf pan. Fill the crust with the spaghetti, and top with the olives and the cheese.

3 Bake for about 20 to 30 minutes or until the cheese has melted and the crust is light golden-brown. Remove from the oven, invert the pan onto a serving platter, slice, and serve.

Spaghetti Pie

makes about 4 to 6 servings

SPAGHETTI WITH BUTTER AND PARMESAN CHEESE

makes about 4 to 6 servings

1 pound spaghetti, cooked and drained

2 ounces grated Parmesan cheese

PANTRY

¼ cup melted butter or margarine

In a bowl, combine the pasta and the butter. Sprinkle with the cheese and serve.

SPANISH-STYLE PASTA WITH ONION SAUCE

makes about 4 to 6 servings

1½ pounds yellow onions, sliced

¼ cup Madeira

1 package (16 ounces) pasta of choice, cooked and drained

¼ cup grated Romano cheese

PANTRY

1 cup butter or margarine

1 tablespoon sugar

In a saucepan, sauté the onions in the butter for about 5 minutes or until tender. Add the sugar and cook over low heat, stirring occasionally, for about 1 hour. Add the wine and cook for about 3 minutes or until heated. Remove from the heat, pour over the pasta, sprinkle with the cheese, and serve.

THAI FETTUCINI

makes about 4 servings

1 can (14 ounces) Thai coconut milk

4 cups broccoli florettes, cooked and drained

1 large red bell pepper, stemmed, seeded and diced

1 package (8 ounces) fettucini, cooked al dente and drained

PANTRY

2 tablespoons curry powder

In a bowl, combine the coconut milk and the curry powder. Add the broccoli and the peppers. Pour over the pasta and serve.

Cooking note: More curry can be added for a spicier flavor.

1 package (8 ounces) spaghetti, cooked and drained
⅔ cup (canned) chicken broth
½ cup grated Parmesan or Romano cheese

PANTRY
5 tablespoons melted butter or margarine

In a saucepan, combine the butter, the pasta, and the broth. Cook for about 5 minutes or until thoroughly heated. Remove from the heat, sprinkle with the cheese, and serve.

WHITE SPAGHETTI

makes about 4 servings

¼ cup slivered almonds
1 package (8 ounces) medium egg noodles, cooked and drained
1 tablespoon poppy seeds

PANTRY
3 tablespoons butter or margarine

In a skillet, sauté the almonds in the butter for about 5 to 7 minutes or until browned. Add the pasta and the poppy seeds. Continue to cook for about 5 minutes or until thoroughly heated. Remove from the heat and serve.

ASIAN-STYLE ALMOND-POPPY NOODLES

makes about 4 servings

---

1 cup ham, cooked and chopped
1 cup cooked shrimp
1 package (10 ounces) frozen mixed vegetables, thawed and drained
2½ cups cooked pasta of choice

PANTRY
2 tablespoons sesame oil
Salt and pepper to taste

In a wok, stir-fry the ham in the oil for about 5 minutes or until well-coated with the oil. Add the shrimp, stir-fry for

about 1 minute and add the vegetables. Cook, stirring occasionally, for about 2 to 5 minutes or until the vegetables are just tender. Add the pasta and season to taste. Cook for about 10 minutes or until thoroughly heated. Remove from the heat and serve.

Cooking note: For variation, serve with Oriental-style sauce on the side.

HAM AND VEGGIE STIR-FRY

makes about 4 servings

Vegetables

Our heightened awareness of the great health benefits of eating vegetables has been matched by our inventiveness in designing mouthwatering vegetable recipes. From broccoli and Brussels sprouts to string beans and squash, in this chapter you'll find savory and satisfying dishes to suit the whole family. Today, vegetable dishes are not just a side dish, but the whole meal.

GREEK-STYLE GREEN BEANS

This abundantly filled chapter will thrill you with such delicious fare as Apple-Glazed Carrots, where apple jelly, mustard, and baby carrots are blended into something that tastes more like dessert than a vegetable side dish. And, since we never met an asparagus dish we didn't love, you'll find everything from Asparagus Rolls and Asparagus Parmesan to Asparagus with Cheese, to name

just a few. We also couldn't take our hands off of eggplant. Baked Eggplant and Tomatoes is as savory and succulent as it sounds. There are Baked Leeks Italiano, Baked Potatoes and Pears, and exotic dishes, such as Bhugia, where green peas, potatoes, and red bell peppers are sautéed in butter to savory perfection. Even the kids will be asking for seconds.

BAKED RED ONIONS

AUNTIE'S HOT PEPPERS

Apple-Glazed Carrots

makes about 4 servings

1 package (14½ ounces) baby carrots
¼ cup unsweetened apple juice
¼ cup apple jelly

PANTRY
1¼ teaspoons prepared mustard

In a saucepan, combine the carrots and the apple juice. Bring to a boil and reduce to a simmer. Cover and cook for about 5 to 7 minutes or until just tender. Remove the cover and continue to cook for about 10 minutes or until most of the liquid has evaporated. Blend in the jelly and the mustard. Cook, stirring occasionally, for about 5 minutes or until the jelly has melted and the carrots are glazed. Remove from the heat and serve.

Asparagus in Its Own Juice

makes about 2 to 4 servings

¾ pound fresh asparagus, trimmed and pared

PANTRY
2 tablespoons butter or margarine
Salt and pepper to taste

In a large saucepan, combine the butter and the asparagus and cover with water. Bring to a boil and cook, stirring occasionally, for about 20 minutes or until tender and the liquid has evaporated. Remove from the heat, season to taste and serve.

Asparagus Parmesan

makes about 4 to 6 servings

2 pounds fresh asparagus, trimmed and outer skin pared
2 ounces grated Parmesan cheese

PANTRY
2 tablespoons melted butter or margarine

1 Position the rack in the center of the oven and preheat to 350 degrees F. Lightly grease a baking sheet.

2 In a saucepan, cover the asparagus with water. Bring to a boil, cover, and cook for about 12 minutes or until just tender.

3 Arrange the asparagus on the prepared baking sheet, drizzle on the butter, and sprinkle with the cheese.

4 Bake for about 10 to 15 minutes or until the cheese is lightly browned. Remove from the oven and serve.

ASPARAGUS ROLLS

makes about 10 to 20 servings

20 slices of bread, crusts removed

1 jar (5 ounces) pimiento cheese spread

1 package (10 ounces) frozen asparagus spears, cooked and drained

Spread one side of the bread slices with the cheese and place an asparagus spear diagonally across. Pull up the corners of the bread and press firmly to seal. Wrap several of the rolls together in waxed paper or plastic wrap and refrigerate until ready to serve.

ASPARAGUS WITH CHEESE

makes about 4 servings

1 package (10 ounces) frozen asparagus spears, thawed and drained

½ cup shredded Swiss cheese

2 tablespoons pimiento, chopped

2 teaspoons sesame seeds, toasted

PANTRY

1 teaspoon salt

1 Position the rack in the center of the oven and preheat to 350 degrees F. Have an 8-inch square baking dish available.

2 In a skillet, cover the asparagus with lightly salted water. Bring to a boil and cook for about 10 minutes or until tender. Drain.

3 In a bowl, combine the asparagus, the cheese, and the pimiento.

4 Arrange in the baking dish and top with the sesame seeds. Bake for about 5 to 10 minutes or until the cheese has melted. Remove from the oven and serve.

Baked Beets with Onions

makes about 4 servings

4 cups beets, diced
1 cup yellow onions, chopped

PANTRY
¼ cup butter or margarine

1 Position the rack in the center of the oven and preheat to 375 degrees F. Lightly grease a 1½-quart baking dish.

2 In a bowl, combine the beets, the onions and the butter.

3 Arrange in the prepared baking dish, add ¼ cup of boiling water and cover. Bake for about 1 hour or until tender. Remove from the oven and serve.

Baked Carrots

makes about 4 to 6 servings

18 baby carrots
½ cup light-brown sugar

PANTRY
½ cup butter or margarine
⅓ teaspoon cinnamon
⅓ c. boiling water

1 Position the rack in the center of the oven and preheat to 350 degrees F. Have a baking dish available.

2 In a bowl, blend the butter, the sugar, the cinnamon and ⅓ cup of boiling water.

3 Arrange the carrots in the baking dish and pour the butter mixture over the top. Cover and bake for about 1 hour or until the carrots are just tender. Remove from the oven and serve.

Baked Carrot and Apple Casserole

makes about 6 servings

4 cups fresh carrots, cut into ½-inch pieces
3 cups apples, peeled and sliced
¼ teaspoon ground nutmeg

PANTRY
2 tablespoons butter or margarine
¼ cup honey

1 Position the rack in the center of the oven and preheat to 350 degrees F. Lightly grease a baking dish.

2 In a saucepan, combine the carrots and ½ cup of water. Cook over low heat for about 15 minutes or until tender. Drain.

3 In a bowl, combine the apples, the carrots, and the honey.

4 Arrange in the prepared baking dish, dot with the butter and cover. Bake for about 40 minutes or until the apples are tender. Remove from the oven, sprinkle with nutmeg, and serve.

1 package (8 ounces) carrots, trimmed, pared and diced

2 fennel bulbs, trimmed, pared and diced

PANTRY

2 tablespoons butter or margarine

1 Position the rack in the center of the oven and preheat to 400 degrees F. Lightly grease a baking pan.

2 In a saucepan, cover the carrots and the fennel with lightly salted water and bring to a boil. Cook for about 10 to 12 minutes or until tender. Drain, add the butter, and mash.

3 Arrange in the prepared baking pan and bake for about 10 minutes or until the top starts to form a crust. Remove from the oven and serve.

BAKED CARROTS AND FENNEL

makes about 4 servings

8 medium carrots, trimmed, pared, sliced and boiled

½ cup ham, cooked and diced

2 tablespoons heavy cream

PANTRY

2 tablespoons butter or margarine

Salt and pepper to taste

1 In a bowl, mash the carrots.

2 In another bowl, using a wire whisk or an electric mixer, blend the butter and the cream. Add the carrots and the ham, season to taste, and serve.

Cooking note: For variation, sprinkle a little brown sugar over the carrots.

BAKED CARROTS AND HAM

makes about 4 servings

4 heads of chicory, cored and sliced in half lengthwise

2 tablespoons safflower oil

PANTRY

2 teaspoons melted butter or margarine

2 tablespoons dried mixed herbs, crushed

1 Position the rack in the center of the oven and preheat to 400 degrees F. Lightly grease a large baking pan.

2 In a small bowl, blend the oil, the butter, and the mixed herbs.

3 Arrange the chicory in the prepared baking pan. Pour the oil and butter mixture over the top. Bake for about 30 to 40 minutes or until just tender and the leaves are light golden-brown. Remove from the oven and serve.

BAKED CHICORY

makes about 4 servings

Baked Eggplant and Tomatoes

makes about 4 to 6 servings

1 medium eggplant, trimmed and sliced

3 medium tomatoes, halved

3 tablespoons grated Parmesan cheese

PANTRY

⅓ cup olive oil

Salt and pepper to taste

1 Position the rack in the center of the oven and preheat to 350 degrees F. Lightly grease a shallow baking dish.

2 In a colander, sprinkle the eggplant slices with salt, set aside for about 30 minutes or until the eggplant has released its liquids, and pat dry.

3 In a skillet, sauté the eggplant in the oil, turning occasionally, for about 5 minutes or until browned.

4 Arrange in the prepared baking dish and add the tomato halves. Sprinkle with the Parmesan cheese and season to taste. Bake for about 15 minutes or until thoroughly heated. Remove from the oven and serve.

Baked Leeks Italiano

makes about 4 to 6 servings

3 leeks, green tops removed and bulb cut into bite-sized pieces

4 ounces Bel Paese cheese, sliced

PANTRY

4 tablespoons butter or margarine

2 cups milk

1 Position the rack in the center of the oven and preheat to 350 degrees F. Lightly grease a 1-quart baking dish.

2 In a saucepan, combine the butter, the milk, and the leeks. Cover and cook at a low simmer, stirring occasionally, for abut 20 minutes or until tender.

3 Arrange the leeks in the prepared casserole, cover with the cheese, and bake for about 10 minutes or until the cheese has melted. Remove from the oven and serve.

4 large yellow onions, cut partially into 8 wedges
4 teaspoons chicken bouillon granules

PANTRY
4 teaspoons butter or margarine
Salt and pepper to taste

1 Position the rack in the center of the oven and preheat to 350 degrees F. Lightly grease a 13 x 9-inch baking pan.

2 Arrange the onions, cut-side down, in the prepared baking pan.

3 Bake for about 30 minutes, turn the onions over and sprinkle the tops with the bouillon granules and the butter. Season to taste and continue to bake for about 10 to 15 minutes or until tender. Remove from the oven and serve.

BAKED ONION BLOOMS

makes about 4 servings

---

4 large red onions, cut partially into 8 wedges
¼ cup flavored bread crumbs

PANTRY
2 tablespoons butter or margarine
Salt and pepper to taste

1 Position the rack in the center of the oven and preheat to 350 degree F. Lightly grease a 13 x 9-inch baking pan.

2 Arrange the onions cut-side down in the prepared baking pan and dot with the butter. Sprinkle with the bread crumbs and season to taste. Bake for about 40 to 45 minutes or until the onions are tender. Remove from the oven and serve.

BAKED RED ONIONS

makes about 4 to 6 servings

---

2 pounds butternut squash, cleaned and cut into pieces
1 teaspoon fresh rosemary, finely chopped

PANTRY
2 tablespoons butter or margarine
2 tablespoons honey

1 Position the rack in the center of the oven and preheat to 375 degrees F. Lightly grease a 13 x 9-inch baking pan.

2 Arrange the squash cut-side down in the prepared baking pan. Bake for about 35 minutes or until tender.

3 In a bowl, blend the butter, the honey, and the rosemary.

4 Turn the squash pieces over and brush with the honey mixture. Continue to bake for about 20 minutes or until lightly browned. Remove from the oven and serve.

BAKED SQUASH WITH ROSEMARY AND HONEY

makes about 6 servings

BAKED SWISS CHARD

makes about 4 servings

½ pound Swiss chard, shredded
1 package (6 ounces) sliced Swiss cheese
6 tablespoons bread crumbs

PANTRY

3 tablespoons melted butter or margarine
1 tablespoon flour
Salt and pepper to taste

1 Position the rack in the center of the oven and preheat to 350 degrees F. Grease an 8-inch square baking pan, with 1 tablespoon of butter and sprinkle the bottom with 2 tablespoons of bread crumbs.

2 In the prepared pan, arrange the chard on top of the bread crumbs. Top with 2 tablespoons bread crumbs, add the cheese, sprinkle with the flour, and drizzle on 1 tablespoon of butter. Season to taste, top with the remaining bread crumbs and drizzle on the remaining butter. Bake about 15 minutes or until the cheese has melted and the chard is wilted. Remove from the oven and serve.

BAKED TOMATOES

makes about 2 servings

2 large plum tomatoes, cut in half lengthwise
1 tablespoon grated Parmesan cheese
1 cup bread crumbs

PANTRY

1 tablespoon butter or margarine
1 teaspoon crushed dried thyme

1 Position the rack in the center of the oven and preheat to 350 degrees F. Lightly grease an 8-inch square baking pan.

2 Arrange the tomatoes in the prepared baking pan cut-side up. Sprinkle with the cheese, the bread crumbs, and the thyme. Cover, bake for about 10 minutes, remove the cover and continue to bake for 10 minutes longer or until the cheese has melted. Remove from the oven and serve.

3 medium red onions, peeled
¼ cup balsamic vinegar
Butter-flavored cooking spray

PANTRY
Salt and pepper to taste

Balsamic Roasted Onions

makes about 4 servings

1 Position the rack in the center of the oven and preheat to 375 degrees F. Lightly grease an 8-inch square baking dish.

2 Lightly coat the outside of the onion with the butter-flavored cooking spray and season to taste.

3 Arrange the onions as close as possible to one another in the prepared baking dish. Bake for about 70 minutes or until tender. Transfer the onions to a warming plate.

4 Add ¼ cup of water to the baking dish and stir to loosen the sediment. Place the pan over a low heat and add the vinegar. Continue to cook, stirring frequently, for about 2 to 3 minutes or until the mixture starts to thicken.

5 Cut the onions in half lengthwise, brush the cut surface with the gravy, season to taste and serve.

---

2 large beefsteak tomatoes, cut in half crosswise, juice and seeds removed
½ teaspoon fresh basil leaves, snipped

PANTRY
2 tablespoons olive oil
Salt and pepper to taste

Barbecued Tomatoes

makes about 4 servings

1 Position the grill about 4 inches from the heat. Lightly grease a shallow baking dish that can go over direct heat.

2 Arrange the tomatoes on the prepared dish and drizzle with the oil.

3 Place the dish at the edge of the grill and cook for about 10 minutes or until thoroughly heated. Remove from the grill, season to taste, garnish with snipped basil, and serve.

Cooking note: Cooking time for grilling recipes depends on the heat source.

Bean-Stuffed Squash

makes about 4 servings

2 medium large acorn squash, stemmed, seeded and halved

1 package (about 9 ounces) sliced green beans in butter sauce, prepared

¼ cup walnuts or pine nuts, chopped

PANTRY

1 tablespoon butter or margarine

3 tablespoons honey

1 Position the rack in the center of the oven and preheat to 350 degrees F. Lightly grease a shallow baking dish.

2 Arrange the squash in the prepared baking dish cut-side down. Bake for 30 to 40 minutes or until tender.

3 In a bowl, combine the beans, the honey, and the walnuts.

4 Turn the squash cut-side up and stuff with the bean mixture. Bake for about 5 minutes or until thoroughly heated. Remove from the oven and serve.

Beets Tokay

makes about 4 to 6 servings

2 cans (16 ounces each) sliced beets

1½ cups Basic White Sauce (see page 398)

½ cup celery, diced

1 cup seed Tokay grape halves, seeded

PANTRY

1 tablespoon butter or margarine

1 Position the rack in the center of the oven and preheat to 350 degrees F. Lightly grease a shallow baking dish.

2 In a bowl, combine the beets, the sauce, the celery, and the grapes. Pour into the prepared baking dish, cover and bake for about 25 minutes or until thoroughly heated. Remove from the oven and serve.

Blushing Onions

makes about 4 servings

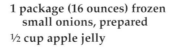

1 package (16 ounces) frozen small onions, prepared

½ cup apple jelly

PANTRY

¼ cup (bottled) chili sauce

1 tablespoon butter or margarine

1 In a bowl, combine the onion, the jelly, and the chili sauce.

2 In a saucepan, melt the butter and blend in the onion mixture. Bring to a boil and reduce to a simmer. Cook for about 10 minutes or until tender. Remove from the heat and serve.

1 can (29 ounces) sauerkraut,
   washed and drained
1 cup beer
¼ teaspoon caraway seeds

PANTRY
1 tablespoon butter or margarine

BOHEMIAN SAUERKRAUT

makes about 6 servings

1 Position the rack in the center of the oven and preheat to 375 degrees F. Lightly grease a 1½-quart baking dish.

2 Arrange the sauerkraut in the prepared baking dish, drizzle on the beer, sprinkle with the caraway seeds and cover. Bake for about 15 to 20 minutes or until thoroughly heated. Remove from the oven and serve.

---

6 medium-sized artichokes,
   stemmed, outer leaves
   trimmed
1 lemon slice
½ cup salad dressing of choice

BOILED ARTICHOKES

makes about 4 to 6 servings

In a saucepan, cover the artichokes with lightly salted water. Add the lemon slice, bring to a boil and cover. Cook for about 15 to 20 minutes or until just tender. Remove from the heat and serve with the salad dressing on the side.

Cooking note: When the artichokes are done, the outer leaves will pull away easily.

269

Vegetables

1½ pounds bok choy
3 tablespoons peanut oil

PANTRY
⅓ teaspoon salt
4 garlic cloves, diced

BOK CHOY IN GARLIC OIL

makes about 4 servings

1 In a bowl, combine the bok choy, the salt, and the garlic.

2 In a wok, stir-fry the bok choy in the oil for about 15 minutes or until wilted. Remove from the heat and serve.

Braised Belgian Endive

makes about 4 to 8 servings

8 medium heads Belgian endive, cut in half lengthwise

½ cup chicken broth

PANTRY

3 tablespoons butter or margarine

2 tablespoons canola oil

In a large skillet, heat the butter and the oil. Add the endive and cook for about 15 minutes or until the outer leaves are browned on both sides. Add the broth and cover. Cook for about 10 to 15 minutes or until the liquid has almost evaporated. Remove from the heat, top with the remaining liquid, and serve.

Braised Celery Hearts

makes about 4 servings

4 celery hearts, washed and trimmed

¾ cup canned chicken stock

¼ cup dry white wine

PANTRY

2 tablespoons butter or margarine

Salt and pepper to taste

1 In a saucepan, cover the celery with lightly salted water, bring to a boil, and cook for about 5 minutes or until just tender. Drain and pat dry.

2 In a skillet, sauté the celery in the butter, turning occasionally, for about 5 to 10 minutes or until golden-brown. Add the stock and the wine, season to taste, and cover. Simmer for about 20 minutes or until thoroughly heated. Remove from the heat, transfer celery to a serving platter, top with a little of the stock, and serve.

Braised Cucumbers

makes about 3 to 4 servings

1 teaspoon beef bouillon granules

3 medium cucumbers, peeled, cut in half lengthwise and in half crosswise

PANTRY

2 tablespoons butter or margarine

1 In a small bowl, blend the bouillon granules and 1 tablespoon of boiling water.

2 In a skillet, sauté the cucumber in the butter, turning occasionally, until lightly browned. Add the bouillon, reduce to a low simmer, and cover. Cook for about 5 minutes or until tender. Remove from the heat and serve.

8 leeks, trimmed, to about 8
   inches and partly cut
   lengthwise
1 tablespoon dry white wine
¼ cup parsley

PANTRY
4 tablespoons butter or
   margarine

BRAISED LEEKS
makes about 4 servings

1 Position the rack in the center of the oven and preheat to 350 degrees F. Lightly grease a shallow baking pan.

2 Place the leeks in the prepared baking pan, dot with 3 tablespoons of the butter, and fill the pan halfway with water. Transfer to the stove top and bring to a boil. Add the wine and cover.

3 Bake for about 30 minutes or until tender. Remove from the oven, drain, top with the remaining butter, garnish with parsley, and serve.

---

1 pound fresh squash, diced
1 stalk leek

PANTRY
4 tablespoons vegetable oil
1 tablespoon sugar

BRAISED SQUASH
makes about 4 servings

In a skillet, sauté the squash in the oil for about 10 minutes or until tender. Add the leek, the sugar, and ½ cup of water. Bring to a boil and reduce to a simmer. Cover and cook for about 10 minutes or until thoroughly heated. Remove from the heat, drain, and serve.

---

1 pound fresh white button
   mushrooms
1 pound fresh broccoli florettes
2 cups (bottled) Italian dressing

BROCCOLI AND MUSHROOMS
makes about 4 servings

1 In a 3-quart microwave-proof baking dish, combine the broccoli and ¼ cup boiling water. Cover and microwave on high heat for about 1 minute. Drain and rinse in cold water.

2 In a bowl, combine the broccoli, the mushrooms, and the dressing. Cover with plastic wrap and refrigerate, turning several times, for at least 8 hours before serving.

BROILED TOMATOES

makes about 6 servings

4 large firm tomatoes, halved
½ cup grated Parmesan cheese

PANTRY
4 tablespoons melted butter or
    margarine
1 teaspoon dried oregano,
    crushed

1 Position the broiler rack about 4 inches from the heat. Lightly grease a shallow baking pan.

2 In the prepared baking pan, arrange the tomatoes cut-side up. Drizzle with the butter and sprinkle with the oregano and the cheese. Broil for about 5 minutes or until the cheese has melted. Remove from the oven and serve.

BROWN SUGAR GLAZED SQUASH

makes about 6 servings

4 cups squash, cubed
1½ tablespoons packed brown
    sugar
2 tablespoons lemon juice

PANTRY
⅓ cup melted butter or
    margarine
Salt and pepper to taste

1 Position the rack in the center of the oven and preheat to 400 degrees F. Lightly grease a shallow baking pan.

2 In a bowl, combine the squash, the butter, the sugar, and the lemon juice and season to taste.

3 Arrange in the prepared baking pan, cover, and bake for about 20 minutes. Remove the cover and bake for an additional 15 minutes or until tender. Remove from the oven and serve.

BROWN SUGAR GLAZED SWEET POTATOES

makes about 6 servings

6 sweet potatoes, boiled, pared
    and halved
1 cup brown sugar, firmly
    packed

PANTRY
2 tablespoons butter or
    margarine

1 Position the rack in the center of the oven and preheat to 375 degrees F. Lightly grease a baking dish.

2 In a bowl, combine the sugar and enough water to make a syrupy mixture.

3 Arrange the sweet potatoes on the prepared baking dish. Pour syrup over, dot with butter, and cover. Bake for about 10 minutes and remove the cover. Continue to bake, basting for about 10 minutes or until the potatoes are glazed. Remove from the oven and serve.

1 pound Jerusalem artichokes, trimmed, pared and thinly sliced

PANTRY
2 tablespoons butter or margarine
Salt and pepper to taste

In a skillet, sauté the artichokes in the butter for about 6 to 7 minutes or until tender and lightly browned. Remove from the heat, season to taste, and serve.

BROWNED JERUSALEM ARTICHOKES

makes about 3 to 4 servings

---

12 medium fresh Brussels sprouts, trimmed

PANTRY
1 tablespoon butter or margarine
⅛ teaspoon white pepper

1 Cut an "X" into the base of each sprout.

2 In a saucepan, cover the sprouts with 1½ cups of water. Bring to a boil and reduce to a simmer. Cover

and cook for about 10 minutes or until tender. Drain, cool slightly, and slice in half lengthwise.

3 In a saucepan, cook the sprouts over medium heat for about 10 minutes or until lightly browned. Remove from the heat, transfer to a serving plate, pour the butter over, season with the white pepper, and serve.

BRUSSELS SPROUTS

makes about 2 servings

---

2 packages (10 ounces each) frozen Brussels sprouts, thawed and drained
⅓ cup grated Monterey Jack or Tillamook cheese
1½ cups hot Mornay Sauce (see page 413)

PANTRY
1 tablespoon melted butter or margarine

1 Position the broiler rack about 6 inches from the heat. Have a 1½-quart baking dish available.

2 Arrange the sprouts in the prepared baking dish, pour on the sauce, sprinkle with the cheese, and drizzle on the butter.

3 Broil for about 4 to 5 minutes or until lightly toasted on top. Remove from the broiler and serve.

BRUSSELS SPROUTS AU GRATIN

makes about 6 servings

BRUSSELS SPROUTS IN BEER

makes about 6 to 8 servings

2 pounds Brussels sprouts, trimmed
6 bacon strips
½ cup beer or ale

PANTRY
2 garlic cloves, minced

1 Position the rack in the center of the oven and preheat to 350 degrees F.

2 Cut an "X" into the base of each sprout.

3 In a saucepan, cover the sprouts with lightly salted water. Bring to a boil and cook for about 1 minute. Drain and dip into cold water bath. Drain, pat dry and cut into halves lengthwise.

4 In an oven-proof skillet, sauté the bacon for about 5 minutes or until it loses its pinkish color. Add the sprouts and cook for 5 minutes or until thoroughly heated. Pour in the beer, bring to a boil and reduce to a simmer. Cover and cook for about 4 minutes or until tender.

5 Bake for about 15 minutes or until the bacon is crisp. Remove from the oven and serve.

BRUSSELS SPROUTS IN PECAN SAUCE

makes about 2 to 4 servings

1 pound fresh Brussels sprouts, trimmed
¼ cup chopped pecans

PANTRY
3 tablespoons butter or margarine
Salt and pepper to taste

1 Cut an "X" into the base of each sprout.

2 In a saucepan, cover the sprouts with lightly salted water. Bring to a boil and cook for about 10 minutes or until tender. Drain and transfer to a warming plate.

3 In a skillet, cook the sprouts in the butter for about 10 minutes or until lightly browned. Add the pecans and cook for about 2 minutes or until thoroughly heated. Remove from the heat, pour the sauce from the skillet over, season to taste, and serve.

1 package (10 ounces) frozen
  baby Brussels sprouts in
  butter sauce
⅓ cup crumbled blue cheese
1 tablespoon bacon bits

BRUSSELS SPROUTS WITH BLUE CHEESE

makes about 3 servings

1 Position the grill about 4 inches from the heat.

2 Place the sprouts on a large piece of aluminum foil. Pull up the four edges, seal, and puncture the top with little holes.

3 Place on the grill and cook for about 30 minutes or until tender and slightly browned. Remove from the grill, open the foil, sprinkle the sprouts with cheese and bacon bits, and serve.

Cooking note: Cooking time for grilling recipes depends on the heat source.

3 shallots, peeled and minced
1½ pounds Brussels sprouts,
  trimmed and separated into
  leaves

PANTRY
3 tablespoons butter or
  margarine

BRUSSELS SPROUTS WITH SHALLOTS

makes about 6 to 8 servings

In a skillet, sauté the shallots in the butter for about 10 minutes or until tender. Add the Brussels sprout leaves and stir-fry for about 5 minutes or until just tender. Remove from the heat and serve.

2 cups small Brussels sprouts,
  trimmed and cut in half
¼ cup walnuts, chopped
¼ teaspoon ground nutmeg

PANTRY
1 tablespoon butter or margarine

BRUSSELS SPROUTS WITH WALNUTS

makes about 4 servings

In a bamboo steamer over boiling water, steam the sprouts for about 7 to 8 minutes or until tender. Remove from the heat, add the walnuts and the nutmeg, and serve.

Buddhist Mock Fish

makes about 4 servings

1 large potato, pared and thinly sliced
1 small white onion, thinly sliced
½ pound snow peas
10 woodear mushrooms, soaked, trimmed and sliced

PANTRY
2 tablespoons vegetable oil
1 teaspoon sugar
Salt and pepper to taste

In a skillet, sauté the onions in the oil for about 5 minutes or until translucent. Add the peas and the mushrooms, and stir-fry for about 1 minute. Season to taste and add the sugar. Add ⅓ cup of water and bring to a boil. Continue to cook for about 7 minutes or until the peas are just tender. Add the potatoes and cook for about 15 minutes or until thoroughly heated. Remove from the heat and serve.

Butter-Fried Parsnips

makes about 4 servings

2 pounds fresh parsnips, trimmed, pared and diced
¼ teaspoon nutmeg

PANTRY
¼ cup butter or margarine
Salt and pepper to taste

1 In a saucepan, cover the parsnips with lightly salted water. Bring to a boil and cook for about 20 to 25 minutes or until tender.

2 In a skillet, sauté the parsnips in the butter for about 5 minutes or until lightly browned Sprinkle with the nutmeg and cook for about 2 minutes or until thoroughly heated. Remove from the heat, season to taste, and serve.

Buttery Peas and Zucchini

makes about 2 servings

1 package (10 ounces) frozen peas in butter sauce, prepared
1 medium zucchini, trimmed and cut into strips
1 tablespoon dried pimiento

PANTRY
Salt and pepper to taste

In a skillet, cook the zucchini in 2 tablespoons of water for about 5 minutes, stirring and turning until the water has evaporated and the zucchini is just tender. Add the peas and pimiento, season to taste, and serve.

3 large Shiitake mushrooms

2 medium cakes tofu, drained

1 pound cabbage, cored and sliced

3 tablespoons (bottled) Mirin sauce

PANTRY

3 tablespoons sesame oil

3 tablespoons soy sauce

1 In a bowl, cover the mushrooms with hot water and set aside for about 30 minutes. Drain. Trim and cut into ¼-inch strips.

2 In a wok, stir-fry the cabbage and the mushrooms for about 1 to 2 minutes or until the cabbage is wilted. Reduce the heat and crumble the tofu over the top. Add the soy sauce and the Mirin sauce. Continue to cook, stirring occasionally, for about 5 minutes or until thoroughly heated. Remove from the heat and serve.

CABBAGE AND BEAN CURD

makes about 4 to 6 servings

---

2 cups frozen lima beans, thawed and drained

2 cups frozen whole kernel corn, drained

¼ cup almonds, blanched and slivered

¼ cup chopped ripe olives

PANTRY

2 tablespoons butter or margarine

1 In a saucepan, cover the beans with lightly salted water. Bring to a boil and cook for about 10 minutes. Add the corn and simmer for an additional 10 minutes or until the vegetables are tender.

2 In a skillet, sauté the almonds in the butter for about 10 minutes or until toasted. Add the vegetables and the olives. Cook for about 5 minutes or until thoroughly heated. Remove from the heat and serve.

CALIFORNIA SUCCOTASH

makes about 4 to 6 servings

1½ pounds fresh parsnips, trimmed, pared, cooked, and quartered

PANTRY

3 tablespoons butter or margarine

3 tablespoons clover honey

1 In a large saucepan, melt the butter and the honey over low heat.

2 Add the parsnips, stir until coated, and cover. Simmer over low heat for about 5 minutes or until thoroughly heated. Remove from the heat and serve.

CANDIED PARSNIPS

makes about 4 to 6 servings

CANDIED SWEET POTATOES

makes about 4 to 6 servings

6 sweet potatoes, pared and cut into slices

1½ cups brown sugar, firmly packed

PANTRY

¼ teaspoon salt

1 Position the rack in the center of the oven and preheat to 350 degrees F.

2 Arrange the potato slices in a heavy skillet and add 1½ cups of water. Add the sugar and the salt and cover. Bake for about 30 minutes. Remove the cover and continue to bake for about 30 minutes or until the liquid has evaporated. Remove from the oven and serve.

CARROT AND TURNIP CASSEROLE

makes about 4 servings

3 medium carrots, trimmed, pared and cut into julienne strips

2 medium turnips, trimmed, pared and cubed

1 cup Basic White Sauce (see page 398)

½ cup bread crumbs

PANTRY

1 tablespoon butter or margarine

Salt to taste

1 Position the rack in the center of the oven and preheat to 350 degrees F. Lightly grease a baking dish.

2 In a saucepan, cover the carrots and the turnips with lightly salted water, and cook for about 15 minutes or until tender.

3 Arrange the carrots and turnips in the prepared baking dish and pour the sauce over the top. Sprinkle with the bread crumbs and bake for about 10 to 12 minutes or until the bread crumbs are toasted. Remove from the oven and serve.

CARROT MASHED POTATOES

makes about 4 servings

3 medium potatoes, pared, diced and boiled

1 medium carrot, trimmed, pared and sliced

PANTRY

1 tablespoon butter or margarine

½ cup milk

Salt and pepper to taste

1 In the container of a blender or food processor, combine the carrots and ½ cup of boiling water. Process on high speed until chopped.

2 In a bowl, combine the potatoes, the carrots, the milk, and the butter, and mash until smooth. Season to taste and serve.

4 large carrots, trimmed, pared and sliced
1 cup dark ale or stout

PANTRY
1 tablespoon butter or margarine
1 teaspoon sugar
Salt and pepper to taste

In a saucepan, combine the butter, the carrots and the ale. Bring to a boil and reduce to a simmer. Cook, stirring frequently, for about 10 minutes or until tender. Blend in the sugar, season to taste, and serve.

CARROTS IN ALE

makes about 4 servings

1½ cups carrots, sliced, boiled and drained
½ cup sweetened apple cider
1 cup light cream or half and half

PANTRY
2 tablespoons butter or margarine
2 tablespoons flour
1 tablespoon sugar
Salt and pepper to taste

1 In the top of a double boiler over boiling water, melt the butter, blend in the flour and stir to make a roux.

2 Blend in the cream and the cider over direct heat and bring to a boil. Cook, stirring frequently, for about 10 minutes or until thickened. Add the carrots and the sugar, and season to taste. Cover and cook for about 15 minutes or until thoroughly heated. Remove from the heat and serve.

CARROTS IN CREAMED SWEET CIDER

makes about 4 servings

---

1 pound carrots, trimmed, pared and thinly sliced
1 teaspoon light-brown sugar
1 tablespoon fresh thyme, snipped
2 teaspoons fresh parsley, snipped

PANTRY
1 tablespoon butter

In a saucepan, cover the carrots with lightly salted water. Bring to a boil, add the sugar, and stir until dissolved. Reduce to a simmer and cook for about 12 to 15 minutes or until just tender. Drain. Blend in the butter, the thyme, and the parsley, and serve.

CARROTS WITH THYME AND PARSLEY

makes about 4 servings

CARROTS WITH VINEGAR

makes about 4 servings

1½ pounds carrots, trimmed, pared and diced
¼ cup yellow onions, minced

PANTRY

3 tablespoons red wine vinegar
½ teaspoon dried basil, crushed
Salt and pepper to taste

In a microwave-proof dish, combine the carrots and the onion. Add the vinegar and the basil, and cover. Microwave on high heat, stirring occasionally, for about 10 minutes. Uncover and continue to microwave on high heat for an additional 5 minutes or until the liquid has evaporated and the vegetables are just tender. Remove from the oven, season to taste, and serve.

CAULIFLOWER IN CREAMED CIDER

makes about 4 servings

1½ cups cauliflower florettes, boiled and drained
1 cup heavy cream
½ cup unsweetened apple cider

PANTRY

2 tablespoons butter
2 tablespoons flour
1 tablespoon sugar
Salt and pepper to taste

1 In the top of a double boiler over boiling water, melt the butter, blend in the flour, and stir to make a roux.

2 Blend in the cream, the sugar, and the cider.

3 Cook over boiling water, stirring frequently, for about 10 minutes or until thickened. Add the cauliflower, season to taste, and cover. Cook for about 15 minutes or until tender. Remove from the heat and serve.

CAVOLFIORE ALLA ROMANA

makes about 4 to 6 servings

1 head of cauliflower, trimmed and separated into florettes
1 teaspoon fresh oregano, snipped

PANTRY

2 tablespoons olive oil
2 garlic cloves, chopped
2 tablespoons (canned) tomato sauce

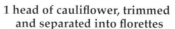
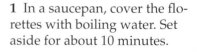

1 In a saucepan, cover the florettes with boiling water. Set aside for about 10 minutes.

2 In a skillet, sauté the garlic in the oil for about 5 minutes or until tender. Add the oregano and the cauliflower. Stir-fry for about 5 minutes or until slightly browned. Blend in the tomato sauce, remove from the heat, sprinkle with the cheese, and serve.

1 large celery, leaves removed and trimmed
2 tablespoons chives, minced
2 tablespoons (bottled) Italian dressing

1 Separate the stalks and cut diagonally into slices.

2 In a saucepan, cover the celery with lightly salted water. Bring to a boil and cook for ˌ ˌut 10 minutes or until te ˌ . Drain. Remove from ˌ ˌat, blend in the chiv ˌ ˌl the dressing, an ˌ ˌe.

CELERY WITH CHIVES

makes about 4 servings

---

1 bunch of chard, broken into small pieces
2 tablespoons heavy cream

PANTRY
1 tablespoon melted butter or margarine
Salt and pepper to taste

1 In a small bowl, blend the butter and the cream, and season to taste.

2 In a bamboo steamer over boiling water, steam the chard for about 5 minutes or until wilted. Remove from the heat, top with the cream mixture, and serve.

CHARD À LA CREME

makes about 4 servings

---

1 can (14½ ounces) asparagus spears
1 can (10½ ounces) cheddar cheese soup
2 hardboiled eggs, chopped
1 cup buttered bread crumbs
½ cup almonds or pecans, chopped

PANTRY
1 tablespoon butter or margarine

1 Position the rack in the center of the oven and preheat to 375 degrees F. Lightly grease a 1-quart baking dish.

2 In a bowl, combine the asparagus, the soup, the eggs, and ½ cup of the bread crumbs.

3 Pour into the prepared baking dish and top with the remaining bread crumbs and the almonds. Bake for about 20 minutes or until thoroughly heated. Remove from the oven and serve.

CHEESY ASPARAGUS

makes about 2 servings

CHEESY QUICK POTATOES

makes about 4 servings

1 package (4 ounces) instant mashed potatoes
½ cup shredded mild cheddar cheese

Prepare the potatoes according to the package directions, stir in the cheese while still hot, and serve.

CHILLED CUCUMBERS WITH RED RADISHES

makes about 6 to 8 servings

5 small cucumbers, peeled, trimmed and cubed
16 red radishes, stemmed, trimmed and halved
1 tablespoon Honey Soy Sauce (see page 405)

PANTRY
¼ cup vegetable oil
3 tablespoons (bottled) rice vinegar

1 In a skillet, sauté the cucumbers and the radishes in the oil for about 5 minutes. Blend in the soy sauce and the vinegar. Continue to cook for about 2 to 3 minutes or until just tender.

2 Pour into a bowl, cover with plastic wrap, and refrigerate for about 4 hours before serving.

CHINESE CABBAGE WITH SHEEP'S CHEESE

makes about 4 servings

1 cup red onion, chopped
2½ cups Chinese cabbage, sliced
½ cup sheep's cheese, diced
¼ cup peanut oil

PANTRY
1 tablespoon rice vinegar
1 tablespoon dried thyme
Salt and pepper to taste

1 In a wok, stir-fry the onions and in the oil for about 5 minutes or until translucent.

2 In a bowl, combine the onions, the thyme, the vinegar, the cabbage, and the cheese, and season to taste. Cover with plastic wrap and refrigerate for at least 1 hour before serving.

3 medium cucumbers, peeled, trimmed and cut into strips

PANTRY

3 tablespoons soy sauce
1 teaspoon sesame oil

In a bowl, combine the cucumbers, the soy sauce, and the oil. Cover with plastic wrap and refrigerate for at least 2 hours before serving.

Chinese Chilled Cucumbers

makes about 4 servings

---

1 package (3½ ounces) ramen noodles, carefully separated
1 bunch scallions, trimmed and chopped
¼ cup sunflower seeds, toasted
1 package (8 ounces) prepared cole slaw

PANTRY

2 tablespoons vegetable oil
2 tablespoons red wine vinegar

1 In a skillet, sauté the noodles in the oil for about 10 minutes or until lightly browned. Transfer to a warming plate.

2 In the same skillet, sauté the scallions and the sunflower seeds for about 5 minutes or until the scallions are tender. Transfer to a warming plate.

3 In a bowl, combine the cole slaw, the noodles, the scallions, and the seeds. Sprinkle with the vinegar and serve.

Chinese Cole Slaw

makes about 4 to 6 servings

---

2 cans (16 ounces each) green beans, drained
1 can (10¾ ounces) cream of celery soup
1 can (16 ounces) bean sprouts, drained
1 can (3 ounces) French's™ fried onion rings

PANTRY

1 tablespoon butter or margarine

1 Position the rack in the center of the oven and preheat to 350 degrees F. Lightly grease a 2-quart baking dish.

2 Arrange the green beans in the prepared baking dish, and add the soup and the bean sprouts. Bake for about 30 minutes, top with onion rings, and bake for an additional 5 minutes or until the rings are golden-brown. Remove from the oven and serve.

Chinese Green Bean Casserole

makes about 8 to 10 servings

CHINESE TARO BALLS

makes about 4 to 6 servings

1 pound taro root, pared and grated
1 tablespoon rice flour
2 tablespoons rice wine

PANTRY
1 cup vegetable oil
1 tablespoon cornstarch or arrowroot

1 In a bowl, combine the taro root, the flour, the cornstarch and the wine. Pinch off small pieces of dough and roll into balls.

2 In a wok, stir-fry the balls in the oil for about 10 minutes until crisp and golden-brown. Transfer to a rack covered with paper towels, drain, and serve.

Cooking note: This dish can be served warm or cold.

BRUSSELS SPROUTS AND CHIVES

makes about 6 servings

2 packages (10 ounces each) baby Brussels sprouts in butter sauce, prepared
2 teaspoons prepared mustard
2 tablespoons chives, chopped

In a bowl, combine the sprouts, the mustard, and the chives, and serve.

CORN AND OKRA

makes about 4 servings

4 tablespoons leftover bacon drippings
1½ cups fresh okra, sliced
1 small white onion, minced
2 cups fresh whole kernel corn

In a skillet, cook the okra, the onion, and the corn in the bacon drippings. Cook on low heat for about 10 to 12 minutes. Add 1 cup of water and cover. Cook for about 20 minutes or until tender. Remove from the heat, drain, and serve.

2 pounds Jerusalem artichokes, cleaned, pared and cut into ½-inch slices

2 pounds potatoes, pared, cooked and mashed

½ cup grated cheese of choice

PANTRY

1 tablespoon butter or margarine

1 tablespoon flour

1 Position the rack in the center of the oven and preheat to 400 degrees F. Lightly grease a pie plate.

2 In a saucepan, cover the artichokes with lightly salted water. Bring to a boil and cook for 5 to 10 minutes or until tender. Drain, reserving the water.

3 In a saucepan, melt the butter, blend in the flour, and stir to make a roux. Stir in about 1 cup of the reserved water and bring to a boil. Cook, stirring constantly, for about 10 minutes or until thickened.

4 Line the prepared pie plate with the mashed potatoes to form a crust. Place the artichokes in the crust and top with the sauce and the cheese.

5 Bake for about 25 minutes or until lightly browned. Remove from the oven and serve.

CHOKE PIE

makes about 4 servings

16 small yellow onions

¼ cup chicken broth

PANTRY

1 teaspoon sugar

Salt and pepper to taste

3 tablespoons butter or margarine

1 Position the rack in the center of the oven and preheat to 450 degrees F. Lightly grease a shallow baking pan.

2 In a saucepan, combine the broth and butter, stirring until the butter is melted.

3 Trim the bottom of each onion horizontally. Make vertical cuts from the top of each onion to the bottom, ¼ inch apart, all the way around the onion. Arrange the onions in the prepared baking pan, and sprinkle with the sugar and season to taste. Pour the broth over the top and cover. Bake for about 45 minutes or until tender. Remove from the oven and serve.

Cooking note: The baking pan must be large enough to allow for the onion flowers to spread open.

CHRYSANTHEMUM ONIONS

makes about 8 servings

CORN ON THE COB WITH HONEY MUSTARD SAUCE

makes about 6 servings

1 package (six ears) frozen corn on the cob, prepared

½ cup (bottled) honey mustard sauce

1 tablespoon fresh parsley, chopped

PANTRY

1 tablespoon melted butter or margarine

In a small bowl, blend the mustard sauce, the butter, and the parsley. Brush on the corn and serve.

COUNTRY FRIED CABBAGE

makes about 4 servings

2 tablespoons leftover bacon drippings

1 medium head of cabbage, shredded

In a skillet, sauté the cabbage in the bacon drippings, stirring frequently, for about 15 minutes or until lightly browned. Cover and reduce the heat. Cook, stirring occasionally, for about 10 minutes or until just tender. Remove from the heat and serve.

CREAMED GREEN BEANS

makes about 6 servings

1 cup fresh mushrooms, sliced

4 cups green beans, cooked

1 cup sour cream or unflavored yogurt

PANTRY

2 tablespoons butter or margarine

Salt and pepper to taste

In a saucepan, sauté the mushrooms in the butter for about 10 minutes or until tender. Add the beans and the sour cream, and season to taste. Remove from the heat and serve.

1 cup carrots, diced
1 cup green peas
1 cup Basic White Sauce (see
 page 398)
Garlic salt to taste
Onion salt to taste

PANTRY
Pepper to taste

1 In a saucepan, cover the carrots and the peas with lightly salted water. Bring to a boil and cook for about 12 to 15 minutes or until the peas are tender. Drain and reserve the liquid.

2 In a serving bowl, combine the vegetables and the sauce. Season to taste and serve.

Cooking note: For variation, add a little garlic paste to the sauce.

CREAMED PEAS AND CARROTS

makes about 4 to 6 servings

1½ cups potatoes, diced
¾ cup carrots, finely minced
1 cup unflavored yogurt

PANTRY
1 tablespoon butter or margarine
Onion or garlic powder to taste
Dried basil to taste, crushed

1 Position the rack in the center of the oven and preheat to 375 degrees F. Lightly grease a baking dish.

2 In a saucepan, cover the potatoes with lightly salted water. Bring to a boil and cook for about 15 minutes or until tender.

3 In a bowl, combine the potatoes, the carrots, and the yogurt. Season with onion or garlic powder and dried basic to taste.

4 Arrange the potatoes in the prepared baking dish and bake for about 10 to 15 minutes or until thoroughly heated. Remove from the oven and serve.

CREAMED POTATOES AND CARROTS

makes about 4 servings

CREAMED RADISHES

makes about 4 servings

1½ cups large radishes,
  trimmed, pared and sliced
1¼ cups Basic White Sauce (see
  page 398)
1 tablespoon anise powder

PANTRY
Salt and pepper to taste

1 In a saucepan, cover the
radishes with lightly salted
water. Bring to a boil and
cook for about 15 to 20 minutes or until tender.

2 Remove from the heat,
drizzle on the sauce, season
to taste, garnish with anise
powder, and serve.

CREAMED SPINACH

makes about 8 servings

2 packages (10 ounces each)
  frozen chopped spinach,
  prepared
⅓ cup sour cream

PANTRY
¼ teaspoon nutmeg

In a bowl, blend the spinach,
the sour cream, and the nutmeg, and serve.

CREAMED SPINACH WITH CHÈVRE

makes about 4 to 6 servings

3 packages (10 ounces each)
  spinach leaves
2 ounces fresh soft goat cheese
  (chèvre)
1 large shallot, peeled and
  minced
1 tablespoon lemon zest, grated

PANTRY
Salt and pepper to taste

1 In a saucepan, combine the
spinach about 2 inches of
water. Bring to a boil and
reduce to a simmer. Cook,

constantly pressing down
with a spoon, for about 10
minutes or until wilted.
Drain, reserving ½ cup of
water, and transfer to a
warming plate.

2 In a skillet, blend the
cheese, the shallots, and the
reserved liquid. Bring to a
boil and cook, stirring occasionally, for about 10 minutes
or until reduced by half.
Remove from the heat, season
to taste, pour on top of the
spinach, garnish with lemon
zest, and serve.

1 to 1½ pounds white turnips, pared and cut into bite-size cubes
2 cups Basic White Sauce (see page 398)

PANTRY
Celery salt to taste
Pepper to taste

1 In a saucepan, cover the turnips with lightly salted water. Bring to a boil and cook for about 10 minutes or until tender. Drain.

2 In a bowl, combine the turnips and the sauce, season to taste, and serve.

CREAMED TURNIPS

makes about 4 servings

1½ cups fresh corn kernels
2 cups okra, sliced
½ cup heavy cream

PANTRY
¼ cup butter or margarine
Salt and pepper to taste

In a skillet, cook the corn in the butter over low heat, stirring frequently, for about 10 to 15 minutes or until lightly browned. Add the okra, cover, and continue to cook, stirring occasionally, for about 10 minutes or until tender. Remove the cover, season to taste, blend in the cream, and cook for about 5 minutes or until thoroughly heated. Remove from the heat and serve.

CREAMY OKRA AND CORN

makes about 4 servings

6 medium green bell peppers

PANTRY
2 tablespoons butter or margarine
2 tablespoons flour
2 cups milk
Salt and pepper to taste

1 Position the broiler rack about 4 inches from the heat.

2 Arrange the peppers on the broiler pan and broil, turning frequently, for about 10 min-

utes or until charred. Remove from the broiler and cool.

3 Under running water, cut off the pepper tops and scrape out the seeds and pith. Remove the charred skin and dice the peppers.

4 In a saucepan, combine the butter and the diced peppers. Blend in the flour and the milk, and cook, stirring occasionally, for about 10 minutes or until thickened. Remove from the heat, season to taste, and serve.

CREAMY PEPPERS

makes about 4 to 6 servings

CREAMY SKILLET CORN

makes about 4 to 6 servings

6 to 8 ears of corn
¼ cup heavy cream
Garlic salt to taste

PANTRY

2 tablespoons butter or
    margarine
1 garlic clove, minced
Pepper to taste

1 Scrape the corn off the cobs.

2 In a skillet, sauté the garlic in the butter for about 5 minutes or until tender. Add the corn and cook for about 5 minutes or until thoroughly heated. Add the cream and reduce to a slow simmer. Cook for about 8 to 10 minutes or until tender. Remove from the heat, season to taste, and serve.

CREOLE-STYLE OKRA

makes about 4 servings

1 cup okra, sliced
1 medium yellow onion, minced
½ cup green bell peppers, diced
½ cup tomatoes, diced

PANTRY

1 tablespoon butter or margarine
Salt and pepper to taste

1 In a saucepan, cook the okra in about ½ cup of lightly salted water over low heat for about 10 to 15 minutes or until tender.

2 In a skillet, sauté the onion and the peppers in the butter for about 5 minutes or until the onions are translucent. Add the tomatoes and season to taste. Add the okra and continue to cook for about 10 minutes or until thoroughly heated. Remove from the heat and serve.

CRISPY POTATO WEDGES

makes about 4 to 6 servings

4 white potatoes, baked and cut lengthwise into 6 wedges

PANTRY

1 cup vegetable oil for frying
Salt and pepper to taste

1. In a deep-fryer, heat the oil to 375 degrees F. Fry the potatoes for about 10 to 15 minutes or until light golden-brown. Transfer to a wire rack covered with paper towels to drain. Season to taste and serve.

4 medium potatoes, pared and
  shredded

PANTRY
1 cup vegetable oil
Salt and pepper to taste

1 In a deep fryer, preheat the
oil to 375 degrees F.

2 Soak the shredded potatoes
in ice water for about 10 minutes. Drain and pat dry.

3 Fry the potatoes in the hot
oil for about 5 minutes or
until light golden-brown.
Transfer to a rack covered
with paper towels to drain.
Season to taste and serve.

Cooking note: When frying
the potatoes, add small
amounts at a time to prevent
the potatoes from sticking
together.

CRISPY SHREDDED POTATOES

makes about 4 servings

---

1 pound turnips, trimmed and
  shredded

PANTRY
3 tablespoons sesame oil
1 tablespoons soy sauce
1 teaspoon sugar
Salt and pepper to taste

1 In a saucepan, sauté the
turnips in the oil until well
coated. Add the soy sauce, the
sugar, and enough water to
cover. Continue to cook for
about 10 minutes.

2 Remove from heat and
drain. Transfer to a platter
and serve hot.

CRISPY SHREDDED TURNIPS

makes about 4 servings

---

2 cans (13 ounces each) diced
  carrots, drained
1 can (10 ounces) cream of
  mushroom soup
½ medium yellow onion,
  minced
1 bag (11 ounces) potato chips,
  crushed

PANTRY
1 tablespoon butter or margarine

1 Position the rack in the center of the oven and preheat to
350 degrees F. Lightly grease a
1-quart baking dish.

2 Arrange a layer of carrots
in the prepared baking dish.
Pour in the soup and top with
the onions.

3 Reduce the heat to 325
degrees F. Bake for about 20
minutes or until thoroughly
heated. Sprinkle with the
potato chips and continue to
cook for about 5 minutes or
until the chips are heated.
Remove from the oven and
serve.

CRUNCHY CARROT CASSEROLE

makes about 4 to 6 servings

CUCUMBERS IN SOUR CREAM

makes about 6 to 8 servings

2 medium cucumbers, sliced and patted dry

1 tablespoon white onion, minced

1 cup sour cream or unflavored yogurt

2 tablespoons tarragon vinegar

1 In a bowl, sprinkle the cucumber lightly with salt, cover and set aside for about 30 minutes.

2 In another bowl, using a wire whisk or an electric mixer, combine the sour cream and vinegar. Add the onions and the cucumbers. Cover with plastic wrap and refrigerate for about 1 hour before serving.

Cooking note: For variation, garnish with parsley, chives, or watercress.

CURRIED CABBAGE

makes about 4 servings

1 teaspoon red onions, minced
6 cups cabbage, shredded

PANTRY
2 tablespoons butter or margarine
½ teaspoon curry powder

In a saucepan, sauté the onions in the butter for about 5 minutes or until tender. Add the curry powder and the cabbage, cover, and cook, stirring occasionally, for about 10 minutes or until tender. Remove from the heat and serve.

Cooking note: Add more curry for a spicier flavor.

Vegetables

CURRIED GREEN BEANS

makes about 6 servings

6 cups chicken broth
1 pound fresh green beans, trimmed
1 can (8 ounces) bamboo shoots

PANTRY
2 tablespoons vegetable oil
2 tablespoons Thai curry paste

In a Dutch oven, stir-fry the curry paste in the oil until fragrant. Add the broth, green beans, and bamboo shoots. Bring to a boil and cook, stirring, for about 15 minutes. Reduce to a simmer and continue cooking until the green beans are tender. Remove from the heat and serve.

Cooking note: Make sure there is sufficient liquid during cooking.

1 package (10 ounces) frozen
  green peas
1 can (16 ounces) pearl onions,
  drained

PANTRY

3 tablespoons butter or
  margarine
1 teaspoon curry powder

1 In a saucepan, cook the peas according to the package directions. Drain and reserve 1 tablespoon of the cooking liquid.

2 Return the peas to the pan, add the onions, butter, curry powder, and reserved liquid. Heat, stirring occasionally, until thoroughly cooked. Remove from the heat and serve.

CURRIED PEAS AND ONIONS

makes about 4 to 6 servings

---

1 small white onion, minced
3 cups potatoes, cooked and
  diced
½ cup fresh or canned chicken
  broth

PANTRY

2 tablespoons butter
½ teaspoon curry powder
Salt and pepper to taste

In a skillet, sauté the onions in the butter for about 5 minutes or until lightly browned. Add the potatoes and the broth. Cook for about 20 minutes or until tender and most of the liquid has evaporated. Blend in the curry powder and cook for about 2 minutes or until thoroughly heated. Remove from the heat, season to taste and serve.

Cooking note: Add more curry for a spicier flavor.

CURRIED POTATOES

makes about 4 servings

---

2 pounds fresh dandelion
  greens, stemmed and cleaned

PANTRY

1 tablespoon butter or margarine
Salt and pepper to taste

In a saucepan, bring the greens and ½ cup of water to a boil. Cook for about 15 minutes or until tender. Drain, chop, add the butter, season to taste, and serve.

Cooking note: Dandelion greens should be used before they have bloomed to avoid the bitter taste.

DANDELION GREENS

makes about 4 servings

DELUXE VEGETABLE BRAISE

makes about 4 servings

1½ cups cauliflower florettes
1½ cups fresh green beans, trimmed and snapped
1½ cups broccoli florettes
1½ cups zucchini, sliced

PANTRY
3 tablespoons vegetable oil
Cashew nuts, crushed

In a wok, sauté the cauliflower in the oil for about 3 minutes or until well-coated. Add ½ cup of water, cover and cook, stirring occasionally, for about 4 minutes. Add the beans, cover, and cook for about 4 minutes. Add the broccoli and the zucchini, cover and cook, stirring occasionally, for about 7 minutes or until the vegetables are just tender. Remove from the heat, drain, and serve.

Cooking note: For variation, garnish with crushed cashews.

DRIED BALSAMIC TOMATOES

makes about 4 servings

4 fresh medium tomatoes, cut into ½-inch slices
¼ cup balsamic vinegar

PANTRY
¼ cup olive oil

1 Position the rack in the center of the oven and preheat to 250 degrees F. Lightly grease a baking or cookie sheet.

2 Arrange the tomatoes on the prepared baking sheet and drizzle with the vinegar and the oil. Bake for about 3 hours or until the tomatoes are dried. Remove from the oven, cool, and serve.

Cooking note: The dried tomatoes may be stored in a zip-lock bag and kept in the refrigerator for up to 2 weeks.

2 small eggplants, trimmed, pared and cut into ½-inch slices
½ pound Mozzarella cheese, thinly sliced

PANTRY
1 cup olive oil
1½ cups (canned) tomato sauce

EGGPLANT PARMIGIANA

makes about 4 to 6 servings

1 Position the rack in the center of the oven and preheat to 400 degrees F. Lightly grease a 3-quart baking pan.

2 In a skillet, sauté the eggplants in the oil, turning occasionally, for about 10 minutes or until both sides are browned. Transfer to a rack covered with paper towels and drain.

3 Arrange half of the eggplants in the prepared baking pan, pour on half of the tomato sauce, and top with half of the cheese. Repeat. Bake for about 15 minutes or until the cheese has melted. Remove from the oven and serve.

4 medium parsnips, trimmed, cooked and mashed
1 medium egg, beaten

PANTRY
¼ cup flour
1 tablespoon butter or margarine
Salt and pepper to taste

ENGLISH PARSNIP CAKES

makes about 4 servings

1 In a bowl, combine the parsnips, the flour, and the egg, and season to taste. Work the dough until smooth and form into four patties.

2 In a skillet, fry the patties in the butter for about 10 to 15 minutes or until both sides are browned and crisp. Transfer to a rack covered with paper towels to drain. Season to taste and serve.

ENGLISH BUBBLE AND SQUEAK

makes about 4 servings

2 cups cabbage, shredded
1 medium onion, minced
2 cups potatoes, mashed

PANTRY
2 tablespoons butter or margarine

1 Position the rack in the center of the oven and preheat to 350 degrees F. Have a baking or cookie sheet available.

2 In a saucepan, cover the cabbage with lightly salted water. Bring to a boil and cook for about 10 minutes or until wilted.

3 In a skillet, sauté the onions in the butter for about 5 minutes or until translucent. Add the cabbage, stirring frequently for about 2 to 3 minutes, and blend in the potatoes.

4 Transfer onto the baking sheet and form into a large round. Bake for 10 minutes or until both sides are browned. Remove from the heat, cut into wedges, and serve.

ENGLISH-STYLE LEEKS

makes about 4 servings

2 pounds medium leeks, trimmed and quartered
1 cup Basic White Sauce (see page 398)
4 ounces grated cheddar cheese

PANTRY
1 teaspoon butter or margarine

1 Position the broiler rack about 6 inches from the heat. Lightly grease a shallow baking pan.

2 In a saucepan, cover the leeks with lightly salted water. Bring to a boil and reduce to a simmer. Cook for about 10 minutes or until tender.

3 Arrange the leeks in the prepared pan, pour on the sauce, and sprinkle with grated cheese. Broil for about 10 minutes or until the cheese has melted. Remove from the broiler and serve.

1 pound haricot beans, soaked
  overnight and drained
2 sage leaves
2 tablespoons tomato puree

PANTRY
¼ cup vegetable oil

1 In a saucepan, just cover
the beans with water. Bring to
a boil and cook, stirring occasionally, for about 50 minutes
or until tender. Drain

2 In a skillet, heat the oil and
add the sage leaves and the
beans. Reduce to a low simmer and cook, stirring frequently, for about 20 minutes
or until the beans have
absorbed the oil. Blend in the
tomato purée and cook for
about 5 minutes or until thoroughly heated. Remove from
the heat and serve.

FAGIOLI ALL-UCCELLETTO (HARICOT BEANS)

makes about 4 to 6 servings

---

2 pounds small new potatoes,
  cooked and drained
1 cup grated Swiss cheese
1 container (8 ounces) whipped
  cream cheese
1 cup caviar

1 Position the rack in the center of the oven and preheat to
350 degrees F. Have a shallow
baking dish available.

2 Core the potatoes, stuff
with the cream cheese and
caviar, and sprinkle with the
cheese.

3 Arrange the potatoes in the
prepared baking dish and
cook for about 10 minutes or
until the cheese has melted.
Remove from the oven and
serve.

FILLED NEW POTATOES

makes about 18 servings

FORESTER'S POTATOES

makes about 4 to 6 servings

3 cans (4 ounces each) sliced mushrooms, drained
1 pound russet potatoes, pared and thinly sliced
2 tablespoons fresh basil leaves

PANTRY

1 tablespoon butter or margarine
4 large cloves garlic, minced
Salt and pepper to taste

1 Position the rack in the center of the oven and preheat to 350 degrees F. Lightly grease a 13 x 9-inch baking dish.

2 In a bowl, combine the mushrooms, the potatoes, the garlic, and the basil, and season to taste.

3 Arrange in the prepared baking dish and bake for about 40 to 45 minutes or until tender. Remove from the oven and serve.

FRENCH-STYLE FRIED SHALLOTS

makes about 4 servings

2 cups graisse de canard (rendered duck fat)
12 large shallots, trimmed and peeled
1 teaspoon five spice powder

PANTRY

¼ teaspoon pepper

In a saucepan, sauté the shallots, the spice powder, and the pepper in the duck fat for 5 minutes. Reduce to a simmer and cook for about 20 minutes or until tender. Transfer to a rack covered with paper towels, drain, and serve.

Cooking note: Duck fat can be found in specialty food stores. The shallots can be refrigerated for about 2 weeks and used as a garnish for different dishes.

FRIED BAMBOO SHOOTS WITH CHILI SAUCE

makes about 4 servings

2½ pounds fresh bamboo shoots
2 teaspoons (bottled) Chinese chili sauce

PANTRY

½ cup vegetable oil
3 tablespoons sesame oil
1 tablespoon soy sauce
1 tablespoon sugar

1 In a saucepan, cover the bamboo shoots with water. Bring to a boil and cook for about 25 minutes or until tender. Drain and cut into strips.

2 In a deep fryer, heat the oil to about 375 degrees F. Fry the bamboo shoots for about 10 minutes or until light golden-brown. Transfer to a warming plate.

3 In a saucepan, combine the oil, the chili sauce, the bamboo shoots, and the soy sauce. Cook for about 5 to 10 minutes or until thoroughly heated. Remove from the heat, top with the sugar, and serve.

1 pound fresh bean spouts,
  heads and tails removed
3 medium green bell peppers,
  stemmed, seeded and diced
2 tablespoons white rice wine
5 tablespoons peanut oil

PANTRY
Salt and pepper to taste

1 In a bowl, cover the bean sprouts with ice water and set aside.

2 In a skillet, sauté the sprouts and the peppers in the oil for about 3 minutes. Add the wine, season to taste, and cook for about 3 minutes or until just tender. Remove from the heat and serve.

FRIED BEAN SPROUTS WITH BELL PEPPERS

makes about 4 servings

---

4 cups cooked beets, sliced

PANTRY
2 tablespoons butter or
  margarine
Salt and pepper to taste

In a skillet, sauté the beets in the butter for about 5 minutes. Season to taste and continue to cook for about 15 minutes or until thoroughly heated. Remove from the heat and serve.

FRIED BEETS

makes about 6 servings

---

1 medium onion, chopped
4 cups cooked Brussels sprouts

PANTRY
2 tablespoons butter or
  margarine
Salt and pepper to taste

In a skillet, sauté the onions in the butter for about 5 minutes or until lightly browned. Add the sprouts and cook for about 5 minutes or until thoroughly heated. Remove from the heat, season to taste, and serve.

FRIED BRUSSELS SPROUTS

makes about 6 servings

FRIED CAULIFLOWER

makes about 4 to 6 servings

4½ cups cauliflower florettes, cooked

2 eggs, beaten until light

1½ cups bread crumbs

PANTRY

1 cup vegetable oil

Salt and pepper to taste

1 In a deep fryer, heat the oil to about 350 degrees F.

2 Dip the florettes into the eggs, roll them around in the bread crumbs, and place in the hot oil. Cook for about 15 minutes or until light golden-brown. Transfer to a rack covered with paper towels, drain, season to taste, and serve.

FRIED CORN

makes about 6 servings

4 cups whole cooked corn

3 tablespoons green bell pepper, trimmed, seeded and minced

Garlic salt to taste

PANTRY

¼ cup butter or margarine

Pepper to taste

In a skillet, sauté the corn and the peppers in the butter, stirring occasionally, for about 20 minutes or until tender. Remove from the heat, season to taste, and serve.

FRIED CUCUMBERS

makes about 6 servings

4 medium cucumbers, pared, sliced and patted dry

¾ cup bread crumbs

1 egg, slightly beaten

PANTRY

3 tablespoons butter or margarine

1 Dredge the cucumber slices in the bread crumbs, dip them into the egg, and roll them in the bread crumbs.

2 In a skillet, sauté the cucumbers in the oil, turning occasionally, for about 10 minutes or until both sides are browned. Transfer to a rack covered with paper towels, drain, and serve.

1 large eggplant, trimmed, pared and cut into ½-inch slices

¾ cup peanut oil

2 ounces Parmesan cheese, grated

1 teaspoon parsley, chopped

PANTRY

Salt and pepper to taste

1 In a bowl, cover the eggplant with boiling water and set aside for about 4 minutes. Drain and pat dry.

2 In a skillet, sauté the eggplant in the oil for about 15 minutes or until tender and both sides are browned. Remove from the heat, season to taste, top with the cheese, garnish with parsley, and serve.

FRIED EGGPLANT WITH PARMESAN CHEESE

makes about 4 servings

---

1 package (10 ounces) frozen green peas, thawed and drained

PANTRY

3 tablespoons butter or margarine

1 tablespoon sugar

2 garlic cloves, minced

Pepper to taste

In a saucepan, sauté the peas in the butter, stirring frequently, for about 2 minutes. Add the sugar and continue to cook, stirring until the sugar has dissolved. Add the garlic and the pepper to taste. Cover, reduce to a simmer and cook for about 5 minutes or until tender. Remove from the heat and serve.

FRIED GREEN PEAS WITH GARLIC

makes about 4 servings

---

6 large green bell peppers, stemmed, seeded and cut into 8 pieces each

PANTRY

2 tablespoons butter or margarine

Salt and pepper to taste

1 In a saucepan, cover the peppers with water and bring to a boil. Cook for about 3 minutes or until just tender.

2 In a skillet, stir-fry the peppers in the butter for about 5 minutes or until light golden-brown. Remove from the heat, season to taste, and serve.

FRIED GREEN PEPPERS

makes about 4 to 6 servings

Fried Green Tomatoes

makes about 4 servings

1 pound medium green tomatoes, pared and sliced

1 large red bell pepper, stemmed, seeded and diced

½ cup cream

PANTRY

1 tablespoon butter or margarine

Salt and pepper to taste

In a skillet, stir-fry tomatoes and the peppers in the butter for about 1 minute. Blend in the cream, reduce to a simmer and cook for about 15 minutes or until the peppers are tender. Remove from the heat, season to taste, and serve.

Fried Lettuce

makes about 4 servings

1 pound Bibb lettuce

PANTRY

5 tablespoons sesame oil

1 garlic clove, mashed

Salt and pepper to taste

In a skillet, sauté the garlic in the oil for about 5 minutes or until lightly browned. Add the lettuce and stir-fry for about 1 to 2 minutes or until the leaves are a bright green. Remove from the heat, season to taste, and serve.

Fried Salsify

makes about 4 to 6 servings

½ pound salsify, cooked and cut into bite-sized pieces

PANTRY

½ cup flour

1 cup vegetable oil

Salt and pepper to taste

1 In a bowl, combine the flour and the salsify, and season to taste.

2 In a deep fryer, heat the oil to 350 degrees F. Stir-fry the salsify, for about 5 minutes or until browned. Transfer to a rack covered with paper towels, drain, and serve.

Cooking note: Salsify is also know as oyster plant.

1 cup potatoes, cooked and
    mashed
3 cups potatoes, grated
2 eggs, beaten until foamy

PANTRY
1 tablespoon vegetable oil
Salt and pepper to taste

1 In a bowl, combine the
mashed potatoes, the grated
potatoes, and the eggs, and
season to taste.

2 In a skillet, heat the oil and
drop in the batter ¼ cup at a
time, forming pancakes. Cook
for about 10 to 15 minutes or
until both sides are golden-
brown. Transfer to a rack
covered with paper towels,
drain, and serve.

GERMAN-STYLE
POTATO PANCAKES

makes about 8 servings

---

3 bacon slices, cooked and
    crumbled, drippings reserved
1 small yellow onion, chopped
3 tablespoons light-brown
    sugar, firmly packed
1 pound carrots, trimmed, pared,
    sliced, cooked and drained

In a skillet, sauté the onion
in the bacon drippings for
about 5 minutes or until
translucent. Add the carrots
and the sugar. Cook, stirring
frequently, for about 5 to 10
minutes or until thoroughly
heated and glazed. Remove
from the heat, sprinkle with
the bacon, and serve.

GLAZED CARROTS
WITH BACON

makes about 2 servings

---

1 pound celeriac root
1 tablespoon molasses
⅛ teaspoon nutmeg

PANTRY
2 tablespoons butter or
    margarine
Ginger powder to taste

1 In a saucepan, cover the
celeriac with lightly salted
water and bring to a boil.
Cook for about 10 minutes or
until tender. Drain and cut
lengthwise into slices.

2 In a skillet, blend the butter,
the molasses, the nutmeg, and
the ginger powder to taste.
Cook for about 1 minute and
add the celeriac. Cook, stirring frequently, for about 5 to
10 minutes or until thoroughly heated and glazed. Remove
from the heat and serve.

GLAZED CELERIAC

makes about 4 to 6 servings

GRANDMOTHER'S CORN PUDDING

makes about 4 servings

2 cups uncooked sweet corn
1¼ cups light cream

PANTRY

1 tablespoon butter or margarine
Salt to taste

1 Position the rack in the center of the oven and preheat to 350 degrees F. Lightly grease a 1½-quart baking dish.

2 In the container of a blender or food processor, combine the corn, the salt to taste, and ¼ cup of the cream. Process on high speed until smooth.

3 Pour into the prepared baking dish and top with the remaining cream. Bake for about 1 hour or until a cake tester inserted into the center comes out clean. Remove from the oven and serve.

AU GRATIN POTATOES

makes about 4 servings

6 medium Idaho potatoes, pared and diced
2 cups heavy cream

PANTRY

¼ cup melted butter or margarine
1½ teaspoons minced garlic

1 Position the rack in the center of the oven and preheat to 350 degrees F. Lightly grease a 13 x 9-inch baking pan.

2 Sprinkle the garlic in the prepared baking pan and add the potatoes. Drizzle with the butter and top with the cream. Cover and bake for about 10 minutes. Remove the cover and continue to bake for about 40 minutes or until tender and light golden-brown. Remove from the heat and serve.

GREAT VALLEY CELERY

makes about 4 to 6 servings

1½ cups celery, diced
1 ripe avocado, peeled, seeded and diced
1 cup (bottled) French dressing
1 tablespoon prepared horseradish

In a saucepan, combine the celery, the dressing, and the horseradish over low heat. Cook for about 10 minutes; do not allow it to boil. Transfer to a bowl with the avocados, cover with plastic wrap and refrigerate for about 24 hours before serving.

1 medium yellow onion, chopped

1 pound fresh green beans, trimmed

2 medium tomatoes, chopped

2 medium tomatoes, minced

PANTRY

1 tablespoon vegetable oil

1 tablespoon olive oil

Salt and pepper to taste

In a Dutch oven, sauté the onions in the oil for about 5 minutes or until tender. Add the beans, cover, and cook for about 10 to 12 minutes or until the beans start to wilt. Add the chopped tomatoes and cook for about 10 minutes or until the tomatoes have the consistency of purée. Season to taste, add the minced tomatoes and the oil, and continue to cook for about 10 minutes or until the beans are tender. Remove from the heat and serve.

Cooking note: Don't allow the mixture to burn or to become crusty.

GREEK-STYLE GREEN BEANS

makes about 4 to 6 servings

2 cans (16 ounces each) cut green beans, drained

1 can (10¾ ounces) condensed cream of mushroom soup

1 can (2¾ ounces) French's™ fried onions

PANTRY

¾ cup milk

Salt and pepper to taste

1 Position the rack in the center of the oven and preheat to 350 degrees F. Lightly grease a 1½-quart baking dish.

2 In a bowl, combine the beans, the milk, the soup, and half of the onions, and season to taste. Pour into the prepared baking dish.

3 Bake for about 30 minutes and top with the remaining onions. Continue to bake for about 5 minutes or until the onions are light golden-brown. Remove from the oven and serve.

GREEN BEAN CASSEROLE

makes about 6 servings

Green Beans Lyonnaise

makes about 4 servings

4 bacon slices, diced
¼ cup yellow onions, minced
1 teaspoon tarragon vinegar
4 cups green beans, cooked

PANTRY
Salt and pepper to taste

1 In a skillet, sauté the bacon, stirring frequently, for about 10 minutes or until crisp. Transfer to a warming plate.

2 In the same skillet, sauté the onions for about 5 minutes or until translucent. Add the vinegar, the bacon, and the beans. Cook for about 5 minutes or until thoroughly heated. Remove from the heat, season to taste, and serve.

Green Beans Parmesan

makes about 8 to 10 servings

2 pounds fresh green beans, trimmed and cut in half lengthwise
½ cup grated Parmesan cheese
½ cup (bottled) salad oil
¼ cup (bottled) garlic-flavored vinegar

PANTRY
½ cup butter or margarine

1 In a saucepan, cover the beans with water and bring to a boil. Reduce to a simmer and cook for about 15 minutes or until tender.

2 In a bowl, combine the beans, the oil, the vinegar, and the cheese. Cover with plastic wrap and refrigerate for at least 1 hour before serving.

Cooking note: For variation, top with minced red onions.

Green Beans Amandine

makes about 8 servings

3 packages (10 ounces each) frozen green beans, cooked and drained
½ cup blanched almonds, sliced

In a skillet, sauté the almonds in the butter for about 10 minutes or until lightly browned. Add the beans and cook for about 5 minutes or until thoroughly heated. Remove from the heat and serve.

½ pound green beans, trimmed, cooked and drained

¼ cup red bell peppers, diced

2 tablespoons sesame seeds, toasted

1 tablespoon fresh lemon juice

PANTRY

½ teaspoon sesame oil

Salt and pepper to taste

In a bowl, combine the beans, the peppers, the sesame seeds, the oil, and the seasoning to taste. Sprinkle with the lemon juice and serve.

GREEN BEANS WITH SWEET RED PEPPERS

makes about 2 to 4 servings

½ pound green beans, trimmed and cut into 2-inch pieces

2 bacon slices

1 tablespoon shallots, minced

PANTRY

2 teaspoons white wine vinegar

1 In a saucepan, cover the beans with lightly salted water. Cook until tender. Drain and transfer to a shallow bowl.

2 In a skillet, sauté the bacon for about 10 to 15 minutes or until crispy. Drain and crumble.

3 In the same skillet, sauté the shallots for about 10 minutes or until a light golden-brown. Remove from the heat and blend in the vinegar. Drizzle over the beans, top with the bacon, and serve.

GREEN BEANS WITH BACON DRESSING

makes about 2 servings

---

1 package (32 ounces) frozen hash brown potatoes, thawed

1 can (4 ounces) diced green chilis, drained

1 can (10¾ ounces) cream of chicken soup

1 cup sour cream

PANTRY

1 tablespoon butter or margarine

1 Position the rack in the center of the oven and preheat to 400 degrees F. Lightly grease a 13 x 9-inch baking pan.

2 In a bowl, combine the chilis, the soup, and the sour cream.

3 Arrange the potatoes in the prepared baking pan, top with the chili mixture, and cover.

4 Bake for about 30 minutes or until tender. Remove from the oven and serve.

Cooking note: For variation, top with grated cheese.

GREEN CHILI HASH BROWNS

makes about 6 to 8 servings

Green Tomato Casserole

makes about 6 servings

3 cups green tomatoes, sliced
2 large eggs
½ cup small curd cottage cheese

PANTRY
1 tablespoon butter or margarine
½ cup milk
Salt and pepper to taste

1 Position the rack in the center of the oven and preheat to 375 degrees F. Lightly grease a 9-inch baking pan.

2 In a bowl, using a wire whisk or an electric mixer, blend the eggs, the milk, and the cottage cheese.

3 Arrange the potatoes in the prepared baking pan and top with the cheese mixture. Bake for about 40 minutes or until the liquid has been absorbed. Remove from the oven, season to taste, and serve.

Grilled Fennel with Caraway

makes about 4 servings

4 fennel bulbs, trimmed, sliced, cooked and drained
¼ cup grated cheese of choice
1 tablespoon caraway seeds

PANTRY
3 tablespoons melted butter or margarine
Salt and pepper to taste

1 Position the broiler rack about 4 inches from the heat. Lightly grease a baking pan.

2 Arrange the fennel in the prepared baking pan and sprinkle with the caraway seeds. Broil for about 4 to 6 minutes or until both sides are lightly browned. Remove from the oven, drizzle with the butter, season to taste, top with the cheese, and serve.

1 pound large red potatoes, pared and cut into ⅛-inch slices

¾ cup coarsely grated Gruyère cheese

1 large egg

PANTRY

1 cup scalded milk

Salt and pepper to taste

GRUYÈRE POTATOES AU GRATIN

makes about 2 servings

1 Position the rack in the center of the oven and preheat to 400 degrees F. Lightly grease a 1½-quart baking dish.

2 In a saucepan, cover the potato slices with lightly salted water and bring to a boil. Cook for about 10 minutes or until tender.

3 In a small bowl, using a wire whisk or an electric mixer, blend the egg and the milk until thickened.

4 Arrange the potatoes, in three layers in the prepared baking dish. Sprinkle the first two layers with some of the cheese, and season to taste. Pour the egg and milk mixture on the top and sprinkle with the remaining cheese. Bake for about 30 minutes or until lightly browned. Remove from the oven and serve.

1 acorn squash (about 1¼ pounds), halved and seeded

1 package (10 ounces) frozen broccoli, cooked and drained

1 package (10 ounces) frozen carrots, cooked and drained

½ cup shredded American cheese

PANTRY

1 tablespoon melted butter or margarine

Salt and pepper to taste

HARVEST SQUASH

makes about 4 to 6 servings

1 Position the rack in the center of the oven and preheat to 400 degrees F. Have a 12 x 9-inch baking dish available.

2 Arrange the squash halves in the baking dish cut-side down and bake for about 30 minutes or until tender.

3 Turn the squash cut-side up, drizzle with the butter and fill with the vegetables. Season to taste and sprinkle with the cheese. Continue to bake for about 3 to 5 minutes or until the cheese has melted. Remove from the oven, cut, and serve.

Herbed Corn and Peas

makes about 4 servings

2 cups green peas, cooked
2 cups whole kernel corn, cooked

PANTRY

1 teaspoon butter or margarine
⅛ teaspoon dried marjoram, crushed
¼ dried parsley, crushed
Salt and pepper to taste

In a saucepan, combine the peas and the corn and ¾ cup of water. Blend in the marjoram and the parsley, and cover. Cook over low heat for about 3 minutes and blend in the butter. Cover and continue to cook for about 3 minutes or until thoroughly heated and the liquid has been absorbed. Remove from the heat, season to taste, and serve.

Holiday Candied Beets

makes about 4 servings

2 medium beets, pared and diced
2 cups orange juice

PANTRY

2 cups sugar
½ cup honey

In a saucepan, combine the sugar, the juice and the honey. Cook, stirring frequently, for about 3 minutes or until the sugar has dissolved. Add the beets, reduce to a simmer and cover. Cook for about 40 minutes or until tender. Remove from the heat and serve.

Cooking note: For variation, use orange marmalade instead of honey.

Honey Glazed Carrots

makes about 4 servings

1 pound baby carrots
⅛ teaspoon star anise

PANTRY

⅓ cup butter or margarine
⅓ cup honey

In a saucepan, cover the carrots halfway with water. Bring to a boil and cook for about 10 to 15 minutes or until tender. Reduce to a simmer and add the butter, the honey, and the anise. Bring to a boil and cook for about 5 minutes or until the liquid has evaporated and the carrots are glazed. Remove from the heat and serve.

Honeyed Sweet Potatoes

makes about 6 servings

6 medium sweet potatoes, pared and cut into ¼-inch slices lengthwise

5 tablespoons fresh orange juice

PANTRY

1 tablespoon butter or margarine

¼ cup honey

Salt and pepper to taste

1 Position the rack in the center of the oven and preheat to 350 degrees F. Lightly grease a baking dish.

2 In a saucepan, cover the potatoes and cover with lightly salted water and bring to a boil. Cook for about 15 to 20 minutes or until tender.

3 Arrange the potatoes in the prepared baking dish. Top with the honey, pour the juice over, and season to taste. Bake for about 30 minutes or until thoroughly heated and glazed. Remove from the oven and serve.

Cooking note: This recipe is not for yams (see glossary).

Honey-Lemon Glazed Onions

makes about 6 servings

3½ cups white pearl onions, cooked

3 tablespoons lemon juice

PANTRY

¼ cup butter or margarine

6 tablespoons honey

In a skillet, combine the butter, the lemon juice, the honey, and the onions. Cook over low heat, stirring frequently for about 8 to 10 minutes or until tender. Remove from the heat and serve.

AUNTIE'S HOT PEPPERS

makes about 6 servings

1 pound long hot peppers, stemmed and seeded

1 can (8 ounces) Italian plum tomatoes, drained

PANTRY

1 tablespoon olive oil

3 garlic cloves, minced

1 In a small bowl, place the tomatoes, crushing about 5 of them.

2 In a skillet, sauté the peppers and the garlic in the oil for about 10 minutes or until tender. Add the tomatoes and cook, stirring occasionally, for about 10 minutes or until thoroughly heated. Remove from the heat, season to taste, and serve.

HUNGARIAN ASPARAGUS

makes about 6 servings

2½ cups cooked asparagus pieces

1 cup buttered bread crumbs

¼ cup sour cream, whipped

PANTRY

1 tablespoon butter or margarine

1 Position the rack in the center of the oven and preheat to 350 degrees F. Lightly grease an 8-inch square baking pan.

2 Arrange the asparagus in the prepared baking dish, sprinkle with the crumbs, and top with the sour cream.

3 Bake for about 10 minutes or until the crumbs are toasted. Remove from the oven and serve.

Cooking note: For variation, roll the asparagus in the crumbs before baking.

1 medium eggplant
1 small yellow onion, chopped
1 teaspoon fresh lemon juice

PANTRY
1 tablespoon butter or margarine
¼ cup mayonnaise
Salt and pepper to taste

1 Position the rack in the center of the oven and preheat to 350 degrees F. Lightly grease a shallow baking pan.

2 Bake the eggplant in the prepared baking pan for about 50 minutes or until just tender. Remove from the oven, pare the eggplant, and cut into bite-sized cubes.

3 In the container of a blender or food processor, combine the eggplant, the mayonnaise, the onion, and purée until smooth. Season to taste, drizzle on the lemon juice, and serve.

Cooking note: For variation, add diced cucumbers and tomatoes to the eggplant purée.

ISRAELI EGGPLANT SALAD
makes about 4

---

1 small white onion, minced
2 pounds broccoli rabe,
    trimmed, with florettes cut off

PANTRY
¼ cup olive oil
2 garlic cloves, minced

In a skillet, sauté the garlic and the onion in the oil for about 5 minutes or until the onions are translucent. Add the broccoli rabe and continue to cook for about 10 to 15 minutes or until tender. Remove from the heat and serve.

Cooking note: This dish goes well with gilled meats. Broccoli rabe can be found in specialty stores during autumn and spring.

ITALIAN BROCCOLI RABE
makes about 4 to 6 servings

Johnny Cake with Broccoli

makes about 4 servings

1 box (8½ ounces) corn muffin mix, prepared
½ cup fresh broccoli florettes, chopped
¼ cup Swiss cheese, grated
¼ cup almonds, chopped

PANTRY

1 tablespoon butter or margarine

1 Position the rack in the center of the oven and preheat to 350 degrees F. Lightly grease an 8-inch square baking pan.

2 In a bowl, combine the muffin mixture and the broccoli. Pour into the prepared baking pan.

3 Bake for about 20 minutes and sprinkle with the cheese and the almonds. Bake for an additional 5 minutes or until the cheese has melted and a cake tester inserted into the center comes out clean. Remove from the oven and serve.

Lemon-Zucchini Slices

makes about 4 servings

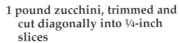

1 pound zucchini, trimmed and cut diagonally into ¼-inch slices
1 teaspoon safflower oil
2 tablespoons fresh lemon juice

PANTRY

1 tablespoon butter or margarine
Salt and pepper to taste

1 Position the rack in the center of the oven and preheat to 400 degrees F. Lightly grease a shallow baking pan.

2 In a bowl, combine the zucchini and the oil.

3 Arrange the zucchini in the prepared baking pan and bake for about 10 minutes. Turn over and season to taste. Continue to bake for about 10 to 15 minutes or until tender. Remove from the heat, sprinkle with the lemon juice, and serve.

Lima Beans with Scallions

makes about 4 servings

1 package (16 ounces) frozen lima beans, thawed and drained
2 scallions, trimmed and chopped
2 tablespoons peanut oil

PANTRY

1 teaspoon sugar

1 In a saucepan, cover the beans with water. Bring to a boil and cook for about 2 minutes or until tender.

2 In a skillet, stir-fry the lima beans in the oil for about 1 minute or until the beans are well-coated. Reduce to a simmer, add 2 tablespoons of water, and blend in the sugar and the scallions. Continue to stir-fry for about 1 to 2 minutes or until thoroughly heated. Remove from the heat, add 2 tablespoons of water, and serve.

18 shallots, peeled
1½ cups Madeira
¾ cup (canned) chicken broth

PANTRY
3 tablespoons honey

In a saucepan, sauté the shallots in the butter, stirring frequently, for about 10 minutes or until a light golden-brown. Blend in the wine, the broth, and the honey. Bring to a boil and reduce to a simmer. Cook, stirring occasionally, for about 15 minutes or until the liquid has thickened. Remove from the heat and serve.

MADEIRA-GLAZED SHALLOTS

makes about 3 to 4 servings

---

1 winter squash, stemmed, pared and seeded

PANTRY
1½ tablespoons butter or margarine
Ground nutmeg to taste

1 Position the rack in the center of the oven and preheat to 350 degrees F. Lightly grease a baking dish.

2 Cut the squash into cubes and arrange in the prepared baking dish. Bake for about 20 minutes or until tender.

3 In a bowl, mash the squash. Using a wire whisk or an electric mixer, blend in the butter until fluffy. Sprinkle with nutmeg and serve.

MASHED WINTER SQUASH

makes about 4 servings

---

1 pound fresh broccoli florettes
1 pound fresh mushrooms, trimmed
2 cups dressing of choice

1 In a 3-quart microwave-proof dish, combine the broccoli and 1 cup of water and cover. Microwave on high heat for about 1 minute. Drain and rinse in cold water.

2 In a bowl, combine the broccoli, the mushrooms and the dressing. Cover with plastic wrap and refrigerate for at least 8 hours before serving.

MICROWAVE BROCCOLI AND MUSHROOMS

makes about 4 servings

Microwaved Pea Pods Oriental

makes about 4 servings

1 package (10 ounces) frozen pea pods, thawed
1 tablespoon peanut oil

PANTRY
1 tablespoon soy sauce

In a microwave-proof dish, microwave the pea pods on high heat for about 3 minutes or until thoroughly heated. Add the oil and the soy sauce, and continue to microwave on high heat for about 1 to 2 minutes or until just tender. Remove from the oven and serve.

Minted Cherry Tomatoes

makes about 4 servings

24 cherry tomatoes
1 teaspoon dried mint, crushed

PANTRY
1 tablespoon olive oil

In a skillet, cook the tomatoes in the oil, stirring occasionally, for about 3 minutes. Add the mint and cook for about 2 minutes or until thoroughly heated.

Cooking note: For variation, quarter the tomatoes before cooking.

Mushroom-Pimiento Peas

makes about 3 servings

1 package (10 ounces) frozen green peas, cooked and drained
1 can (8 ounces) sliced mushrooms, drained
2 cans (4 ounces each) chopped pimientos

PANTRY
3 tablespoons butter or margarine

In a saucepan, sauté the peas, the mushrooms, and the pimientos in the butter for about 10 minutes or until thoroughly heated. Remove from the heat and serve.

1 package (8 ounces) fresh mushrooms, trimmed and sliced

1 jar (30 ounces) spaghetti sauce

¼ cup fresh parsley, snipped

PANTRY

1 tablespoon vegetable oil

In a saucepan, sauté the mushrooms in the oil for about 3 to 4 minutes or until tender. Add the tomato sauce, bring to a boil, and reduce to a simmer. Cover and cook for about 4 to 5 minutes or until thoroughly heated. Remove from the heat, add the parsley, and serve.

MUSHROOMS STEWED IN SPAGHETTI SAUCE

makes about 4 servings

1½ cups (canned) whole kernel corn, drained

3 eggs, separated

PANTRY

¼ cup flour

Salt and pepper to taste

1 Lightly grease a skillet and preheat.

2 In the container of a blender or food processor, combine the corn, the egg yolks, the flour, and season to taste. Process on high speed until smooth.

3 In a bowl, using a wire whisk or an electric mixer, beat the egg whites until stiff. Fold in the corn mixture.

4 Drop by spoonfuls into the prepared skillet, forming small patties. Cook for about 15 minutes or until both sides are light golden-brown. Remove from the heat and serve.

NEW ENGLAND CORN OYSTERS

makes about 4 servings

Normandy Potatoes

makes about 8 servings

6 white potatoes, pared and thinly sliced

1 envelope (1¼ ounces) onion soup mix

PANTRY

¼ cup butter or margarine

Salt and pepper to taste

1 Position the rack in the center of the oven and preheat to 400 degrees F. Lightly grease a shallow baking dish.

2 In a bowl, blend 1½ cups of boiling water, the soup mix, and the butter.

3 Arrange the potatoes in the prepared baking dish, top with the soup mixture, and season to taste. Bake for about 40 to 50 minutes or until tender and most of the liquid has been absorbed. Remove from the oven and serve.

O'Brien Potatoes

makes about 4 to 6 servings

2 medium red onions, sliced

3 tablespoons green peppers, diced

4½ cups potatoes, diced

PANTRY

3 tablespoons butter or margarine

Salt and pepper to taste

In a skillet, sauté the onions and the peppers in the butter for about 10 minutes or until the peppers are just tender. Add the potatoes, lower the heat, and cover. Continue to cook, stirring occasionally, for about 25 to 30 minutes or until tender. Remove from the heat, season to taste, and serve.

Okra Cooked in Stewed Tomatoes

makes about 6 servings

2 cups okra, cooked

1 can (16 ounces) stewed tomatoes

PANTRY

1 tablespoon butter or margarine

Salt and pepper to taste

In a saucepan, simmer the okra and the tomatoes in the butter for about 5 minutes or until thoroughly heated. Remove from the heat, season to taste, and serve.

**1 pound fresh okra, trimmed
and sliced**
½ cup buttermilk
2 cups self-rising cornmeal

PANTRY
1 teaspoon salt

1. In a deep fryer, preheat the oil to 375 degrees F.

2 In a bowl, combine the okra, the salt and the buttermilk. Set aside for about 30 minutes and drain.

3 In the cornmeal, dredge the okra until well-coated.

4 Place the okra in the deep fryer and cook for about 10 to 15 minutes or until both sides are light golden-brown. Transfer to a rack covered with paper towels, drain, and serve.

OKRA FRANÇAISE
makes about 6 servings

**3½ cups small white pearl
onions**

PANTRY
1 teaspoon salt
⅓ cup warm honey
½ cup (bottled) ketchup
1 tablespoon melted butter or
margarine

1 Position the rack in the center of the oven and preheat to 375 degrees F. Lightly grease a baking dish.

2 In a saucepan, cover the onions with lightly salted water. Bring to a boil and cook for about 5 minutes or until tender.

3 In a bowl, combine the honey, the ketchup, and the butter.

4 Arrange the onions in the prepared baking dish and top with the ketchup mixture. Bake for about 45 minutes or until thoroughly heated. Remove from the heat and serve.

ONION CASSEROLE
makes about 6 servings

ONIONS IN MUSHROOM SAUCE

makes about 4 servings

10 small white onions
¼ cup grated cheese of choice
1 can (10¾ ounces) cream of mushroom soup

PANTRY
1 tablespoon butter or margarine

1 Position the rack in the center of the oven and preheat to 375 degrees F. Lightly grease a baking dish.

2 Arrange the onions in the prepared baking dish, pour in the soup, and sprinkle with cheese. Cover and bake for about 30 minutes. Remove the cover and continue to bake for about 10 minutes or until the cheese has melted and the onions are tender. Remove from the oven and serve.

ORANGE-KISSED BRUSSELS SPROUTS

makes about 4 to 6 servings

1 pound Brussels sprouts, trimmed and halved
⅓ cup fresh orange juice
1 teaspoon grated orange rind

PANTRY
Salt and pepper to taste

1 In a bamboo steamer over boiling water, steam the sprouts, covered, for about 15 minutes or until tender.

2 In a saucepan, combine the sprouts, the orange rind, and the orange juice. Cook, stirring frequently, for about 5 minutes or until thoroughly heated. Remove from the heat, season to taste, and serve.

ORANGE BEETS

makes about 3 to 4 servings

1 can (14 ounces) beets, drained and liquid reserved
1 tablespoon orange rind

PANTRY
1 tablespoon cornstarch
2 tablespoons sugar

1 In a bowl, blend the cornstarch and 2 tablespoons of water.

2 In a saucepan, combine the reserved liquid and add the orange rind. Bring to a boil and reduce to a simmer. Cook for about 5 minutes or until the liquid is reduced to one-third of a cup. Blend in the cornstarch mixture and continue to cook, stirring frequently, for about 5 minutes or until thickened. Add the beets and cook for about 10 minutes or until thoroughly heated. Remove from the heat, add the sugar, and serve.

6 medium baking potatoes, pared and cut into chunks

PANTRY

¼ cup melted butter or margarine
1 garlic clove, minced
Salt and pepper to taste

1 Position the rack in the center of the oven and preheat to 375 degrees F. Lightly grease a 13 x 9-inch baking dish.

2 In a bowl, blend the butter and the garlic, and season to taste. Add the potatoes.

3 Arrange the potatoes in the prepared baking dish and bake for about 55 to 60 minutes or until tender and lightly browned. Remove from the oven and serve.

Oven-Roasted Potatoes

makes about 6 servings

---

12 small russet potatoes, pared and halved lenghtwise
Fresh flat-leafed parsley, separated into 24 leaves

PANTRY

6 tablespoons melted butter or margarine
Salt and pepper to taste

1 Position the rack in the center of the oven and preheat to 450 degrees F. Pour the butter into a shallow baking pan.

2 Arrange the potatoes cut side up in the prepared baking pan. Top with the parsley leaves and season to taste. Bake for about 40 minutes or until tender and light golden-brown. Remove from the oven and serve.

Parsley Leaf Potatoes

makes about 6 to 8 servings

---

8 small new potatoes, pared
¼ cup fresh parsley, snipped

PANTRY

1 tablespoon butter or margarine
Salt and pepper to taste

1 In a bamboo steamer over boiling water, arrange the potatoes on a wire rack. Cover and steam for about 15 to 20 minutes or until tender.

2 In a bowl, combine the potatoes, the butter, and the parsley. Season to taste and serve.

Parsley Potatoes

makes about 4 servings

Parsnips Glazed with Sweet Mustard

makes about 6 servings

8 parsnips, trimmed, pared and halved lengthwise

3 tablespoons brown sugar, firmly packed

PANTRY

1 tablespoon butter or margarine

½ teaspoon dry mustard

1 Position the rack in the center of the oven and preheat to 400 degrees F. Lightly grease a shallow baking pan.

2 In a saucepan, cover the parsnips with 1 inch of lightly salted water. Bring to a boil and cover. Cook for about 20 minutes or until tender.

3 Arrange the parsnips in the prepared baking pan, and sprinkle with the sugar and the mustard. Cover and bake for about 10 minutes. Remove the cover and continue to cook, basting frequently, for about 10 minutes or until glazed. Remove from the oven and serve.

Peas and Parsnips

makes about 4 to 6 servings

1 package (10 ounces) frozen green peas, thawed and drained

1¼ cups parsnips, finely diced

PANTRY

1 tablespoon melted butter or margarine

In a saucepan, cover the parsnips and the peas with lightly salted water. Bring to a boil and reduce to a simmer. Cover and cook, stirring occasionally, for about 12 to 15 minutes or until the parsnips are tender. Remove from the heat, drain, drizzle on the butter, and serve.

Vegetables

1 package (10 ounces) frozen
peas, cooked and drained
1 cup lettuce, shredded
1 tablespoon fresh parsley,
snipped

PANTRY
1 cup butter or margarine

In a saucepan, cook the peas
in the butter for about 5 minutes or until thoroughly heated. Remove from the heat,
add the lettuce, sprinkle with
parsley, and serve.

Peas Elegante

makes about 4 to 6 servings

---

1 package (10 ounces) frozen
green peas, cooked and
drained
1 can (8 ounces) sliced
mushrooms, drained
2 cans (4 ounces each)
pimientos, chopped

PANTRY
3 tablespoons butter or
margarine
Salt and pepper to taste

In a saucepan, cook the peas,
the mushrooms, and the
pimientos in the butter for
about 5 minutes or until thoroughly heated. Remove from
the heat, season to taste, and
serve.

Peas with Mushroom and Pimiento

makes about 3 to 4 servings

---

4 large green bell peppers,
stemmed, seeded and cut into
¼-inch rings
4 egg whites, beaten until stiff,
but not dry

PANTRY
1 cup vegetable oil
½ cup flour

1 In a deep fryer, preheat the
oil to about 350 degrees F.

2 Dredge the pepper rings in
the flour and dip in the egg
whites. Place in the hot oil
and fry for about 5 to 10 minutes or until lightly browned.
Transfer to a rack covered
with paper towels, drain,
and serve.

Pepper Fry

makes about 4 servings

Pickled Onion Rings

makes about 6 servings

1 large red onion, thinly sliced

PANTRY
1 teaspoon salt
¼ cup sugar
½ cup rice vinegar

1 In a bowl, sprinkle the onions lightly with salt. Set aside for about 5 minutes and pat dry.

2 In another bowl, combine the sugar and the vinegar. Add the onions and set aside for about 2 hours before using.

Cooking note: This can be refrigerated for up to 2 weeks.

Pickled String Beans

makes about 6 servings

4 pounds string beans, trimmed
2 tablespoons pickling spices

PANTRY
1 cup sugar
1 cup rice vinegar
1 teaspoon salt

1 In a bowl, combine the sugar, the vinegar, and the spices.

2 In a soup kettle, cover the beans with lightly salted water. Bring to a boil and cook for about 15 minutes or until tender. Add the pickling mixture and continue to cook for about 10 minutes or until thoroughly heated. Remove from the heat and serve.

Piselli Alla Napoletana

makes about 4 servings

¼ cup onions, chopped
2 pounds fresh green peas, shelled
1½ teaspoons tomato paste, dissolved in ⅔ cup of boiling water

PANTRY
2½ tablespoons olive oil

In a saucepan, sauté the onions in the oil for about 5 minutes or until translucent. Add the peas and cook, stirring frequently, for about 2 minutes. Add the tomato mixture, bring to a boil, and reduce to a simmer. Cover and cook, stirring occasionally, for about 25 minutes or until tender and most of the liquid has been absorbed. Remove from the heat and serve.

4 medium potatoes, pared and
    thinly sliced
3 medium yellow onions,
    chopped
½ cup bread crumbs

PANTRY
2 tablespoons butter or
    margarine
Salt and pepper to taste

POTATO AND
ONION CAKE

makes about 4 servings

1 Position the rack in the center of the oven and preheat to 350 degrees F. Lightly grease an 8-inch square baking dish.

2 Arrange the potatoes in the prepared baking dish, top with the onions, season to taste, and sprinkle with the bread crumbs. Cover and bake for about 15 minutes. Uncover and continue to bake for 20 minutes or until tender and lightly browned. Remove from the oven and serve.

---

8 medium Idaho potatoes,
cooked and mashed
½ cup flavored bread crumbs

PANTRY
1 cup milk
1 tablespoon flour
Salt and pepper to taste

POTATO MUSH

makes about 4 servings

1 In a small bowl, combine the flour and 1 tablespoon of milk.

2 In a saucepan, combine the potatoes and the milk, and bring to a boil. Cook, stirring frequently for about 2 minutes. Add the flour mixture, season to taste, and cook for about 3 minutes or until thoroughly heated and the liquid has been absorbed. Remove from the heat, top with the bread crumbs, and serve.

---

3 pounds russet potatoes,
    boiled, pared and puréed
¼ cup leftover meat drippings
1 large yellow onion, minced

PANTRY
Salt and pepper to taste

POTATO PANCAKE

makes about 6 to 8 servings

1 In a bowl, combine the potatoes and the onions, and season to taste.

2 In a skillet, cook the potato mixture in the meat drippings over low heat for about 25 minutes or until both sides are lightly browned. Remove from the heat, cut into wedges, and serve.

POTATO PUDDING

makes about 4 servings

2 pounds potatoes, pared and
  grated

2 large eggs, beaten

1 can (8 ounces) mushroom
  stems and pieces, drained

¼ cup yellow onion, minced

PANTRY
Salt and pepper to taste

1 Position the rack in the center of the oven and preheat to 350 degrees F. Lightly grease a 13 x 9 inch-baking pan.

2 In a bowl, combine the potatoes, the eggs, the mushrooms, the onion, and season to taste. Pour into the prepared baking pan and cover.

3 Bake for about 30 minutes. Remove the cover and continue to bake for an additional 30 minutes or until lightly browned. Remove from the oven and serve.

Cooking note: For variation, top with grated cheese and bake for an additional 5 minutes or until the cheese has melted.

POTATO TORTILLAS

makes about 6 servings

3 medium potatoes, pared and
  sliced

4 medium eggs, beaten

PANTRY
¼ cup olive oil
Salt and pepper to taste

1 In a skillet, sauté the potatoes in the oil for about 15 minutes or until just tender. Mash the potatoes and continue to cook, stirring occasionally, for about 5 minutes or until tender.

2 In a bowl, combine the potatoes and the eggs, and season to taste.

3 In the same skillet, cook the potato mixture in the oil over low heat for about 25 minutes or until both sides are lightly browned. Remove from the heat, cut into wedges, and serve.

3 pounds russet potatoes, pared and diced

8 bacon slices, diced

PANTRY

1 cup flour

1 tablespoon melted butter or margarine

1 In a saucepan, cover the potatoes with lightly salted water for about 20 minutes or until tender.

2 In a bowl, using a wire whisk or an electric mixer, combine the potatoes and the flour.

3 On a lightly floured surface, roll out the dough to about ¼-inch thick and cut into strips.

4 Position the rack in the center of the oven and preheat to 375 degrees F. Lightly grease a shallow baking pan.

5 Arrange the strips of dough in the prepared baking pan, top with the bacon, and drizzle with the butter. Bake for about 20 minutes or until the bacon is crisp. Remove from the oven and serve.

POTATOES AND NOODLES

makes about 4 servings

---

4 medium baking potatoes, pared and cut in half lengthwise

PANTRY

8 tablespoons butter or margarine, room temperature

1 Position the grill about 6 inches from the heat.

2 Spread 2 tablespoons of butter on 4 of the potato halves. Wrap a buttered and an unbuttered potato half together in aluminum foil and arrange on the grill. Cook, turning occasionally, for about 30 minutes or until tender. Remove from the grill and serve.

Cooking note: Cooking time for grilling recipes depends on the heat source.

POTATOES ON A GRILL

makes about 4 servings

POTATOES WITH BACON

makes about 6 servings

8 bacon slices, diced
6 medium potatoes, pared and
thinly sliced

PANTRY
1 tablespoon butter or margarine
1 tablespoon flour
2½ cups milk
Salt and pepper to taste

1 Position the rack in the center of the oven and preheat to 350 degrees F. Lightly grease a baking pan.

2 In a skillet, sauté the bacon for about 15 minutes or until crisp.

3 Arrange half of the potatoes in the prepared baking pan. Sprinkle the top with half of the bacon and dust lightly with the flour. Repeat. Pour the milk on top and cover. Bake for about 45 minutes, remove the cover, and season to taste. Continue to bake for about 15 minutes or until the liquid has been absorbed. Remove from the oven and serve.

POTATOES WITH CAPER BUTTER

makes about 4 servings

4 medium russet potatoes, pared
and boiled
1 tablespoon capers, drained
1 tablespoon cider vinegar

PANTRY
¼ cup butter or margarine

In a saucepan, melt the butter and cook until lightly browned. Remove from the heat and add the vinegar and the capers. Pour over the potatoes and serve.

POTATOES WITH OLIVES

makes about 4 to 6 servings

1 onion, sliced
2 pounds russet potatoes, pared
and thinly sliced
¼ pound black Italian olives

PANTRY
6 tablespoons olive oil
Salt and pepper to taste

In a skillet, sauté the potatoes in the oil for about 5 minutes and reduce to a simmer. Add the onions, cook for about 5 minutes, season to taste, and add the olives. Continue to cook for about 5 minutes or until tender. Remove from the heat and serve.

1½ pounds russet potatoes,
pared and thinly sliced

12 ounces leeks, trimmed and
thinly sliced

PANTRY

2 tablespoons melted butter or
margarine

1½ teaspoons dried basil,
crushed

Salt and pepper to taste

1 Position the rack in the center of the oven and preheat to
350 degrees F. Lightly grease a
5-inch round baking pan.

2 Arrange a layer of the potatoes in the prepared baking
pan and top with the leeks.
Sprinkle with the basil and
season to taste. Repeat, ending with the potatoes. Press
down firmly and drizzle with
the butter. Bake for about 50
to 60 minutes or until tender
and lightly browned. Remove
from the oven, slice, and
serve.

POTATO-
LEEK CAKE

makes about 4 to 6 servings

---

1 bunch (8 ounces) carrots,
trimmed, pared and diced

1 rutabaga (8 ounces), trimmed,
pared and diced

1 tablespoon brandy or rum

PANTRY

2 tablespoons butter or
margarine

1 Position the rack in the center of the oven and preheat to
400 degrees F. Lightly grease a
baking pan.

2 In a saucepan, cover the
carrots and the rutabaga with
lightly salted water and bring
to a boil. Cook for about 10 to
12 minutes or until tender.

3 In a bowl, combine the carrots, the rutabaga, the butter,
and the brandy. Pour the mixture into the prepared baking
pan. Bake for about 10 minutes or until the top becomes
crusty. Remove from the oven
and serve.

POTCH

makes about 4 servings

Vegetables

Quick Celery and Snap Beans

makes about 4 servings

2 cups (canned) snap beans, drained

½ cup celery, sliced and cooked

PANTRY

1 tablespoon butter or margarine

Salt and pepper to taste

In a saucepan, combine the butter, the beans, the celery, and ½ cup of water. Bring to a boil and reduce to a simmer. Cover and cook for about 10 minutes or until tender. Remove from the heat, season to taste, and serve.

Radish Fry

makes about 6 servings

3 bunches of fresh radishes, trimmed and sliced

PANTRY

2 tablespoons vegetable oil

Salt and pepper to taste

Listed as 11. Should be 12

In a skillet, stir-fry the radishes for about 10 to 15 minutes or until lightly brown. Remove from the heat, season to taste, and serve.

Raspberry Yams

makes about 6 servings

6 medium yams, pared and cooked

1 package (10 ounces) frozen raspberries, thawed and drained

2 tablespoons brown sugar

PANTRY

2 tablespoons butter or margarine

1 Position the rack in the center of the oven and preheat to 350 degrees F. Lightly grease a baking dish.

2 Arrange the yams in the prepared baking dish and top with the raspberries, the sugar, and the butter. Bake, basting frequently, for about 20 minutes or until thoroughly heated. Remove from the oven and serve.

1 can (15 ounces) ratatouille
2 tablespoons red wine of choice
¾ cup grated cheddar cheese

RATATOUILLE AU GRATIN

makes about 4 servings

1 Position the broiler rack about 4 inches from the heat. Have a shallow baking dish available.

2 In a saucepan, cook the ratatouille and the wine for about 2 minutes or until slightly heated.

3 Pour into the baking dish and top with the cheese. Broil for about 10 minutes or until the cheese has melted. Remove from the broiler and serve.

---

1 large head of red cabbage, trimmed, cored and finely shredded
1 large yellow onion, sliced
¼ cup black or red currant juice

PANTRY
2 tablespoons butter or margarine

RED CABBAGE

makes about 4 servings

In a saucepan, sauté the cabbage and the onions in the butter for about 2 minutes. Pour in the juice and reduce to a simmer. Cover and cook for about 20 to 25 minutes or until just tender. Remove from the heat and serve.

---

4 medium red onions, cut into wedges
4 slices bacon, quartered
2 tablespoons safflower oil
1 tablespoon watercress, chopped

SKEWERED RED ONIONS WITH BACON

makes about 4 servings

1 Position the broiler rack about 4 inches from the heat. Have a shallow baking pan available.

2 Arrange the onion and bacon alternately on four lightly greased metal skewers. Rest the skewers at an angle to avoid touching the bottom of the baking pan. Drizzle with the oil and broil, turning frequently, for about 8 to 10 minutes or until the bacon is crisp. Remove from the oven, garnish with watercress, and serve.

Roasted Garlic Potatoes

makes about 6 to 8 servings

1 can (14½ ounces) chicken broth

11 medium russet potatoes, pared and thinly sliced

PANTRY

1 tablespoon butter or margarine

1 tablespoon garlic powder

1 Position the rack in the center of the oven and preheat to 400 degrees F. Lightly grease a 13 x 9-inch baking pan.

2 In a bowl, blend the broth and the garlic powder.

3 Arrange the potatoes in the prepared baking pan and pour the broth mixture over the top. Cover and bake for about 40 minutes. Remove the cover and bake for an additional 15 minutes or until tender. Remove from the oven and serve.

Roasted Squash with Spinach and Cheese

makes about 4 servings

2 acorn squash (about 1 pound each), halved and seeded

1 package (10 ounces) frozen chopped spinach, thawed and drained

1 cup shredded Gruyère cheese

¼ cup walnuts, chopped

1 Position the rack in the center of the oven and preheat to 400 degrees F. Lightly grease a shallow baking tray.

2 Arrange the squash cut-side down on the prepared baking tray and bake for about 20 to 25 minutes or until tender.

3 In a bowl, combine the spinach, three-quarters of the cheese, and the walnuts.

4 Turn the squash over and fill with the spinach mixture. Sprinkle the remaining cheese over the top and continue to bake for about 15 minutes or until the cheese has melted. Remove from the oven and serve.

Vegetables

1 medium rutabaga, trimmed,
    pared and diced
2 medium onions, minced

PANTRY

3 tablespoons butter or
    margarine
Salt and pepper to taste

RUTABAGA PURÉE

makes about 4 to 6 servings

1 In a saucepan, cover the rutabaga about half way with lightly salted water. Bring to a boil and cover. Cook for about 10 minutes until tender. Remove from the heat and drain.

2 In a bowl, using a wire whisk or an electric mixer, purée the rutabaga until almost smooth. Add the butter and continue to blend for about 1 minute or until smooth. Add the onion, season to taste, and serve.

---

1 medium yellow onion, sliced
1 medium head of cabbage,
    trimmed, cored and finely
    shredded
⅛ teaspoon powdered saffron
½ cup (canned) beef stock

PANTRY

Salt and pepper to taste

SAFFRON CABBAGE

makes about 4 to 6 servings

In a non-stick skillet, sauté the onions for about 5 minutes or until tender. Add the cabbage, the saffron, and the stock and bring to a boil. Cover and cook for about 10 to 12 minutes or until tender. Drain, season to taste, and serve.

---

1 pound potatoes, pared and cut
    into even slices
1 can (20 ounces) sauerkraut
1 tablespoon caraway seeds
12 frankfurters, cooked

SAUERKRAUT WITH POTATOES AND FRANKFURTERS

makes about 4 servings

1 In a saucepan, cover the potatoes with lightly salted water and bring to a boil. Cook until just tender. Drain.

2 In another saucepan, combine the sauerkraut and the caraway seeds, and cook for about 5 minutes or until thoroughly heated. Remove from the heat, top the sauerkraut with the franks, and serve with the potatoes on the side.

Cooking note: For variation, spread mustard on the franks.

Sautéed Bok Choy

makes about 4 servings

1 small head of bok choy, separated and the leaves cut into 4 sections crosswise
3 tablespoons safflower oil
1 medium yellow onion, sliced

In a wok, stir-fry the onions for about 5 minutes or until tender. Add the bok choy. Stir-fry for about 3 minutes and cover. Cook for about 5 minutes or until wilted. Remove from the heat and serve.

Sautéed Collards and Onions

makes about 12 servings

6 pounds collard greens, trimmed and coarsely chopped
2 cups white onions, minced

PANTRY
2 tablespoons vegetable oil
4 garlic cloves, minced
Salt and pepper to taste

1 In a large pot, cover the collard greens with lightly salted water. Bring to a boil and cook for about 4 minutes or until just tender.

2 In a Dutch oven, sauté the garlic and the onions in the oil for about 5 minutes or until tender. Add the collard greens and sauté for about 5 minutes or until tender. Remove from the heat, season to taste, and serve.

Vegetables

Sautéd Okra

makes about 4 to 6 servings

1 pound fresh okra, stemmed and cut lengthwise into narrow strips

PANTRY
3 tablespoons butter or margarine
Salt and pepper to taste

In a skillet, stir-fry the okra for about 3 minutes and season to taste. Cover and simmer over low heat for about 10 minutes. Remove the cover and continue to cook, stirring occasionally, for about 5 minutes or until the liquid has been absorbed. Remove from the heat and serve.

1 medium yellow onion, sliced

1 package (10 ounces) spinach, thawed and drained

3 tablespoons safflower oil

In a wok, stir-fry the onion in the oil for about 5 minutes or until tender. Add the spinach, stir-fry for about 3 minutes, and cover. Cook for about 5 minutes or until wilted. Remove from the heat and serve.

SAUTÉED SPINACH

makes about 4 servings

2 pounds fresh spinach, cooked and chopped

⅓ cup seedless raisins, plumped in boiling water and drained

3 tablespoons pine nuts

1 cup dark bread croutons

PANTRY

2 tablespoons vegetable oil

1 garlic clove, minced

Salt and pepper to taste

1 In a skillet, sauté the garlic and the pine nuts in the oil, stirring frequently, for about 5 minutes or until the garlic is lightly browned. Add the spinach and the raisins, and salt and pepper to taste. Cook for about 5 minutes or until thoroughly heated. Remove from the heat, garnish with croutons, and serve.

SAUTÉED SPINACH AND RAISINS

makes about 4 servings

½ cup yellow onion, grated

¼ cup fresh parsley or cilantro, minced

8 ears of corn, cooked al dente

½ cup Tartar Sauce (see page 411)

1 Position the broiler rack about 4 inches from the heat.

2 In a bowl, combine the sauce, the onion, and the parsley.

3 Arrange the corn in a baking dish and top with the onion mixture. Broil for about 3 to 4 minutes or until the top is lightly browned. Remove from the broiler and serve.

SAVORY BROILED CORN WITH TARTAR SAUCE

makes about 4 servings

SAVORY ROASTED POTATOES

makes about 6 to 8 servings

4 large russet potatoes, pared and cut into bite-sized cubes
¼ cup chicken broth
1½ teaspoons onion salt

PANTRY
¼ cup butter or margarine

1 Position the rack in the center of the oven and preheat to 350 degrees F. Have a baking or cookie sheet available.

2 In a bowl, combine the potatoes and the butter. Arrange on the baking sheet and sprinkle with the onion salt.

3 Bake for about 40 minutes. Pour the broth over the potatoes and continue to bake for about 20 minutes or until tender and the liquid has been absorbed. Remove from the oven and serve.

Cooking note: For variation, replace the onion salt with onion powder.

SAVORY SPINACH CASSEROLE

makes about 4 to 6 servings

2 packages (10 ounces each) frozen chopped spinach, cooked and drained
1 package (8 ounces) Neufchatel cheese, at room temperature
⅓ cup grated Parmesan cheese

PANTRY
¼ cup milk, at room temperature

1 Position the rack in the center of the oven and preheat to 350 degrees F. Have a 1-quart casserole available.

2 In a bowl, using a wire whisk or an electric mixer, blend the milk and the cheese.

3 Place the spinach in the casserole, top with the milk and cheese mix, and sprinkle with the Parmesan cheese.

4 Bake for about 20 minutes or until thoroughly heated. Remove from the oven and serve.

4 cups shredded cabbage, cooked

2 cups Basic White Sauce (see page 398)

¼ cup soft bread crumbs

PANTRY

1 teaspoon butter or margarine

Salt and pepper to taste

1 Position the rack in the center of the oven and preheat to 350 degrees F. Lightly grease a shallow baking dish.

2 Arrange half of the cabbage in the prepared baking dish, top with the half of the sauce, and season to taste. Repeat and sprinkle with the bread crumbs.

3 Bake for about 5 to 6 minutes or until the bread crumbs are toasted. Remove from the oven and serve.

SCALLOPED CABBAGE

makes about 4 servings

---

1 large red onion, sliced

5 cups carrots, diced, cooked and drained

½ pound Velveeta™ cheese, sliced

1½ cups crackers, crushed

PANTRY

½ cup butter or margarine

1 Position the rack in the center of the oven and preheat to 350 degrees F. Lightly grease a 1½-quart baking dish.

2 In a skillet, sauté the onions for about 5 minutes or until tender.

3 Layer the carrots and the cheese in the prepared baking dish. Top with the onions and sprinkle with the crackers. Bake for about 30 minutes or until the top is toasted. Remove from the oven and serve.

SCALLOPED CARROTS

makes about 4 servings

Vegetables

Scalloped Potatoes

makes about 6 to 8 servings

6 medium potatoes, pared and thinly sliced

PANTRY

Salt and pepper to taste
1 tablespoon flour
½ cup milk
2 tablespoons butter or margarine

1 Position the rack in the center of the oven and preheat to 350 degrees F. Lightly grease a shallow baking dish.

2 Arrange half of the potatoes in the prepared baking dish, season to taste, sprinkle with 1½ teaspoons flour, and dot with 1 tablespoon of butter. Repeat and pour the milk over.

3 Cover and bake for about 1 to 1½ hours or until tender. Remove from the oven and serve.

Cooking note: For variation, sprinkle chopped onions between the potato layers.

Scalloped Snap Beans

makes about 4 servings

1½ pounds snap beans, cooked and drained
1 can (10¾ ounces) cream of tomato soup
½ cup grated pepper cheese
½ cup soft bread crumbs

PANTRY

1 tablespoon butter or margarine

1 Position the rack in the center of the oven and preheat to 350 degrees F. Lightly grease a shallow baking dish.

2 Arrange the beans in the prepared baking dish and pour on the soup. Sprinkle with the cheese and the bread crumbs. Cover and bake for about 10 minutes. Remove the cover and continue to bake for about 20 minutes or until the bread crumbs are toasted. Remove from the oven and serve.

2 can (16 ounces each) stewed
   tomatoes
Onion juice to taste
½ cup dry bread crumbs

PANTRY

Salt and pepper to taste
2 tablespoons butter or
   margarine

1 Position the rack in the center of the oven and preheat to
400 degrees F. Lightly grease a
baking dish and sprinkle with
¼ cup bread crumbs.

2 In a bowl, blend the tomatoes and the onion juice to
taste.

3 Pour into the prepared baking dish. Top with the remaining bread crumbs and dot
with the butter. Bake for
about 20 minutes or until the
bread crumbs are toasted.
Remove from the oven and
serve.

SCALLOPED TOMATOES
makes about 6 servings

**1 cup broccoli florettes, cooked
   and drained**
**2 teaspoons sesame seeds,
   toasted**
**2 teaspoons Honey Soy Sauce
   (see page 405)**

PANTRY

1 tablespoon melted butter or
   margarine

1 In a bowl, blend the butter,
the sesame seeds, and the soy
sauce.

2 Add the broccoli, toss gently to coat, and serve.

SESAME BROCCOLI
makes about 4 servings

**4 cups beets, trimmed, pared
   and shredded**

PANTRY

2 tablespoons butter or
   margarine
1 tablespoon red wine vinegar
1 teaspoon sugar
Salt and pepper to taste

In a saucepan, combine the
butter, the beets, the vinegar,
the butter and 2 tablespoons
of water. Cover and cook, stirring occasionally, for about 10
minutes or until just tender.
Remove from the heat, add
the sugar, season to taste, and
serve.

SHREDDED BEETS
makes about 4 to 6 servings

Shredded Parsnips

makes about 4 to 6 servings

9 parsnips, trimmed, pared and coarsely shredded

PANTRY

1 cup vegetable oil
Salt and pepper to taste

1 In a bowl, cover the shredded parsnips with ice water and refrigerate for at least 1 hour. Drain and pat dry.

2 In a deep fryer, preheat the oil to 350 degrees F.

3 Place the parsnips in the hot oil and stir-fry for about 5 minutes or until light golden-brown. Transfer to a rack covered with paper towels and drain. Seasoning to taste and serve.

Shredded Sweet Potatoes with Scallions

makes about 2 servings

1 pound sweet potatoes, pared and shredded
¼ cup scallion, minced
1 teaspoon fresh lemon juice

PANTRY

1½ tablespoons olive oil
½ teaspoon ground cumin powder

In a skillet, sauté the potatoes and the cumin in the oil for about 15 minutes or until just tender. Add the scallions and the lemon juice, and continue to cook for about 2 minutes or until tender. Remove from the heat and serve.

Skillet Hash

makes about 4 servings

2 large yellow onions, chopped
2 medium potatoes, pared, diced and cooked
1 slice (about ¾ to 1 pound) corned beef, diced
1 can (16 ounces) baked beans in tomato sauce

PANTRY

1 tablespoon vegetable oil
Salt and pepper to taste

In a skillet, sauté the onions for about 5 minutes or until tender. Add the potatoes, the beef, and the beans, and season to taste. Cook, stirring occasionally, for about 5 minutes or until thoroughly heated. Flatten the ingredients with a spatula and continue to cook for about 3 minutes or until the bottom has browned. Remove from the heat, cut into wedges, and serve.

1¼ pounds snow peas, trimmed
  and cut lengthwise into 3
  strips
2½ tablespoons (bottled) lemon
  oil
1½ teaspoons poppy seeds

PANTRY
Salt and pepper to taste

1 In a bamboo steamer over
boiling, steam the peas for
about 7 to 8 minutes or until
just tender.

2 In a bowl, combine the
peas, the oil, and the poppy
seeds, season to taste, and
serve.

Snow Peas Tossed with Lemon Oil

makes about 4 servings

2 pounds fresh asparagus,
  trimmed and cut into 2-inch
  pieces
1 scallion, trimmed and minced
½ cup (bottled) Oriental-style
  salad dressing

PANTRY
½ teaspoon dried red pepper
  flakes, crushed

1 In a saucepan, bring 1 quart
of lightly salted water to a
boil and add the asparagus.
Return to a boil and cover.
Continue to cook for about 3
minutes or until just tender.
Drain and rinse thoroughly
under cold water.

2 In a bowl, combine the
asparagus, the scallion, the
salad dressing, and the pepper flakes. Cover with plastic
wrap and refrigerate for at
least 1 hour before serving.

Spicy Chilled Asparagus

makes about 4 servings

1 pound fresh carrots, trimmed,
  pared, and sliced
6 pieces dried red chile peppers
½ cup (bottled) teriyaki baste
  and glaze

PANTRY
2 tablespoons vegetable oil

In a wok, sauté the peppers in
the oil until darkened.
Remove the peppers and add
the carrots. Stir-fry for about 4
minutes or until just tender.
Add the teriyaki baste and
glaze, and cook for about 5
minutes or until the carrots
are glazed. Remove from the
heat and serve.

Spicy Glazed Carrots

makes about 4 servings

Spinach Casserole

makes about 6 servings

2 packages (10 ounces each) frozen chopped spinach, thawed and drained

1 container (16 ounces) sour cream

1 envelope (1 ounce) onion soup mix

PANTRY

1 tablespoon butter or margarine

1 Position the rack in the center of the oven and preheat to 350 degrees F. Lightly grease a 1-quart baking dish.

2 In a bowl, combine the spinach, the sour cream, and the soup mix.

3 Arrange in the prepared baking dish and bake for about 30 minutes or until thoroughly heated. Remove from the oven and serve.

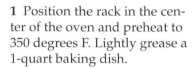

Spinach Loaf

makes about 2 to 4 servings

1 cup brown rice, cooked
1 cup celery, chopped
2 cups spinach, cooked
1 tablespoon wheat germ

PANTRY

1 tablespoon butter or margarine

1 Position the rack in the center of the oven and preheat to 400 degrees F. Lightly grease a 6 x 4-inch baking pan.

2 In a bowl, combine the rice, the celery, the wheat germ, and the spinach. Press into the prepared baking pan and bake for about 30 minutes or until thoroughly heated. Remove from the oven and serve.

Spinach Sauté

makes about 4 servings

1 pound fresh spinach, stemmed

PANTRY

3 tablespoons sesame oil
Salt and pepper to taste

In a saucepan, sauté the spinach in the oil for about 5 minutes or until wilted. Season to taste and serve.

1½ pounds fresh spinach, stemmed

1 tablespoon (bottled) chili oil

PANTRY

1 medium garlic clove, minced

In a Dutch oven, sauté the garlic in the oil for about 5 minutes or until tender. Add the spinach and cover. Cook for about 5 minutes or until wilted. Remove from the heat, season to taste, and serve.

SPINACH WITH CHILI OIL

makes about 3 to 4 servings

---

2 medium onions, finely chopped

2 tablespoons green pepper, finely chopped

2 packages (10 ounces each) frozen spinach, cooked and drained

PANTRY

¼ cup butter or margarine

In a skillet, sauté the onion and the pepper in the butter, stirring occasionally, for about 5 minutes or until the onions are lightly browned. Add the spinach and cook for about 5 minutes or until thoroughly heated. Remove from the heat and serve.

SPINACH WITH ONION AND PEPPER

makes about 6 servings

---

2 cups yellow summer squash, diced

3 medium yellow onions, thinly sliced

PANTRY

3 tablespoons butter or margarine

Salt and pepper to taste

In a skillet, sauté the squash and onions in the butter. Cover and simmer over low heat, stirring occasionally, for about 20 to 30 minutes or until tender. Remove from the heat, season to taste, and serve.

SQUASH AND ONION SAUTÉ

makes about 4 servings

Squash in Syrup

makes about 6 servings

¾ cup dark-brown sugar, firmly packed

1 winter squash (about 3 to 4 pounds), stemmed, seeded and cut into wedges

PANTRY

2 tablespoons butter or margarine

1 Divide the sugar among the squash wedges. Arrange in a large skillet skin-side down. Add 2 tablespoons of water, top with the butter and cover. Cook over low heat for about 30 minutes or until tender.

2 Scoop out the pulp, top with the liquid left in the pan, and serve.

Steamed Ginger Rice with Snow Peas

makes about 4 to 6 servings

2 cups long-grain rice, uncooked

1 teaspoon ginger root, finely grated

¼ pound snow peas, chopped

In a saucepan, bring 4 cups of water to a boil. Add the rice and the ginger, reduce to a slow simmer, and cover. Cook for about 20 minutes or until tender. Add the peas and cover. Cook for about 2 minutes or until thoroughly heated. Remove from the heat, fluff, and serve.

Steamed Mushrooms

makes about 4 to 6 servings

1 pound fresh white button mushrooms, trimmed and thinly sliced

PANTRY

1 tablespoon butter or margarine

In the top of a double boiler over simmering water, combine the butter and the mushrooms, and cover. Cook for about 20 minutes or until tender. Remove from the heat, season to taste, and serve.

1 pound fresh spinach, stemmed

3 tablespoons orange rind, finely chopped

1 tablespoon fresh orange juice

¼ cup chopped nuts of choice

In a large skillet, combine the spinach, the orange rind, and the orange juice, and cover. Cook over high heat, stirring occasionally, for about 5 minutes or until just tender. Remove from the heat, garnish with chopped nuts, and serve.

STEAMED ORANGE SPINACH

makes about 2 to 4 servings

---

4 single taro corns, trimmed, pared and cut into bite-sized cubes

¼ cup Swiss chard, chopped

½ cup (bottled) oyster sauce dressing

PANTRY

¼ cup vegetable oil

2 garlic cloves, crushed

1 In a saucepan, cover the taro with lightly salted water. Soak for about 20 minutes and bring to a boil. Cook for about 10 to 15 minutes or until tender.

2 In a skillet, sauté the garlic in the oil for about 5 minutes or until lightly browned. Add the chard and cook over low heat for about 5 minutes or until wilted. Add the taro and cook for about 5 minutes or until thoroughly heated. Remove from the heat and serve with the dressing on the side.

STEAMED TARO WITH SWISS CHARD

makes about 4 servings

---

2 medium acorn squash (about 2 to 2½ pounds), stemmed, seeded and cut in half lengthwise

PANTRY

2 tablespoons butter or margarine

⅓ cup milk

Salt and pepper to taste

1 In a bamboo steamer over boiling water, cover and steam the squash cut-side down for about 20 minutes or until tender. Remove from the steamer and scoop out the pulp.

2 In a saucepan, combine the pulp, the butter, and the milk. Simmer over low heat for about 5 minutes or until thoroughly heated. Remove from the heat, season to taste, and serve.

STEWED ACORN SQUASH

makes about 4 servings

Stewed Tomatoes

makes about 4 servings

2½ cups quartered tomatoes
¼ teaspoon light-brown sugar, firmly packed

PANTRY
4 teaspoons butter or margarine
4 teaspoons flour

In a saucepan, combine the butter, the tomatoes, the sugar and the flour. Cook over low heat, stirring frequently, for about 10 minutes or until thoroughly heated. Remove from the heat and serve.

Cooking note: For variation, try adding sautéed onions, mushrooms, and Worcestershire sauce and top with grated cheese of choice.

Stir-Fried Bean Sprouts

makes about 4 to 8 servings

10 dried mushrooms, trimmed and chopped
4 shallots, sliced
8½ ounces fresh bean sprouts
¼ cup (bottled) oyster sauce

PANTRY
2 tablespoons vegetable oil
1 garlic clove, minced

In a wok, stir-fry the garlic, the mushrooms and the shallots in the oil for about 2 to 3 minutes. Add the bean sprouts and cook for about 5 minutes. Blend in the oyster sauce and stir-fry for about 2 to 3 minutes or until tender. Remove from the heat and serve.

Cooking note: For variation, add dry sherry while cooking.

Stir-Fried Broccoli and Mushrooms

makes about 4 servings

1 small white onion, cut into wedges
2 cups broccoli florettes
2 cups mushrooms, sliced

PANTRY
2 tablespoons vegetable oil
1 large garlic clove, minced

In a wok, stir-fry the onion and garlic in the oil for about 5 minutes or until tender. Add the broccoli and the mushrooms and season to taste. Stir-fry for about 5 minutes or until the broccoli is just tender. Remove from the heat and serve.

Vegetables

3 tablespoons peanut oil
1 pound fresh spinach, trimmed
1 slice (about ¼ to ½ pound) boiled ham, cut into thin strips

PANTRY

½ teaspoon sugar
Salt and pepper to taste

In a large skillet, stir-fry the spinach in the oil for about 5 minutes or until the leaves are coated with the oil. Add the sugar and the ham, and stir-fry for about 5 minutes or until thoroughly heated. Remove from the heat, season to taste, and serve.

STIR-FRIED SPINACH

makes about 4 servings

---

1 boneless, skinless chicken breast, cut into strips
1 teaspoon safflower oil
1 cup of mixed vegetables
½ teaspoon sesame seeds

1 In a wok, stir-fry the chicken in the oil for about 3 to 5 minutes or until tender. Transfer to a warming plate.

2 In the same wok, stir-fry the vegetables and the sesame seeds for about 5 minutes or until just tender. Add the chicken and stir-fry for about 3 minutes or until thoroughly heated. Remove from the heat and serve.

STIR-FRIED VEGETABLES

makes about 4 servings

347

Vegetables

---

1 pound frozen whole kernel corn, thawed and drained
1 pound frozen baby lima beans, thawed and drained
1½ cups Basic White Sauce (see page 398)

PANTRY

Salt and pepper to taste

In a large saucepan, cover the corn and the beans with lightly salted water. Bring to a boil and cook, stirring occasionally, for about 12 to 15 minutes or until just tender. Remove from the heat, drain, and return to the pot. Blend in the white sauce and cook for about 5 minutes or until thoroughly heated. Remove from the heat, season to taste, and serve.

SUCCOTASH

makes about 8 to 10 servings

Sweet and Sour Beets

makes about 4 servings

2 bunches fresh beets, trimmed, pared and coarsely grated

PANTRY
2 tablespoons rice vinegar
1 teaspoon sugar
2 tablespoons butter or margarine
Salt and pepper to taste

In a saucepan, combine the beets, 3 or 4 tablespoons of water, the vinegar, and the sugar. Cover and simmer for about 10 minutes or until tender. Remove from the heat, add the butter, season to taste, and serve.

Sweet Beets with Applesauce

makes about 4 to 6 servings

1 can (16 ounces) diced beets, drained
1 cup (bottled) unsweetened applesauce

PANTRY
1 tablespoon butter or margarine
Salt and pepper to taste

In top of a double boiler over boiling water, mash the beets into a purée. Blend in the applesauce and season to taste. Remove from the heat, blend in the butter, and serve.

Sweet 'n' Sour Spinach

makes about 6 servings

3 cups cooked spinach, finely chopped

PANTRY
1 teaspoon sugar
1 tablespoon rice wine vinegar
Salt and pepper to taste
2 tablespoons butter or margarine

1 In a bowl, combine the spinach, the sugar, and the vinegar, and season to taste.

2 In a saucepan, cook the spinach mixture in the butter, stirring frequently, over low heat for about 5 minutes or until thoroughly heated. Remove from the heat and serve.

Vegetables

2 cans (16 ounces each) sweet potato halves, drained
1 cup fresh cranberries
1½ cups miniature marshmallows
½ cup orange marmalade

PANTRY
1 tablespoon butter or margarine

1 Position the rack in the center of the oven and preheat to 350 degrees F. Lightly grease a 10 x 6-inch baking pan.

2 Arrange the potatoes in the prepared baking pan. Top with the cranberries and the marmalade. Bake for about 30 minutes or until tender.

3 Sprinkle with the marshmallows and broil for 3 to 4 minutes or until the marshmallows are lightly browned. Remove from the broiler and serve.

Cooking note: For variation, garnish with chopped pecans.

SWEET POTATO BERRY BAKE

makes about 6 to 8 servings

---

1 medium sweet potato, pared and diced
1 cup fresh broccoli, chopped
½ cup low-fat cottage cheese
1 tablespoon sesame seeds

1 In a saucepan, bring the potatoes and 1 cup of water to a boil and cook for about 15 minutes. Add the broccoli and reduce to a simmer. Continue to cook for about 5 to 6 minutes or until the potatoes are tender.

2 In a bowl, combine the potatoes, the broccoli, the cottage cheese, and the sesame seeds, and serve.

SWEET POTATOES AND BROCCOLI

makes about 2 to 3 servings

SWEET POTATOES WITH APPLESAUCE

makes about 6 servings

3 large sweet potatoes, pared and cut into bite-sized pieces
¼ cup brown sugar, firmly packed
2 cups unsweetened applesauce

PANTRY
¼ cup butter or margarine

1 Position the rack in the center of the oven and preheat to 350 degrees F. Lightly grease a baking dish.

2 In a saucepan, cover the potatoes with lightly salted water and bring to a boil. Cook for about 15 minutes or until just tender.

3 Arrange the potatoes in the prepared baking dish. Dot with the butter, sprinkle with the sugar, and spoon the applesauce over the top. Bake for about 30 minutes or until tender. Remove from the oven and serve.

Cooking note: This recipe uses sweet potatoes, not yams (see glossary).

SWEET WHIPPED CARROTS

makes about 4 servings

8 medium carrots, trimmed, pared, sliced and boiled
2 tablespoons heavy cream
¼ cup seedless raisins, plumped

PANTRY
2 tablespoons butter or margarine
Salt and pepper to taste

1 In a bowl, mash the carrots.

2 Using a wire whisk or an electric mixer, blend in the butter and the cream until smooth. Add the raisins, season to taste, and serve.

Cooking note: For variation, plump the raisins in brandy.

2 ounces Swiss cheese, grated

6 medium fresh tomatoes, halved

PANTRY

¼ cup mayonnaise

½ teaspoon paprika

1 Position the broiler rack about 4 inches from the heat. Have a baking pan available.

2 In a bowl, using an electric mixer, blend the mayonnaise, the cheese, and the paprika.

3 Arrange the tomatoes cut side up on the baking pan and spread the cut surfaces with the cheese mixture. Broil for about 3 to 5 minutes or until the tops are lightly browned. Remove from the oven and serve.

Cooking note: For variation, try different kinds of cheeses.

SWISS BROILED TOMATOES

makes about 6 servings

1 small head of cauliflower, trimmed and cut into florettes

2 teaspoons tandoori spice mix

1 tablespoon fresh lemon juice

⅔ cup unflavored yogurt

PANTRY

1 tablespoon butter or margarine

1 Lightly grease a shallow baking dish.

2 In a saucepan, bring the cauliflower florettes to a boil in 1 quart of lightly salted water. Cook for about 5 minutes or until tender. Drain and arrange in the prepared baking pan.

3 In a small bowl, blend the spice mix, the lemon juice, and the yogurt. Pour over the cauliflower and cover. Set aside for about 1 hour.

4 Position the rack in the center of the oven and preheat to 350 degrees F.

5 Uncover cauliflower and bake for about 30 minutes or until tender and lightly browned. Remove from the oven and serve.

TANDOORI CAULIFLOWER

makes about 4 servings

Tart and Hot Turnips

makes about 4 to 6 servings

2 cups turnips, thinly sliced

¼ teaspoon red pepper flakes, crushed

PANTRY

½ cup rice vinegar

2 teaspoons sugar

1 In a bowl, sprinkle the turnip slices lightly with salt and set aside for 30 minutes. Drain and pat dry.

2 In a bowl, combine the turnips, the vinegar, the sugar, and the pepper. Cover with plastic wrap and refrigerate, stirring occasionally, for at least 8 hours before serving.

Tiny Corn Casserole

makes about 4 servings

½ pound sliced bacon

2 cups whole kernel corn

2 cups creamy-style corn (canned)

1 large egg, beaten until foamy

PANTRY

1 teaspoon butter or margarine

Salt and pepper to taste

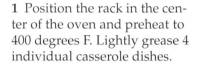

1 Position the rack in the center of the oven and preheat to 400 degrees F. Lightly grease 4 individual casserole dishes.

2 Reserve 4 bacon slices and set aside. Chop the remaining slices into small pieces.

3 In a skillet, sauté the bacon pieces for about 5 minutes or until crisp and drain off the bacon drippings. Blend in the whole kernel and the creamy-style corn, and season to taste.

4 Arrange in the prepared casserole dishes and top with the reserved bacon slices. Bake for about 30 minutes or until thoroughly heated and the bacon is crisp. Remove from the oven and serve.

1 can (16 ounces) tomatoes,
   drained, reserving the juice
3 cups green or red cabbage,
   shredded
1 teaspoon instant beef bouillon
   granules

In a skillet, combine the
reserved juice and the bouillon granules. Bring to a boil
and cook for about 1 minute
or until the granules have dissolved. Reduce to a simmer,
add the cabbage, and cook for
about 3 minutes. Add the
tomatoes and cover. Cook for
about 15 minutes or until the
cabbage is tender. Remove
from the heat and serve.

TOMATO AND CABBAGE STEW

makes about 2 servings

6 firm fresh tomatoes
2½ cups pinto beans, cooked
3 broiled bacon slices, halved
¼ cup grated cheese of choice

PANTRY
1 tablespoon butter or margarine

1 Position the rack in the center of the oven and preheat to
350 degrees F. Lightly grease a
13 x 9-inch baking pan.

2 Cut the tops off the tomatoes, scoop out the centers,
and fill with the beans.
Arrange in the prepared baking pan and bake for about 20
minutes or until the tomato
skins start to wrinkle. Top
with the bacon slices and continue to bake for about 10
minutes or until the bacon has
browned. Remove from the
oven, garnish with grated
cheese, and serve.

TOMATOES STUFFED WITH BEANS

makes about 6 servings

Tomatoes Stuffed with Spinach

makes about 6 servings

6 firm fresh tomatoes
2 cups spinach, cooked
½ medium yellow onion, minced
½ cup grated cheese of choice

PANTRY
1 tablespoon melted butter or margarine

1 Position the rack in the center of the oven and preheat to 375 degrees F. Lightly grease a 13 x 9-inch baking dish.

2 In a bowl, blend together the spinach, the butter, and the onion.

3 Cut the tops off the tomatoes, scoop out the centers, and fill with the spinach mixture.

4 Arrange in the prepared baking pan and bake for about 20 minutes or until the tomato skins start to wrinkle. Top with the cheese and continue to bake for about 10 minutes or until the cheese has melted. Remove from the oven and serve.

Tropical Sweet Potatoes

makes about 8 to 10 servings

4 cups sweet potatoes, sliced and cooked
½ cup flaked coconut, toasted
1 can (15 ounces) coconut cream

PANTRY
1 tablespoon melted butter or margarine

1 Position the rack in the center of the oven and preheat to 350 degrees F. Lightly grease a 13 x 9-inch baking pan.

2 Arrange the sweet potatoes in overlapping rows in the prepared baking pan and drizzle with the butter.

3 In a saucepan, bring the coconut cream to a boil. Cook, stirring occasionally, for about 10 minutes or until the cream has reduced to about two-thirds. Pour over the potatoes and sprinkle with the flaked coconut.

4 Bake for abut 20 minutes or until bubbly. Remove from the oven and serve.

1 pound fresh asparagus,
   trimmed
½ cup grated Monterey Jack
   cheese
1 cup bread crumbs

PANTRY
1 tablespoon butter or margarine

1 Position the rack in the center of the oven and preheat to 350 degrees F. Lightly grease a baking dish.

2 In a bamboo steamer over boiling water, steam the asparagus for about 10 minutes or until just tender. Drain, reserving the liquid, and cut the asparagus into 1-inch pieces.

3 Arrange, in alternating layers with the bread crumbs in the prepared baking dish. Dot with the butter and drizzle the reserved liquid over the top.

4 Bake for about 15 minutes. Sprinkle with the cheese and continue to bake for about 5 minutes or until the cheese has melted. Remove from the oven and serve.

TWICE-COOKED ASPARAGUS

makes about 4 servings

12 medium potatoes, unpared
   and quartered lengthwise

PANTRY
1 teaspoon garlic powder
½ teaspoon chili powder

1 Position the rack in the center of the oven and preheat to 400 degrees F. Have a baking or cookie sheet available.

2 In a large pot, cover the potatoes with lightly salted water and bring to a boil. Cover and cook for about 30 minutes or until tender.

3 In a small bowl, blend the garlic and chili powder.

4 Arrange the potatoes on the baking sheet and sprinkle with the garlic and chili powder. Bake for about 15 minutes or until light golden-brown. Remove from the oven and serve.

TWICE-COOKED POTATOES

makes about 6 to 8 servings

Two-Potato Fries

makes about 6 servings

¾ **pound baking potatoes, cut into wedges**

¾ **pound sweet potatoes, cut into wedges**

PANTRY

1 tablespoon vegetable oil

¼ teaspoon paprika

1 Position the rack in the center of the oven and preheat to 400 degrees F. Lightly grease a baking or cookie sheet.

2 In a bowl, combine the potatoes, the oil, and the paprika. Arrange on the prepared baking sheet.

3 Bake for about 30 minutes or until both sides are browned and just tender. Remove from the oven, season to taste, and serve.

Cooking note: This recipe uses sweet potatoes, not yams (see glossary).

Vegetable Burger

makes about 6 to 8 servings

½ **cup mixed dried vegetables, soaked in hot water and drained**

2 **pounds ground beef**

¼ **cup grated Romano cheese**

PANTRY

1 tablespoon vegetable oil

¼ teaspoon onion powder

1 In a bowl, combine the vegetables, the beef, the cheese, and the onion powder. Form into 8 patties.

2 In a skillet, sauté the patties in the oil for about 30 minutes, turning and browning on both sides. Remove from the heat and serve.

2 pounds turnips, trimmed, peeled and chopped
2 large eggs
¼ cup light cream
½ cup bread crumbs

PANTRY
1 tablespoon melted butter

Vegetable Pudding

makes about 3 to 4 servings

1 Position the rack in the center of the oven and preheat to 350 degrees F. Lightly grease a shallow baking dish.

2 In a saucepan, cover the turnips with lightly salted water. Boil for about 20 minutes or until just tender.

3 In a bowl, using a wire whisk or an electric mixer, blend the cream and the eggs until smooth. Add the bread crumbs and the turnips.

4 Pour into the prepared baking dish and bake for about 40 minutes. Drizzle with the melted butter and continue to bake for about 10 minutes or until lightly browned. Remove from the oven and serve.

1 pound carrots, trimmed, pared and sliced diagonally
2 teaspoons light-brown sugar, firmly packed
1 tablespoon cilantro, snipped fresh

PANTRY
2 tablespoons butter or margarine

Vichy Carrots

makes about 3 to 4 servings

In a saucepan, cover the carrots with lightly salted water. Bring to a boil and reduce to a simmer. Cook for about 20 minutes or until most of the water has evaporated. Add the butter and the sugar, and cook, stirring frequently, for about 3 minutes or until the carrots are lightly glazed. Remove from the heat, sprinkle with the cilantro, and serve.

WALNUT-SAUTÉED SNOW PEAS AND WATER CHESTNUTS

makes about 4 servings

2 tablespoons walnut oil
2 cups fresh snow peas, trimmed
1 can (8 ounces) sliced water chestnuts, drained

PANTRY
¼ teaspoon sesame oil
Salt and pepper to taste

In a skillet, sauté the peas in the oil, stirring frequently, for about 3 minutes. Add the chestnuts and continue to cook, stirring occasionally, for about 2 to 3 minutes or until just tender. Remove from the heat, drizzle with sesame oil, season to taste, and serve.

WINE-GLAZED SHALLOTS

makes about 4 to 6 servings

18 shallots, peeled
1½ cups Zinfandel
¾ cup apple juice

PANTRY
1½ tablespoons butter or margarine
6 tablespoons sugar
Salt and pepper to taste

In a skillet, sauté the shallots in the butter over low heat, stirring frequently, for about 5 minutes or until lightly browned. Blend in the sugar and the wine. Cook, stirring occasionally, for about 3 minutes or until the sugar has dissolved. Cover and simmer for about 20 minutes or until the liquid has thickened. Blend in the apple juice and continue to cook for about 5 minutes or until tender. Remove from the heat, season to taste, and serve.

Cooking note: Any dry red wine could be used in this recipe.

WINE-SOAKED ONIONS

makes about 6 to 8 servings

4 cups onions, thinly sliced
2 cups dry white wine
½ cup fresh parsley, snipped

PANTRY
Salt and pepper to taste

In a container with a tight-fitting lid, combine the onions, the wine, and the parsley. Season to taste, cover and refrigerate for about 5 days before serving.

2 medium yams, pared and
  thinly sliced
1 large Macintosh apple, cored
  and thinly sliced
¼ cup unsweetened applesauce
½ cup apple cider

PANTRY
1 tablespoon butter or margarine
1 tablespoon cinnamon

1 Position the rack in the center of the oven and preheat to 400 degrees F. Lightly grease an 8-inch square baking dish.

2 In a bowl, blend the applesauce and the apple cider.

3 Layer the yams and the apples in the prepared baking pan. Pour the apple mixture over the top and sprinkle with the cinnamon. Cover and bake for about 40 minutes or until tender. Remove from the oven and serve.

YAM AND APPLE CASSEROLE

makes about 4 servings

---

3 yellow bell peppers, trimmed,
  seeded and cut into ½-inch
  squares
1 cup fresh bread crumbs

PANTRY
2 tablespoons olive oil
1 medium garlic clove, minced

In a skillet, sauté the peppers in the oil for about 10 minutes or until just tender. Add the garlic and the bread crumbs. Continue to cook, stirring occasionally, for about 5 minutes or until the bread crumbs are browned and the peppers are tender. Remove from the heat and serve.

YELLOW BELL PEPPER SQUARES

makes about 2 to 4 servings

Zesty Grilled Potatoes

makes about 6 servings

4 medium potatoes, unpared
½ cup Italian dressing

PANTRY
Salt and pepper to taste

1 Position the grill about 3 inches from the heat.

2 In a saucepan, cover the potatoes with lightly salted water. Cook for about 20 minutes or until tender.

3 Arrange the potatoes in a shallow baking pan and cover with the dressing. Set aside for about 1 hour, turning occasionally to coat. Remove from the dressing and transfer to the grill.

4 Grill the potatoes for about 16 to 20 minutes or until both sides are golden-brown. Remove from the grill, season to taste, and serve.

Cooking note: Cooking time for grilling recipes depends on the heat source.

Zucchini Pie

makes about 6 servings

4 cups zucchini, finely diced
½ cup yellow onion, minced
2 large eggs, beaten
½ cup bread crumbs

PANTRY
Salt and pepper to taste

1 Position the rack in the center of the oven and preheat to 375 degrees F. Lightly grease a 9-inch pie plate.

2 In a bowl, combine the zucchini, the onions, the eggs, and the bread crumbs, and season to taste.

3 Press into the prepared pie plate and bake for about 25 minutes or until tender. Remove from the oven, cut into wedges, and serve.

3 cups zucchini, grated, drained and patted dry
3 large eggs, beaten
½ cup whole wheat flour
1 cup grated mozzarella cheese

PANTRY
¼ teaspoon salt
1½ cups (bottled) tomato sauce

1 Position the rack in the center of the oven and preheat to 450 degrees F.

2 On a flat, lightly floured surface, combine the zucchini, the eggs, the flour, and the salt. Knead the dough until smooth and spread out to fit a 12-inch round pizza pan.

4 Bake for about 20 minutes or until just firm. Remove from the oven and reduce the temperature to 350 degrees F.

5 Spread the tomato sauce on the crust and top with the cheese. Bake for about 10 minutes or until the cheese has melted. Remove from the oven and serve.

Cooking note: For variation, add your favorite toppings.

ZUCCHINI PIZZA CRUST

makes about 6 servings

½ cup peanut oil
3 zucchinis (each about 8 inches long), trimmed, pared and cut crosswise into ½-inch slices
2 ounces grated Romano cheese
2 tablespoons fresh parsley, chopped

PANTRY
Salt and pepper to taste

In a skillet, sauté the zucchini in the oil for about 20 to 25 minutes or until tender and both sides are lightly browned. Remove from the heat, season to taste, top with the cheese, garnish with parsley, and serve.

ZUCCHINI ROMANO SAUTÉ

makes about 6 servings

Zucchini Supreme

makes about 4 servings

**1 pound zucchini, trimmed and
  sliced**
**1 can (8 ounces) mandarin
  orange sections, drained**
**¼ cup pecans or almonds,
  chopped**

PANTRY
¼ teaspoon ground nutmeg

1 In a bamboo steamer over
boiling water, steam the zucchini for about 10 minutes or
until tender.

2 In a bowl, combine the zucchini, the orange wedges, the
nutmeg, and the pecans, and
serve.

Broccoli and Pine Nuts

makes about 3 to 4 servings

2 pounds fresh broccoli florettes
3 tablespoons fresh lime juice
¼ cup pine nuts, toasted

PANTRY
1 tablespoon butter or margarine

1 In a steamer over boiling
water, steam the florettes for
about 2 minutes.

2 In a skillet, stir-fry the broccoli in the butter for about 3
minutes or until tender.
Remove from the heat, sprinkle with the lime juice and the
nuts, and serve.

Broccoli with Sesame Oil

makes about 4 servings

2 pounds fresh broccoli florettes
**1 teaspoon sesame seeds,
  toasted**

PANTRY
1 teaspoon sesame oil
1 teaspoon soy sauce

1 In a saucepan, bring 1½
quarts of lightly salted water
to a boil. Add the florettes
and cook for about 2 to 3 minutes or until just tender. Rinse
in ice cold water and drain.

2 In a bowl, combine the oil,
the soy sauce, and the seeds.
Add the broccoli and serve.

2 pounds fresh broccoli florettes

PANTRY
¾ cup olive oil
½ cup rice wine vinegar
2 teaspoons mustard powder
2 garlic cloves, minced

1 In a steamer set over boiling water, steam the florettes for about 2 to 4 minutes or until just tender. Rinse under cold water and drain.

2 In a bowl, blend the oil, the vinegar, the mustard, and the garlic. Add the broccoli and serve.

BROCCOLI WITH VINAIGRETTE

makes about 4 to 6 servings

---

2 large russet potatoes, scrubbed and cut into slices
¼ cup (bottled) Italian salad dressing

PANTRY
Salt and pepper to taste

1 Position the broiler rack about 4 inches from the heat.

2 In a plastic bag, combine the potatoes and the dressing.

3 Remove the potatoes from the bag, arrange them on the broiler pan, and broil, turning once, for about 12 to 15 minutes or until tender. Remove from the oven, season to taste, and serve.

BROILED POTATO SLICES

makes about 4 servings

---

11 cups shredded cabbage

PANTRY
⅓ cup sugar
⅓ cup ketchup
⅓ cup white vinegar

1 In a small saucepan, combine the sugar, the ketchup, and the vinegar and bring to a boil. Cook, stirring frequently, for about 3 minutes or until the sugar has dissolved.

2 In a large bowl, combine the cabbage and the hot dressing, cover with plastic wrap, and refrigerate for at least 3 hours before serving.

BARBECUED SLAW

makes about 6 to 8 servings

Brussels Sprouts and Carrot Salad

makes about 4 servings

1 package (10 ounces) frozen Brussels sprouts, thawed and drained

1 package (10 ounces) frozen sliced carrots, thawed and drained

½ cup lemon-shaker dressing

1 In a saucepan, combine the sprouts and the carrots, and cover with water. Bring to a boil and reduce to a simmer. Cover and cook for about 10 minutes or until tender. Drain and pat dry. Dip into a cold water bath. Drain and pat dry.

2 In a bowl, combine the vegetables and the dressing. Cover with plastic wrap and refrigerate for at least 4 hours before serving.

Brussels Sprouts with Nuts

makes about 4 servings

1 pound Brussels sprouts, trimmed

¼ cup hazelnuts, toasted and ground, or almonds, sliced

PANTRY

2 teaspoons olive oil

⅛ teaspoon ground cardamom

1 Cut an "X" into the base of each sprout.

2 In a steamer over boiling water, steam the sprouts for about 7 to 8 minutes or until tender.

3 In a bowl, combine oil, the nuts, and the cardamom. Add the sprouts and serve.

Potato Celery Bake

makes about 4 servings

6 medium potatoes, pared and diced

1 can (10½ ounces) cream of celery soup

½ cup wine of choice (optional)

PANTRY

5 tablespoons butter or margarine

Salt and pepper to taste

1 Position the rack in the center of the oven and preheat to 350 degrees F. Lightly grease a 1½-quart baking dish.

2 Arrange the potatoes in the prepared baking dish. Dot with the butter and pour in the soup and ½ cup of water (or the wine). Cover and bake for about 1 hour or until tender. Remove from the oven, season to taste, and serve.

1½ **pounds fresh bamboo shoots**

¼ **pound fresh mustard greens, leaves only**

PANTRY

1 teaspoon sugar

1 cup vegetable oil

Salt and pepper to taste

1 In a saucepan, cover the bamboo shoots with water and bring to a boil. Cook for about 25 minutes. Drain and cut into strips.

2 In a deep fryer, heat the oil to about 375 degrees F. Fry the bamboo shoots for about 10 minutes or until light golden-brown.

3 In a bowl, combine the bamboo shoots and the sugar.

4 In the same deep fryer, fry the leaves for about 10 to 15 minutes or until crisp. Remove from the heat, season to taste, top with the bamboo shoots, and serve.

Cooking note: The greens may cause the oil to splatter.

FRIED BAMBOO SHOOTS WITH MUSTARD GREENS

makes about 4 servings

4 **large russet potatoes, baked and halved lengthwise**

4 **large eggs**

¼ **cup white onion, finely minced**

2 **tablespoons watercress, minced**

PANTRY

1 tablespoon butter or margarine

Salt and pepper to taste

1 Position the rack in the center of the oven and preheat to 350 degrees F. Have a shallow baking dish available.

2 Scoop most of the potato out of the skins. Mash, add the butter, and salt and pepper to taste.

3 Arrange the potato shells in the baking dish. Sprinkle the insides of the shells with the onion. Fill with the mashed potato.

4 Make a shallow hollow on top of each potato and drop an egg in each one.

5 Bake for about 15 minutes or until the eggs are cooked. Remove from the oven, garnish with watercress, and serve.

POTATOES FILLED WITH EGGS AND ONIONS

makes about 4 servings

POTATOES ELEGANTE

makes about 4 to 6 servings

1 cup grated Parmesan cheese
6 medium potatoes, thinly sliced
2 tablespoons chives, chopped

PANTRY
⅓ cup melted butter or
   margarine
Salt and pepper to taste

1 Position the rack in the center of the oven and preheat to 400 degrees F. Lightly grease an 8-inch pie plate and sprinkle with some of the cheese.

2 Layer half of the potatoes in the prepared pie plate and brush with the butter. Sprinkle with cheese and repeat.

3 Bake for about 1 hour or until tender and the cheese has melted. Remove from the oven, season to taste, garnish with chives, and serve.

REFRIGERATOR POTATOES

makes about 8 to 10 servings

9 large russet potatoes, cooked, drained and mashed
2 packages (3 ounces each) cream cheese
1 cup sour cream or unflavored yogurt

PANTRY
2 tablespoons butter or
   margarine

1 In a bowl, using a wire whisk or an electric mixer, blend the potatoes, the cream cheese, the sour cream, and the butter. Beat until light and fluffy. Arrange in a baking dish, cover and refrigerate for about 30 minutes.

2 Position the rack in the center of the oven and preheat to 350 degrees F.

3 Bake the potatoes for about 30 minutes or until thoroughly heated. Remove from the oven and serve.

Cooking note: Leftover potatoes can be refrigerated for up to 2 weeks and can be reheated several times.

1 package (10 ounces) frozen
  baby Brussels sprouts in
  butter sauce, prepared.
½ cup seedless green grapes
2 tablespoons slivered almonds
2 tablespoons dry white wine

In a bowl, combine the Brussels sprouts, the grapes, and the wine. Garnish with slivered almonds and serve.

Royal Brussels Sprouts

makes about 3 to 4 servings

1 large stalk broccoli, sliced
  lengthwise
3 tablespoons peanut oil

PANTRY
1 tablespoon soy sauce

In a skillet, sauté the broccoli in the oil for about 2 minutes. Blend in the soy sauce, ¼ cup of water, and season to taste. Cover and continue to cook, stirring occasionally, for about 6 to 7 minutes or until just tender. Remove from the heat and serve.

Sautéed Broccoli

makes about 4 servings

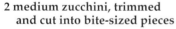

2 medium zucchini, trimmed
  and cut into bite-sized pieces
1½ teaspoons sesame seeds,
  toasted
1 teaspoon Honey Soy Sauce
  (see page 405)
1 tablespoon fresh lemon juice

PANTRY
1 tablespoon sesame oil
Salt and pepper to taste

1 On the rack of a bamboo steamer over boiling water, steam the zucchini for about 5 minutes or until tender.

2 In a bowl, combine the zucchini, the oil, the sesame seeds, and the soy sauce, and season to taste. Sprinkle with the lemon juice and serve.

Sesame Zucchini

makes about 2 servings

Soft Sauerkraut with Mustard

makes about 4 servings

1 pound sauerkraut (in glass or plastic container)
1 cup light cream

PANTRY
1 teaspoon prepared mustard

In a saucepan, combine the sauerkraut, the cream, and the mustard. Simmer for about 20 minutes or until tender. Remove from the heat and serve.

Soy Sauce Potatoes

makes about 4 servings

2 medium potatoes, pared and cut into bite-sized cubes

PANTRY
¼ cup (bottled) soy sauce
½ cup sugar
Salt and pepper to taste

In a saucepan, combine the potatoes, 2 cups of water, the soy sauce, the sugar, and season to taste. Cook uncovered, stirring occasionally, for about 20 minutes or until just tender. Remove from the heat and drain, reserving the cooking liquid. Serve with the reserved liquid on the side.

Vegetable Cheese Filling

makes about 2 servings

1 small zucchini, trimmed
1 large tomato, peeled, seeded and diced
2 ounces (canned) green chilis, rinsed, seeded and chopped
¾ cup shredded cheddar cheese

1 In a saucepan, cover the zucchini with water. Bring to a boil and cover. Cook for about 5 minutes or until just tender. Drain and dice.

2 In a bowl, combine the zucchini, the tomato, the chilis, and the cheddar, and serve.

Cooking note: This can be used as a filling for sandwiches or as a topping for fruits and vegetables.

VEGETABLE LOAF

makes about 6 servings

1 large yellow onion, sliced
1 medium carrot, trimmed, pared and sliced
2 cups cornmeal mush, cooked
6 bacon slices

PANTRY
¼ cup peanut butter
1 tablespoon flour

1 Place a 9 x 5-inch loaf baking pan in the freezer 1 hour before cooking.

2 In a saucepan, cover the onions and the carrots with lightly salted water. Bring to a boil and reduce to a simmer. Cook for about 7 to 10 minutes or until tender.

3 In a bowl, mash the carrots and onions into a purée. Blend in the cornmeal mush and the peanut butter. Pour into the prepared loaf pan and refrigerate for about 1 hour. Cut into ½-inch slices and dust with the flour.

4 In a skillet, sauté the bacon for about 5 to 7 minutes or until browned. Transfer to a warming plate.

5 In the same skillet, sauté the vegetable slices for about 20 minutes or until both sides are lightly browned. Remove from the heat and serve with the bacon on the side.

1891 CREAMED CABBAGE

makes about 4 servings

1 medium head of cabbage, thinly sliced
½ cup heavy cream

PANTRY
1 tablespoon butter or margarine
Salt and pepper to taste

In a saucepan, combine the cabbage and 1 cup of water. Bring to a boil and reduce to a simmer. Cook for about 15 minutes or until tender. Drain the liquid and blend in the cream and the butter, and season to taste. Cook for about 5 minutes or until thoroughly heated. Remove from the heat and serve.

SQUAW CORN

makes about 4 servings

4 bacon slices, cut into 1-inch pieces
½ green bell pepper, diced
2 cups whole kernel corn
2 large eggs, beaten

PANTRY
Salt and pepper to taste

In a skillet, sauté the bacon for about 5 minutes or until browned. Add the pepper and continue to cook for about 5 minutes or until just tender. Add the corn and continue to cook, over low heat, for about 5 minutes. Add the eggs and continue to cook, stirring occasionally, for about 5 minutes or until the eggs have set. Remove from the heat, season to taste, and serve.

STEAMED SHREDDED CABBAGE

makes about 4 to 6 servings

1 small head of bok choy, cut into ½-inch slices and salted
¼ cup sesame seeds, toasted
¼ cup peanut oil, heated

In a steamer over boiling water, steam the cabbage for about 5 minutes or until tender. Remove from the heat, top with the hot oil, sprinkle with the sesame seeds, and serve.

STEAMED SPINACH

makes about 6 servings

2 pounds fresh spinach, trimmed

PANTRY
¼ cup olive oil
1 garlic clove, minced
Salt and pepper to taste

In a steamer over boiling water combine the oil, the garlic, and the spinach. Cover and steam for about 5 to 10 minutes or until tender. Remove from the heat, season to taste, and serve.

STIR-FRIED CELERY

makes about 4 servings

4 cups celery, diagonally sliced
1½ cups white mushrooms, sliced
1½ cups pea pods
3 scallions, trimmed and sliced

PANTRY
3 tablespoons vegetable oil

In a wok, stir-fry the celery in the oil for about 3 minutes or until just tender. Add the mushrooms, the pea pods, and the onions. Sir-fry for about 5 minutes or until thoroughly heated. Remove from the heat and serve.

Cooking note: For variation, add Oriental-style sauce while cooking and garnish with slivered almonds and thinly sliced orange rind.

Desserts

CUSTARD IN A PUMPKIN

When it comes to desserts, the 4-Ingredient cook is an aficionado of fruit and all the great ways there are to whip them into sweet wonders. Since most desserts require a number of ingredients and a significant amount of time, we've found that fruit can deliver all the pleasures of baked sweets without the fuss. Here are mouthwatering treats, including Zabaglione, Apricot Kumquat Balls, Bananas Wrapped in Tortillas, Blueberry Couscous Cake, and Carambola with Strawberries. Included, too, are interesting ways to prepare Baked Apples. Our dessert fruits can be prepared in a multitude of ways: they are baked in Hawaiian Baked

GRILLED SOMERSET ORANGES

TOMATO SPICE CAKE

Peaches, grilled Fruit Kebabs, or fried in Fried Plantains in Butter. Anyway you slice it, our quick-to-prepare desserts are sweet indeed.

Almond Cookie Shells

makes about 6 servings

3 large egg whites, beaten
½ cup sliced almonds, toasted

PANTRY
2 tablespoons sugar
2 tablespoons flour

1 Position the rack in the center of the oven and preheat to 350 degrees F. Lightly grease a muffin tray.

2 In a bowl, combine the eggs, the flour, the sugar, and the almonds. Pour the mixture into the prepared muffin cups to create shells.

3 Bake for about 10 minutes or until just done. Remove from the oven, turn the muffin cups over, remove the shells, and let them cool before serving.

Cooking note: These shells can be used with favorite dessert fillings.

Almond Custard Filling for Tarts

makes about 4 to 6 servings

2 large eggs, beaten until foamy
1 teaspoon almond extract

PANTRY
1 cup milk
2½ tablespoons sugar

1 Position the rack in the center of the oven and preheat to 375 degrees F. Have 6 small prebaked tart shells ready.

2 In a bowl, blend the eggs, the milk, the sugar, and the almond extract. Pour into the prepared tart shells.

3 Bake for about 30 minutes or until a cake tester inserted into the center comes out clean.

4 Remove from oven and serve.

6 medium Macintosh apples, cored
¾ cup mincemeat

PANTRY
1 tablespoon butter or margarine
1 cup sugar

1 Position the rack in the center of the oven and preheat to 300 degrees F. Lightly grease a 13 x 9-inch baking pan.

2 In a small bowl, blend the sugar and 2 cups of water.

3 Fill the centers of each apple with 2 tablespoons of the mincemeat. Arrange in the prepared baking pan and pour in the sugar water.

4 Bake for about 1 hour or until tender. Remove from the oven and serve with the pan juices on the side.

Cooking note: This dish can be served with a main course or for dessert.

APPLES STUFFED WITH MINCEMEAT

makes about 6 servings

---

4 dried apricots, chopped
5 to 6 dried kumquats, chopped
½ cup powdered sugar

In the container of a blender or food processor, process the apricots and the kumquats until finely minced. Pour the mixture into a bowl and shape into small balls. Roll in the sugar until completely covered. Set aside to dry and serve.

APRICOT-KUMQUAT BALLS

makes about 4 servings

Desserts

---

1 medium avocado, pared, seeded and cut into 8 wedges
1 medium pink grapefruit, pared and separated into 8 wedges
1 small red onion, thinly sliced
1 tablespoon (bottled) poppy seed sauce

In a bowl, combine the avocado and the grapefruit. Top with the onion slices, drizzle with the sauce, and serve.

AVOCADO AND GRAPEFRUIT SALAD

makes about 4 servings

BAKED APPLES WITH RAISINS

makes about 2 servings

2 medium Granny Smith apples, pared and cored
2 tablespoons golden raisins
½ cup fresh orange juice

PANTRY
1 tablespoon butter or margarine
½ teaspoon cinnamon

1 Position the rack in the center of the oven and preheat to 350 degrees F. Lightly grease an 8-inch square baking pan.

2 Fill the apples with the raisins and arrange in the prepared baking pan. Pour the juice over the apples and sprinkle with the cinnamon. Bake for about 1 hour or until tender. Remove from the oven and serve.

BAKED BANANAS

makes about 4 servings

4 firm bananas, peeled and cut in half lengthwise
2 tablespoons fresh lemon juice
1 tablespoon lemon or orange rind
¼ cup brown sugar, firmly packed

PANTRY
¼ cup melted butter or margarine

1 Position the rack in the center of the oven and preheat to 350 degrees F. Lightly grease a 13 x 9-inch baking pan.

2 Arrange the bananas flat side down in the prepared baking pan. Brush with the lemon juice, sprinkle with the sugar, and drizzle with the butter.

3 Bake for about 15 minutes or until thoroughly heated. Remove from the oven, sprinkle with the rind, and serve.

BANANAS AU GRATIN

makes about 4 to 6 servings

8 large bananas, peeled and thinly sliced
1 tablespoon confectioner's sugar
6 scoops vanilla ice cream

PANTRY
2 tablespoons melted butter or margarine

1 Position the rack in the center of the oven and preheat to 400 degrees F. Lightly grease 6 custard dishes. Arrange the dishes on a baking or cookie sheet.

2 Divide the bananas among the prepared dishes. Lightly brush with the butter and sprinkle with the sugar.

3 Bake for about 8 minutes. Transfer to the broiler and broil for about 2 minutes or until the tops have browned. Remove from the oven, top with the ice cream, and serve.

2 (8 inches in diameter) flour
  tortillas
2 small bananas, peeled
1 tablespoon peanut butter
1 tablespoon grape jelly

Place the tortillas in a
microwave-proof dish and
microwave on high heat for
about 10 to 20 seconds or
until thoroughly heated.
Spread the tortillas with the
peanut butter and the jelly.
Place the bananas in the centers of the tortillas. Fold the
edges over the bananas, jelly-
roll fashion, and secure with a
toothpick. Return to the
microwave and microwave
on high heat for about 10 seconds or until thoroughly heated. Remove from the
microwave and serve.

BANANAS WRAPPED IN TORTILLAS

makes about 2 servings

¼ cup powdered sugar
1½ cups flaked coconut
2 cans (11 ounces each)
  mandarin orange sections,
  drained
2 large bananas, peeled and
  thinly sliced

1 In a small bowl, combine
the sugar and the coconut.

2 In a serving dish, arrange
half of the orange slices and
top with the sugar mixture.
Layer on half of the banana
slices and top with the sugar
mixture. Repeat. Cover with
plastic wrap and refrigerate
for at least 1 hour before serving.

BANANA, ORANGE AND COCONUT AMBROSIA

makes about 4 servings

---

6 cups sweetened apple juice
1 tablespoon vanilla extract
1 pint fresh blueberries
3 cups couscous

1 In a saucepan, combine
the apple juice, the vanilla
extract, and the couscous and
bring to a boil. Cook, stirring
occasionally, for about 15 to
20 minutes or until thickened.
Remove from the heat and
blend in the blueberries.

2 Pour into a 13 x 9-inch dish
and cover with plastic wrap.
Refrigerate for about 2 hours
before serving.

BLUEBERRY COUSCOUS CAKE

makes about 4 to 6 servings

Carambola with Strawberries

makes about 6 servings

2 cups sliced carambola (starfruit)

2 cups fresh strawberries, halved

¾ cup Champagne

PANTRY

¼ cup sugar

In a bowl, sprinkle the carambola with the sugar and refrigerate for about 2 hours. Add the strawberries, pour the Champagne over the fruit and serve.

Chinese Baked Apples

makes about 6 servings

6 medium Macintosh apples, stemmed and cored

¼ teaspoon grated fresh ginger root

¾ cup date jam or preserves

PANTRY

1 tablespoon butter or margarine

1 Position the rack in the center of the oven and prehcat to 300 degrees F. Lightly grease a 13 x 9-inch baking pan.

2 Fill each apple with 1 scant tablespoon of jam and arrange in the prepared baking pan. Coat apples with the remaining jam and sprinkle with the ginger. Bake for about 20 minutes or until tender. Remove from the oven and serve.

Desserts

Chinese Fruit Compote

makes about 6 servings

2 large Macintosh apples, pared, cored and cut into wedges

2 medium oranges, pared and separated into sections

1 small cantaloupe, pared, seeded and cut into bite-sized cubes

1 can (14 ounces) lychee nuts, drained

1 tablespoon fresh lemon juice

In a bowl, combine the apples, the oranges, the cantaloupe, the nuts, and the lemon juice. Cover with plastic wrap and refrigerate for about 4 hours before serving.

1 small pumpkin, seeded, most
   of the pulp removed and the
   top reserved
3 large eggs
½ cup light-brown sugar, firmly
   packed
1 can (14 ounces) coconut milk

1 In a bowl, using a wire
whisk or an electric mixer,
blend the eggs, the sugar, and
the coconut milk. Pour the
mixture into the pumpkin
and replace the top.

2 In a bamboo steamer over
boiling water, steam the
pumpkin for about 40 min-
utes or until the custard has
set. Remove from the heat
and serve.

CUSTARD IN A PUMPKIN

makes about 4 to 6 servings

---

6 large winesap apples, peeled,
   cored and sliced
¼ cup lemon juice
¾ pound peanut brittle, finely
   crushed

PANTRY
1 tablespoon butter or margarine

1 Position the rack in the center of the oven and preheat to
325 degrees F. Lightly grease a
baking dish.

2 Arrange the apples in the
prepared baking dish. Sprinkle with the lemon juice and
top with the peanut brittle.
Bake for about 40 minutes or
until tender. Remove from the
oven and serve.

ESCALLOPED APPLES

makes about 6 to 8 servings

---

4 large winesap apples,
   stemmed, pared, cored and
   chopped
½ cup light corn syrup
¼ cup fresh lemon juice

PANTRY
1 tablespoon sugar

In the container of a blender
or food processor, combine
the apples, the corn syrup, the
lemon juice, and the sugar.
Process until smooth and
transfer to a bowl. Cover with
plastic wrap and refrigerate
for about 1 hour before serving.

FRESH APPLESAUCE

makes about 4 to 6 servings

Fried Plantains in Butter

makes about 4 servings

2 large plantains, peeled and sliced

1 tablespoon coconut oil

1 tablespoon sweetened lemon juice

PANTRY

¼ cup butter or margarine

In a skillet, sauté the plantains in the butter and the oil, turning frequently, for about 4 minutes or until browned on both sides. Transfer to a rack covered with paper towels. Drain, sprinkle with the lemon juice, and serve.

Frosted Kumquats

makes about 4 servings

1 large egg white, beaten until stiff

14 dried kumquats

½ cup powdered sugar

1 Place the egg and the sugar in separate bowls.

2 Dip the kumquats in the egg white and roll in the sugar until completely coated. Place on a rack and dry for 5 minutes. Roll again in the sugar and serve.

Frosted Litchi

makes about 4 servings

1 large egg white, beaten until stiff

1 can (11 ounces) litchi, drained

½ cup powdered sugar

1 Place the egg and the sugar in separate bowls.

2 Dip the litchi in the egg white and roll in the sugar until completely coated. Place on a rack and dry for 5 minutes. Roll again in the sugar and serve.

2 large honeydew melons, tops and bottoms cut off

1 can (8 ounces) crushed pineapple, drained

2½ cups red seedless grapes

2 small cantaloupes, pared, seeded, and cut into bite-sized pieces

1 Scoop out the seeds and pulp from the honeydew melons. Cut the pulp into bite-sized pieces and reserve. Wash the melon shells and turn upside down on a rack covered with paper towels to dry. Place in plastic bags and refrigerate for at least 4 hours.

2 In a bowl, combine the reserved honeydew pulp, the pineapple, the grapes, and the cantaloupes. Cover and refrigerate for at least 1 hour. Arrange the fruit mixture inside the melon shells and serve.

FRUIT IN HONEYDEW SHELLS

makes about 24 servings

4 large cantaloupes, pared and cut into 1½-inch chunks

4 large honeydew melons, pared and cut into 1½-inch chunks

1 watermelon, rind removed and melon cut into 1½-inch chunks

3 tablespoons fresh lemon or orange juice

1 In a bowl, combine the cantaloupe, the honeydew, and the watermelon. Drizzle with the lemon juice. Cover with plastic wrap and refrigerate for at least 2 hours.

2 Position the broiler rack about 4 inches from the heat.

3 Arrange 2 cantaloupe chunks, 2 honeydew melon chunks, and 2 watermelon chunks on each of the two metal skewers. Place in a baking pan.

4 Broil for about 10 to 15 minutes or until thoroughly heated and slightly brown. Remove from the oven and serve.

Cooking note: For variation, top with fresh chopped mint.

FRUIT KEBABS

makes about 2 servings

GINGER-STUFFED APRICOTS

makes about 4 servings

1 pound dried apricots, halved
½ teaspoon ginger preserves
½ cup powdered sugar

1 In a bamboo steamer over boiling water, steam the apricots for about 15 minutes or until tender. Remove from the heat and cool.

2 Spoon the preserves into the centers of half of the apricots. Top with the unfilled apricot halves and press together to seal. Roll in the sugar until completely coated. Set aside for about 1 hour and serve.

GRAPEFRUIT WITH PORT

makes about 6 servings

3 pink grapefruits, halved, segments loosened and pitted
2 tablespoons powdered sugar
2 tablespoons white port
3 ounces Stilton cheese, crumbled

1 Position the broiler rack about 4 inches from the heat.

2 Arrange the grapefruit cut side up in a baking pan. Sprinkle with the sugar, the wine, and the cheese. Broil for about 5 minutes or until the cheese has melted and slightly browned. Remove from the oven and serve.

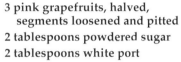

GRILLED HONEY APPLES

makes about 4 to 6 servings

3 medium Macintosh apples, peeled, cored and sliced into ¾-inch rings

PANTRY
¼ cup butter or margarine
⅓ cup honey

1 Position the grill about 6 inches from the heat.

2 Arrange the apple rings on foil. Dot with the butter and drizzle with the honey. Bring the edges of the foil together and seal.

3 Place on the edge of the grill. Cook, turning occasionally, for about 12 to 15 minutes or until just tender. Remove from the grill and serve.

Cooking note: Cooking time for grilling recipes depends on the heat source.

2 large navel oranges, halved, segments loosened and pitted

¾ cup finely grated cheddar cheese, at room temperature

2 tablespoons Triple Sec

4 pecan halves

1 Position the broiler rack about 6 inches from the heat.

2 In a small bowl, combine the cheese and the liqueur.

3 Arrange the oranges cut side up in a baking pan and top with the cheese mixture. Broil for about 5 minutes or until the cheese has melted and slightly browned. Remove from the oven, garnish with pecan halves, and serve.

Cooking note: For variation, top with mint leaves.

Grilled Somerset Oranges

makes about 4 servings

---

8 firm medium peaches, dipped in boiling water and skins removed

½ cup light brown sugar, firmly packed

½ cup canned unsweetened pineapple juice

1 cup coconut-flavored whipped cream

1 Position the rack in the center of the oven and preheat to 350 degrees F. Lightly grease an 8-inch square baking dish.

2 Arrange the peaches in the prepared baking dish. Sprinkle with the sugar and pour on the juice. Cover and bake for about 20 minutes. Remove the cover and continue to bake, basting occasionally, for about 10 minutes or until the peaches are glazed. Remove from the oven and serve with the whipped cream on the side.

Cooking note: This dish can be served hot or cold.

Hawaiian Baked Peaches

makes about 8 servings

Irish Apple Mash

makes about 4 servings

1 pound Granny Smith apples, pared, cored and diced

2 pounds potatoes, pared, cooked and mashed

PANTRY

1 tablespoon sugar

2 tablespoons butter or margarine

1 In a saucepan, combine the apples and the sugar. Add water to just cover the apples and bring to a boil. Cook, stirring occasionally, for about 10 to 15 minutes or until tender.

2 In a bowl, combine the apples, the potatoes, and the sugar, and serve.

Jewish Apple and Matzo Kugel

makes about 4 to 6 servings

6 matzos, broken into pieces, dipped in water and squeezed dry

1 medium Granny Smith apple, pared and diced

2 large eggs, separated

PANTRY

1 tablespoon vegetable shortening

Sugar to taste

Salt and pepper to taste

1 Position the rack in the center of the oven and preheat to 350 degrees F. Lightly grease a baking dish.

2 In a small bowl, using a wire whisk or an electric mixer, beat the egg whites until stiff but not dry. Set aside.

3 In another bowl, using a wire whisk or an electric mixer, beat the egg yolks until smooth. Add the matzo, the apples, the shortening, and sugar, and season to taste.

4 Gently fold in the egg whites.

5 Pour the mixture into the prepared baking dish and bake for about 1 hour or until the top is light golden-brown. Remove from the oven and serve.

½ cup dried lotus seeds, cleaned and skins removed

¼ cup pearl tapioca

⅓ cup dried seedless loganberries

PANTRY

Sugar to taste

In a saucepan, cover the lotus seeds with water. Bring to a boil and reduce to a simmer. Cover and cook for about 40 minutes or until tender. Blend in the tapioca, bring to a boil and reduce to a simmer. Cover and cook for about 30 minutes. Blend in the berries and cook for about 30 minutes or until tender. Blend in the sugar to taste. Remove from the heat and serve.

LOTUS SEED AND LOGAN PUDDING

makes about 4 servings

⅔ cup shredded or flaked coconut

3 cans (11 ounces each) mandarin orange sections, drained

PANTRY

⅓ cup sugar

1 In the container of a blender or food processor, process the coconut until fine.

2 In a serving dish, arrange the orange sections, and sprinkle with the sugar and the coconut. Cover with plastic wrap and refrigerate for at least 1 hour before serving.

MANDARIN ORANGE AMBROSIA

makes about 4 servings

1½ cups yellow mung beans

¼ cup coconut milk, beaten

PANTRY

2 tablespoons arrowroot or cornstarch

1 cup sugar

1 In a bowl, cover the beans with 2 cups of water. Set aside for about 20 minutes. Drain.

2 In a small bowl, blend the arrowroot and ¼ cup of hot water.

3 In a saucepan, just cover the beans with water. Bring to a boil and reduce to a simmer. Cook for about 15 minutes and add the arrowroot mixture and the sugar. Continue to cook for about 15 minutes, or until the water has been absorbed. Remove from the heat, top with the coconut milk, and serve.

Cooking note: This dish can be served hot or cold and can be refrigerated for up to 1 week.

MUNG BEAN PUDDING

makes about 4 servings

OLD-FASHIONED FRIED PEACHES

makes about 4 servings

6 fresh peaches, pared, halved and seeded
¼ cup brown sugar, firmly packed
1 cup whipped cream

PANTRY

2 tablespoons butter or margarine
1 teaspoon cinnamon or nutmeg

In a skillet, melt the butter, and add the peaches cut side up. Fill the peaches with sugar. Cover and cook over low heat for about 10 to 15 minutes or until tender. Remove from the heat, sprinkle with the cinnamon, and serve with whipped cream on the side.

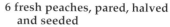

ORANGE DELIGHT

makes about 4 to 6 servings

2 cups small-curd cottage cheese
2 cup (canned) crushed pineapple, drained
1 large package orange-flavored gelatin
2 cups whipped cream

In a bowl, combine the cottage cheese, the pineapple, the gelatin, and the whipped cream. Refrigerate for about 2 hours before serving.

PEARS POACHED IN GRAPE JUICE

makes about 4 servings

½ cup red grape juice
4 firm pears, stems removed
4 mint leaves

PANTRY

3 tablespoons sugar
¾ teaspoon cinnamon
¾ teaspoon allspice

1 In a saucepan, combine the grape juice, ½ cup of water, the sugar, the cinnamon, and the allspice. Bring to a boil and cook, stirring frequently, for about 3 minutes or until the sugar has dissolved.

Reduce to a simmer, add the pears and cover. Cook, turning the pears frequently, for about 15 minutes or until just tender. Transfer to a warming plate.

2 Return the grape juice mixture to a boil and cook for about 10 minutes or until the liquid is reduced by half. Spoon over the pears, garnish with mint, and serve.

1 can (20 ounces) pineapple
  chunks, drained and chilled
3 tablespoons plum wine
½ cup sweetened flaked coconut

In a bowl, combine the pineapple, the wine, and the coconut. Refrigerate for about 1 hour before serving.

PINEAPPLE PLUM WINE AMBROSIA

makes about 4 servings

---

2 packages (15 ounces each) nut
  bread mix
1¼ cups golden raisins
2 large eggs, beaten
1 can (30 ounces) pumpkin pie
  filling

1 Position the rack in the center of the oven and preheat to 400 degrees F. Lightly grease two muffin pans.

2 In a bowl, combine the bread mix and the raisins.

3 In a second bowl, blend the eggs and the pie filling. Add the bread mix and the raisins, stirring until just moistened. Pour into the prepared muffin cups, filling about two-thirds full.

4 Bake for about 15 to 20 minutes or until a cake tester inserted into the center comes out clean. Remove from the oven, cool, and serve.

PUMPKIN RAISIN MUFFINS

makes about 3 dozen

Desserts

---

1 can (16 ounces) creamed rice
  pudding
3 tablespoons sweetened cocoa
  powder mix
2 tablespoons chocolate cookies,
  crushed

In a bowl, combine the rice and 2 tablespoons cocoa powder. Sprinkle the top with remaining cocoa powder and refrigerate for about 1 hour. Garnish with crushed chocolate cookies and serve.

QUICK CHOCOLATE RICE

makes about 2 to 3 servings

Roman-Style Custard

makes about 3 servings

3 large egg yolks, beaten

PANTRY
2 cups milk
¼ cup honey
¾ teaspoon ground nutmeg
(reserve ½ teaspoon for
garnish)

1 Position the rack in the center of the oven and preheat to 325 degrees F. Have a 1-quart baking dish available.

2 In a saucepan, combine the milk and the honey. Cook over low heat for about 10 minutes or until thoroughly heated. Remove from the heat, and blend in the egg yolks and ¼ teaspoon nutmeg.

3 Pour into the baking dish and bake for about 1 hour or until set. Remove from the oven, garnish with nutmeg, and serve.

Sweet Apple and Potato Purée

makes about 4 servings

4 medium russet potatoes, pared and cut into eighths
3 large Granny Smith apples, cored and quartered

PANTRY
1 tablespoon honey
¼ teaspoon ground cinnamon
1 tablespoon butter or margarine
Salt and pepper to taste

1 In a saucepan, cover the potatoes and the apples with 1 cup water. Bring to a boil and reduce to a slow simmer. Cover and cook for about 15 to 20 minutes. Blend in the honey and the cinnamon. Continue to cook for about 10 minutes or until the potatoes are tender.

2 Remove from the heat, add the butter, mash until smooth, season to taste, and serve.

Sweet Rice Cakes

makes about 4 servings

1 pound sweet rice flour
1 pound black bean paste

PANTRY
¾ cup sugar

1 In a bowl, combine the flour, 3 cups of water, and the sugar. Pour into a lightly greased baking pan. Place the pan inside of a larger pan filled with boiling water. Steam for about 30 minutes or until cake tester inserted into the center comes out clean.

2 Form into small, flat patties. Spoon 1 tablespoon of the bean paste into the centers of the patties, seal the edges, and roll into balls. Flatten the balls slightly and serve.

Desserts

1 package double layer spice
  cake mix (prepared)
1 can (10¾ ounces) condensed
  tomato soup

1 Position the rack in the center of the oven and preheat to
350 degrees F. Have a baking
dish available.

2 In a bowl, blend the cake
mix and the soup.

3 Pour into the baking dish
and bake for about 20 to 30
minutes or until a cake tester
inserted into the center comes
out clean. Remove from the
oven and serve.

Cooking note: For variation,
top with cream cheese frost-
ing.

TOMATO SPICE CAKE

makes about 8 to 12 servings

1 medium (about 4 pounds)
  pumpkin, stemmed, seeded,
  pared and cut into bite-sized
  pieces
½ cup walnuts, ground

PANTRY
2 tablespoons sugar

In a Dutch oven, combine the
pumpkin, the sugar, and 1
cup of water. Bring to a boil
and reduce to a simmer.
Cover and cook for about 30
minutes or until tender.
Remove from the heat,
drain, cool to room
temperature, garnish
with ground walnuts,
and serve.

TURKISH PUMPKIN DESSERT

makes about 6 servings

5 egg yolks
½ cup Marsala, port or sherry
18 crackers of choice

PANTRY
¾ cup sugar
Salt to taste

In the top of a double boiler
over a boiling water, using a
wire whisk or an electric
mixer, beat the egg yolks with
1 tablespoon water, until
foamy and light. Blend in the
sugar, the salt to taste, and the
wine, and continue to beat
until thick and fluffy (do not
allow to boil). Remove from
the heat and serve with crackers on the side.

ZABAGLIONE

makes about 6 servings

Beverages

To quench your thirst for everything made with 4-or-less ingredients, we've included a short chapter on beverages.

You'll find coffees, including Amaretto Coffee, Calypso Coffee, and Gaelic Coffee. Here, too, are surprising elixirs, such as Beef Cooler; a juicy delight for the kids called Jungle Juice, and the best Tomato Juice Cocktail this side of horseradish. Enjoy!

AMARETTO COFFEE

Amaretto Coffee

makes about 1 serving

1½ teaspoons instant coffee crystals
3 tablespoons Amaretto
Dessert cream

In a microwave-proof cup, blend together ¾ cup water and the coffee. Cover and microwave on high heat for about 1 to 1½ minutes or until steaming hot. Blend in the Amaretto, add the dessert cream and serve.

Anise Milk

makes about 4 servings

1 teaspoon anise seed, crushed

PANTRY
1 quart milk
1 tablespoon sugar

In a saucepan, heat the milk for about 5 minutes or until it comes to the boiling point. Blend in the sugar and the anise, remove from the heat and serve.

Cooking note: This drink can be served cold and anise extract can be substituted for anise seeds.

Banana Liqueur

makes about 1 quart

2 medium bananas, peeled and sliced
1 teaspoon vanilla extract
1 cup vodka

PANTRY
1 cup sugar

1 In the container of a blender or a food processor, combine the bananas, the vanilla, the vodka, and the sugar. Process on high speed until smooth. Blend in the remaining vodka and process on high speed for about 30 seconds or until smooth. Pour into a jar with a tight-fitting cover.

2 Place in a dark area, shaking several times, and let ferment for about 1 week. Shake, strain through a sieve, pour into a bottle, and use as desired.

Cooking note: The flavor of this liqueur will enhance with age.

1 can (10½ ounces) beef broth
½ cup club soda, chilled
4 lemon wedges

In a bowl, blend the broth and the club soda. Serve over ice with lemon wedges on the side.

BEEF COOLER

makes about 3 to 4 servings

---

4 teaspoons dark-brown sugar, firmly packed
¾ cup dark rum
1¼ cups extra strong fresh coffee
⅔ cup heavy cream, chilled

In a saucepan, combine the sugar, the rum, and the coffee. Cook, stirring frequently, for about 3 minutes or until the sugar has dissolved. Remove from the heat, top with the chilled cream, and serve.

Cooking note: For variation, whip the cream before topping the coffee.

CALYPSO COFFEE

makes about 4 cups

---

4 teaspoons light-brown sugar, firmly packed
¾ cup Scotch whiskey
1¼ cups freshly made coffee
⅔ cup heavy cream, chilled

In a saucepan, combine the sugar, the whiskey, and the coffee. Cook, stirring frequently, for about 3 minutes or until the sugar has dissolved. Remove from the heat, top with the chilled cream, and serve.

Cooking note: For variation, whip the cream before topping the coffee.

GAELIC COFFEE

makes about 4 cups

JUNGLE JUICE

makes about 12 servings

5 bananas, peeled and sliced

5 medium Valencia oranges, pared, pith removed, seeded and sliced

5 lemons, pared, pith removed, seeded and sliced

PANTRY

Sugar to taste

In the container of a blender or food processor, combine the bananas, the oranges, and the lemons. Process on low speed until just chopped and add sugar to taste. Pour the mixture into a bowl and refrigerate for about 1 hour before serving.

TOMATO JUICE COCKTAIL

makes about 10 servings

1 can (46 ounces) tomato juice

½ to ¾ teaspoon Tabasco™ sauce

6 small limes, thinly sliced

PANTRY

2 teaspoons dried cumin, crushed

Salt to taste

In a bowl, blend the juice, the cumin, the Tabasco sauce, and the salt to taste. Cover with plastic wrap and refrigerate for at least 1 hour. Garnish with lime slices and serve.

Cooking note: For variation, add vodka to make a "Bloody Mary."

VANILLA-ALMOND COFFEE

makes about 1 cup

⅓ cup ground coffee

1 teaspoon vanilla extract

½ teaspoon almond extract

¼ teaspoon anise seeds

In the container of a blender or food processor, combine the coffee, the vanilla extract, the almond extract, and the anise seeds. Process on high speed until smooth. Pour into a container with a tight-fitting cover.

Cooking note: To prepare coffee, use 1 cup water with the coffee blend in your home coffeemaker.

2 cups seedless grapes, chilled
2 cups fresh orange juice
1½ tablespoons Triple Sec
6 mint leaves

In a small bowl, blend the orange juice and the liqueur. Pour over the grapes, garnish with mint, and serve.

Orange Juice with Grapes

makes about 6 servings

Sauces, Dips, Condiments, and Dressings

RUJAK MANIS

The 4-Ingredient cook is a well-prepared chef. At a moment's notice, you can scan the pantry to see what's cooking. And you know that a certain sauce or a spicy condiment will wake up the flavor in a particular food. In fact, one of the most important tools of the well-prepared chef is having a great repertoire of sauces and dressings at your fingertips. Here are recipes aplenty to help you become the great 4-Ingredient cook. For sauces, there's Almondine Butter Sauce, where the almonds are stir-fried deep golden-brown to unleash their flavor; a Basic Marinade-Barbecue Sauce, which utilizes Russian and French Dressing; and a Cilantro Pesto, which contains pungent miso spread. You'll also find toppings, fillings,

APPLE BUTTER

BASIC WHITE SAUCE

seasonings, spreads, dips, mustards, mayonnaises, and special-flavored butters.

Learn these recipes well and you'll never worry about what to prepare for dinner again.

ALMONDINE BUTTER SAUCE

makes about ⅔ cup

PANTRY
⅓ cup butter or margarine
½ cup sliced almonds
¼ cup lemon juice from concentrate

In a saucepan, stir-fry the almonds in the butter until deep golden-brown. Remove from the heat, stir in the lemon juice, and serve over fish or vegetable dishes.

ALMOND TOPPING FOR CASSEROLES

makes about 1½ cups

1 cup bread crumbs
½ cup almonds, chopped

PANTRY
2 tablespoons butter or margarine
1 teaspoon Seasoning Salt (see page 14)

In a saucepan, combine the butter, the bread crumbs, and the salt. Cook, stirring frequently, for about 5 minutes or until browned. Add the almonds and cook for about 3 minutes or until lightly toasted. Remove from the heat and serve.

APPLE BUTTER

makes about 4 servings

1 jar (32 ounces) unsweetened applesauce

PANTRY
1½ teaspoons ground cinnamon
½ teaspoon ground cloves
½ teaspoon ground allspice

1 In a saucepan, combine the applesauce, the cinnamon, the cloves, and the allspice. Cook over low heat for about 50 to 60 minutes or until thickened.

2 Pour the mixture into a bowl, cover with plastic wrap, and refrigerate for about 1 hour before serving.

1 jar (18 ounces) orange
   marmalade
¼ cup prepared horseradish

PANTRY
¼ cup mustard

1 In the container of a
blender or food processor,
combine the marmalade, the
mustard, and the horseradish.
Process on high speed until
smooth.

2 Pour the mixture into a
bowl, cover with plastic wrap,
and refrigerate for about 1
hour before serving.

Basic Dipping Sauce

makes about 2⅓ cups

½ cup (bottled) Italian dressing
½ cup (bottled) Russian
   dressing

1 In the container of a
blender or food processor,
combine the two dressings
and process on high speed
until smooth.

2 Pour the mixture into a
bowl, cover with plastic wrap,
and refrigerate until ready to
use.

Basic Marinade-Barbecue Sauce

makes about 1 cup

PANTRY
¼ cup mayonnaise
1 teaspoon onion powder
¼ teaspoon celery salt

In a bowl, using a wire whisk
or an electric mixer, beat
together the mayonnaise, the
onion powder, and the celery
salt until smooth. Cover with
plastic wrap and refrigerate
until ready to use.

Basic Mayonnaise Spread

makes about 8 servings

BASIC PARMESAN CHEESE SAUCE

makes about 4 servings

¾ cup Basic White Sauce (see below)
¼ cup ricotta or cottage cheese
¼ cup grated fresh Parmesan cheese

In the top of a double boiler over boiling water, blend the sauce and the ricotta cheese. Add the Parmesan cheese and cook for about 3 to 5 minutes or until the cheese has melted. Remove from the heat and serve.

BASIC WHITE SAUCE

makes about 2½ cups

PANTRY
3 tablespoons butter
⅓ cup flour
2½ cup milk
Salt and pepper to taste

In a saucepan, melt the butter and blend in the flour to make a roux. Cook, stirring frequently, for about 1 minute. Blend in ½ cup of milk and continue to cook, stirring frequently, for about 5 minutes or until smooth. Blend in 2 cups of milk and continue to cook for about 5 minutes or until thickened. Remove from the heat, season to taste, and serve.

Cooking note: The consistency of this sauce can be altered by the amount of milk used.

BOURBON SAUCE

makes about 1¾ cups

1 cup powdered sugar, sifted twice
1 large egg, lightly beaten
½ cup bourbon or brandy

PANTRY
½ cup butter or margarine

1 In a small bowl, combine the sugar and the egg.

2 In the top of a double boiler over boiling water, melt the butter, and blend in the egg mixture. Cook, stirring frequently, for about 15 minutes or until thoroughly heated. Remove from the heat, blend in the bourbon, and cool to room temperature.

1 cup yellow onion, minced
2 tablespoons sour cream or
  unflavored yogurt

PANTRY
1 tablespoon butter or margarine
1 pinch of ground nutmeg

In a saucepan, sauté the onions in the butter for about 5 minutes or until tender. Blend in the nutmeg and the sour cream, and serve.

BROILED ONION TOPPING

makes about 4 to 6 servings

PANTRY
½ cup salt
¾ cup minced garlic
¼ cup black pepper
¼ cup cayenne pepper

In a bowl, combine the salt, the garlic, the black pepper, and the cayenne pepper. Pour into a jar with a tight-fitting cover and refrigerate until ready to use.

CAJUN SEASONING

makes 1¼ cups

1 carton (16 ounces) cottage
  cheese
2 tablespoons Dundee-style
  marmalade
2 tablespoons brandy or
  unblended malt whisky
1 tablespoon lemon juice

PANTRY
2 tablespoons sugar

1 In the container of a blender or food processor, combine the cheese, the marmalade, the sugar, the brandy, and the lemon juice. Process on low speed until smooth.

2 Pour the mixture into a bowl, cover with plastic wrap, and refrigerate at least 2 hours before serving.

CALEDONIAN CREAM

makes about 2½ cups

CELERY CRANBERRY RELISH

makes about 4 servings

1 pound cranberries, chopped
1 medium Granny Smith apple, cored and chopped
2 cups celery, chopped
1 teaspoon fresh lemon juice

PANTRY
1½ cups granulated sugar

In the top of a double boiler over boiling water, combine the cranberries, the apples, and the celery. Blend in the sugar and the lemon juice. Cook for about 10 to 15 minutes or until tender. Remove from the heat and transfer into a container with a tight-fitting cover. Refrigerate for at least 2 days before using.

CHIPOTLE MAYONNAISE

makes about 1 cup

½ cup sour cream
2 chipotle chilis

PANTRY
½ cup mayonnaise
⅛ teaspoon dried oregano, crushed

1 In the container of a blender or food processor, combine the mayonnaise, the sour cream, the oregano, and the chilis. Process on high speed until smooth.

2 Pour mixture into a container with a tight-fitting cover and refrigerate for at least 1 day before using.

CHINESE MUSTARD

makes about ½ cup

PANTRY
¼ cup dry mustard
½ teaspoon salt
2 teaspoons vegetable oil

In a saucepan, bring ¼ cup of water to a boil. Blend in the mustard, the salt, and the oil. Remove from the heat and serve.

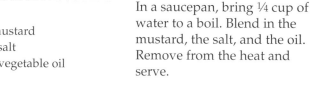

CHINESE-STYLE SALT AND PEPPER

makes about 1 cup

⅔ cup sea salt

2 tablespoons whole Szechwan peppercorns

1 teaspoon whole black peppercorns

1 Preheat a dry skillet over high heat and then reduce to medium heat. Add the salt and peppercorns, and cook, stirring frequently, for about 3 minutes or until lightly browned.

2 In the container of a blender or food processor, process on high speed until smooth.

3 Pour through a fine sieve and cool to room temperature before using.

CILANTRO PESTO

makes about ¾ to 1 cup

1 large bunch cilantro leaves, chopped

¼ cup walnuts, chopped

¼ cup mellow white miso spread (see note)

PANTRY

2 medium garlic cloves, chopped

¼ cup olive oil

1 In the container of a blender or food processor, combine the garlic, the cilantro, the oil, the walnuts, and the miso spread. Process on low until smooth.

2 Pour into a bowl, cover with plastic wrap and refrigerate until ready to use.

Cooking note: Miso is a Japanese paste of fermented soy beans. It can be found in health food or Asian stores.

COCONUT CREAM DRESSING

makes about ½ cup

½ cup sour cream or unflavored yogurt

3 tablespoons unsweetened flaked coconut

1 tablespoon lime juice

PANTRY

1 tablespoon honey

In a bowl, using a wire whisk or an electric mixer, blend the sour cream, the honey, the coconut, and the lime juice until smooth. Pour into a container with a tight-fitting lid and refrigerate for at least 2 hours before serving.

CREAM SAUCE

makes about 1½ cups

1 can (10½ ounces) cream of mushroom soup

PANTRY
¾ cups milk

In a saucepan, heat the soup for about 3 minutes. Blend in the milk and cook, stirring frequently, for about 8 to 10 minutes or until thoroughly heated. Remove from the heat and serve.

Cooking note: The consistency of this sauce can be altered by the amount of milk used.

CREAMY COTTAGE CHEESE DRESSING

makes about 1 cup

1 cup cream-style cottage cheese
1 tablespoon lemon juice

PANTRY
2 tablespoons sugar
2 tablespoons milk

1 In the container of a blender or food processor, combine the cottage cheese, the sugar, and the lemon juice. Process on high speed until smooth. Blend in the milk and process on high-speed until thickened.

2 Pour into a bowl, cover with plastic wrap, and refrigerate until ready to use.

GARLIC DRESSING

makes about ½ cup

½ teaspoon white pepper

PANTRY
⅓ cup white wine vinegar
¼ cup olive oil
½ teaspoon garlic powder

In a bowl, blend the vinegar, the oil, the garlic powder, and the white pepper. Pour into a jar with a tight-fitting cover and refrigerate until ready to use.

1 cup ginger preserves
2 tablespoons sherry
2 tablespoons plum wine
½ teaspoon grated fresh ginger

In a saucepan, combine the preserves and the sherry. Bring to a boil and remove from the heat. Blend in the wine and the ginger, and serve.

Ginger Wine Sauce

makes about 2 servings

---

3 egg yolks
1 egg
4 tablespoons lemon juice
¾ cup beef or chicken consommé, heated

PANTRY
Salt and pepper to taste

1 In a small bowl, using a wire whisk or an electric mixer, blend the egg yolks and the egg together.

2 In the top of a double boiler over boiling water, combine the eggs, the lemon juice, and the consommé. Cook, stirring frequently, for about 5 minutes or until thickened. Remove from the heat, season to taste, and serve.

Cooking note: This is traditionally served with a meat dish.

Grecian Egg and Lemon Sauce

makes about 4 servings

---

1 package (8 ounces) cream cheese, room temperature
2 tablespoons pineapple preserves
⅓ cup flaked coconut

In a small bowl, using a wire whisk or an electric mixer, blend the cheese, the pineapple preserves, and the coconut. Cover with plastic wrap and refrigerate for about 1 hour before using.

Hawaiian Coconut Spread

makes about 1⅓ cups

Hawaiian Pineapple Sauce

makes about 4 to 6 servings

1 can (8 ounces) crushed pineapple, juice reserved
2 tablespoons lemon or lime juice

PANTRY

1 tablespoon cornstarch or arrowroot

1 In a saucepan, blend the reserved juice and the cornstarch. Bring to a boil and reduce to a simmer. Cook, stirring frequently, for about 5 minutes or until thickened.

2 In the container of a blender or food processor, combine the juice mixture, the pineapple, and the lemon juice. Process on high speed until smooth.

3 Pour back into the same saucepan and cook for about 5 to 10 minutes or until thoroughly heated. Remove from the heat and serve.

Homemade Zucchini-Pineapple Preserves

makes about 8 pints

4 pounds zucchini, shredded
1 can (46 ounces) unsweetened pineapple juice
1½ cups (bottled) lemon juice

PANTRY

3 cups sugar

1 In a Dutch oven, combine the zucchini, the pineapple juice, the lemon juice, and the sugar. Bring to a boil and reduce to a simmer. Cook, stirring occasionally, for about 20 minutes.

2 Pour the mixture into sterilized jars and store.

Honey Orange Sauce

makes about 1⅔ cups

1½ cups orange juice
1 teaspoon grated orange zest

PANTRY

2 tablespoons cornstarch or arrowroot
¼ cup honey

In a saucepan, combine the cornstarch, the orange juice, and the honey. Bring to a boil and cook, stirring occasionally, for about 10 minutes or until thickened. Remove from the heat, blend in the orange zest, and serve.

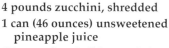

HONEY SOY SAUCE

makes about 1¾ cups

¾ cup honey
1 cup soy sauce

In a saucepan, combine the honey and the soy sauce, and cook over low heat for about 5 minutes or until bubbles start to form around edge of the pan. Remove from the heat, cool to room temperature, and serve.

HONEY SPICE BUTTER

makes about ½ cup

½ cup butter or margarine at room temperature
2 teaspoons honey
½ teaspoon ground cinnamon
½ teaspoon ground nutmeg

In a bowl, using a wire whisk or an electric mixer, blend the butter, the honey, the cinnamon, and the nutmeg. Cover with plastic wrap and refrigerate for at least 1 hour before using.

HOT ARTICHOKE SPREAD

makes about 2 servings

1 cup salad dressing of choice
1 cup grated Parmesan cheese
1 can (14 ounces) artichoke hearts, drained and chopped

1 Position the rack in the center of the oven and preheat to 350 degrees F.

2 In a bowl, using a wire whisk or an electric mixer, combine the salad dressing, the cheese, and the artichoke hearts.

3 Spoon into a 2-cup casserole and bake for about 20 minutes or until lightly browned. Remove from the oven and serve.

405

Sauces, Dips, Condiments, and Dressings

IMITATION BUTTER

makes about 4 servings

PANTRY

1 pint lowfat cottage cheese
¼ cup nonfat dry skim milk
2 packages Butterbuds™ natural
  butter flavor

In the container of a blender
or food processor, combine
the cottage cheese, ¼ cup
water, the milk, and the But-
terbuds. Process on high until
smooth. Spoon the mixture
back into the cottage cheese
container, cover tightly, and
refrigerate for at least 2 hours
before serving.

Cooking note: Use as a
spread, not a substitute for
butter or vegetable shortening
in cooking or baking.

MINT SAUCE

makes about 8 servings

**2 tablespoons dried mint leaves,
crushed**
½ cup cider vinegar

PANTRY

2 tablespoons sugar

1 In the container of a
blender or food processor,
combine the mint, the sugar,
and the vinegar. Process on
high speed until smooth.

2 Pour the mixture into a
bowl, cover with plastic wrap,
and refrigerate for at least 1
hour before using.

MUSHROOM SAUCE

makes about 2 servings

**1¼ cup white mushrooms,
sliced**

PANTRY

¼ cup butter or margarine
⅓ cup flour
½ cup milk
Salt and pepper to taste

In a saucepan, sauté the
mushrooms in the butter for
about 10 to 15 minutes or
until tender. Blend in the flour
and cook, stirring frequently,
for about 3 to 5 minutes or
until thickened. Blend in the
milk, bring to a boil, reduce to
a simmer, and cook, stirring
frequently, for about 3 to 4
minutes or until smooth and
thickened. Remove from the
heat, season to taste, and
serve.

PANTRY
⅓ cup white wine or cider
   vinegar
Salt and pepper to taste
1 cup olive oil

1 In the container of a blender or food processor, combine the vinegar and the oil, and season to taste. Process on high speed until smooth.

2 Pour into a bowl, cover with plastic wrap and refrigerate until ready to use.

OLIVE OIL VINAIGRETTE
makes about 10 servings

---

2 tablespoons orange marmalade

PANTRY
¼ cup butter or margarine, softened

In a bowl, blend the butter and the marmalade until smooth, cover with plastic wrap, and refrigerate until ready to use.

ORANGE BUTTER
makes about ⅓ cup

---

1 cup Basic White Sauce (see page 398)
⅓ cup shredded Parmesan cheese
Garlic salt to taste

PANTRY
½ teaspoon dry mustard powder

In a the top of a double boiler over boiling water blend the sauce, the cheese, the mustard, and the garlic salt. Cook, stirring occasionally, for about 3 minutes or until smooth. Remove from the heat and serve.

PARMESAN CHEESE SAUCE
makes about 2 servings

Pasta and Pizza Sauce

makes about 4 servings

½ **pound ground beef**
1 cup chopped pepperoni

PANTRY
1 jar or can (30 ounces) spaghetti
   sauce

In a non-stick skillet, sauté the meat for about 5 minutes or until it loses its pinkish color. Drain and add the pepperoni and the spaghetti sauce. Bring to a boil and reduce to a simmer. Cook, stirring frequently, for about 8 minutes or until thoroughly heated. Remove from the heat and serve.

Royal Butter

makes about 2 cups

1 package (8 ounces) cream
   cheese, room temperature
¼ **cup prepared horseradish,**
   drained

PANTRY
½ butter or margarine, room
   temperature
¼ cup mayonnaise

In a bowl, using a wire whisk or an electric mixer, blend the butter, the cheese, the mayonnaise, and the horseradish. Cover with plastic wrap and refrigerate until ready to use.

Rujak Manis (Indonesian Sauce for Fruit)

makes about 6 servings

¼ **cup Ketjap manis**
½ **piece Thai chili**
½ **-inch fresh ginger root, pared**
1 teaspoon fresh lime juice

1 In the container of a blender or food processor, combine the Ketjap manis, the chili, the ginger, and the lime juice. Process on high speed until smooth.

2 Pour into a bowl, cover with plastic wrap and refrigerate for at least 1 hour before using.

Cooking note: Ketjap manis is an Indonesian sauce similar to soy sauce, except sweeter.

1 can (6 ounces) salmon, drained and flaked

1 can (4 ounces) tiny deveined shrimp, drained

PANTRY

½ cup mayonnaise

In a bowl, using a wire whisk or an electric mixer, combine the salmon, shrimp, and the mayonnaise until just smooth. Cover with plastic wrap and refrigerate for about 1 hour before using.

SALMON MAYONNAISE

makes about 4 servings

½ cup bacon, diced

1 cup red onion, sliced

4 cups (canned) stewed tomatoes

8 ounces pasta of choice, cooked

PANTRY

¼ cup flour

Salt and pepper to taste

1 In a small bowl, blend the flour with ⅛ cup of water.

2 In a skillet, sauté the bacon, stirring frequently, for about 5 minutes or until just crispy. Add the onions and continue to cook for about 5 minutes or until lightly browned. Add the tomatoes and simmer for about 10 minutes. Blend in the flour mixture and season to taste. Cook for about 10 to 15 minutes or until thickened. Remove from the heat and serve over the pasta.

SAVORY TOMATO SAUCE

makes about 4 to 6 servings

---

1 package (1½ ounces) spaghetti sauce mix

1 can (12 ounces) vegetable juice cocktail

PANTRY

2 tablespoons canola oil

In a saucepan, blend the sauce mix, the vegetable juice, 1 cup of water, and the oil. Bring to a boil and reduce to a simmer. Cook, stirring occasionally, for about 25 minutes or until thoroughly heated and thickened. Remove from the heat and serve.

SAVORY SAUCE FOR FISH

makes about 2½ cups

Sesame Vegetable Topping

makes about 2 servings

2 tablespoons onion, finely chopped
2 teaspoons sesame seeds
½ cup buttered cracker crumbs

PANTRY
2 tablespoons vegetable oil

In a skillet, sauté the onion in the oil for about 5 minutes or until lightly browned. Add the seeds and cook, stirring frequently, for about 1 minute. Remove from the heat, add the crumbs, and serve.

Sour Cream Stuffing

makes about 4 servings

1 package (8 ounces) stuffing mix
2 large eggs
½ cup sour cream

1 In a bowl, sprinkle the stuffing mix with a little water. Cover with plastic wrap and set aside for about 1 hour or until the water has been absorbed.

2 Prepare the stuffing mix according to the directions on the package, using the eggs and the sour cream, and serve.

Sweet and Sour Sauce

makes about 1½ cups

1 cup (bottled) French dressing
¼ cup (bottled) chili sauce
¼ cup pickle relish

1 In the container of a blender or food processor, combine the dressing, the chili sauce, and the relish. Process on high speed until smooth.

2 Pour the mixture into a bowl, cover with plastic wrap, and refrigerate until ready to use.

½ cup sweet bean paste (miso)
2 tablespoons ginger preserves
1 tablespoon ginger brandy

In a bowl, blend the bean paste, the preserves, and the brandy. Cover with plastic wrap and refrigerate until ready to use.

SWEET RED BEAN SPREAD

makes about ⅔ cup

1½ teaspoons lemon juice
Hot sauce (bottled) to taste

PANTRY
½ cup mayonnaise
½ teaspoon dried basil

In a bowl, using a wire whisk or an electric mixer, blend the mayonnaise, the lemon juice, the basil, and the hot sauce until smooth. Cover with plastic wrap and refrigerate for at least 1 hour before using.

TARTAR SAUCE

makes about ½ cup

½ cup white wine

PANTRY
3 tablespoons butter or
    margarine
⅓ cup flour
2½ cups milk
Salt and pepper to taste

In a saucepan, melt the butter and blend in the flour to make a roux. Cook, stirring frequently, for about 1 minute. Blend in ½ cup of the milk and continue to cook, stirring frequently, for about 5 minutes or until smooth. Blend in 2 cups of milk and continue to cook for about 5 minutes or until thickened. Reduce the heat to low, blend in the wine, and cook for 3 to 5 minutes. Remove from the heat, season to taste, and serve.

Cooking note: The consistency of this sauce can be altered by the amount of milk used.

WHITE WINE SAUCE

makes about 2 servings

CALZONE FILLING

makes about 6 servings

12 ounces bulk pork sausage
½ cup pizza sauce
1 can (4 ounces) sliced
   mushrooms
1 package shredded mozzarella

In a bowl, combine the sausage, the pizza sauce, the mushrooms, and the mozzarella. Cover with plastic wrap and refrigerate until ready to use.

MORNAY SAUCE

makes about 4 servings

¼ cup grated Gruyère cheese
2 tablespoons light cream
2 teaspoons Dijon mustard
2 egg yolks, beaten
2 tablespoons (bottled) hot
   sauce

PANTRY
2 tablespoons butter
1 tablespoon flour
½ cup of milk
Salt and pepper to taste

1 In a bowl, blend the eggs and the hot sauce.

2 In a skillet, combine the butter and the flour, and cook over low heat, stirring occasionally, for about 2 minutes to make a roux.

3 Remove from the heat and blend in the milk and the cheese.

4 Return to the heat and blend in the egg yolks. Cook for about 4 minutes, but do not allow to come to a boil. Remove from the heat, season to taste, and serve

SWEET MAYONNAISE

makes about 1 cup

2 tablespoons Amaretto
1 teaspoon cardamom powder

PANTRY
¾ cup mayonnaise
1 teaspoon onion powder

1 In a bowl, blend the mayonnaise, the Amaretto, the onion powder, and the cardamom. Cover with plastic wrap and refrigerate until ready to use.

INDEX